Edward Healy Thompson

The Life of M. Olier

Founder of the Seminary of St. Sulpice

Edward Healy Thompson

The Life of M. Olier
Founder of the Seminary of St. Sulpice

ISBN/EAN: 9783741173165

Manufactured in Europe, USA, Canada, Australia, Japa

Cover: Foto ©Andreas Hilbeck / pixelio.de

Manufactured and distributed by brebook publishing software (www.brebook.com)

Edward Healy Thompson

The Life of M. Olier

THE
LIFE OF M. OLIER,

Founder of the Seminary of S. Sulpice.

BY

EDWARD HEALY THOMPSON, M.A.

"Tempus est ut incipiat judicium a domo Dei."
1 Pet. iv. 17.

LONDON:
BURNS AND LAMBERT, 17 PORTMAN STREET,
PORTMAN SQUARE;
AND 63, PATERNOSTER ROW.
1861.

ADVERTISEMENT.

THIS biography is founded entirely on the work of the Abbé Faillon, entitled *Vie de M. Olier, Fondateur du Séminaire de S. Sulpice, accompagnée de Notices sur un grand nombre de Personnages contemporains.* 2 vols. (Second Edition, 1853.) The present writer has but sought to reproduce in an English form and in his own way what is there so admirably depicted.

The limits to which he was confined have obliged him to make considerable reductions in the narrative, but he has proceeded throughout on the principle of condensing rather than omitting, and has not unfrequently introduced into the body of the work some of the striking traits contained in the very copious notes with which that author's volumes are enriched. To represent the man and his mission in the world—to bring out into full relief the idea with which he was possessed, and the principles by which he was guided—has been the main endeavour of the writer; he has, however, made it a special object to retain what constitutes an attractive feature in the original life—the notices of M. Olier's contemporaries, many of whom were persons not only distinguished for eminent spiritual attainments, but favoured with high supernatural gifts, and has been careful to include all such circumstantial details as tend to illustrate the state of religion, and what may be called the religious habits of society, at the time. For this reason, among others, he has drawn attention to some of the most famous shrines of our Lady and other places of pilgrimage, which were the objects of popular devotion, and it has been a matter of no slight interest to him to observe in how many instances that devotion, in the present day, has not only reassumed its ancient forms, but continued to run in its ancient channels.

M. Faillon enjoyed one inestimable advantage, as compared with the previous biographers of M. Olier, in having access to the *Mémoires* which the servant of God composed in obedience to his director, the Père Bataille; a task which he performed with all the simplicity and sincerity of a child. The manuscript may be said to consist of two parts: one recording the lights vouchsafed him with respect to religious direction; the other containing, together with many passages of his life, a particular account of the dealings of God with his soul, his interior trials and supernatural favours, and the mysterious ways by which he was prepared and fashioned by Divine grace for his extraordinary mission. The first was composed with the persuasion that it would one day be published, and serve to the edification of many souls; the second was intended for the eyes of his director alone, a fact which it is necessary to note, as explaining why we find him entering into so many personal details, and employing terms which, but for the positive command of his spiritual guide, would have been repugnant to the humility of one who entertained so profound a contempt for himself. Each sheet, as it was written, was put into F. Bataille's hands, who, after the death of his saintly penitent, committed the whole to the keeping of the directors of the Seminary.

For the satisfaction of the reader, it may be well to add, that the following pages have been revised in their progress through the press by one whose name would be a sufficient guarantee for theological competency, as well as for the care and exactness with which the task has been executed.

CONTENTS.

CHAPTER I.
EARLY YEARS OF M. OLIER—HIS CONVERSION.

His birth and baptism at Paris. First indications of his vocation and mission. His devotion to the Blessed Virgin. Natural liveliness of his disposition. His family removes to Lyons. An adventurous feat. He receives the tonsure, and a benefice. S. Francis de Sales foretells his future services to the Church; blesses him on his deathbed. He receives peculiar favours from God. Desires to embrace the religious state. Returns with his family to Paris, and enters the University. Attends the schools of the Sorbonne. Becomes abbé of Pébrac; a fashionable preacher; and a man of the world. Marie de Gournay; effects of her prayers. M. Olier goes to Rome to study Hebrew; his sight affected. He makes a pilgrimage to Loreto, and becomes a changed man.—*Page* 1.

CHAPTER II.
COMMENCEMENT OF HIS APOSTOLIC LIFE—HIS VOCATION, AND ELEVATION TO THE PRIESTHOOD.

Death of his father; he is summoned home. His mother's character and conduct. His extraordinary devotion in instructing the poor of Paris, and young scholars. Consequent anger and scorn of his relatives and acquaintances. Influence of his example. Assists his cousin, Mlle. de Bussy, to become a Carmelite nun. Kisses the feet and the sores of the poor. Pilgrimage to Our Lady of Chartres. His corporal austerities. The Mother Desgranges. The Mother Agnes of Langeac is supernaturally bidden to pray for him. His pilgrimages in order to ascertain his vocation. Sermon at S. Paul's. His vocation shown to him in a dream. Is admitted to holy orders, and takes S. Vincent de Paul as his director. Employed by the saint in giving country missions; his unceasing exertions affect his health. Prepares to receive the priesthood; his first Mass. He vows a perpetual servitude to Mary; his piety towards her. The Conferences of S. Lazarus.—*Page* 15.

CHAPTER III.

APPARITION OF MOTHER AGNES DE LANGEAC — MISSION INTO AUVERGNE—ATTEMPTED REFORM OF THE ABBEY OF PÉBRAC—DEATH OF MOTHER AGNES.

M. Olier prepares to evangelize the parishes dependent on his abbey of Pébrac; his associates. Retreat at S. Lazarus; apparition of a Dominican nun. Mission into Auvergne; his charity and humility. Visit to the convent at Langeac; recognition of Mother Agnes. He sets about reforming his abbey; his plans defeated. Mother Agnes takes him as her spiritual guide; her last farewell and death. Letter of M. Olier to her religious. His practice of holy poverty. He is offered a bishopric.—*Page* 31.

CHAPTER IV.

FATHER DE CONDREN—M. OLIER TAKES HIM AS HIS DIRECTOR.

Extraordinary gifts of this holy man. His disciples; MM. de Foix, du Ferrier, Brandon, de Bassancourt, and Amelote. S. Vincent de Paul urges M. Olier to accept the bishopric. M. Olier is moved to take F. de Condren for his director; follows his counsels. His devotion to the Blessed Sacrament, and to the Mother of God. Declines taking his doctor's degree. Is directed to engage in country missions. Makes a preparatory retreat; F. de Condren's spiritual maxims, and prayer; subsequently adopted by M. Olier for the Seminary of S. Sulpice. Dangerous passage of the Seine.—*Page* 44.

CHAPTER V.

SECOND MISSION INTO AUVERGNE.

Preparations for the mission; indignation of M. Olier's family. His powerful preaching; personal humility; and charity to the poor. His manner of instructing little children. His assiduity in prayer, and transports of Divine love. M. Meyster; his extraordinary conversion; F. de Condren's opinion of him. Success of the missions. Attempt on M. Olier's life. Co-operation of the country clergy. Conferences established at Puy. Retreat given at Pébrac. Instances of his disinterestedness and poverty of spirit. Marie de Valence. Illness of M. Olier, and remarkable recovery. Visit from his mother; death of his sister. He receives the gift of a higher order of prayer, and of a more perfect dependence on the Spirit of Christ. Return to Paris; various missions in and about the capital.—*Page* 55.

CHAPTER VI.

THE NUNS OF LA RÉGRIPPIÈRE—FATHER BERNARD—M. DE QUÉRIOLET—M. BOURDOISE—MISSIONS OF BRITTANY, PICARDY, ETC.

M. Olier visits his priory of Clisson. Goes thence to the convent of La Régrippière; his conduct there. Conversion of the Sister de Vauldray, and of other nuns. Visit to Nantes; the Mother de Bressand; Sister Marie Boufard. Françoise Madeleine de la Roussière; miraculous favour vouchsafed to her. Reform of La Régrippière continued; visit to the Abbey of Fontevrault. M. Olier resumes his studies. Father Bernard, "the poor priest." M. de Quériolet; account of his life and conversion. M. Adrien Bourdoise; his character and demeanour; sends M. Olier on a mission near Chartres. Mission at Illiers; conversion of the Bellier family. Françoise Fouquet; her great sanctity. M. Olier is nominated coadjutor to Bishop of Châlons; declines the proffered dignity. The associates choose M. Amelote for their superior. Mission at Amiens; conversion of a Swedish colonel, and of his men. Accusations brought against the missionaries. M. Bourdoise instructs them in the ceremonies of the Church.—*Page* 71.

CHAPTER VII.

TRIALS OF M. OLIER, INTERIOR AND EXTERIOR—DEATH OF F. DE CONDREN—SEMINARY OF CHARTRES—REFORM OF LA RÉGRIPPIÈRE COMPLETED.

M. Olier's two petitions to God. His extraordinary trials; withdrawal of spiritual gifts, suspension of bodily and mental powers, interior darkness and distress, fears, and scruples of conscience, temptations to vainglory. He is treated with contempt and distrusted; interdicted from preaching and hearing confessions. F. de Condren's last conversation with him, and with M. du Ferrier. His death, and appearance to M. Olier. The French Oratory. M. Olier is delivered from his trials; chooses M. Picoté for his director. He and his associates take up their residence at Chartres; but without result. Conversion of the Sister de la Troche. The association at Chartres is dissolved.—*Page* 95.

CHAPTER VIII.

SEMINARY OF VAUGIRARD—M. OLIER'S STATE OF UNION WITH GOD.

Madame de Villeneuve advises an establishment at Vaugirard. M. Olier retires to Notre Dame des Vertus, where he receives intimations of the Divine will. Withdrawal of all his associates excepting M. de Foix and M. du Ferrier. They engage a house at

Vaugirard; their manner of life. Fathers Tarrisse and Bataille. M. Olier takes the latter for his director. His extraordinary state of union with God; his interior light and joy, and supernatural gifts. He makes a vow of servitude to Jesus. The three solitaries solemnly consecrate themselves at Montmartre. Letter of M. Bourdoise, and the reply; he visits Vaugirard. Extraordinary influence exercised by Marie de Gournay. M. Olier's gift of science and eloquence. Providential aids. Cardinal de Richelieu's proposal. MM. de Gondrin, de Queylus, de Poussé, Hurtevent, and de Cambiac, with others, join the community. M. de Bassancourt visits Vaugirard, and remains. M. Amelote applies, and is refused; his true vocation. M. de Sainte-Marie. Supernatural lights of M. Olier; exemplified in his preaching. M. Copin requests the associates to take charge of his parish during his absence. Donation of M. de Rochefort. M. Olier's insight into Holy Scripture. He is chosen superior of the community.—*Page* 111.

CHAPTER IX.

THE SPIRIT OF THE SEMINARY OF VAUGIRARD—REMOVAL TO S. SULPICE.

Objections entertained against M. Olier's undertaking, arising from the fact of past failures. No ecclesiastical seminary had as yet been permanently established in France; M. Olier the first to succeed. His instructions to his ecclesiastics. The one object of his teaching, union with Jesus Christ in His acts and intentions. Brother Claude; his exalted sanctity, and extraordinary gifts; his first meeting with M. Olier. Parish of S. Sulpice; M. de Fiesque offers the *cure* to M. Olier. Advice of F. Tarrisse; aid rendered by Marie de Gournay. The three great objects of M. Olier's vocation. Anger of his family; his charitable judgment of their conduct. Retreat under F. Bataille. His installation at S. Sulpice. Establishment of the Seminary and Community. The general respect and confidence with which the servant of God is regarded. Summary of his meditations during his retreat.—*Page* 135.

CHAPTER X.

FRIGHTFUL STATE OF THE PARISH OF S. SULPICE—M. OLIER ESTABLISHES A COMMUNITY OF PAROCHIAL CLERGY.

M. Olier's twofold task. The *faubourg* S. Germain; condition of the inhabitants, moral and religious. State of the clergy; M. Olier would have them adopt a community life; his address to them, and conduct towards them. Formation of a community of parish priests; their regulations and duties. M. Olier's maxims for confessors. His vow of perfection, and personal example. His rules are adopted by other parishes of Paris. He is consulted by several bishops on the subject of diocesan seminaries.—*Page* 160.

CHAPTER XI.

M. OLIER'S REFORMS AT S. SULPICE—HIS COADJUTORS.

He institutes catechetical instructions for children; his manner of teaching them. Instructions for servants, beggars, and aged poor; the general catechism; discourses for work-people; conferences for heretics. Sacrilegious practice of the Lutherans. Father Véron;- his method of controversy. Clément the cutler, and Beaumais the draper. Conduct of the Calvinists; M. Olier's efforts for their conversion. He sets up a bookstall. His zeal for the beauty and order of God's house; reforms in the parish church; observance of the Canonical Hours. His love of souls; his fervour in preaching. Conversion of a merry-andrew. Reform of the guilds. Great increase of penitents. The church crowded. Extract from M. Olier's Considerations on the Canonical Hours.—*Page* 174.

CHAPTER XII.

M. OLIER'S REFORMS, CONTINUED.

He institutes the confraternity of the Blessed Sacrament; establishes the Perpetual Adoration. His rebuke to the Princesse de Condé. Exposition and solemn Benediction. Infrequent communion and indevotion to Mary among the effects of Jansenistic teaching; M. Olier's counter-teaching and practice. Anne Auger Granry. M. Olier's love of the poor. Brother John of the Cross. Re-organization of the Confraternity of Charity. Mme. Leschassier and her daughter. Mme. Legras. Confessors not allowed to give alms to their penitents. His zeal against sin, and charity to sinners. His perseverance in prayer for his flock. Awful death of an abandoned woman. His courage in protecting the innocent. Mme. Pollalion. M. Olier's labours for the suppression of vice. Conversion of actors. M. Crétenet. Father Yvan. M. Olier's liberality towards the clergy, and zeal in undertaking their defence. Case of the Curé of Arcueil.—*Page* 195.

CHAPTER XIII.

ATTEMPT TO EXPEL M. OLIER FROM S. SULPICE—ERECTION OF THE SEMINARY INTO A COMMUNITY.

He encounters opposition in various quarters; expectation of persecution. He purchases a site for a new seminary. Renews his solemn engagement at Montmartre. A conspiracy is formed to expel him from the parish. M. de Fiesque is induced to publish a formal charge against him; case of the Abbey of Clisson. The presbytery is attacked by a furious mob, and M. Olier is seized and dragged out. Generous conduct of S. Vincent de Paul. The servant of God is conveyed to the Luxembourg; his extraordinary humility and charity. His petition to the Council of State; it is referred to the Parliament of Paris. Exertions of friends in his behalf; his simple piety. The Parliament orders his re-instatement. Renewed violence on the part of his enemies; his faith and courage. A strange procession; decree of the Parliament against its authors. M. Olier's charity towards his enemies. He is advised by his friends to quit the parish, and is offered the bishopric of Rodez; his admirable replies. He refers the matter to the Abbé of S. Germain, who withdraws his opposition. The dispute with M. de Fiesque is definitively concluded; generosity of M. Olier and his friends. He exchanges the Abbey of Pébrac for that of Cercanceau. His filial piety. The Seminary of S. Sulpice is erected into a community.—*Page* 214.

CHAPTER XIV.

M. OLIER'S INFLUENCE IN THE WORLD.

He commences building a new parish church, and erects a chapel of ease. Many conversions effected by his conversation; his influence with persons living in the world. The Association of the Passion; composed principally of military men; the Baron de Renty; the Marquis de la Motte Fénelon; Abraham de Fabert; M. du Four. A singular adventure. Death-bed of M. de la Roque Saint-Chamarant. Influence of the association in discouraging duelling; public protestation of its members. Edict of Louis XIV. The Marquis de Fénelon and his son. M. Olier's instructions to the Princesse de Condé on the right use of worldly grandeur. His rebukes to fine ladies. Mme. de Rantzau. Anecdote of the Duchesse d'Aiguillon. Mlle. de Portes. The Sisters of Christian Instruction. Death of Marie de Gournay. Revival of pilgrimages; increase of devotion and respect for the clergy.—*Page* 234.

CHAPTER XV.

PILGRIMAGES AND JOURNEYS.

Failing health of M. Olier; his reluctance to take repose. He visits Clairvaux, Dijon, and Citeaux. At Beaune he makes acquaintance with Venerable Margaret of the Blessed Sacrament; their spiritual relations. His journey to S. Claude; danger on the way; he venerates the body of the saint. Visits the tomb of S. Francis de Sales at Annecy, and receives a divine intimation. Passes by Geneva; makes the acquaintance of Mme. d'Herculais at Grenoble. The Grande Chartreuse. S. Antoine de Vienne. The Mother Françoise de Mazelli. The Holy Places of Provence. The Mother Madeleine de la Trinité. The Mother de S. Michel. M. Olier's recollection and devotion. His liberality to the poor. Instances of his admirable humility. His visit to the tomb of S. Vincent Ferrer, and to S. Anne d'Auray. Farewell to the nuns of La Régrippière. His devotion to S. Martin of Tours. His influence with the provincial clergy. Sacrilegious robbery at S. Sulpice; public act of reparation. Discovery of the culprit.—*Page* 256.

CHAPTER XVI.

THE TROUBLES OF THE FRONDE.

Outbreak of the sedition. Penitential observances enjoined by M. Olier. His measures for the relief of the destitute. His perilous expedition to S. Germain-en-Laye. He resigns his two priories of Clisson and Bazainville. Relaxation of morals consequent on the siege; mission given by F. Eudes. Dearth of provisions; sufferings of the people. M. Olier organizes a system of relief. The Company of Charity. Orphanages. The Council of Charity. Numerous charitable institutions. Conduct of the Princesse de Condé; her death. Louis XIV. at the church of S. Sulpice. M. Olier's advice to the Queen-mother. Renewal of the civil war. M. Olier opens an asylum for country girls and destitute nuns. Establishment of the Filles du Saint Sacrement in fulfilment of the Queen-mother's vow. The nuns of Notre Dame de Miséricorde. Mme. de Saujeon and the Duke of Orleans.—*Page* 277.

CHAPTER XVII.

THE SEMINARY OF S. SULPICE—ITS ESTABLISHMENT AND INTERIOR SPIRIT.

The Blessed Virgin shows M. Olier, in a vision, the model of the Seminary. The work commenced; description of the building. Devotion to the Interior Life of Jesus, the leading idea of the Seminary. Devotion to the interior life of Mary. Mary the channel of all graces. S. John the Evangelist, one of the patrons of S. Sulpice. Masses for the intentions of the Blessed Virgin. Other patrons: S. Joseph, S. Dominic, S. Francis of Assisi, S. Francis of Paula, S. Martin, S. Denis, S. Ambrose, and S. Gregory. The Presentation of the Blessed Virgin, the principal feast of the Seminary. The President Molé becomes its civil patron. The letters-patent of the crown registered by the Parliament of Paris.—*Page* 296.

CHAPTER XVIII.

M. OLIER'S METHOD OF SPIRITUAL TRAINING.

His exalted idea of the ecclesiastical state. The virtues necessary for clerics; simplicity and modesty; self-humiliation; mortification of the senses. Perfection of his own practice. Interior mortification; obedience and fidelity to rule. Prayer. Study of the Gospels, and of the Scriptures generally. M. Olier's reverence for the Bible. Observance of the ceremonial of the Church, and of its interior spirit. Training in parochial duties. Fervour and regularity of the Seminarists. Necessity of theological proficiency; true motives and dispositions for study. Rules of conduct in public disputations. M. Blanlo. Method of prayer approved by M. Olier.—*Page* 309.

CHAPTER XIX.

M. OLIER AND JANSENISM.

Austerity a supposed sign of adhesion to the heresy. M. Olier suspected of favouring it; his public protest. Dishonesty of the party; M. Olier's letter to a parishioner. His vigilance and zeal; he is accused of false doctrine. M. du Hamel; his system of public penance. Infrequency of communion. M. Olier's discourse against Jansenism. Fury of the party; F. Des Mares publishes his "Christian and Charitable Remonstrance." The Hôtel de Liancourt. Conference with Des Mares and others at S. Sulpice. Affair of the Duke de Liancourt; M. Arnauld condemned by the Sorbonne. Practical effects of Jansenistic teaching. M. Olier defeats a notable scheme of the party. His precautions to guard the Seminary against its influences.—*Page* 330.

CHAPTER XX.

THE COMMUNITY OF S. SULPICE—ITS CONSTITUTION AND INTERIOR SPIRIT.

Jansenism unable to gain a footing in S. Sulpice. M. de Foix made Bishop of Pamiers; his after history. Removal of M. du Ferrier; his end. Efforts of the Jansenists to subvert M. Olier's influence. Attempt to introduce the Oratorians into the parish. Revelation made to the servant of God by the Blessed Virgin. His reliance on Divine Providence in the choice of subjects for the Community. Vocations of M. Souart, M. de Bretonvilliers, and M. Tronson. The novitiate or "interior seminary." Protestation to be made by each member of the community. The spirit of servitude. Practical rules; schedule of self-examination. M. Olier's instructions respecting the use of wordly goods and the care of health. The noviciate removed from Vaugirard to Avron, and afterwards to Issy.—*Page* 348.

CHAPTER XXI.
ESTABLISHMENT OF PROVINCIAL SEMINARIES.

The community of S. Sulpice a local institution, not a congregation. M. Olier establishes seminaries in the dioceses of Bordeaux, Pamiers, and Rodez. State of the diocese of Limoges. Circumstances attending the foundation of a seminary at Nantes; M. René Lévêque. M. Olier's personal influence with the country clergy; effect of his addresses in Provence; seminary of Aix. He submits the rules and general plan of S. Sulpice to the collective episcopate. Summary of his memorial. His deference to episcopal authority, exemplified in his conduct respecting a seminary at Avignon. Foundation of a seminary at Viviers; its beneficial results. Effects of M. Olier's eloquence at Puy; M. de Maupas and M. de Lantages. Seminaries of Clérmont and S. Flour; deplorable condition of latter diocese. M. Olier withdraws his priests from Clermont-Lodève; his letter to M. du Bosquet on the occasion. The Seminary of S. Sulpice confirmed by the Holy See. Testimony borne by the Bishops of France in favour of the servant of God and of S. Sulpice in 1730.—*Page* 369.

CHAPTER XXII.
VARIOUS MISSIONARY ENTERPRISES.

M. Olier's desire to go as a missionary into the East. Revelation made to him respecting the Seminary of Foreign Missions. He organizes a mission to the Protestants of the Vivarais and the Cévennes. M. de Queylus made Curé of Privas. Success of the mission in that town; and in Jaujac, Viviers, Thueyts, &c. M. Olier's zeal for the recovery of England to the faith; he holds conferences with Charles II., and receives his abjuration. Sorrow manifested by Charles on hearing of his death; papers found in the king's cabinet. The Marquis of Worcester and the Earl of Bristol. Meeting of M. Olier and M. de la Dauversière. Formation of the Society of Our Lady of Montreal. Foundation of the Seminary of Ville Marie. Arrangement with the English government.—*Page* 387.

CHAPTER XXIII.
M. OLIER'S LAST ILLNESS AND DEATH.

He is seized with a violent fever, and resigns his parish. His recovery. M. de Bretonvilliers is appointed his successor. M. Olier's spirit of self-accusation. His tranquillity under painful disorders. Retires to Péray. His devotion to the Holy Cross. He is struck with paralysis, and conveyed to Paris. His unalterable patience, and desire of suffering. Interior darkness and desolation; his spirit of self-sacrifice. The Bishop of Grenoble desires to resign his see in M. Olier's favour. His health improves; he tries the waters of Bourbon. Makes a vow to the Blessed Virgin, and has the happiness of again saying Mass. Visits our Lady of Puy. Unites the *cure* of S. George with the seminary in that town, and authenticates the saint's relics. Instances of his humility. Visits the tomb of the Venerable Mother Agnes. Performs two pilgrimages; and retires into S. Sulpice. Vision of Jesus bearing His cross. His devotion to the mystery of the Resurrection; his aspirations of Divine love. His last instructions. His death-bed. S. Vincent de Paul receives his last sigh. Exposition of his body; print of a cross on his forehead. He is buried in the chapel of the Seminary. Desecration of his remains at the Revolution. — *Page* 402.

CHAPTER XXIV.

SUPERNATURAL GIFTS AND GRACES.

M. Olier's personal appearance, and intellectual powers. His gift of reading the secrets of men's hearts. Extraordinary influences exercised by him. His power of relieving mental suffering; and healing bodily diseases. Miraculous cure of Mlle. Manse. Appearance of the man of God to a hospital-nun of Montreal. Miraculous cures of a deaf priest; Pierre Trescartes; Marguerite Vieillard; M. Boucaut; M. Colomb; M. de Béget; Anne Feulha; François Néron; and Françoise de l'Espinasse du Passage. Declaration of the writer.—*Page* 423.

APPENDIX .... *Page* 439

LIFE OF M. OLIER.

CHAPTER I.

His early years—His conversion.

It would be little in accordance with the spirit or the mission of the holy man who is the subject of this narrative, if his biographer were to commence the history of his life with an enumeration of his ancestors. Suffice it, therefore, to say that he came of a distinguished family, which had borne many of the highest offices in the state, and had gained itself an honourable name in various departments of the public service. His father was Jacques Olier de Verneuil, secretary and master of requests to Henry IV., who, in the year 1599, espoused Mary Dolu, Lady of Ivoy, in Berri. As is often observable in the case of those whom God has chosen to accomplish any great work for His glory, both parents, although (as we shall see) they showed a culpable eagerness to promote their son's worldly advancement, were diligent in the performance of their religious duties, and edified their household by their numerous virtues.

They had eight children, the youngest of whom was born in Paris, on Saturday, September 20th, 1608, and on the same day received in baptism the name of Jean, by which he was always called in his own family. But in the world he was known as Jean Jacques, the latter being the name of his patron, S. James the Less, which he took, as it would appear, at his confirmation. Almost immediately after his birth, he was put out to nurse (as was the custom in those days) in the *faubourg*

S. Germain, and, what is worthy of remark, in the very parish with which his fame is for ever associated, that of S. Sulpice; as though (to adopt his own words) God would that he should breathe in his earliest infancy the air of the place in which it was His will that he should serve Him in his maturer years. The street to which he was taken was called the Rue S. Sulpice, and pious affection did not fail to note that as, when that prodigy of theological science, the great S. Thomas Aquinas, was 'a child, the surest way of quieting him was to put a book into his hands, so the infant who was destined in afterlife to shed such lustre on the priesthood, was never better pleased than when he was carried by his nurse to the neighbouring church. The sight of its interior was sure to stop in an instant all cries and tears, when caresses and other attempts at diversion had failed of effect. This result, indeed, may be attributed to the natural force of novelty and change of scene on the mind of a little child, and not to any immediate influence of divine grace; but not so a circumstance which M. Olier has himself recorded. He was in his seventh year when, being in a church for the purpose of hearing mass, at the moment the priest passed on his way to the altar, the thought suddenly flashed upon him, how pure and holy must they be who are set apart to offer the Adorable Sacrifice. So deep was the impression made on his soul, that it was never afterwards effaced. It seemed, he says, to his childish mind as though priests must live a life wholly hid in God; so that it was with wonder he saw them act like ordinary men while performing their awful function. Anything, even though it were but a movement of the head, which indicated that they were conscious of visible things around them, was a surprise and a shock to him; he thought they were angelic beings the moment they had vested, or at least as soon as they had ascended the steps of the altar. It was indeed a childish ignorance, but it was no less an earnest of his own future vocation, and of the mission which, in the providence of God, he was designed to fulfil in sanctifying the clergy of France.

The devotion which his parents, and especially his

father, entertained towards the Blessed Virgin, was shared and indeed surpassed by this pious child. It was a pleasure to him to reflect that his mother's name was Mary, and that he was born in a street called Notre-Dame-d'Argent.* He never began his lessons without invoking the aid of his august patroness, and it seemed to him as though he were unable to learn anything by heart unless he first repeated a "Hail Mary." He would go and tell her in his childish way everything he was going to do, and ask her consent, preferring to act always, not as from the motive of his own choice, but simply at her bidding. When he had new clothes, though it were but a single article of dress, he would present himself humbly before her image in the cathedral of Notre Dame, and beg her never to let him offend her Divine Son as long as he should wear them. As he grew older, he was tempted to omit this ceremony, as something irksome and absurd, which nobody thought of performing except himself; but he declares that he was very soon punished for his negligence, for scarcely a day was allowed to pass before his new clothes were lost, or torn, or visited with some disaster, which he took as a warning not to refuse this act of homage to his heavenly benefactress.

When he was eight years old, he was put to school, where he displayed a quickness and a power of comprehension very remarkable in so young a boy. At the same time his natural liveliness of disposition began to develop itself in ways which gained for him among his elders a character for unruliness and insubordination which he scarcely deserved. He seems to have been one of those children whose faults are attributable rather to an exuberance of animal spirits, and an inability

---

* "Our Lady of Silver;" so called from the silver image which was placed in a niche at the corner of the street by Francis I., in reparation for a sacrilegious outrage committed by the heretics. This image, however, having been stolen and replaced by another of less costly material, the street gradually resumed its old name of *Roi de Sicile*, which it took from Charles of Anjou, count of Provence, and king of Naples and Sicily, who had a mansion in it.

to control their physical energies, than to any habitual disobedience or self-will. The result, however, was, that he was always running risks and getting into trouble. His own account of himself is, that such was his recklessness and want of thought, that, but for the special interposition of Providence, he must frequently have been killed, or crippled for life. "I never looked where I was treading, or whither I was going; I was for ever falling down, or running against something, and hurting myself. Once, I remember, I tumbled into a well, and had a most narrow escape of my life; at another time I fell with my head under a cart-wheel, which would have crushed it to pieces, but that for some unexplained cause the horse suddenly stopped. I was the source of continual alarms to everybody in the house." With his mother he seems not to have been a particular favourite; and she thought to bring him into subjection by constantly chiding, thwarting, and chastising him; a method of proceeding which was calculated to have anything but a salutary effect on a high-spirited boy.

In the year 1617, his father being raised by Louis XIII. to the honourable post of Intendant of Lyons, the family quitted Paris and took up its residence in that city, where Jean Jacques with his brothers attended the classes of the Jesuit fathers. There his fearless and adventurous spirit soon found an occasion of indulging itself. One day, when playing with a bird, it escaped from his hands and flew on to the roof of a house. In an instant he had made the sign of the cross, and invoking his angel-guardian, had sprung from a window upon the roof and secured the truant; not, however, without raising a cry of terror from those who had witnessed the hazardous feat; for the window from which he had leapt, and which was on the third story, was below the level of the adjoining roof on which he had succeeded in alighting; and, had he missed his footing, he would have been dashed to pieces on the pavement below. "My master" (he writes), "whom the noise had summoned to the spot, and who was seized with terror when he beheld my perilous position, punished me as I deserved; nor to this day can I think of the danger I so recklessly incurred without a shudder, and a fervent thanksgiving to God, who bestowed such fatherly care upon me at a time when I was quite unconscious of His mercies."

Being destined by his family to the ecclesiastical state, he had received the tonsure when he was eight years old, and, through an abuse which prevailed in France in those days, he was at the same time put in possession of a benefice. But his restless activity, and the heedlessness and almost violence of his disposition, which, instead of diminishing, increased as he grew older, appeared to his parents so incompatible with the moderation, gravity, and recollection which befit a priest, that they began to have serious misgivings on the subject of their son's vocation, and were preparing to turn their thoughts to some other profession, when their doubts were set at rest, and their minds reassured, by the authoritative voice of no less a person than S. Francis de Sales. This holy prelate, on his occasional visits to Lyons, had been struck with the piety and rectitude of the Intendant, and had admitted him to his intimate friendship. The mother of our youth, fearful of offending God by thrusting into the sacred ministry one who was destitute of a true vocation, opened her heart to the saint, and besought him to make the matter a subject of special prayer, in order to ascertain the Divine will. S. Francis acceded to her request, and the result we learn from one of M. Olier's personal friends, who was present on the occasion. He had gone to assist at the saint's mass in the chapel of the Visitation convent at Lyons, and on the bishop's leaving the altar, Madame Olier presented her children to him for his blessing. S. Francis embraced them one after another, and began speaking with affectionate interest about them all, when their mother interposed with renewed expressions of uneasiness respecting Jean Jacques, who, she said, was an unruly, headstrong boy on whom correction was thrown away. "Well, well," said the saint mildly, "we must not be hard upon young people; high spirits are not a sin; and now take comfort from what I say, for I tell you that God has chosen this good child to do great service in His

Church." He then laid his hands on the boy's head, embraced him tenderly, and gave him his benediction.

Nor did the holy prelate's solicitude for the child end thus; he wished at once to aid in bringing about the accomplishment of his own prediction. He had long entertained a design of resigning his bishopric to his coadjutor, and retiring to a hermitage, beautifully situated on the borders of the Lake of Annecy, which he had caused to be restored. Here he intended devoting the remainder of his days to the training of young ecclesiastics: five or six cells were already constructed, and of one of these it was his wish that Jean Jacques should be the occupant. He desired to have the boy always with him, and this desire was fully reciprocated by young Olier, who, from the day that S. Francis adopted him, in a manner, as his child, never called him by any other name than the endearing one of father. But this design, which promised so much both for the Church of France and for our pious youth, was not destined to be realized: a few days after, and the labours of the saint had ceased on earth, and he was gone to his glorious rest in heaven. Francis was at this time in the train of the duke of Savoy, whom he had accompanied to Avignon. M. Olier's father would fain have had him occupy a portion of his house, which was very spacious, and close to the convent of the Visitation; but Francis declined this and other similar offers of hospitality, by saying that, foreseeing the difficulty there might be of procuring suitable quarters, he had already engaged a lodging; and it was then discovered that he had fixed upon a little room belonging to the gardener of the convent, which was a very temple of the winds, and, moreover, was troubled with a smoky chimney. To all renewed offers of better accommodation, the saint did but pleasantly reply, that he was never better than when he fared badly. In this comfortless apartment Francis de Sales was seized with his last illness, and hither thronged all the friends of the great bishop, to beg his prayers and receive his benediction. In the crowd came Madame Olier, with her children; it was the feast of the Holy Innocents, and when he beheld the child of his election, kneeling with tearful, earnest countenance at his bedside, can we doubt that the dying saint, as he gently raised his hand and blessed him, poured out upon him all the tenderest feelings of a father's heart, and consecrated him, as it were, for the accomplishment of a work which himself had not had time even to commence? M. Olier, as may be supposed, ever throughout his life had recourse to the saint's intercession with the most assured confidence; and, as we shall see in the course of this history, believed that to him he was indebted for numerous and extraordinary graces.

Our youth had now reached his fourteenth year, a critical age for one of his determined character and ardent temperament; but we have his own testimony to the fact that he was withheld by a peculiar operation of Divine grace from falling into irregular courses. If he were unhappily guilty of any infidelity, a cloud seemed to settle on his mind, otherwise so lively and active, and he was unable to apply himself to his studies. "I observed," he says, "that I lost all capacity of learning when I was out of the state of grace. No sooner did I commit any sin, than my understanding seemed to become dark and obfuscated; and I could neither apprehend nor retain anything until I had been to confession. I remember well, that when I had to pass a public examination, I was obliged for a considerable time before to be careful to keep myself in the state of grace; and nothing at this time surprised me more than to see persons living in sin, and yet capable both of learning and of using the knowledge they had acquired. I wondered how this could be, imagining that everybody was affected like myself." So marvellously was God pleased to guard this chosen soul from contracting early habits of sin; nor were these the only signs of the special protection with which he was favoured. One day, in his fifteenth year, he had swum across a wide river, intending to rest himself on the other side; but finding strangers unexpectedly on the opposite bank, he attempted, from a motive of modesty, to return without recovering breath. Scarcely, however, had he reached the middle of the stream, when he felt himself quite exhausted, and unable to proceed. He was in the very act of sinking, when his foot caught the point of a stake fixed in the bottom; and on this he succeeded in steadying himself until assistance was rendered him. A deliverance from death, which depended apparently on so slight an accident, made a deep impression on his mind.

About this time he had a strong desire to embrace the religious state, and his first attraction was towards the Carthusians, many of whose houses he visited as opportunity served; he next turned his attention to the Franciscans, and even went so far as to beg them to receive him; but it was the will of God that he should sanctify himself, and be instrumental in sanctifying others, in the secular life. He had finished his humanities, as classical studies were called, at Lyons; and his father being again promoted to the high office of a Counsellor of State, our youth returned with his family to Paris, where he was entered at the far-famed University. He had for his professor of philosophy one of the ablest men of the day, Peter Padet, of the *College d'Harcourt;* and of the manner in which he acquitted himself in his new studies, it is sufficient to say that it fully corresponded with the expectations which his friends had formed of him. A public act, which he kept in Latin and Greek, extending over the whole course of philosophy, was crowned with universal applause; and his professor paid him the compliment of declaring that, in maintaining his thesis, as well as in his replies, he had achieved the highest possible success.

On leaving the *College d'Harcourt,* he attended the schools of the Sorbonne, where he equally distinguished himself. His father spared no expense to obtain him the advantage of the best instructors, and gave him as his master in theology one of the most celebrated doctors of the time, Nicholas Lemaistre, who in the subsequent reign was made Bishop of Lombez. Under the direction of this learned and pious divine, the young Olier made himself profoundly acquainted with the scholastic writers, and at the same time acquired a thorough knowledge of Greek, which was of infinite service to him in the study of the Holy Scriptures, as well as of the Greek fathers.

The honours he reaped at this time were so much the more flattering to his parents as they were due entirely to his own talents and exertions, and they began to indulge the most sanguine hopes of the distinguished part he was to play in the world. With his birth, connections, and personal advantages, it seemed to them that their son might attain to the highest dignities in Church and state. A miserable spirit of worldliness took possession of them, the more miserable and odious as exhibited in persons who made profession of piety, and who indeed, under ordinary circumstances, were accustomed to act from religious motives. Not only did they cast about how best to secure the favour and influence of those who might further their child's advancement, but they even endeavoured to excite ambitious views in the youth himself, suggesting to him many little ways by which he could recommend himself to notice and promote his worldly prospects. Even while at Lyons, his father had procured him a second benefice in the shape of a priory; he now obtained for him the richer preferment of the abbey of Pébrac, in the diocese of S. Flour (of which we shall hear more in the sequel), and to this was soon added a second priory, that of Bozainville, in the diocese of Chartres. Besides these more substantial dignities, he was at the same time elected honorary canon of the chapter of S. Julien de Brioude, a distinction which he shared with two bishops and a brother abbot. This was in 1626, when he had attained his eighteenth year; and now in his quality of abbé, although but a layman, for it does not appear that he had received even minor orders, he was entitled to preach; and as preaching would be a means of exhibiting his talents before the world, he ascended the pulpit, and delivered himself of brilliant orations which gained him an extensive popularity, and were the especial delight of his infatuated mother, who, although, as it has been intimated, she had hitherto shown him no particular affection, could not resist the charms of an eloquence which tickled the ears and won the applause of the intellectual crowd. At length she seemed to have become sensible of her son's good qualities, when, as he says, "I had a throng of fine people about me, and was all the fashion, preaching beautiful sermons, abounding in rhetorical tropes and vain conceits, but in which not a word was uttered against the manners of the world, its pride and its covetousness."

M. Olier had now entered on his career of ambition and, it must be added, of dissipation, with all the habitual ardour of his character. He was to become a great man, and to become a great man, he must pay court to the great; and this could only be effectually accomplished by frequenting their assemblies and mixing in all the gay society of the capital. Behold then our future reformer as the spruce young abbé, the graceful courtier, the brilliant wit, the writer of epigrams, the utterer of smart sayings and pretty compliments in *salon* and in *boudoir*, with his retinue of servants, his couple of carriages, and his well-appointed household; for his parents grudged no expenditure which could help to give him consequence and conduce to his advancement. And well did the young man respond to their liberality: his address and good looks, the ease and frankness of his manners, the charm of his conversation, his incontestable abilities, joined to the consideration in which his family were held, obtained him a ready admittance into the highest circles; and so he enjoyed life, and made full use of his liberty, and was fast becoming an accomplished man of the world and a lover of its pleasures, if not a sharer in its vices; till at last his parents were filled with dismay at his dissipated courses, and awoke, as from an evil dream, to behold their child about to plunge into a vortex of sin, to the very edge of which they had themselves beguiled him by their criminal vanity and folly.

His mother, who, though not insensible to the world's attractions, had a great horror of sin, was deeply distressed, and never ceased to pray with tears to God for the conversion of her son; many holy souls also, who mourned in secret over the miseries of the time, made the young abbé the subject of their intercessions; but there was one pre-eminently to whose prayers M. Olier always attributed the mercy he obtained, and who is so remarkable a person in herself, and plays so important a part in this history, as to call for more particular notice. This was Marie de Gournay, widow of David Rousseau, one of the twenty-five licensed victuallers of Paris. A country-girl of mean parentage, she retained in her married state, when she might have lived in ease and comfort, her predilections for a hard and simple life; and her humility was equal to her love of poverty. So vile and little was she in her own eyes, that she could not endure to spend upon herself; her clothes were never of the newest, and her food consisted for the most part of scraps which others had left. Her one sole study was to imitate the blessed Mother of God, and in all things to conform her interior dispositions to those with which that incomparable Virgin performed her ordinary actions. Fearful of attracting the esteem of others, she avoided everything which might obtain her the character of being a person of piety, and during the twenty years she pursued her avocation, engaged continually in waiting on her guests, she never testified by speech or manner the intimate union she enjoyed with God. Not but that numbers who frequented the house were indebted to her for many spiritual blessings; and by some timely word, apparently of the simplest and most ordinary kind, she led many a hardened sinner to repentance, on whom reproof and admonition had been tried in vain; still no one would have suspected the extraordinary sanctity that lay hid beneath an exterior in nowise distinguishable from that of a thousand other women of her class. At her husband's death she chose for herself one of the most uncomfortable rooms in the house, for it was so situated as never to be free from noise and bustle, from which she suffered much; but there she made a solitude for herself in which to commune alone with Him who was the one object of all her thoughts and affections. Her constant prayer was that God would take her to Himself; and so great were the satisfactions she derived in the reception of the most

Holy Eucharist, that It seemed to serve her for meat and drink, and she sometimes passed whole days without any other nourishment.

This poor woman, so humble in her origin, leading so obscure a life, and engaged in what would generally be regarded as a most unspiritual calling, was possessed with one longing desire—the sanctification of the clergy, and the reformation in particular of the parish of S. Sulpice, in which she resided. One day that M. Olier, then in his twentieth year, was returning with a party of friends, young ecclesiastics like himself, from the fair of S. Germain, a woman apparently of the lowest order, in a voice which betokened the anguish of her heart, said to them, "Ah, sirs, I have long prayed for your conversion, and I hope God will even yet hear my prayer." It was Marie de Gournay, whose perseverance and confidence in God were at length to have a most complete reward; for we learn from M. Olier himself, that of five or six young abbés, all of good family, who frequented a house by the side of S. Sulpice's church, separated from her own only by a wall, there was not one who ultimately did not yield to grace and quit the world to follow Christ. For himself, it would seem as if from that moment he felt moved to abandon the gay life he was leading; he was no longer at his ease, and would say to his companions, "Somebody, I am sure, is praying for me." The heavenly Mother for whom, amidst all his frivolity and sin, he had retained a tender devotion, had, on her part, not forsaken him; many of her holiest servants joined their prayers to hers; and now grace after grace was knocking at his heart, and though it was eighteen months before his conversion was completed, the struggle with himself had already begun. "I did not love the world," he says; "I could not find any satisfaction in it, yet I was for ever falling, despite the sweet attractions of God's love, His unceasing solicitations, and the poignant remorse I was sure to suffer after sinning, nay, notwithstanding I sought the powerful aid of the sacraments of the Church."

Such was his state of mind when he determined on

going into Italy, not for any object connected with his spiritual interests, but from a motive in which a desire of worldly distinction had a considerable share. Having lost the grace of God, he had acquitted himself only with ordinary success on the occasion of taking his degree of bachelor of arts, and he was resolved to recover his superiority. It was his ambition to excel, and to do something which should exalt him above the common herd of scholars and learned men; he therefore conceived the design of making himself master of Hebrew, with the view of maintaining a thesis in that language at the Sorbonne. Only at Rome could he obtain the instruction he needed, and to Rome accordingly he repaired. But God had other designs respecting him. Scarcely had he arrived in the Eternal City, when he was troubled with an affection of the eyes, which effectually prevented all application to study, excluded him from general society, and induced an apprehension that he might altogether lose his sight. The most skilful physicians failed to arrest the progress of the malady, and at length, all human means proving without avail, the sufferer bethought him of having recourse to supernatural aid, and he resolved to go on a pilgrimage to the Holy House of Loreto*.

He left Rome towards the end of May, and notwithstanding the increasing heats, he, in a spirit of penance, retained his winter dress and commenced his journey on foot. Unaccustomed to laborious exercise, and enfeebled by the remedies used to mitigate his disorder, the fatigue, especially for the few first days, seemed too much for his strength; but he refreshed and encouraged himself with continual communings with God and His blessed Mother; sometimes reciting the rosary, at others composing a pious canticle in honour of the Queen of heaven. There remained but one day more of his arduous journey, when he was attacked by a fever which com-

---

* An account of the *Santa Casa*, or Holy House of Loreto, as well as of the evidences on which the tradition rests, will be found in the *Rambler*, vol. vii. pp. 383—408.

pelled him to stop upon the road; and when at length it abated, and he again resumed his way, his bodily powers but ill corresponded with his ardent desire to reach his destination, and it was with the utmost difficulty he could drag himself along. The nearer, however, he drew to the holy place, the more his soul was filled with interior consolations, and when at last he beheld from a distance the church of Loreto, he experienced the liveliest emotions of tenderness and joy. "My heart," he says, "was wounded as it were with an arrow, and all inflamed with a holy love of Mary."

On entering the town, his companions would have sent immediately for a physician, but such was his impatience to throw himself at the feet of the miraculous image, that they did not venture to oppose his wishes. On his way he was accosted by a woman possessed, who, though he wore no cassock, nor had any other distinguishing mark about him, cried to him in Italian, "French abbé, be converted, and live as a man of God, or it will go ill with thee." On entering the great church, he threw himself on his knees, and, with his countenance bathed in tears, implored the immaculate Virgin, that should he ever be in danger of falling again into sin, she would obtain for him the boon of death. At that instant he was completely cured; the fever left him, so that the physician, whom his friends had brought, found his pulse so moderate and regular, that he supposed he had finished his journey in a carriage; and as the eyes of his mind were divinely enlightened, so those of his body were miraculously healed: the disorder had ceased, and never troubled him more. At the same time he received an extraordinary gift of prayer, and passed the whole night within the church in fervent supplications, with abundance of tears. Into the Holy House he did not dare to enter, until he had cleansed his soul by a humble confession of his sins.

The supernatural graces with which he had been favoured at this holiest of shrines, wrought so complete a transformation in him, that he could scarcely be recognized as the same man. He returned to Rome, as he had come, on foot, occupying himself by the way in adoring God for His great mercies, and extolling the glories of his august patroness.

CHAPTER II.

Commencement of his apostolic life—His vocation; and elevation to the priesthood.

LONGING to give himself entirely to God, and fearing to lose his soul should he return to the world, M. Olier had thoughts of entering the monastic state in some convent of Italy. To this end he visited several Carthusian houses, and especially that in the isle of Capri; and all he there witnessed of the angelic lives of the inmates, only inflamed his heart with a more ardent desire of giving himself up to divine contemplation. Strong, however, as was his attraction to the solitary life, he was still in doubt as to what was the will of God respecting him, when an event happened which summoned him back to France. This was the death of his father, after a long and painful illness, which he had borne with the most exemplary patience, exhibiting throughout the same tender devotion to the Most Holy Virgin for which he had been remarkable all his life. The loss of one he so dearly loved, deeply wounded the sensitive and affectionate heart of M. Olier, and for a day and a night he never ceased giving passionate vent to his sorrow.

His mother was most urgent for him to return, and with that mixture of piety and worldliness which is frequently to be found in imperfect souls, she was equally anxious that he should be a model of ecclesiastical virtue, and at the same time aspire to the highest offices in the Church. For two of her sons she had already provided to her perfect satisfaction. The eldest, François Olier de Verneuil, had been made a master of requests, while her seventh son, Nicolas Edouard Olier de Fontenelle, had succeeded his father as *grand audiencier* of France; and it was now the desire of her heart to see Jean Jacques occupying the honourable position of almoner to the king, which she had been for some time soliciting for him. That there was a large fund of worldliness in his mother's character, there unhappily cannot be a doubt; even her affection for her child, and the estimation in which she held him, seemed to vary with the hopes she entertained of his success in the world. Thus she received him on his return with the most lively demonstrations of regard, protesting that he was now her only consolation and support, and lavishing every manner of endearment upon him, so long as she thought he might second her ambitious views; but no sooner did she perceive that honours and distinctions had no longer any attraction for him, than her behaviour altogether changed; for M. Olier never for an instant wavered in his resolution to withdraw entirely from the world: "Although," he says, "I made no outward demonstration, yet from the moment that God called me at Loreto, my only pleasure was in communing with Him; all else was a burden and a torment to me. My longing desire, and the very end of my being, was to speak of God." And yet he kept silence, and for nine months led a hidden life, revealing his intentions to no one, not even to his confessor; until on Christmas Day, in making a general confession of his past life, he avowed his determination to belong henceforth entirely to God, and to devote himself unreservedly to His service.

As though to make his rupture with the world as irrevocable as possible, he proceeded to commit an outrage on conventional proprieties, such as it never overlooks or pardons. He, a young, well-bred, refined, accomplished gentleman, but lately one of its own most favoured votaries, began to make himself the friend and associate of the rabble, and that openly, and even in appearance ostentatiously, as though to defy and put to scorn all public opinion. And, in truth, he seemed to be beside himself, like the great patriarch S. Francis, when, in obedience to the divine call, he stripped himself of his clothes before his father's face, and went forth into the world an outcast and a beggar, having left all for Christ; he felt (he says) impelled by movements of zeal which he could not have resisted without a consciousness that he was opposing the grace of God, and neglecting that on which his perseverance in his vocation depended. He entered, then, on the practice of an apostleship the like of which the gay world of Paris had never witnessed. Day after day he went into its crowded streets, and selecting the most miserable objects he could find—the more ragged and squalid, the better to his taste—with a sweetness and a tenderness which nothing but divine charity could have taught him, led them in a troop to his mother's house, where he rendered them such services as they individually required, instructed them in the truths of salvation, and distributed alms among them according to their needs. Not being a priest, nor indeed even in holy orders, he could but prepare them for confession, and then send them, under the charge of a trusty servant, to a young and devoted priest, with whom he was united in the closest ties of friendship. This was François Renar, who, despite a natural repugnance for hearing confessions, discharged this charitable office at the church of the Capucins du Marais, where he remained daily in his confessional from six o'clock until noon. The sick, M. Olier caused to be conveyed to the hospital, himself accompanying them. At the same time he devoted himself to the instruction of young scholars, and especially such as aspired to the ecclesiastical state, assembling them together for this purpose in his own apartment. This act of devotion was even more obnoxious to his friends than the care he expended on the poor, as, to their minds, there was something especially derogatory in performing the part of a schoolmaster, and that towards persons who were every way his inferiors. They could no longer keep any measures with him, but gave full vent to their indignation and contempt, and at length proceeded so far as to drive his beggars and his scholars out of the house, and compel him to transfer his reception-room to a part of the premises which, as he says, reminded him of the stable of Bethlehem.

Had this, however, been all, the world at large might have ignored his eccentricities, and even have regarded them with a patronizing pity; so far, it might appear, he had had the decency to withdraw himself and the objects of his folly from the public eye, and retreat with them into the privacy of his maternal dwelling. But as yet it had formed no adequate conception of the audacity with which he was prepared to brave its wrath and set it at defiance. Soon this madcap of an abbé might be seen, in open day and in the most frequented places, surrounded by a crowd of wretched people, whom he was instructing, or with whom he was conversing, or to whose tale of sorrow he was listening, with the same animated air, the same unconscious grace, the same interested attention, for which he was distinguished when, but a few short months ago, he paid his nightly *devoirs* at the court of fashion, wit, and beauty. It may readily be conceived what rage and scorn such conduct would provoke in his old acquaintance, the more as he was plainly invulnerable to all the shafts of ridicule that were lanched against him. One day he was catechising a poor man at the door of Nôtre Dame, when a cavalier, richly dressed, approaching the servant who accompanied M. Olier, said to him, in a voice loud enough to be heard by all around, " Tell your master he is mad!" The young abbé heard the words, but continued his instructions with an expression on his countenance of such sweetness and humility as would have covered any generous-hearted person with confusion. Faithful to the light within him, he minded neither taunt, nor sneer, nor affronts that were still more hard to bear; his courage never quailed, his ardour never cooled, and if ever he offered apology for his singularity, it was in some such simple words as these: " The rich and the great never want for instruction, there are plenty who are ready enough to act as their teachers; but the poor, who for the most part are far better disposed, are overlooked and abandoned, because in them vanity finds nothing on which to feed."

Scoffers, of course, there were, numerous enough; nor were there wanting those good worthy men, after their fashion, who shook their heads or smiled significantly when the young abbé's name was mentioned, and gravely lamented, or loudly condemned, his ill-misguided zeal, the mere vagary, as they called it, of an ill-balanced, enthusiastic mind. But a few generous souls there were whom the example of such heroic charity roused to emulation; so that not many years elapsed before the sight of young men, well and even nobly born, teaching beggars and outcasts was no longer a novelty in the streets of Paris. Among the first was M. Renar, the young priest already mentioned; but all were not endowed, especially at the outset of their labours, with the holy shamelessness of our abbé. One, in particular, there was, who would move to a distance, or escape into a house, if he saw any of his old acquaintance approaching; but M. Olier sweetly reproached him for his cowardice, showing him the folly of being ashamed of caring for the poor, if we would not have the Son of God ashamed of us before His Father and the holy angels.

Madame Olier, and his relatives generally, as we have seen, regarded the occupations in which he was engaged as a dishonour to the family, and their dislike of his proceedings was not a little aggravated by an event which now happened. His cousin, Mlle. de Bussy, a young lady on whose wealth and beauty they reckoned for obtaining the honours and advantages of a great alliance, announced her intention of entering the convent of the reformed Carmelite nuns; and in this intention she had the encouragement and support of M. Olier. The opposition she encountered on the part of her friends was violent and prolonged, but it was met by a resistance no less determined, and in the end triumphant, on the part of the young abbé. This was a crime not soon to be forgiven by his family, and their resentment showed itself in renewed insults and reproaches. M. Olier bore all with the utmost patience, believing, in his humility, that his friends were animated by a purer intention in opposing, than he himself was in pursuing, his charitable labours. When his mother treated him with more unkindness than usual, he would go to the church of Nôtre Dame, and throwing himself on his knees before his favourite image, would say, in the anguish of his heart, " I take thee for my mother, Most Holy Virgin, for my own rejects me : O Mary, deign to be a mother to me." His devotion to the Queen of Heaven had never ceased to express itself in modes very similar to those which he had adopted when a child. If he happened to have anything that could be called beautiful or costly, it was sure to find its way to the church of Nôtre Dame. His cousin, on leaving the world, he says, must needs stuff his wardrobe with her diamonds and jewellery, and other cast-off vanities, but they were soon distributed among the different churches of the capital, and a large proportion was expended in the decoration of the cathedral of Nôtre Dame.

Desirous and even careful as he was to avoid annoying his relatives needlessly, M. Olier set no bounds to his fervour, so far as the mortification of his own natural inclinations was concerned ; and the same charity which impelled him to brave the scorn of the world for the sake of the poor and miserable, led him to the performance of acts still more extraordinary and heroic. After teaching some poor wretch his catechism, he would kneel and kiss his feet ; and were the object of his love and compassion afflicted with any noisome sore, he would beg to be allowed to kiss it also ; nay, he would apply his lips to loathsome ulcers, the very sight of which filled the passers by with horror. One of his biographers, M. de Bretonvilliers, relates that on sixteen different occasions he was himself an eye-witness of this marvellous act of charity. After a visit to his favourite church of Nôtre Dame, it was not unfrequently his custom, on going out, to kiss the feet of all the poor he found at the door or within the enclosure, as well as of all whom he met on the bridges and in the streets : he beheld

Jesus Christ in His suffering poor, and by an impulse he was unable to resist, he did Him homage in their persons.

M. Olier, however, was as humble and obedient as he was ardent and courageous, and at a word from his confessor, who suggested to him that such extraordinary actions, performed so publicly, might only have the effect of exciting notice and admiration, he instantly abandoned the practices of which we have spoken. He no longer kissed the sores of the poor with his bodily lips, but he kissed them still, he says, in spirit. "For," he adds, "our interior ought to be greater than our exterior; and what we do exteriorly ought to appear to us so little, in comparison with what, in our interior, we desire to do for God's great majesty, as to make us blush for shame. Thus what we do will be full of humility and charity, the two conditions which ought to accompany all our actions, and which constituted the spirit in which our Lord performed everything He did." But though he was careful to avoid any public display, yet when he was walking in the country, in places where there was no danger of incurring notoriety, he would kiss both the feet and the sores of the poor he met, never omitting to bestow an alms upon them; and he believed these meetings were ordered by a special providence, so as to afford consolation to the sufferers, as well as edification to himself. One day he met three poor persons one after another, in whom his piety recognized a likeness to Jesus, Mary, and Joseph. "The first," he says, "that passed was an old man, the next was a good woman, the third a young man. I questioned them as to their faith, and received satisfactory replies. The last of them, who represented to me Jesus Christ, affected me much; his body was frightfully burnt, one arm shrunk and withered, and even bared to the bone. I asked him, among other things, how he met with such an accident; he told me it was through endeavouring to save his children from the flames. Nothing could have corresponded more perfectly with my imagination; the likeness between this poor man and my Saviour, covered with wounds in endeavouring to save His children, moved me deeply. 'Ah! God bless you,' I answered to every word he spoke. After consoling him and giving him my benediction, he went away much comforted, nor was I less so than he, for he had let me kiss his sores."

Another feature in the circumstance which pleased M. Olier was, that this poor man told him he came from Nôtre Dame de Chartres, as he felt he had thus an opportunity of thanking our blessed Lady, in the person of this poor sufferer, for the mercies she had lately shown him in that celebrated church. Not long after his return from Rome, God was pleased, for his greater purification, to visit him with a most grievous trial. It was his habit to confess and receive communion every day, but so sensitive was he to every little imperfection, and so scrupulous did his conscience become, that at last he confessed as many as three times in a morning, and would even summon the priest from the altar, when he was preparing to say Mass, in order to give him absolution. This was Father Dufour, chaplain of St. Paul's, who had been almoner to S. Francis de Sales. In vain did this good priest endeavour to remove his scruples by the suggestion of all the motives applicable to such a case; although he implicitly obeyed every direction given him by his confessor his fears remained, and only the Hand that had smitten him could give the relief he needed. He resolved once more to have recourse to the Mother of Mercy, and to seek her aid at the shrine of Our Lady of Chartres,* which had been the resort of pious

* The history of this celebrated shrine dates (strange to say) from pagan times, before the birth of Christ. Tradition says that on the height where now stands the cathedral church of Chartres, there was, in times anterior to Christianity, an altar dedicated to "the Virgin who should bear a son" (Virgini parituræ). This expectation of a Deliverer, the son of a virgin, is proved by incontestable monuments to have widely prevailed among the nations, whether as a remnant of the primitive patriarchal faith, or by reason of a special revelation, or that it was derived from the Jews who, at the period of Alexander's conquests, were dispersed about the world, or from all three causes combined. Altars with a similar import are also said to have existed in several other places; as, for example,

CHAP. II.]   HIS CORPORAL AUSTERITIES.   23

pilgrims from time immemorial. It was the middle of winter when he left Paris, in true pilgrim guise, on foot; but such was the ardour of his devotion, and so pleasing to his heavenly patroness was the simplicity of his faith, that from the moment he entered the cathedral church, even before he had visited the subterranean chapel in which her image stood, he found himself delivered from all his scruples.

The reader will not need to be told, that proportioned to his tenderness towards others was his severity towards himself. Very high sanctity is always accompanied with extraordinary mortifications, and M. Olier was no exception to the rule. The gay young abbé, whose life had been all softness and delicacy, who affected magnificence, not from a vulgar love of display, but as it gratified a refined and elegant taste, now dealt hardly with himself, that he might have the more to bestow in alms upon the poor, and kept aloof from society, that he might occupy his leisure in prayer. His austerities were practised with all the secrecy possible, but his servant discovered that he was in the habit of removing the mattress from his bed and lying on the palliasse, restoring everything to its place in the morning, in order to escape observation; and so effectually were his precautions taken, that it was some years before his practice became known to any but the confidential servant in question. In short, he was as ingenious in contriving mortifications and as indefatigable in denying himself, as men of the world are studious of their ease and unwearied in the pursuit of pleasure. Nor was this love of solitude and mortification the effect of an over-wrought imagination, or an indiscreet zeal; he was but following the leadings of divine grace, and preparing himself for the work to which God was calling him. He had a mission to perform in the order of Providence—a mission no less than that of permanently reforming the clergy of France,

at Nogent, Autun, Dijon, &c. In Christian times the shrine of Our Lady of Chartres became a most frequented place of pilgrimage.

and he was now being tried and fitted for the office. A vocation so extraordinary demanded extraordinary graces and a perfection of holiness corresponding thereto. This is the clue to his conduct during the interval we are now considering, and may prepare us for all that is supernatural in the accounts that follow.

Ever since the change that had passed upon him at Loreto, M. Olier had been travailing, as it were, in the throes of a second conversion, and a few holy souls were specially called to assist at the birth. Of Marie de Gournay we have already spoken; of another, M. Olier made the acquaintance when visiting his abbey of Pébrac in the year 1631. This was Mother Desgranges, Superioress of the nuns of Our Lady of Brioude, whose venerable age and exalted virtues inspired him with a filial reverence and affection. He seemed to behold in her a representative of that heavenly Mother to whose love and service he was pre-eminently devoted; and the admonitions she gave him were received with as much docility as though they had come from the lips of the Blessed Virgin herself. In a letter he addressed to her, and which has been preserved, he begs her, in the most earnest terms, to continue still to nourish his soul with her salutary counsels, and to obtain for him a more perfect love and devotion to Jesus and Mary. But the person who was directly commissioned by Heaven to intercede for the future founder of S. Sulpice, was Mother Agnes of Jesus, Prioress of the Dominican Convent of S. Catherine de Langeac, who was, and is still to this day, held in the highest veneration throughout Auvergne, Velay, and the neighbouring provinces, and whom the Church has declared Venerable for her virtue and heroic sanctity. This holy nun never ceased her prayers for the sanctification of the clergy, and the conversion of the poor country-people, who, for want of zealous pastors, were plunged in ignorance and vice; and one day, when she was beseeching her Divine Spouse, with many tears, to close her earthly exile and admit her to His presence, our Lord said to her, "I have still need of thee for the sanctification of a soul who shall promote My glory."

HIS DOUBTS ABOUT HIS VOCATION.

Shortly afterwards, the Blessed Virgin, towards whom the Mother Agnes entertained a devotion, remarkable even among saints, appeared to her, clothed with light, and said, "Pray to my Son for the Abbé of Pébrac." Pébrac was only six miles distant from Langeac, but the Mother Agnes had never seen M. Olier, nor even heard his name; and it was not until three years afterwards that they beheld each other, and that in the manner and under the circumstances which will be related in the next chapter. Meanwhile she offered not only her most fervent prayers, but her extraordinary austerities, for the sanctification of the soul which had been thus commended to her charity; and such was the ardour with which she sought to satisfy the Divine justice by her sufferings for the sins of which that soul was guilty, that (as we learn from M. Olier himself) she scourged herself so cruelly that the walls of her cell were sprinkled with her blood.

At this time M. Olier had no director,* nor was he aware of the necessity of such a guide, in order to determine his vocation and make progress in spiritual perfection. He was still doubtful whether it might not be God's will that he should enter some reformed religious order, and to obtain the light he needed he ceased not to implore the aid of his heavenly patroness. To this end he made several pilgrimages in her honour; besides repairing to Our Lady of Virtues, Our Lady of Angels, and other noted shrines in the neighbourhood of Paris, his devotion led him to go twice, on foot, to the famous

---

* It is hardly necessary to observe that the office of a confessor is simply to receive the penitent's confession; that of a director, to guide the soul in the ways of the spiritual life. Of course, the two may be combined in the same person; and when the ordinary confessor happens to possess the qualifications necessary for the difficult office of direction, such combination is deemed highly desirable; but in themselves they are essentially distinct. Every pious Catholic, in a matter of difficulty which concerns conscience, would consult his confessor, or any other good priest, but (whatever expressions may be used in common parlance) this does not constitute him a *director*.

sanctuary of Our Lady of Liesse.* It was his habit thus to prepare himself for the more worthy celebration of her feasts, and one of these occasions was in the month of August, 1632 (during, therefore, the exhausting heats of summer), in preparation for the Feast of the Assumption. He went, accompanied by his servants, chanting litanies on the way, or composing, as was his wont, simple canticles in her praise. He wished, moreover, to recommend to her the success of a sermon he was to deliver on that day in the church of St. Paul, in Paris. He was subject at this period to a feeling of nervous trepidation whenever he had to preach in public, which distressed him the more that he feared it was occasioned by a secret desire of human esteem. Many times he made an offering of himself to God, that, if such were His will, he might suffer the confusion of being unable to proceed; but no such result ever followed, although the agitation remained. On the day in question, while mounting the pulpit, he was more than usually disturbed; nevertheless, he began his sermon, and continued it for some time without the slightest hesitation, when he suddenly lost all presence of mind; but, confident in the assistance of his powerful patroness, he went on giving utterance to whatever came to his lips, although he knew not what he was saying; and so it was that, without any sensible effort of memory or thought, he delivered himself of all he had prepared, and that so fluently and so forcibly, that no one but himself was aware of his embarrassment. Of this the parish register bore witness, for there it stood recorded that on Sunday, August 15th, 1632, being the Feast of the Assumption of the Blessed Virgin Mary, M. Jean Jacques Olier preached in the afternoon, and *acquitted himself both well and learnedly.*†

It was in the November following that he received his first intimation of the Divine will, and that by means of

---

* The traditional account of the origin of this celebrated shrine forms No. 13 of " Catholic Legends," published among the volumes of the " Popular Library."

† " Il eut un bel auditoire, et fit tres-bien et tres-doctement."

a dream, although he did not understand its full significance at the time. There was a good and holy priest, who had shown our young abbé many kindnesses, and when he was on his deathbed M. Olier begged his friend to remember him when he came before God, and obtain grace for him to know his vocation. Two or three nights afterwards he saw, in a vision, heaven opened, and Pope S. Gregory the Great seated on a lofty throne, and below him, on another throne, S. Ambrose; below these, again, were the seats of the priests, one of which, under the latter saint, was vacant; and still lower, and even far lower, he beheld a number of Carthusian monks, as though to complete the hierarchy. From his fifteenth year (as has been related) M. Olier had been attracted towards the Carthusian order; but this vision seemed to tell him that it was the will of God that he should serve Him in the ranks of the clergy, whom those great saints had illustrated by their virtues and elevated by their labours. The seat left vacant below S. Ambrose seemed to be reserved for one who, with a zeal akin to that of the holy prelate, should devote himself to the exaltation of the sacerdotal order, and thus render a more needful service to the Church than was rendered by many Carthusian monks. M. Olier paid but little attention to this dream at the time, although it was repeated two successive nights, and yet it left a deep and lasting impression on his mind, the full force of which he did not realize, except on after-thought. He had no longer any desire of the monastic life, and going the next day, as was his custom, to vespers at the house of the Carthusians, he felt within himself such a repugnance to their particular vocation, that (as he says) he never entertained the thought again, although he preserved the utmost respect for the monks themselves, and took great pleasure in visiting them and assisting at their offices, in order to unite himself to their prayers and endeavour to participate in their spirit.

The question of his vocation thus finally settled, it only remained that he should prepare himself to receive holy orders; nor could there be a doubt as to where, or under whose direction, this preparation should be made. The Priests of the Congregation of the Mission, lately established by S. Vincent de Paul, had already commenced a course of spiritual exercises for the younger clergy, and to them M. Olier would naturally have turned for the direction he needed; but it was no longer a matter of choice. For, by the command of the Archbishop of Paris, every candidate for ordination was obliged to enter into a retreat of ten days in the house of the Priests of the Mission. This order had been issued the previous year (February 21st, 1631), at the instance of the zealous Bishop of Beauvais, to whom the matter had been earnestly recommended by one of the most remarkable men of the day, M. Adrien Bourdoise, of whom we shall hear more in this history; and thus it came to pass that our abbé made his preparation for the sub-diaconate under the immediate direction of S. Vincent de Paul, whom he henceforth took as his confessor and spiritual guide.

Near contact with a spirit like that of S. Vincent could not fail to kindle fresh ardour in the breast of M. Olier: his desire now was to labour for the salvation of the poor country-people, and this desire the saint enabled him effectually to fulfil by associating him with the Priests of the Mission, although he was not affiliated to the congregation. Acting under the direction of these apostolic men, he catechised and preached with a zeal that never tired; however exhausted he might be after the arduous duties of the day, if he met a poor man on the way he would stop and speak to him of God; when journeying from place to place he would turn aside from the road to converse with the peasants in the fields, regardless of the fatigue, and even privations, to which he thus exposed himself, for not unfrequently night overtook him while engaged in these labours of love, and he would be compelled to find shelter in a hovel. He had not lost his affection for beggars; but if he met with any in the streets he would take them with him to his lodging, and after ministering to their temporal wants, apply himself to the relief of their spiritual necessities, preparing them to make a general confession with a sweetness and a patience that nothing could disturb. Such unceasing exertions at length affected his health, and he was obliged to resign his post to other labourers. Still, when no longer able to bestow his personal aid, he provided for the continuance of the missions out of his own private means, and procured that spiritual advantage, not only for the places from which he derived any emoluments, as Bazainville and Clisson, but also for several of the parishes of the capital.

A whole year having been devoted to the work of the missions, M. Olier once more retired to the Priory of S. Lazarus, to prepare himself for the reception of the priesthood.* But not content with making the ordinary retreat, he spent three whole months in a course of spiritual exercises, intermitting all other labours. On the feast of St. John Baptist, 1633, he said his first Mass in the chapel of the Carmelite nuns of our Lady des Champs, and on the same day and in the same place Mdlle. de Bussy made her religious profession, M. Olier preaching the sermon. Sister Magdalen of S. John Baptist (such was the name she took in religion) during the forty years she spent, first in Paris and afterwards at Limoges, was a model of sanctity to all around her, and it was observed that she seemed to share in an eminent degree her cousin's profound devotion to the Blessed Sacrament and his tender love of Mary.

This love and confidence in the Holy Mother of God seemed to increase and intensify in his heart from the day he approached the altar. Persuaded that to her, after God, he owed everything in the order of grace, he vowed to her a perpetual servitude, desiring that all he possessed should be at her disposal. He could refuse nothing to those who pleaded in her name. If he had no money about him he would give away his handkerchief, or a book, or a medal: "They are the servants of the great

---

* Of the time when he was admitted to the diaconate, no mention is made by his biographer.

Queen," he would say, "I cannot resist them." It was his delight to have some representation of her before him, whatever he was engaged in, and he never omitted to salute her image wherever he met with it. He always passed in preference through the streets in which such images most abounded; they were, in fact, very numerous in Paris, as the citizens, by way of a protest against Calvinistic impiety, had placed them at many of the corners, and also on the fronts of their houses. He seemed to know instinctively where they were, without being at the trouble of looking for them, and would point them out to his friends in hidden nooks and niches, in order to excite their devotion.

These friends were, for the most part, young ecclesiastics of family, who were also under the direction of S. Vincent de Paul; and it was for their benefit, and at their desire, that the famous conferences of S. Lazarus were instituted, which became the occasion of so many blessings to France. The first meeting was held, with the approbation of the Archbishop, on July 9th, 1633, and these weekly assemblies were ultimately frequented by the ablest and most devoted of the young clergy of Paris. To the success of these *réunions*, as well as to the furtherance of the objects for which they were begun, M. Olier contributed not a little, both by introducing numbers of young men to the conferences, and by himself instituting (as will hereafter appear) assemblies of a similar character in other localities.

CHAPTER III.

Apparition of Mother Agnes de Langeac—Mission into Auvergne —Attempted reform of the Abbey of Pébrac—Death of Mother Agnes.

EVER since his elevation to the priesthood M. Olier had desired to evangelize the parishes which were dependant on the Abbey of Pébrac; but, before entering on his labours, he sought to imbue himself thoroughly with the truths he was about to announce to others. For some time he had felt unable to apply his mind to study, and he now resolved not to have recourse to books, but to occupy himself entirely with prayer. "Prayer," he writes, "is my great book; and a passage I once met with in S. Gregory Nazianzen has confirmed me in this conviction; where he says, that preachers ought not to venture to mount the pulpit until they have ascended the steps of contemplation; they ought to behold in God, and to derive from Him, the truths which they preach." The more he read in this divine book, the more intense became his thirst for the salvation of souls; and he succeeded in getting together a band of missionaries such as has been rarely witnessed. They were all young men of family, and among them were his cousin, M. de Perrochel, afterwards Bishop of Boulogne, and an ardent lover of poverty and of the poor; M. de Barrault, nephew of the Archbishop of Arles; and M. Renar, of whom mention was before made. The whole band was, by M. Olier's desire, placed under the direction of an experienced Priest of the Mission.

All being now arranged, he retired to S. Lazarus for a ten days' preparatory retreat; during which, by the desire of S. Vincent, he preserved complete seclusion and perpetual silence, keeping apart from the rest, and ot even availing himself of the usual liberty of speaking in the hours of recreation. It is at such seasons that God has been pleased to favour the souls of His election with signal supernatural graces, and it was now that there happened to M. Olier the most extraordinary event of his life. He was alone in his chamber, engaged in prayer, when he saw before him a female figure in the garb of a nun. Her countenance wore an expression of exceeding gravity and sadness. Her hands were crossed upon her breast, and in one she held a crucifix, in the other a rosary. By her side, but somewhat behind her, kneeling on one knee, appeared an angel of surpassing beauty, who with one hand bore up the folds of her mantle, in the other held a handkerchief, as though to catch the tears she shed. "I weep for thee," she said, in a tone of deep affliction, which went to M. Olier's heart and filled it with a sweet emotion. These were the only words she uttered. So majestic was her bearing, and such reverence did the angel show her, that he believed it was the Virgin Mother who stood before him, and though he remained seated, he cast himself in spirit at her feet. He thought that in showing him the crucifix and the rosary she meant to teach him that the cross of Christ and devotion to His Holy Mother must be the means of his salvation and the rule of his life. The apparition was repeated shortly after, and it was on this second occasion that M. Olier became convinced that the figure was that of a person then actually alive, and that she was a religious of the order of S. Dominic.

His desire to go at once in search of his mysterious visitor was very strong; but as all the preparations for the mission were finished, he was unable, and indeed unwilling, to interpose any delay. On his way, however, with his companions, to the scene of their labours, his mind was on the alert to receive any intimations that might serve as a clue to further inquiry, for he was persuaded that sooner or later Providence would bring him into personal relations with the object of his search; and when, on reaching Riom, a town of Auvergne, some fifty miles from Langeac, he heard people speak of the Mother Agnes as a marvel of sanctity, and found that she was the prioress of a Dominican house, he began to think that perhaps it was this holy nun who had appeared to him at S. Lazarus. This conjecture took more definite shape in his mind the nearer he approached the neighbourhood of the convent and the more he learnt of her sanctity, and he resolved to go and see her as soon as he could obtain the necessary leisure.

The abbey of Pébrac was situated in the depths of a mountain gorge, near the bed of a torrent which falls into the Allier, and there, in the heart of those savage wilds, the missionaries commenced their labours, passing from village to village and from hamlet to hamlet, proclaiming the kingdom of God and calling on all wanderers to return. M. Olier preached every day, and only left the pulpit to finish in the confessional the conversions he had begun by the force and unction with which he spoke. Then would he assemble the poor people together with all the affection of a father, wait upon them himself with head uncovered, and, when their wants were satisfied, make his own meal of the scraps that remained. Those who were unable to attend the church, or had wilfully absented themselves, or had not yielded to his persuasive exhortations, he would seek out in their own homes, or wherever they were to be found, consoling, admonishing, and conquering, by sheer gentleness and sweetness, souls whom rebuke or menace would have confirmed in their impenitence. In fine, not content with having devoted his days to toil, he would often spend a considerable portion of the night in prayer. One thing this lowly priest had asked of God with earnest supplication, and God had granted his request: it was that in all his charitable labours he might pass for a person of no account, and that the credit of what he did might be given to another. It was therefore with a joyful satisfaction he observed that, both on the journey and at the scene of his ministrations, no one regarded him as the leader and promoter of the expedition; particularly as his whole manner and bearing were so simple and retiring, and he was continually employed in attendance on the poor and in other humble avocations.

M. Perrochel was the one to whom all looked as the principal conductor of the mission; to him, as to the chief, all deference was paid, and to him was the merit of the work referred: "He passed," says M. Olier, "for what he was and since has proved himself to be, a messenger sent from God, a veritable apostle, yea, a living image of our Saviour Jesus Christ." If these words were applicable, as doubtless they were, to the future Bishop of Boulogne, the eulogium they convey was at least as justly due to his saintly friend.

All this time M. Olier had not forgotten his visitor at S. Lazarus, and at length he took advantage of a favourable opportunity to repair to the village of Langeac, which (as has been said) was six miles distant from the abbey of Pébrac. Meanwhile it was observed with surprise by the nuns that Mother Agnes seemed to have a supernatural knowledge of the movements of a body of priests who were on their way to give a mission in Auvergne, and she spoke in particular of M. Olier, and of his coming to the convent, with a pleasure which was the more unaccountable as they knew she had never seen him in her life, nor had the slightest personal acquaintance with him. It was with scarcely less surprise that M. Olier, on arriving at the village inn, received a visit from a lay sister of the convent, who came to salute him in the name of the mother prioress. This act of courtesy naturally led to his paying a visit in return to the priory, but, to his disappointment, the Mother Agnes did not make her appearance in the parlour. She had commissioned the sisters, however, to present him with her rosary, as a mark of her esteem, a circumstance which they did not fail to notice; while to M. Olier himself this gift of a rosary came as a strong presumptive proof that the donor was one and the same person with his mysterious visitor. He repeated his visit several times, and still no Mother Agnes was visible. At last she came into the guest-room accompanied by one of the sisters; but her veil was down, as is the custom of the order, and she began to converse with M. Olier as with an ecclesiastic whom she knew only through the report that had reached her of his zealous labours in those parts. Desirous, however, of satisfying himself as to whether she was the actual person who had appeared to him, he begged her to lift her veil. She did so at his request, and he beheld once more before him the countenance of her who had visited him in his lonely chamber at S. Lazarus. "My mother," he said, "I have seen you elsewhere." "True," she replied; "you saw me twice at Paris, where I appeared to you during your retreat at S. Lazarus. I was directed by the Holy Virgin to pray for your conversion, God having destined you to lay the first foundation of ecclesiastical seminaries in France."[*]

At these words, and at the thought of the solemn mission to which he was called by God, M. Olier, in his humility, remained like one astounded; but when Mother Agnes went on to relate how, in obedience to the divine command, she had for three years offered up her prayers and penances in his behalf, he gave full expression to the feelings of gratitude which filled his heart, and earnestly implored her to continue by her counsels the work of sanctification she had already begun in him. She, on her part, was equally affected; and from this moment was established that confidential intercourse between these two holy souls which conduced most powerfully to the spiritual perfection of both. Agnes availed herself of every opportunity to draw his attention to any imperfection she observed in his conduct; exhorting him

---

[*] Besides the testimony of M. Olier himself, whose veracity is unimpeachable, there are still extant the depositions of twenty-four persons of the highest character, who declared their full and entire belief in the apparition, the particulars of which they had heard from his own lips, and vouched for the general notoriety of the occurrence at the time. But that which invests it with most authority in the minds of Catholics is, that in the course of the proceedings at Rome, preparatory to the canonization of Mother Agnes of Jesus, the apparition formed the subject of a long and searching inquiry, at the end of which the promoter of the faith summed up by saying that its truth was beyond dispute: *Dubitari nequaquam potest quin vera fuerit apparitio.* Allusion is also made to the circumstance in the bull of Pius VII., who conferred on Mother Agnes the title of Venerable.

especially to the practice of humility and self-renunciation, and above all things, of interior mortification, as being the very basis and support of the spiritual life. Her constant wish and prayer for him, as she again and again assured him, was that he might be favoured with an abundance of sufferings and crosses, and she never ceased imploring the blessing of Heaven as well on his present labours as on his future vocation. While M. Olier preached and ministered to the country people, Mother Agnes, in the solitude of her cell, offered herself as a victim to God in his and their behalf, and for the whole people and clergy of France.

One subject there was which, even at their first interview, Agnes did not neglect to press upon him, the reform of his own abbey of Pébrac, promising that while he worked she would pray. This religious house had long presented a deplorable spectacle: all remnant of ancient discipline had disappeared, and the utter contempt of monastic rules had been attended with the introduction of every manner of disorder. M. Olier had already directed his attention to the matter, and had even put S. Vincent de Paul in communication with M. Alain de Solminihac, in the hopes that he who had begun so successfully the reform* of the Canons Regular of S. Austin, in his own abbey of Chancellade, in Guyenne, would undertake a similar work at Pébrac. But, as the abbé was unable at that time to supply the required number of religious to fill the places of the ejected monks, the contemplated arrangement had never been concluded. During his present visit, however, M. Olier had witnessed with his own eyes such irregularities on the part of the inmates of the monastery, as caused him the deepest affliction. That the evil was great he had been well aware, but the scandalous reality far exceeded anything he had previously conceived, and

---

* The Abbé de Chancellade commenced his reforms in the year 1622. He was nominated to the bishopric of Cahors by Louis XIII. in 1637, and died December 31st, 1659. He was a man of most austere and saintly life.

he did not hesitate to declare that not even the poor neglected peasantry had more need of reformation than these unworthy professors of the religious life. By the most touching appeals, and, failing these, by the most alarming representations of their guilt in the sight of an offended God, he endeavoured to recall them to a sense of their responsibilities; but in vain. The defence they set up for themselves, and on which they relied for their justification, was, that they were bound, not by the positive rules of their order, but simply by the measure in which those rules were observed by those who received their vows; declaring that at their profession they had formally protested that they understood them and took them, not according to their literal import, but in the sense in which they were actually fulfilled by the community at the time. To this, however, it was replied, that an individual has no power to frame a rule for himself, nor a superior of an order to dispense with its essential vows—not even the bishop himself. These representations, coupled with the earnest entreaties and remonstrances of M. Olier, at length so wrought upon them, that two-thirds of their number (twelve out of eighteen) had begun to show a disposition to accept a reform, when Mother Agnes laid strict injunction on him to accomplish the work on which he had entered.

Accordingly, on June 1st, 1634, he wrote to the Abbé de Chancellade, beseeching him, with a sort of passionate earnestness, to undertake the reform of his monastery, and promising on his part to consent to any sacrifices the abbé might require. Such an appeal, couched in terms of the deepest humility, produced so powerful an effect on the mind of Alain de Solminihac, that, instead of communicating with M. Olier through one of his religious, as had been suggested in the letter, he set out immediately for the abbey of Pébrac, in order to confer with the writer in person. An arrangement was speedily effected between two men whose object was simply to promote the glory of God, at the price of any labour or loss to themselves. M. Olier offered to surrender the whole revenue of the abbey, together with the abbatial residence, and all the benefices attached, which were capable of supporting as many as forty monks; at the same time he resigned his priory of Vieille Brioude, in order to its being henceforth incorporated with the abbey of Pébrac. Alain, on his own part, undertook to provide such of the present inmates as were unwilling to embrace the intended reform with adequate pensions for their lives; and, the monks agreeing to this, M. Olier proceeded without delay to put the buildings in complete repair, preparatory to delivering them up to the new occupants.

But the spirit of evil, seeing his domains invaded, and his power about to be restrained, instigated one of the principal farmers of the abbey lands to oppose, and for a time to defeat, the contemplated reform. This man, who was virtually the steward of the monastery, and supplied the house with provisions, fearing that his profits would be diminished by the intended changes, insisted so strongly on the injustice of the whole proceeding, and on the injury that would accrue to the abbey, that the monks, one and all, resolved to withdraw their consent, and neither to accept the proposed reform nor to quit a monastery where they had hitherto lived at their ease, free from control or interference of any kind. Their measures were taken with an astuteness and a dissimulation which for the time were successful. It so happened that a work having a similar object, but of a less severe character, was being urged forward at Paris by F. Faure, Superior of the Congregation in that city, with the powerful sanction of the Cardinal de la Rochefoucauld, Abbé of S. Geneviève, who had been commissioned by the Holy See to reform the Canons Regular of S. Austin, in France. To these good and zealous men the monks of Pébrac now made a vehement appeal, and on the 1st of August presented the cardinal with a formal protest against the act of M. Olier; declaring it to be destructive of the true interests of the abbey, and begging that it might be reformed on the model which was advocated by F. Faure, and sanctioned by himself. Unhappily, they found a ready supporter in one whose constant endeavour it seems to have been to thwart the servant of God in his highest aspirations and noblest works. The representations of the refractory monks were seconded by no less a person than Mme. Olier, who was unwilling that so valuable a piece of preferment should be lost to the family; and dreaded moreover lest, to induce his religious subjects to acquiesce in his reforms, her son should himself take the habit, as indeed he had actually proposed. In consequence of this determined opposition, the cardinal summoned M. Olier to Paris, for the purpose of conferring with him on the proposed changes in the abbey; and forbade him meanwhile to proceed any further in the business against the expressed wishes of the monks, or to admit any persons to profession, under pain of their vows being declared null and void. But whether F. Faure was unable to send the necessary number of religious, or that M. Olier refused his consent to what he deemed a partial, and therefore an imperfect correction of a scandalous abuse, so it was that the hopes he had cherished were for the present entirely frustrated, and the monks of his abbey emboldened to persist in their irregular courses. Without doubt, he was opposed at this time to the mitigated reform* of S. Geneviève, but this difference of opinion did not prevent F. Faure and his religious from entertaining the deepest respect

---

* When the reform of the Canons Regular of S. Austin was first contemplated, the Cardinal de la Rochefoucauld had designed to separate them into several independent houses, and in the year 1630 had commissioned the Abbé de Chancellade to reform all the monasteries in the more distant provinces. But F. Faure, Superior of the Paris Congregation, judged that it would be better to have but one corporation, and succeeded in drawing over the cardinal to his opinion; and the arrangement between M. Olier and the abbé was made the occasion of obtaining his authoritative interference. Accordingly, on March 1st, 1635, the cardinal ruled that all the monasteries of Canons Regular in France should be incorporated with that of S. Geneviève, and forbade other houses to receive any religious but such as were sent by the Paris Congregation; and two years afterwards he expressly ordered the houses that had accepted the stricter reform of the Abbé de Chancellade to unite with that congregation. This led to much division and confusion, and four of the monasteries reformed by the abbé continued to maintain their own observances.

for M. Olier, as is plain from the terms employed in the Annals of the Congregation, where he is characterized as " a holy priest, whose memory is in benediction among all good men; a pastor who was animated with a zeal equal to his virtue, to maintain the honour and worship of God in all the churches which Providence had placed under his control."

Meanwhile, during all these anxious negotiations, the work of the mission had been proceeding with astonishing success. The people received the word of God with an avidity which seemed rather to increase than to diminish with time, and conversions were everywhere both numerous and striking. These spiritual conquests filled the soul of Mother Agnes with joy and exultation; nor was she less consoled by the fidelity with which M. Olier responded to the graces which she had obtained for him by her prayers. With such courage and ardour did he follow along the way of perfection, that at the end of the six months during which the mission lasted he appeared to her quite another person to what he had been at the beginning, and she returned most fervent thanks to Mary, to whom, after God, she attributed the marvellous change. All the characteristic faults of a hasty and impetuous nature seemed to have been subdued and eradicated, and he had become altogether an interior man. Perceiving this, and that he was deeply conversant with all the more intricate phases of the spiritual life, she took him henceforth for her director, and confided to him the secret trials of her soul: "Heretofore," she said, "I have regarded you as the child of my prayers and tears; but now I look upon you as my father and guide." He was the master-workman destined in the providence of God to put the crowning stone to the spiritual edifice: under his direction Mother Agnes entered on higher and hitherto untrodden paths of perfection, and enjoyed a light, a peace, and a satisfaction, such as she had never experienced since her entrance into religion. Thus was M. Olier enabled to render back in kind the benefits he had received through the prayers and mortifications of this holy nun; and the union that henceforth subsisted between them, and the knowledge they mutually obtained of each other, became, in the order of Providence, the means by which the sanctity of these two chosen souls was made known to the world. For it was M. Olier who, more than any other person, contributed to inspire the faithful, and especially the clergy of France, with an exalted idea of the heroic virtues and supernatural gifts of the Venerable Mother Agnes; while, on the other hand, it was the Mother Agnes who, divinely enlightened to discern the high qualities and great spiritual endowments of this young priest, foresaw and foretold the nature of the mission he was destined to fulfil, and the extraordinary and complete success with which it should be accomplished.

The time, however, was near at hand when the friends who had been brought together in so wonderful a manner were to be separated, never to meet again in this life. M. Olier (as already stated) was summoned to Paris by the Cardinal de la Rochefoucauld, and about the same time he received a communication from F. de Condren, Superior of the Oratory, urging his immediate return, on account of an affair which very nearly concerned the glory of God. It was with the most lively feelings of grief that Mother Agnes heard of her director's intended departure, but anything which involved the sacrifice of herself was welcomed readily and with joy, as an occasion of more entire conformity to the divine will, and she bade him go at once without delay. On taking leave of him she presented him with her crucifix, saying, "All the time you have been here I have ceased to beg of God that He would take me to himself, but now I bid adieu both to the parlour and the world;" and leaving the apartment, she went and threw herself on her knees before the Blessed Sacrament. There, in the hearing of her nuns, she thanked God and His Virgin Mother for having been permitted to accomplish the work she had been set to do, and for which her life had been prolonged on earth; then praying with great earnestness for him who had been so long the subject of her special intercessions, she besought her Heavenly Spouse no longer to delay her departure to Him, but to admit her into the number of those who bless and adore Him for ever.

That very day, October 12th, 1634, Mother Agnes fell sick, and availing herself of the short time that still remained to her, she wrote to F. de Condren, begging him to undertake the spiritual direction of M. Olier. She wrote also to M. Olier himself, announcing to him that her life was drawing to its close. The prediction was speedily verified, for on the 19th of the same month this saintly woman expired in the 32nd year of her age. M. Olier was in the confessional, at the church of S. Paul, on the morning of All Saints, when the tidings reached him. Deeply affected, he went on the instant to pour out his soul's complaint to Jesus in the tabernacle; and believing that where Jesus is, there also are all His saints, he addressed himself to the venerable mother, begging her, who during her life had shown such sympathy for his sorrow, to obtain him consolation for his loss. "Immediately," he says, "my tears were dried, and I felt no longer capable of grieving, for in my ignorance I had believed that we ought to weep and lament, were it only as a sign of the affection we bore the dead; but this is but a vain custom of the world, as if the saints were not the gainers by quitting this mortal life." Having thus consoled himself, he sought to console in his turn the bereaved religious of Langeac. "My reverend mothers," he wrote, "Jesus Christ abandoned by His Father, the Mother bereft of her Son, be your consolation and support. Yours is no common sorrow, and you may well be allowed to mourn awhile for the loss you have sustained; and yet in one thought we may all find comfort, that God Himself is the gainer by our loss. He now possesses fully and entirely a soul of which, so long as she was unconfirmed in grace, He may be said to have had but a sort of precarious tenure. O my mothers, how can we be losers in that which enriches the very majesty of God? You have lost a sister and you have gained a saint. Besides, ought you not to rejoice in the happiness of your mother? To weep and lament, when the first gush of natural sorrow has had its vent, is as though to regret and deplore the bliss she now enjoys; it is as if you grudged your mother her eternal repose, and would disturb even Paradise itself with your lamentations." He then bids them take heed that no relaxation of discipline creep into the convent, now that their holy superior has left them, enjoins them to wean their hearts from creatures, however holy they may be, and concludes by taking his lesson to himself in terms of the lowliest self-abjection.

As though the more effectually to guard against the consequences he dreaded, from the death of his saintly adviser, he set himself to practise the counsels of perfection, and especially that of holy poverty, with increased devotion. Hitherto, by the advice of S. Vincent de Paul, he had retained his carriage and horses, although, in continuing to use them, he did violence to his own feelings. "I cannot wear the world's livery," he wrote, "or follow its fashions; its retinues, its lacqueys, its equipages,—everything of which it makes most account is repugnant to me, and I suffer a sort of purgatory every time I think of a troop of attendants and a servant to walk behind me." But now, by permission of his director, he sold both carriage and horses, and expended the proceeds on the poor or in supplying fresh missions for country places. He retained only one domestic, and even with that one he would have dispensed but for the express injunction of S. Vincent; this was towards the close of the year 1634.

The reader will not have forgotten the dream M. Olier had, in which he saw S. Ambrose sitting on a throne, with a place for a priest vacant below him. He had ever since felt a particular devotion for this great prelate, and had made a practice of meditating on his virtues and actions as the model he wished to have ever before his eyes in the event of his being raised to the episcopate. Now, there was a holy bishop,[*] who had conceived so high an opinion of M. Olier's piety and zeal, that he was intending to beg the king to nominate

---

[*] Probably M. de Corneillan, Bishop of Rodez.

him as his coadjutor and successor. The matter had been made the subject of prayer for many years, and at length his choice had fallen on this young ecclesiastic. This was the business on which (as already mentioned) F. de Condren had urged his immediate return to Paris; and how and why it terminated in a refusal on M. Olier's part will be seen in the next chapter.

CHAPTER IV.

Father de Condren—M. Olier takes him as his director.

FATHER CHARLES DE CONDREN, who succeeded Cardinal de Berulle, its founder, as superior of the French Oratory, was a man of rare sanctity, and an eminent master of the spiritual life. His genius lay in forming young ecclesiastics for the duties of their sacred ministry, and no one exercised so powerful an influence in preparing the way for the reformation of the clergy of France. The veneration in which he was held by many of the greatest and holiest persons of his day was unbounded. Cardinal de Berulle, himself remarkable for his apostolical virtues, and to whom numbers of zealous and saintly men resorted for instruction and direction, entertained so high a reverence for F. de Condren, that as he passed his room-door he would stoop and kiss the stones on which he had trod, and was in the habit of writing down, on his knees and with head uncovered, anything he had heard from his lips. S. Vincent de Paul (as M. Olier relates) was used to speak of him in terms of admiration which almost seemed exaggerated, and when he heard of his death, cast himself on the ground, and, striking his breast, accused himself, with tears, of not having honoured so holy a man as he had deserved. And S. Jane Frances de Chantal, after an interview she had with him, pronounced upon him an eulogium such as it would be difficult in words to surpass: "If God," said she, "gave to the Church our blessed founder (S. Francis de Sales) for the instruction of men, it seems to me that He has made Father de Condren capable of instructing angels." Lastly, M. Olier himself speaks thus of him: "His exterior was but the appearance, the mere husk and shell of what he really was, being inwardly altogether another self, the very interior of Jesus Christ and His hidden life; so that it was rather Jesus Christ living in F. de Condren, than F. de Condren living in himself. He was like the Host upon our altars; externally one sees only the accidents or appearances of bread, but interiorly it is Jesus Christ. So was it with this great servant of our Lord, so singularly beloved of God. Our Lord who dwelt within him prepared him to preach the Gospel, to renew the primitive purity and piety of the Church; and this it is that this great man desired to do in the heart of his disciples during his sojourn in the world, which was hidden and unknown, like the sojourn of our Lord Himself among men.... The sublimity of his lights was something marvellous: they went so far beyond the reach of ordinary intelligences, that it was not possible to commit to writing all the truths he uttered, so holy were they, and so removed from the gross and common way of conceiving and apprehending things, for he had received all by infusion.* And as it is laid down in theology, that the light of angels is of such a nature, that the lower angels cannot compass without miracle the extent of the light of the higher angels, so was it with his light in respect to other intelligences. On quitting this great man one could only say, 'Oh! how wonderful this is; blessed are they who gather up the crumbs that fall from this heavenly table.'"

His conversational powers were of the highest order, but God seems to have withheld from him the faculty of

---

* Doctrines are said to be *infused*, when they are imparted to the intelligence by the Spirit of God without the aid of study, oral instruction, or any other of the ordinary means by which a knowledge of divine truth is commonly acquired.

expressing his thoughts on paper,—or, if he possessed it, he was unwilling to exercise it from motives of humility and in obedience to the Divine will. When pressed by M. Olier on the subject, he replied, that God would recompense a hundredfold those who mortified themselves in something for His sake, and that commonly they who refrained from writing, out of love for Him, received, as their reward, the gift of enlightening souls, a gift far more advantageous to the Church than that of writing. Yielding, however, to the solicitations of his friends, for whose profit he was always ready to sacrifice his own inclinations, he at last consented to gratify them, and for this purpose retired with a lay brother, who was to act as his amanuensis. Every morning for fifteen days he composed himself to dictate, having first begged the Divine assistance; the brother held his pen in hand ready to commence; but, after a moment's silence, he only said, "Let us wait till to-morrow," for God seemed to close his mouth, and he could find no ability to express himself. Sometimes he would say laughingly to those who urged him to write, "Look now, the Apostles wrote a very few epistles in their lifetime, and I must have written more than a hundred." Conversing, oral teaching, direct personal influence, this was the gift of which he was possessed in an extraordinary degree. He was known sometimes to converse with different persons for as many as fourteen hours together, and such grace accompanied his words, that few left him as they had come. It was not the brilliancy, or the eloquence, or the originality of what he said that wrought such marvellous effects: the secret lay in this, that he spoke as one who lived in God and God in him; he had the unction of the Spirit. Sinners were converted, heretics were reclaimed, the tepid felt their hearts kindle with Divine love, the good and the zealous were enlightened and directed in the ways of perfection.

Such was the man who now summoned our abbé back to Paris. It was F. de Condren's vocation (as we have said) to form young ecclesiastics for their holy state, and before M. Olier went on the mission to Auvergne, he and five others had regularly attended his private conferences. As most of them subsequently took an active part in the establishment of the seminary of S. Sulpice, in conjunction with M. Olier, it will be well to say a few words respecting them here. M. de Caulet, Abbé of S. Volusien de Foix,* and son of a president of the parliament of Toulouse, was a man of a singularly disengaged and mortified life; he was one of F. de Condren's first disciples. M. du Ferrier, who had come to Paris solely with the hope of obtaining preferment by means of his high connections, was so deeply impressed with the piety of M. de Foix, that he also was led to put himself under F. de Condren's direction. Associated with these were two brothers, named Brandon. The eldest had relinquished his post of councillor of state to dedicate himself to the service of God. The younger, who was called M. de Bassancourt, had also given up a high civil appointment with the intention of entering religion; though possessed of considerable property, he was remarkable for his humility and simplicity, and his manners and conversation were so engaging, that he was the delight and ornament of the little society. Perhaps the ablest man of the five was M. Amelote, whom F. de Condren had chosen to instruct MM. Brandon and Bassancourt in theology. For some time, the latter withstood all the father's attempts to gain his confidence; he felt a special repugnance both to his person and to his counsels, and kept aloof from him as much as possible. At length, vanquished by the charm of an address which few who came within the sphere of its attractions could resist, he inquired of the holy man what he would have him do do. F. de Condren replied by prescribing him a rule of life the direct opposite of that which he had laid down for himself. Hitherto he had spent his whole time in study; he was now forbidden, for the space of a year, to do more than read two chapters of Holy Scripture every day, one from the Old Testament, the other from the New. He was to read these on his knees, without any commentary; in the one, adoring God

* Hence called M. de Foix, from the name of his abbey.

the Father preparing the world for the coming of His Son, and in the other listening to Jesus Christ, who desires Himself to be our instructor. This rule, however, was not peculiar to M. Amelote, the other disciples of F. de Condren followed it equally.

Enlightened by the Spirit of God, F. de Condren knew that these were the men whom He had chosen to supply the great need of the Church. He knew that the work was to be accomplished by simple priests, if only to offer to their pupils an example of that abnegation which it would be their endeavour to inculcate; and although he rigorously abstained from even hinting at the motive by which he was actuated, he spoke repeatedly to his disciples of an important office in the Church to which God had destined them, and for the fulfilment of which it was His will that they should not aspire to the episcopate. The veneration with which he inspired them forbade their asking any questions, and, in fact, it was not until eight days before he died that he began to speak openly to them on the subject. The reason for this reserve he himself intimated when, in a letter to the Bishop of Comminge, who wished to establish a seminary in his diocese, he said, "You will not forget that this is not a matter to be talked about. The things of God are kept in the secrecy of His Spirit: to publish them to the world is to reveal them to the devil, who is able to frustrate them by means of those who lend themselves to his malice."* No sooner, therefore, had he learned that there was a design to raise M. Olier to the episcopate, than, fearing lest he should be lured away from the path which Providence had marked out for him, he wrote to him, as we have seen, to come at once to Paris.

M. Olier, though now one of F. de Condren's disciples, was still under S. Vincent de Paul's direction; and whether he was ignorant of the injunction contained in the letter of Mother Agnes to F. de Condren, or that he waited for some clearer intimation of God's will before

---

* So also S. Vincent de Paul used frequently to say, that a good work, divulged before the time, was half destroyed.

withdrawing from so revered a guide, and one to whom he owed so much, he continued to have recourse to him during the remainder of 1634, and for a portion of the following year. And here we cannot but admire in what special and unexpected ways God deals with those whose desire is simply to do His will; great saint as he was, and most experienced and enlightened in the conduct of souls, Vincent de Paul was suffered to remain in ignorance of the designs of Providence in regard to M. Olier, so that he urged him very strongly to accept the bishopric which was offered him, and laboured assiduously to overcome his scruples. He was the more moved to adopt this course, because from the knowledge he had of the secrets of his soul, he was aware that he was in a state of extreme spiritual distress and despondency, with no heart to renew his missionary labours. This interior desolation was, indeed, of a kind of which he had as yet had no experience; and as he found no relief in any of the remedies prescribed by his director, he resolved to go into retreat for the purpose of imploring the Divine assistance. His fidelity had its reward; for when his abandonment seemed most complete, he heard an interior voice saying to him, "F. de Condren will give thee peace," and at the same instant an indescribable calm pervaded his soul, and all its agitations ceased.

To F. de Condren, accordingly, he now betook himself —for to him, and not to S. Vincent de Paul, God had entrusted the task of perfecting the future founder of S. Sulpice for his important mission. S. Vincent resigned the charge of him, not only willingly, but joyfully, into the hands of the superior of an institute to which in times past he had himself resorted for instruction and guidance; and as our abbé ever retained the same deep veneration for his old director, so did the saint's affection and regard for the young priest remain undiminished. He still continued to press upon him the acceptance of the bishopric, made it the constant subject of his prayers, and even went on a pilgrimage to Our Lady of Chartres for the purpose of ascertaining the Divine will. But M. Olier was now under obedience to F. de Condren, and the reply of that holy man was ever the same,—that he should make the matter a subject of frequent prayer, for that he saw in him great obstacles to his becoming a bishop, which our abbé, in his humility, understood to mean that his faults and deficiencies were such as disqualified him for so weighty an office. And yet there were times at which his director let fall expressions which might have shown him that he was actuated by another, and a secret motive; for he would say to him,— "God has other designs respecting you; they are neither so brilliant nor so honourable as the episcopate, but they will be of greater service to the Church." The more also he consulted God in prayer, the more profoundly convinced he became of his own unfitness for the episcopal office. Once, in particular, after making his morning's meditation with much aridity and many involuntary distractions, on the Feast of the Purification, it seemed to him that he ought not so much as to entertain the thought, until he had arrived at a state of pure and perfect union with God, so far removed (he says) from his own "gross, unspiritual condition." A similar impression was made on his mind on another occasion, when he had retired for prayer to the church of S. Germain-des-Prés; and the same day, though he does not relate how, the intention of raising him to the episcopate was entirely abandoned, and he was relieved of a business by which his mind had been greatly harassed and perplexed.

The two devotions which especially characterized the French Oratory were the adoration of Jesus in the Blessed Sacrament * and a singular love and veneration

---

* F. de Condren instituted a society called the "Company of the Holy Sacrament," which numbered among its members ecclesiastics and laymen of every rank, from prelates and princes to merchants and shopkeepers. Its object, besides promoting increased devotion to the Blessed Sacrament, was to relieve the poor and afflicted, and to aid in every charitable work. It met every Thursday, in the afternoon, when some ecclesiastic addressed to the assembled brethren a few words of exhortation, reports were made, and alms were collected, often to a very considerable amount. "These meetings," says M. du Ferrier, "presented a picture of the humility and charity of the primitive Christians." The Company was sup-

for His Virgin Mother; and these also (as we have seen) were remarkably developed in M. Olier even from a child. F. de Condren never ceased inculcating on his disciples this admirable truth, that to be a priest was to be an unceasing adorer of the Blessed Sacrament, and such was the fervour which his exhortations enkindled in the hearts of his disciples, that henceforward the one desire and object of their lives was both by their own examples and by direct precept and instruction to spread abroad in all places a particular devotion to the August Victim who dwells continually on the altar. "I longed to be bread," writes M. Olier, "that I might be changed into Jesus Christ; I wished I were of the nature of oil that I might be always consuming before the Most Holy Sacrament; and I remember that whenever I returned late from the country, and went, as was my custom, to salute our Lord at Nôtre-Dame, on finding the church closed, I used to console myself by looking into the interior through the chinks of the doors; and, seeing the lamps burning, I would say, 'Alas! how happy are you to be all consuming to the glory of God, and burning perpetually to serve as a light to Him!'"

F. de Condren also encouraged him to continue all the little pious practices by which it had been his wont to testify his love and devotion to Mary; and many things which he had been in the habit of doing only as occasion served or inclination prompted, now took the form of regular observances. Every Saturday he went to say Mass at Nôtre-Dame; and he never quitted Paris, or returned to the city, without paying a visit to the same church. He made a practice also of begging the blessing of his august benefactress every time he went out of his room or re-entered it, or lay down on his bed; and (as already mentioned) he always made her an offering of everything he had that was new. Before putting himself under the direction of F. de Condren, he had been accustomed to keep the Saturday in every week as a festival

---

pressed—for what reason does not appear—by Cardinal Mazarin shortly before his death.

in her honour, and to abstain from doing anything he would not have done on a day of obligation; but fearful of carrying the matter to an excess, he had not prevented those about him from pursuing their usual occupations. Now, however, with the approbation of F. de Condren, he never wished any who were in his employment to do servile work on Saturdays, and that at whatever inconvenience to himself, though indeed, he remarks in the simplicity of his faith, "I observed that when I let them work, they were sure to do some damage."

While at Paris, he began to resume his studies, with the view of taking his doctor's degree, but finding that his various practices of piety interfered with his reading, and having some scruples on the subject, he sought the joint advice of F. de Condren and S. Vincent, for he still regarded the latter as in some sort his director. They bade him follow the attractions of grace, and accordingly he retired from the theological course (of which in fact he had no need), and abandoned all idea of proceeding to the doctorate. This determination he applauded all through his life: "I escaped," he says, "what might have been an occasion of pride, and did honour to the Cross; for when it is seen that the people profit by the discourses of an unlearned person, any ray of light he has will be attributed, not to the science of the schools, but to the mercy of God."

Being now free to give full scope to the evangelical zeal with which he was devoured, he experienced an ardent desire to go as a misionary to Canada, and there needed all his personal reverence for F. de Condren, and the sense he entertained of the obedience which was due to such a director, to prevent him from putting his design into execution. That holy man had other views for him and his companions. He wished them to behold with their own eyes the spiritual destitution of the people, and the urgent need there was of good and faithful pastors; and to this end his purpose was to send them into such places as were worst provided in this respect, and especially into parishes in which some great scandal had occurred. It was his object also that they should become thoroughly versed in the duties of the ministry before proceeding to instruct others therein, and by their successful labours should have gained the general confidence of both clergy and people, before laying the foundations of the institutions which he foresaw they were to establish. Country missions, therefore, were what he now enjoined, and though he still maintained a strict reserve as to his ulterior designs, he would say to them from time to time, as they made report of their progress, and sought his advice or correction, "We must go on with these for the present, and afterwards we shall accomplish something better." He made the same remark to each of them, "but no one," says M. du Ferrier, "ventured to ask him any question."

Auvergne, the scene of his former labours, was the point to which M. Olier's desires were all directed, and towards the end of March, 1636, he made a preparatory retreat, under the direction of F. de Condren, in a country-house near Paris. This retreat was the occasion of his receiving interior favours such as he had never yet experienced; certain spiritual maxims were impressed upon his soul with so much force and vividness, that throughout all his after-life they seemed to act like a spur to urge him on to unceasing progress in the way of perfection. He performed the exercises quite alone; his director did not give him any subjects for the four meditations he was to make every day, for an hour each, but left him entirely to the suggestions of the Holy Spirit; neither did he pay him more than a single visit during the whole time, being unable to quit his duties in the city. "It was now," says M. Olier, "that I began to have manifest experience of the guidance of that Divine Spirit, and of the care He has had of me ever since. I remember that I then learnt, for the first time, and to my great astonishment, that Jesus Christ is really present in souls. I was glad to be enlightened on the subject of this great truth by my director. 'Yes,' he said, 'our Lord is really present in our souls: *Christus habitat per fidem in cordibus nostris*. "Christ dwells in our hearts by faith:"—that is, faith is the principle of His dwelling, and His Divine Spirit forms Him therein with His virtues: '*donec formetur Christus in vobis.*' He then said, 'Since this is so, henceforth you must unite all your actions to the Son of God in one of three ways: either by affection, or by disposition, or simply by faith. If you have a sensible experience of Christ's presence, unite yourself to Him by affection. If you have no sensible experience, unite yourself to Him by disposition; that is to say, endeavour to have in you the same thoughts and dispositions with which He performed the same actions; and when you are ignorant of His dispositions, or are unable to form them in your soul, unite yourself to Him simply by faith; that is to say, join in spirit your actions to those of the Son of God, which you will thus offer with your own.'"

These maxims formed the basis of the perfection which M. Olier subsequently inculcated in the seminary of S. Sulpice. F. de Condren also gave him a form of prayer which embodied the great truth he had taught him, and which M. Olier left for the use of the community. It ran thus: *Veni, Domine Jesu [vivens in Maria], et vive in hoc servo tuo, in plenitudine virtutis tuæ, in perfectione viarum tuarum, in sanctitate Spiritus tui [in veritate virtutum tuarum, in communione mysteriorum tuorum] et dominare omni adversæ potestati, in Spiritu tuo, ad gloriam Patris. Amen.* (" Come, Lord Jesus [who livest in Mary], and live in this Thy servant, in the plenitude of Thy power, in the perfection of Thy ways, in the sanctity of Thy Spirit [in the truth of Thy virtues, in the communication of Thy mysteries], and by Thy Spirit overcome all hostile power, to the glory of the Father. Amen.")*

At the close of his retreat he took, as the subject of his meditation, devotion to the Blessed Virgin, which he made in a chapel dedicated to her. His august patroness favoured him with many consolations, and, as he believed, gave evidence of her motherly protection by delivering him from imminent danger when crossing the Seine on

---

* M. Olier added the words between brackets for the use of the seminary.

his return to Paris. The boat was overloaded, and as the wind was boisterous, M. Olier became alarmed; but perceiving an image of our Lady attached to a house on the bank for which he was making, he said to M. de Foix, who was with him, "There is nothing to fear; the Holy Virgin sees us;" and his alarm at once subsided. On beholding once more the towers of Nôtre Dame, his soul was inundated with joy, and he felt again all those tender emotions of love and confidence in Mary which he had experienced when he first came within sight of the holy shrine at Loreto.

CHAPTER V.

Second Mission into Auvergne.

PREPARATIONS were now made for a second mission into Auvergne, but meanwhile M. Olier gratified his zeal for souls by assisting at a retreat given by certain of the ecclesiastics who attended the Conferences of S. Lazarus to the inmates of the female penitentiary, called the Hospital de la Pitié. It was to the members of the Conferences that he also looked to supply his little band of missionaries, and to these S. Vincent de Paul added a few of his own experienced priests. The family of M. Olier were occupied at the time with the preliminaries of a marriage between his eldest brother and Marie Roger, daughter of Nicolas Roger, chamberlain to the queen, Marie de Medicis. The affair was regarded as one of great importance, and but for our abbé it would probably never have been successfully accomplished. He was pressed to stay for the nuptials, which were fixed for an early day, but the mission was now fully organized, and nothing would induce him to delay his departure even for an hour. He was present at the signing of the marriage contract, but on the very eve of its solemnization he left

Paris. His relatives, and especially his mother, who had never become reconciled to the kind of life her son had adopted, so different from that which she had contemplated for him, were supremely indignant at what their pride felt as an affront, and reproached him bitterly with the degradation of going to preach to wretched country-people when he might have been a bishop. His mother's unkindness wounded him deeply; but, repairing to Nôtre-Dame, as usual, to take leave of his heavenly patroness, he felt himself amply consoled for the loss of earthly affection by the evidences which that tenderest of mothers was pleased to give him of her approval and love.

It was in the month of April, 1636, that the missionary expedition set out from Paris. M. Olier was on horseback, an exercise to which he was little accustomed—the rest were in a coach—and for the whole ten or eleven days of their journey (he says) they had neither sun nor rain, the sky remaining obscured in the clouds. Their labours commenced on the Sunday within the octave of the Ascension, in the church of a priory dependant on the Abbey of Pébrac, called S. Ilpise. The peasants assembled in crowds from twenty miles round, and so great was their fervour, that many did not care to take any food all through the day, and numbers passed whole nights in the church or in the porch, waiting three or four days together before they were able to make their confession, although there were twelve or thirteen priests constantly occupied. It was now the month of May, and the heat was intense; not only the building itself, but the churchyard also being filled with people, who blocked up the doors and clung to the windows in their eagerness to catch the words of the preacher.*

---

* The actual number of missionaries does not appear to have been more than six or eight at this time: the rest were priests of the neighbourhood who volunteered their assistance. Such instances of fervour are by no means rare in the history of Home Missions; indeed, they are rather the rule than the exception in a Catholic population. The remarkable feature was, that a devotion so extraordinary should have been manifested in districts destitute of pastors, or provided only with such as were a scandal to their flocks. The

The mission was conducted by the Vincentian father, M. Portail, who in age and experience ranked in the community next to the saint himself, but it was by M. Olier that the principal sermons were preached. The effects produced were truly astonishing, and to no one more than the preacher himself. Before every sermon he knelt in adoration before the Blessed Sacrament, then rising with his soul filled, as it were, with light, and all on fire with Divine love, he gave vent to the flames that devoured him in burning words which kindled a corresponding fervour in the breasts of those who heard him. Before he went into retreat he had laboured under an apprehension that his health was unequal to missionary work, and his physicians had assured him that the weakness of his chest would always prevent his being able to do more than give a short exhortation to religious at the grate. But now he describes himself as feeling stronger after preaching than he was before, and, in after-life, he was able to speak of himself as one of the most robust in the whole community. From M. de Béget, one of his fellow-labourers, we learn both the almost incredible amount of work he was able to perform, and also the great personal humility which appeared in all his actions. "In this mission of S. Ilpise," he writes, "M. Olier chose the least commodious room in the house in which

---

Tablet newspaper, of August 14th, 1858, contained an account of precisely similar scenes in the parish of Headfort, in the Archdiocese of Tuam, during the three days of Jubilee. No less than 4,100 persons received communion, many of whom had waited patiently for the entire three days and nights. The parish being unprovided with a Catholic chapel, Mass was said in a thatched barn or shed. The archbishop sat for two days, hearing confessions, in the open air, ensconced in a corner, and surrounded by a crowd of fervent penitents; while on seats, in and about the shed, twenty-five priests attended on the faithful, who knelt in humble groups, on the stones and gravel, quietly expecting their turn. On the last day of the Jubilee, the archbishop, after administering Confirmation to about 900 persons, mounted on a table, and addressed the assembled multitudes; the yard, the walls, the roofs of the houses, and every conceivable place from which there was even a chance of catching the voice of the preacher, being covered with human beings.

we lodged; it was situated immediately under the roof, and very meanly furnished. During a repast, which we took in common, he stood and read a chapter of the New Testament, with his head uncovered, eating nothing until we had all finished. While the rest took their recreation he would employ himself in distributing alms to the poor of the place; this was his uniform practice after dinner, his object being to dispose them favourably for the catechism which generally followed. After saying vespers he went into the confessional, and it was always the poorest and most wretched who came to cast themselves into his arms, as into a secure harbour of charity."

Not content, however, with receiving all who came to him with a father's tenderness, he would go forth to seek such as were unwilling or unable to attend. He might be seen climbing the steepest hills, under a burning sun, in search of wanderers from the fold; and had they who watched him from below followed on his footsteps, they would have found him in one of those dismal abodes, half dens, half hovels, which the peasants of those parts inhabited, and where lay some sick and destitute creature in a state of abject poverty, filth, and misery, such as at the present day it would be difficult to imagine. But nothing daunted or repelled his ardent charity. The necessities of these unhappy beings evoked his warmest sympathies, and he lavished on them all the care of a loving mother; feeding them with his own hands, content himself with such scraps as they left, dressing their sores, washing their linen, in short, performing for them any office however menial and revolting, even (as it is expressly stated) to the combing of their heads. Then having thus prepared the way to their hearts, he would return another day and instruct them in the doctrines of salvation, of which for the most part they were ignorant. Neither did he fail to provide for their future needs, for after the example of S. Vincent de Paul, he established at Pébrac a confraternity of charity for the relief of the sick and poor. His love of poverty, indeed, which he regarded as the livery of Jesus

Christ, was visible in his own person and attire. The materials of his dress were of the simplest kind, and under his cassock he was not ashamed of wearing clothing so old and threadbare, that the poorest country-people would not have cared to have it as a gift.

One office, however, there was in which he took singular delight, and for which he seemed to have a special gift: it was that of teaching little children. So far from its being to him a wearisome task, or a duty which charity alone might have led him to discharge, he appeared to enjoy it as a sort of mental recreation after the more laborious exertion of preaching and hearing confessions; while the ease and simplicity of his words and manner, the affectionateness, the gentle condescension, almost humility, with which he addressed the very youngest of his audience, or drew from them responses to his questions, and the ingenuity with which he contrived to blend amusement with instruction, won the admiration of all who heard him. By daily catechisings and devotions suited to their age, he prepared them for a general communion, which they made with a fervour and a recollection which drew tears from the beholders. This great act was preceded by a solemn renewal of their baptismal vows, in which he made them repeat several times, and in a louder tone, the promise to honour their father and mother, in the words of the fourth commandment; after which they went through the parish in procession, with a modesty and a piety which showed how deep was the impression his teaching had made upon them.

Nor all this time did he neglect his own sanctification; all the moments he had at his command were given to prayer. M. Valentin, a priest who accompanied him throughout the mission, relates how he never failed to say his office on his knees before the tabernacle, wherever there was a church in which the Blessed Sacrament was reserved, and on one occasion walked twelve miles in order to enjoy the privilege of offering the Holy Sacrifice. In the evening, after saying matins of the following day, he continued at prayer until he was summoned to supper, and he went (says the writer) as though he were walking to execution, being often heard to murmur with an emotion which excited corresponding feelings of love and compunction in the hearts of his colleagues, "*Amor meus crucifixus est.*" Deeply convinced, moreover, that to impetrate the grace of conversion for others, it was necessary to deal hardly with himself, he joined penance to prayer, and chastised his flesh by frequent disciplines and the use of a hair-shirt and a pointed girdle which he carried secretly with him. A zeal so devoted could not fail to draw down blessings on himself, as well as on the objects of his charity, and it was during this mission that he began to experience those extraordinary movements of grace with which he was afterwards so habitually favoured. At S. Ilpise, on Whit-Sunday, being about to retire to rest after the fatigues of the day, he felt himself moved to pray, and at the same instant he was seized with so violent a transport of love that, completely overpowered, he was fain to throw himself on the ground, unable to do more than utter these words, "Love, love, love, I die, I cannot bear this flame." Instead, however, of taking complacency in this token of the Divine favour, he made it an occasion of self-humiliation, accounting it only as a mark of his own weakness and imperfection. "I was so greedy of the caresses of Divine love," he says, "that God was pleased, in condescension to my infirmity, to bestow these sweetnesses upon me, though, could I have borne it, another mode of treatment would have been better for me; as a mother humours a sickly child by giving it sugar because it cries for it, though not in itself particularly wholesome."

But though he thus reproached himself with weakness, his instructions and example, and, doubtless more than all, his prayers and mortifications, were fraught with the most powerful effects; and the labours of the missionaries became in consequence so onerous, that he wrote with the greatest urgency to Vincent de Paul for a fresh supply of priests. The saint was about to respond to his appeal, when Louis XIII. applied to him for an additional number of chaplains for the troops then on active service, and he was therefore unable to spare any of his community. Under these circumstances, several of M. Olier's personal friends volunteered to share his toils; amongst whom was M. Meyster, who subsequently became one of the most celebrated missioners of the time. He was a native of Ath, in the diocese of Cambrai, and had been tutor in a family of distinction, where he led a life of worldly dissipation, and occupied himself solely with unprofitable studies and pursuits. One day, while endeavouring to recover a bird he had shot, and which had fallen on a frozen piece of water, the ice suddenly broke under his feet, and in spite of all his struggles he was unable to extricate himself. He was in the greatest peril, when he heard a voice, as in the air, say distinctly, "You would not do as much for me." Struck with compunction, like another Paul, he cried aloud, "Lord, I will do much more;" and redoubling his efforts, he succeeded as by miracle in escaping a watery grave. From this moment he broke with the world, led a life of poverty and mortification, and applied himself solely to the study of the Sacred Scriptures and of the Fathers. The zeal with which he was inspired for the conversion of sinners led him, in the first instance, to attach himself to S. Vincent de Paul, who, in the year 1634, admitted him into his congregation; but the Priests of the Mission not being at that time bound by any vow, two years later he withdrew from the community, and placed himself under the direction of F. de Condren. That saintly man, in writing to M. Olier at this time, expressed himself thus respecting him: "M. Meyster seems to me to be one of those men who ought to be left to the Divine guidance; the Spirit of God must not be bound in him, neither must he be made to conform to the rules of others. Our part is to treat him with reverence, and to humble ourselves in the consideration that we are not worthy of the grace which God has bestowed upon him. However, we ought to furnish him with materials for his zeal, by affording him opportunities of exercising it. Happy are the people to whom the Lord shall send him." Other friends and colleagues of M. Olier, who were not directly associated with him, undertook similar labours in other parts of the country; and so it came about, as F. de Condren had designed, that they who were afterwards to lay the foundations of the seminary of S. Sulpice, and to awaken the dormant zeal of their brethren in the ministry, both obtained for themselves those abundant and extraordinary graces which fitted them to be the instruments of so great a work, and were experimentally trained for the office which God destined them to fulfil in the Church of France.

Everywhere, as at S. Ilpise, the success of the missions surpassed all expectation. No sooner had the little band of apostles entered a district, than the people flocked from all parts to hear them, regardless of heat and cold, and the privations and even hardships which they had to undergo. Many brought provisions with them for three or four days, lodging the while in barns and out-houses, where they might be heard conversing together in the evening on what they had learnt during the day. Nor was this a merely passing interest: for long after, the peasants would act the part of missionaries in their own families; farmers and labourers would sing the mission hymns while working in the fields, and question each other on the several points of doctrine and duty in which they had been instructed; in particular, it was observed that devotion to the Blessed Virgin increased among the people, and they might be seen with their beads in their hands, saying their rosary, as they went to their daily labours, or returned. Thousands who had neglected the requirements of religion and morality for years now made their peace with God; heretics were reconciled to the Church, and sacrileges of long standing repaired by a good and general confession; ill-gotten goods were restored, enmities healed, lawsuits amicably terminated, with which work of charity one of the missioners well fitted for the task was particularly charged—while whole families, heretofore divided by hatred and strife, were reunited in the bonds of love and amity. Such were the ordinary results of a mission, so that those pastors who cared for their flocks rivalled each other in their anxiety to obtain for their own people an advantage, the value of which was manifested in the effects that were everywhere produced.

Nor was it the peasantry only who profited by the labours of these holy men, the higher classes also responded to the call; and though the instructions were of the simplest kind, and conveyed in the most homely language, the grace of God so touched their hearts, that none evinced a greater fervour of devotion, or a deeper thankfulness for the mercies they had received; many (as we learn from M. Olier) shedding tears at the departure of the missionaries, and being hardly willing to let them go. There seems to have been only one quarter in which a different spirit prevailed; this was at Pébrac. Certain of the richer inhabitants who farmed the abbey lands at a rent considerably below their value, and were therefore as little favourable to a change in the administration of the funds of the monastery as to a reformation in their own irreligious lives, commenced a course of systematic persecution against M. Olier of a very vexatious character. They got together a rabble composed of the most lawless persons in the neighbourhood, and endeavoured by menaces and violence to prevent the lands being taken at a higher price. The better disposed were withheld from interfering, by a dread of the numbers and influence of those who were opposed to them; the more so as the leader of the malcontents was a man who had rendered himself the terror of the country round by his crimes, particularly by an attempt he had made to assassinate one of his adversaries, M. de Montmorency, in his bed. A similar fate was prepared for M. Olier, but was providentially averted. He was returning one evening, alone and badly mounted, from one of his visits of charity among the poor country people, when he found himself suddenly confronted by two men on horseback, accompanied by another on foot, who seemed to act as their spy. They were about twenty paces in advance, and as soon as they saw him they drew each a pistol from his holster and prepared to dispute his passage. It so happened, however, that at this point in the road there was a bridle path which led to a little chapel, in front of which M. Olier had catechised a group of peasants three days before; into this he now turned, and had not proceeded far when he was joined by another priest, who, while riding in the valley below, had mistaken the glare of the pistols for the flashing of a sword, and had hastened at full gallop to the spot. With a courage which seemed like an inspiration, he cried to M. Olier to go boldly forward, and, putting spurs to their horses, the two rode straight up to the men, who thrust back their pistols into the holsters as they approached, and allowed them to pass unmolested. To all this violence and harassing persecution M. Olier opposed only prayer and penance, a most courageous patience, and an entire submission to the Divine will; and God, who never fails those who put their trust in Him, was pleased to manifest His approval by an extraordinary grace. At the end of an alarming illness, with which he was attacked after the termination of the missions, the very man of whom mention has been made as being the chief instigator of the persecution, came, accompanied by his wife and daughters, to visit him as he lay on his sick-bed, and to implore his forgiveness for all the sufferings he had caused him. This circumstance, which, as may be supposed, was the source of peculiar consolation to M. Olier, he interpreted as a special call to resign himself with renewed confidence into the hands of God.

But that which caused the greatest joy to a heart burning with the love of souls, was the zeal with which the country clergy not only co-operated in the immediate work of the mission, but laboured to carry out its objects amongst their flocks, and to render permanent the effects that had already been produced. It was thus that M. Olier entered on his destined office of an ecclesiastical reformer. The parish priests began to preach and to catechise with an earnestness and an assiduity which may be said to have been unprecedented in those parts; while a considerable number of cathedral canons and priors of convents, who hitherto had regarded their obligations as fulfilled in a discharge of the routine duties of their office, now deemed themselves responsible for the spiritual condition of the people among whom they lived, and especially of the inhabitants of those places which were dependencies of their church or monastery. The canons of the cathedral church of Puy were eminently distinguished for the activity they displayed, and at the suggestion of M. Olier weekly conferences were established, after the model of those of S. Lazarus, with the members of which the local clergy became associated. Other chapters soon followed their example; so that in three or four neighbouring dioceses there was always a large body of ecclesiastics engaged in instructing the people, hearing confessions, visiting the prisons and the hospitals, conducting missions, preparing candidates for orders, and acting as the pioneers of the bishop in his visitations. In the autumn of 1636, M. Olier gave a retreat to the clergy of the diocese of S. Flour, as well as to the candidates for ordination, at his own Abbey of Pébrac, assisted by the members of the Conferences of S. Lazarus. He himself bore all the expenses of their maintenance during the time, and also supplied out of his liberality considerable sums in aid of such parishes as from their poverty stood in greatest need of assistance.

The influence he exercised and the confidence he inspired were proportioned to the estimation in which he was held for his sanctity, and especially for his humility and disinterestedness, of which we find the following instances recorded. While at S. Ilpise he requested his grand vicar, one of his own religious, to fetch some papers from Pébrac for which he had occasion, and on his objecting, M. Olier rebuked him somewhat sharply; but a few hours afterwards, thinking he had spoken with needless severity, he sought out the ecclesiastic, and throwing himself at his feet, begged his forgiveness. The Bishop of S. Flour having convened an assembly to regulate the proportion of tithes to be paid by the several benefices of the diocese to the mother church, the prelate himself as well as the assessors generally proposed to exempt the Abbey of Pébrac, in consideration of the mode in which the abbot expended its revenues. But M. Olier, who was present, gave expression to his disapproval of the measure in terms which inspired all who heard him with a still higher opinion of his virtues. "It is not right," he said, "to exempt abbots, who generally enjoy large revenues and do nothing, at the expense of poor *curés*, who work hard and have a very small income." An ecclesiastic who was charged with overlooking the accounts of the former general of his abbey, brought him the schedule for his inspection, together with a sum of 5,000 livres, which was due to him. M. Olier put his signature to the account, without examining it, in spite of the ecclesiastic's remonstrances, and devoted the whole of the money to supplying fresh missions; and such was his liberality, that during the eighteen months they lasted, he expended more than 16,000 livres in the support of the missionaries and relief of the poor. He was as forgetful of himself as he was careful for others. When he went to Vieille Brioude it was observed that of the two beds which were in his apartment he chose the smallest and worst furnished, leaving the other to the priest who accompanied him. His only complaint was of being treated with too much condescension, and M. Reboul, archpriest of S. Flour, relates that in the several journeys he took with him, M. Olier was so occupied with God that it was necessary to remind him of the hours for meals.

It was about this time that he made the acquaintance of Marie Tessonière, commonly called Marie de Valence, from the town in which she lived. This poor widow, who was more than sixty years of age when M. Olier first saw her, was held in the highest esteem by the holiest personages of the day; and S. Francis de Sales had not hesitated to say of her that she was a living relic. She had a particular devotion to the adorable mystery of the Ever Blessed Trinity, and M. Olier believed that to her he was indebted for a share in the same peculiar grace. Like so many other pious souls at this time, she had felt herself especially moved to pray for the secular clergy, and as though she possessed a supernatural insight into M. Olier's future vocation, she assured him that he was destined by God to do a great work for

His glory. Filled with compassion for her great poverty, M. Olier, with the approbation of F. de Condren, bestowed on this holy widow a pension of a hundred livres a year.

The missions were on the point of closing, when M. Olier observed to one of his friends that there needed only a fifteen days' illness to be assured that God had accepted their labours. The token was not long wanting: on the evening of the last day of the mission which had been given at La Motte Canillac, a little town in Auvergne, when on his way back to Langeac, after preaching the final sermon, he experienced a sudden calm in his soul, together with an entire cessation from all pain, a circumstance so unusual with him that it filled him with alarm; for crosses, as he says, had become to him his strength and support, and he felt as if God were forsaking him. But he was speedily reassured; for on entering the convent chapel he was seized with what to his friends and the physicians seemed like a mortal illness. He lay for days in a state of complete stupor, unconscious of aught that was passing around him, and perfectly insensible to pain, even when the doctors bled him, or rather, according to the barbarous method of those times, stabbed him with their lancets. While in this condition it occurred to M. de Foix to try whether the holy and loved Names of Jesus and Mary would have any effect in rousing him from his lethargy. No sooner had he pronounced the sacred syllables than the apparently dying man responded to the sound, though still like one who was wandering in his sleep. To aught else he was insensible, but these blessed Names (he says) could do what a thousand knives and lancets could not do: they penetrated to an interior region of the soul, which the stupor of the mind and numbness of the body had left unaffected.

His mother, on hearing of his danger, hastened to his assistance, but did not arrive until he was convalescent; his health, however, was far from being re-established, when he was afflicted with a complaint in the knee, brought on, it was supposed, by his long-continued prayers. The doctors were ready again with their lancets; but apprehensive, as he well might be, of being crippled for life, if he trusted himself in their hands, he betook him to Her who was his constant refuge in all trials, and made a vow to Notre Dame de Bon Secours of Tournon,* whither he had himself conveyed, all lame as he was. And now his mother beheld what must have been a new and striking spectacle to the haughty town-bred lady. On the day of M. Olier's departure from Langeac, the poor of the neighbourhood collected to the number of three or four hundred, and accompanied him some distance on his way. "He has been to Paradise," they cried, "and has come back again." He was glad, he says, that she should witness this demonstration of affection, if only to put her out of conceit with a heartless world. To the prayers of the poor he attributed his recovery, and also to the intercession of S. Francis de Sales, whose assistance he had implored at the commencement of his malady. His sister, who was greatly averse to the life he had chosen, had died at Paris during his illness, and he could not but contrast her condition with his own. In the heart of a great metropolis, and in the midst of a large circle of acquaintance, she had been suffered to expire without a friend to assist or console her; "while I," he says, "who had forsaken the world, and broken all the ties of family, found friends and brethren without

---

* Within one of the old Gothic gates of Tournon was a vault, open towards the town, in which was a painting of the Blessed Virgin, honoured under the title of Notre Dame de Bon Secours. It was frequented as a sort of oratory by the people round, novenas were performed in it, and many cures were wrought. On the feasts of our Blessed Lady it was always gaily adorned, and from time immemorial had formed one of the stations of the procession on the Rogation Days. The ancient gate and the oratory have disappeared together, but the painting has been preserved in an adjacent house, and is every year exposed to the piety of the faithful on occasion of the Rogation procession, which still makes its halt at the accustomed spot. The Virgin Mother is represented as seated on clouds, and holding the Infant Jesus on her lap. The people much regret the destruction of this old oratory, and there is good reason to hope that it will be replaced by another of modern construction.

number—clergy, religious, and the poor of Christ—as in a very desert, thus verifying that word of the Lord, that he that hath left house, or brethren, or sisters, or mother, for His Name's sake, shall be recompensed a hundred-fold."

In a few days his knee was perfectly cured, without the aid of any other remedy than that of invoking the Blessed Mother of God, and he was able to undertake a retreat of fifteen days, which he passed in complete solitude. It was then that he received the gift of a higher order of prayer than he had hitherto practised, that of interior recollection in God without exercise of the discursive faculty. He also learned a more perfect and complete dependence on the Spirit of our Lord in the direction of his every word and act. Hitherto he had endeavoured in all simplicity to follow the movements of grace, but he had not as yet so perfectly conceived how absolutely the Spirit of Jesus was to be the animating principle of all his words. It was at the same time shown him, as in a figure, what his vocation should be. He seemed to behold a man continually at prayer before the tabernacle, while the priests whom he had instructed were climbing mountains like lions, or rushing everywhere with the rapidity of flames, spreading devotion to the Blessed Sacrament in the wildest and most abandoned places.

The fame of his apostolical labours had preceded him, and on arriving at Paris his humility was shocked by the respect and consideration with which he found himself everywhere received. S. Vincent de Paul said to him, as he clasped him in his arms, "I know not how it is, but the blessing of God accompanies you wherever you go." It was now the spring of 1638, and had he followed the promptings of his own zeal, he would have returned without delay to his beloved missions; but F. de Condren, who never lost sight of the one object he had in view, kept him at Paris with other members of the little community, giving him from time to time occupation of the kind he most desired in or near the capital. Others, his former colleagues, he sent into the country, away from the distractions of Paris,* that they might be more perfectly trained, under the direction of M. Meyster, for the work to which they were designed. In a mission which M. Olier and his friends undertook in the environs of Paris, they had to pass through S. Germain's, where the king and his court were then staying, and M. Olier (whom all the world regarded as on the way to a bishopric) proposed that, to put in practice that love of evangelical poverty which they professed, they should go in one of the common cars of the country, instead of a

---

* The description which M. du Ferrier gives in his Memoirs (still in MS.) of his mode of life, is so characteristic of the times, and of the manners of the clergy, that it deserves insertion. "After spending the morning in study and a few short devotions, I went to dine, by the order of my uncle, who was Grand Master of Malta, with the Abbé de S. Vincent, agent of the clergy. He kept open house, and as he was a fine gentleman, all the great world, courtiers and prelates, were his constant guests. After dinner they amused themselves with chess, backgammon, and ninepins, all which were considered as permissible for ecclesiastics, so that they did not play at cards. Some went for a stroll, or to hear the news of the day. God put it into the heart of F. de Condren to withdraw me from Paris, away from all this frivolity, and to send me with M. de Bassancourt and M. Amelote, into the country, to Champ-Dolent, in Saintonge, there to pass the summer and prepare for saying my first Mass. The Abbé de Séry, a pious and holy man, was our director, and he set me to read and meditate on the 21st chapter of Leviticus, and the Epistle to the Hebrews; we lived in great quiet, dividing our time between prayer, saying office, study, and recreation. This retreat was very useful to me, and made me lament the loss of so many days, which I had so ill employed; and it served to make me sensible of the many miserable attachments of my heart. It was S. Mark's day when we reached Saintonge, and we spent the night at S. Jean d'Angéli. They gave us for dessert some cheese, and several plates of sweetmeats, there being no fruits then in season. My three friends, mortified and abstemious, contented themselves with a little cheese, while I, on the contrary, who was accustomed to gratify all my tastes, ate nothing but sweetmeats, urging them to do the same, but they touched none of them. That night, when we had lain down, through the mercy of God—obtained, doubtless, by the prayers of His three servants whom I had scandalized—my eyes were opened, and, sensible of my past gluttony, I began to have a detestation for it, and made a resolution to despise for the future whatever gratified my senses. I mention this to show the good which persons of a mortified life effect by their example."

coach, as they had hitherto done. It was represented to him that, as some of the ecclesiastics had acquaintances among the courtiers, such a style of equipage would only excite ridicule, and draw down contempt both on themselves and on the expedition. But the servant of God replied, "Our Lord, when He rode into Jerusalem on an ass, showed us what account we ought to make of the world's opinion; nay, was not He, who is Wisdom and Sanctity Itself, mocked and derided? Were not the Apostles laughed to scorn when they announced the Gospel? No, no; let us not stand bargaining, but go forward." So they went, as he wished, in an open waggon, and God accepted the humiliation, and blessed their labours with extraordinary success.

CHAPTER VI.

The Nuns of La Regrippiére—Father Bernard—M. Quériolet—M. Bourdoise—Missions of Brittany, Picardy, &c.

ON his return to Paris, M. Olier prepared himself for a fresh campaign by a spiritual retreat. Two missions were proposed to him, and his director being away, after consulting God in prayer, he resolved to go into Brittany. He repaired accordingly to his Priory of Clisson, intending to join M. Meyster in Saintonge, where the latter was engaged in giving missions, but a severe cold obliged him to defer the journey. To spend the time with greater profit to his soul, he went through all the exercises of a retreat, visiting frequently the chapel of Notre Dame de Toute Joie,* a place of pilgrimage in the close vicinity of

* This chapel was originally erected by Oliver de Clisson, father of the Constable, in thanksgiving for some happy news he received on the spot. It became a frequented place of pilgrimage, thirteen or fourteen parishes going to it in procession at different times of

the monastery, where he did not fail to receive many consolations at the hands of his heavenly patroness. He took occasion, also, to hold frequent conversations with the clergy of those parts.

While thus recruiting himself, he learned that at the village of La Regrippiére, distant six miles from Clisson, there was a priory of nuns of the order of Fontevrault,* who, through their worldliness, frivolity, and contentiousness, had become the scandal of the neighbourhood. The relaxation of all the bonds of discipline, entailing, as it did, the total loss of the interior spirit of religion, had brought a host of all the usual abuses in its train. Yielding to an impulse of zeal, M. Olier, now sufficiently recovered, repaired to the convent, and without disclosing his name, begged the hospitality of the house for himself and an ecclesiastic who accompanied him. It was the 20th of July, 1638. An intermittent fever, which assumed

---

the year. During the war in La Vendée it was delivered to the flames, but though only the walls remained standing, it was not altogether disused as a place of prayer, and a young girl of the neighbourhood undertook to collect alms for its reconstruction. For several years she might be seen sitting among the ruins, and holding out her hand to the passers-by, especially on fair and market days; she employed herself meanwhile in spinning, giving utterance to her complaints in a mournful song. Many laughed at her, some insulted her, few gave her anything, but she continued spinning and singing, neither abashed nor disheartened. At length, when peace was restored, she took a little image of the Blessed Virgin in her hand, and went about the country begging for the chapel. Some gave her money, others promised timber for the building; after a while, some of the better sort contributed more largely, and the chapel was restored. At the present day it is still a place of much resort to the faithful.

* The order of Fontevrault was founded by B. Robert d'Arbrissel, under the rule of S. Benedict. He died in 1117. It had for its object the conversion of profligate women, in order to their consecration to God. The chief peculiarity of the institute was, that in honour of the Blessed Virgin, to whom on the Cross her Divine Son had given authority over S. John, the monks were, equally with the nuns, put under obedience to the mother abbess, who was also the general of the order: a regulation approved by the Pope. There were some sixty houses, or priories, in France, divided among four provinces, and two in England previous to the schism.

the character of an epidemic, prevailed at that time in the district, and the nuns, supposing them to be persons who were seeking a refuge from its attacks, and apprehensive themselves of taking the disorder, refused them admission. The man of God made no complaint, but retiring quietly from the gate, went and took up his quarters in a dilapidated henhouse which he had observed on his approach to the convent. The servants, out of respect for the habit he wore, did not venture to disturb him, and there accordingly he remained, abiding God's time. The humility he had shown under the rebuff he had received, the modesty and charity which appeared in all his words and demeanour, and his continual application to prayer, were not lost upon those who were without the walls, and the favourable opinion they entertained of the priestly stranger was speedily communicated to the inmates of the house. It was not long, therefore, before a message arrived from the nuns, inviting him to take up his abode in the apartments allotted to guests. But M. Olier simply and modestly replied, that he begged the ladies would not trouble themselves further about his accommodation, for that his little lodging was everything he could wish.

The report of the unknown priest who had established himself in the nuns' henhouse, and would not move out, was soon noised abroad, and one of the magistrates of a neighbouring town was curious to see the intruder. Now it so happened that the magistrate in question was an intimate friend of the Olier family, and he no sooner beheld our abbé in his strange retreat, than he hastened to inform the nuns who and what manner of man it was they had shut their doors upon. If before they had been anxious to retrieve their error, it now appeared as if they could not reproach themselves sufficiently for their want of respect to so great a man, and they entreated him to do their house the honour of occupying the most commodious apartment in it. But this priest of the Most High knew well on what errand he had come: he had come to do a work for God, and he would do it in the way God willed. Thanking, therefore, with all courtesy those who had conveyed to him the flattering message, he answered in language to which their ears were but little accustomed, "Jesus, my Master, was pleased to be born in a stable, and to lie long time in a manger; it would not be fitting, therefore, that I should so promptly quit a place in which I fare so well." Disconcerted, as well as surprised, at a refusal so unexpected, the nuns desired at least that the fowls should be removed from the miserable lodging he had chosen. "No," replied he, with a pleasant smile, "these poor birds have done nothing for which they should be driven out; and if the crowing of a cock could convert the prince of the Apostles, I do not despair but that God may make use of the same means to bring about at last my own conversion."

And now a strange feeling began to steal over the inmates of this unhappy house, a mixture of curiosity and fear, with a slight addition of compunction. What was this man come for? Why had he set himself down as if to watch and wait for something that was going to happen to them? What had he to say to them? Had he come to convert them? But they would not be converted—at least not yet. The vainest nun in the house, the gayest, proudest bird among them all (as M. Olier describes her), young, handsome, and clever, who was for ever receiving visits from her acquaintances among the admiring *noblesse*, was seized with a desire to go and talk with him; but unwilling to forsake her pleasures, she thought to arm herself beforehand by making a bargain with God, that she should have three years' reprieve before she was converted. To reach M. Olier she had to go by the convent chapel, and as she passed, a voice seemed to speak to her heart, and to say to her that her hour was come. When she saw the holy man, she thought she beheld S. Francis de Sales, and, deeply moved, resolved at once to change her life. Hastening to the superioress, she said, "Mother, my apostle is come; I must surrender; I can delay no longer." A conversion so unlooked-for and surprising caused a general sensation, and M. Olier was asked to preach on the following day.

Such grace accompanied his words, that not only the sister de Vauldray (the religious in question), but several others, determined to make a retreat of ten days, accompanied with a general confession, a proceeding of which they had previously had not the slightest intention. The lesson he had learnt in his recent retreat was still uppermost in M. Olier's thoughts, and several times during his discourse he repeated the expression, "*Plaire à Dieu*" ("To please God"). The words made a strange impression on his hearers, and haunted their memory like some sweet and solemn tune, so that, instead of the worldly songs and childish phrases which it was usual to hear up and down the house, the nuns went about saying continually "*Plaire à Dieu, Plaire à Dieu.*" Of forty nuns, fourteen were united in a firm determination to live henceforth as true religious. It was S. Mary Magdalen's day, and on the morrow they commenced their retreat, which terminated accordingly on the 1st of August, dedicated to S. Peter *ad vincula;* a coincidence from which M. Olier, who had a particular devotion to those two great patrons and models of penitent souls, did not fail to draw the happiest auguries. He had no difficulty in bringing back these religious to the observance of the community life, which had been virtually abolished in the house, and in banishing the spirit of appropriation * (*propriété*), that fatal source of dissipation and often even of disorder in a convent.

Before M. Olier could complete the reform he had begun at La Regrippiére, he was obliged to leave for Nantes,† proposing to go thence (as has been said) to

---

* It is not easy to render the term *propriété* by any one English word. It signifies that which is the very opposite of the spirit of community, viz., when religious, instead of possessing all things in common, love to appropriate anything to themselves, whether for use or in possession.

† It was while he was at Nantes that M. Olier received the tidings that a son had been born (Sept. 5th, 1638) to Louis XIII. and Anne of Austria, and consequently an heir to the throne of France. A matter of so much importance to the kingdom had been made the subject of constant prayer to God, and his joy and thankfulness to God were proportionately great. His solicitude for

the assistance of M. Meyster in Saintonge, and afterwards to return to Paris. But his presence being still needed for the confirmation and guidance of the religious who had yielded to grace, God allowed him to be attacked by the epidemic already mentioned, which detained him in Brittany until the beginning of the following year. He was taken ill on the Nativity of the Blessed Virgin, a circumstance which he regarded as a special token of her favour; "a recompense," he writes, "for my small labours, the most precious a Christian can receive." From a spirit of devotion to that heavenly Mother, he always reckoned the years of his own life from her birthday, and her Divine Son (he says) never failed on that day to bestow some blessing upon him. His intention had been to remain at Clisson (to which place he had retired from Nantes) until his health was fully re-established, but he was so strongly urged to return to the latter city by Marie Constance de Bressand, mother assistant of the Convent of the Visitation, that he complied with her request. The only accommodation the good nun could offer him was a room in the gardener's cottage; but this, she well knew, would be exactly to his taste, especially as it resembled the lodging which S. Francis de Sales had occupied at Lyons during his last illness. Indeed it was all for the sake of this great prelate that he accepted the invitation. The Mother de Bressand, before entering religion, had had the happiness of being under the saint's direction, and M. Olier hoped to derive much edification from her reminiscences of his habits and conversation, particularly in all that concerned the spiritual life. Nor was he disappointed in his expectations; while she, on her part, seemed to perceive in him so large a measure of the lights and graces of her saintly director, that she was moved to take him as the guide of her soul. It was at this time also that

the interests of religion made him so anxious that the future monarch should be well and Christianly educated, that he would not have shrunk from the responsibility of acting himself as the young Dauphin's preceptor, and, as it appears, he even expressed a wish to undertake the onerous office.

he was brought into spiritual relations with another very holy woman, the Sister Marie Boufard, who was then living in the world, in a state of great poverty and confirmed ill health, but who subsequently entered the Convent of the Visitation, and died, in the odour of sanctity, at the advanced age of 87 years. She supported herself by keeping a school, and such was her reputation for sanctity, that people came from all parts to consult her on affairs of importance. Like M. Olier, she had a profound devotion to the Most Holy Sacrament, and a tender love for the Blessed Virgin, and as God led her by extraordinary ways, and lavished extraordinary favours upon her, the fear of being deluded caused her to accept with particular joy the guidance of one who was competent to direct her with safety along those heights of perfection to which she was called.

During his residence at Nantes M. Olier became the witness of a miraculous circumstance, and one that from its nature would affect him very powerfully. There was in the Convent of the Visitation a nun named Françoise Madeleine de la Roussière, who was consumed with an insatiable hunger for the Divine Eucharist. The evening before communion she might be observed all panting and gasping for the Bread of Life, which to her was the very meat and drink of her soul; her countenance was in a flame, and the perspiration stood in drops upon her forehead, even in the depth of winter. One day, when M. Olier was saying Mass as usual, and was about to communicate this sister, the Sacred Host detached Itself from his fingers, and went of Its own accord into her mouth, as though hastening to satisfy the longing desire of so ardent a soul. The parish priest of Nort likewise beheld the same extraordinary manifestation of the Divine favour.

M. Olier profited by the delay to follow up the work so auspiciously begun at La Regrippiére. He visited the convent on several occasions, and addressed the religious in letters which were no less effectual than his presence and exhortations. Sister de Vauldray remained stedfast in her good resolutions, and showed a most

admirable courage amidst all the discouragements and
sufferings she had now to endure from those who maintained their spirit of independence, and refused to submit
to the yoke of discipline. One crying abuse there was
which he succeeded at this time in abolishing. Surrounding the convent was a thick wood, in which the
nuns were in the habit of walking, and where there was
a pond, which afforded them the amusement of fishing;
but, strange to say, the wood had no inclosure, so that it
was open to all intruders. M. Olier had no wish to
deprive them either of their walks in the wood or of the
recreation of fishing, but he insisted on the necessity of
the grounds being properly inclosed, which accordingly
was done by the erection of a wall. But a reform, such
as alone would satisfy the zeal of M. Olier, was not to
be brought about in a few days, or even months: how he
succeeded in the end we shall see hereafter; but meanwhile the state of this religious house was a matter of
deep anxiety to him, and the subject of his constant
prayers. It was to Sister de Vauldray that he looked
as the instrument, under God, by which the change was
to be effected, and, with F. de Condren's permission, he
continued to correspond with her in the capacity of her
director, even after his return to Paris. Providence also
assisted him in an unlooked-for way. In the beginning
of January, 1639, he felt himself sufficiently recovered
to leave Nantes, but he was unequal to a journey on
horseback (which was now his only means of travelling),
especially in the middle of winter. In this perplexity,
he partook himself to his usual resource of prayer; when
a gentleman of the country, who was aware of his embarrassment, offered him a seat in his coach and six, only
begging to be allowed to go a little out of the way, to
visit an abbey, with the superioress of which he wished
to confer. This was no other than the Abbey of Fontevrault, the mother house of the convent at La Regrippiére. M. Olier had thus an opportunity of preferring
a petition, for the success of which nothing less than a
personal application would have sufficed. He knew that
in the neighbourhood of Fontevrault was a nun, pious

and prudent, and every way qualified, on whose co-operation he could rely for completing the reform he had so much at heart. This nun he now begged the abbess* to send to La Regrippiére. It was not without some trouble that he obtained his request, but the result amply proved both the justice of his representations and the wisdom of yielding to them.

On reaching Paris, M. Olier hastened to confer with F. de Condren, whom he had not seen for six months; and it was with an inexpressible satisfaction that he found his method of prayer, and his mode of disposing himself thereto, approved by so gifted a master of the spiritual life. Under this father's direction, he now resumed his theological and scriptural studies, but his attraction to prayer was so strong, that he asked and obtained permission to make a second hour's meditation in the evening, except on certain days, when, for the sake of study, it was not to be prolonged beyond half-an-hour; but by the mercy of God (he says) he never omitted the full hour's meditation in the morning, however he might be employed.

The course of this history now introduces us to three men, perhaps the most remarkable of their time, at least for what may be called their holy eccentricities. The first is Father Bernard, commonly called "the poor priest." He was a person of original genius, but of great singularity of character, and one who seems to have been sent into the world for the purpose of condemning and confounding its maxims and notions, by what to many would appear to be an indiscreet display of the folly

---

* This was Jeanne Baptiste de Bourbon, natural daughter of Henry IV. From her childhood she was remarkable for piety, and on becoming abbess of Fontevrault she manifested all the virtues of a perfect religious. - Such was her love of poverty and mortification that she shrank from no employment, however menial; washing the dishes, sweeping the cloisters and the kitchen, waiting on the sick night and day, and assisting the dying. Her accomplishments were no less remarkable. Her ordinary reading consisted of one of the Latin fathers, and she composed several treatises of theology and philosophy. She died on the 16th of January, 1670, at the age of 62, having been abbess thirty-three years.

of the religion of the Cross. His delight seemed to be to despise the opinion of the world, and to affront it in every way his zeal could prompt, or his wit devise. Human respect, human prudence, worldly propriety, what men called wisdom, he absolutely scorned, and he gave expression to his scorn in a way which, in its turn, excited the world's contempt; so that, while his friends, and all who were acquainted with his real character, knew him to be a man of great intellectual acuteness, thorough earnestness of purpose, and a most saintly life, to people in general, who knew only just so much of him as he was pleased to let them see, he looked more like a buffoon or a madman. Between this good but eccentric man and M. Olier there sprang up a peculiar friendship, based on the knowledge of each other's estimable qualities, and especially on their mutual zeal for the honour of God, their tender devotion to Mary, and their love of the poor.

The second was M. de Quériolet, who had been converted while leading a life of habitual impiety, in the manner about to be related. He came at this time to Paris, to see F. Bernard, out of respect for his sanctity, and it was from his own lips that M. Olier learnt the following particulars,* in the presence of S. Vincent de Paul, F. de Condren, and the other ecclesiastics with whom the reader has been made acquainted. "You will agree," he said, "in regarding me as an example of the extraordinary mercy of God, when you have heard the narrative of my horrible crimes. Up to the age of thirty-five I passed my life in the practice of every kind of abomination, and in the habitual profanation of the sacraments, which I received that I might have the appearance of being a good Catholic. At last I was possessed with so unaccountable a hatred for the Person of Jesus Christ, that I left the kingdom in order to go to Constantinople, and turn Mahometan. I had learnt that an envoy from the Grand Turk was at Vienna, and I made haste that I

---

* They were taken down by M. du Ferrier at the time, and are to be found in his (unpublished) memoirs.

might be in time to accompany him on his return; but the infinite mercy of God determined otherwise. While passing by night through a forest in Germany, I fell into the hands of robbers, who killed my two attendants. Seeing their guns levelled at me, I made a vow to visit the shrine of Our Lady of Liesse, if God would deliver me from this peril. I was delivered; but, alas! I did not the less persist in my impious intention, and hurried to Vienna for the purpose of joining the envoy; but he had taken his departure. In the hope of overtaking him, for he had left only the day before, I took boat on the Danube, and reached the confines of Hungary, where I was stopped for want of a passport. I then repaired to Venice, waiting an opportunity to embark for Constantinople, and with this view I enlisted as a soldier of the republic, in the garrison from whence the vessels sailed. For six weeks it pleased God that no vessel left for Constantinople, and tired of the life I was leading, I deserted, regardless of the peril I was incurring, and returned to France. At Paris I heard of the death of my father, hastened by his distress at my unhappy determination, of which he was aware. I then turned Protestant, as thinking it more for my interests; but as I was destitute of all religion, on my family offering me what appeared greater advantages, I again professed myself a Catholic. I resumed my practice of making sacrilegious communions, accompanied with the most frightful profligacy. Though I did not drink to intoxication, yet the quantity of wine in which I indulged kept me in such a state of excitement, that I was always engaged in some quarrel. I seemed to have an insatiable thirst for human blood, and killed several persons in encounters and duels. As a protection to myself, I purchased the

lightning, which tore away the roof of the house, the ceiling of the room, and even the top of the bed, leaving me exposed to a storm of rain; I did but commence blaspheming anew, defying the lightning and Him who sent it. A feeling of remorse, however, followed; I had thoughts of changing my life, and went and begged the Carthusians to receive me into their order; but on the third day I took my departure without a word of farewell. From that time I became an absolute atheist, believing neither in God, nor in heaven, devils nor hell."

It was the time at which the diabolical possessions at the Ursuline Convent of Loudon* were agitating all France, and being on his way to the town, M. de Quériolet thought he would go and witness the exorcisms, which to him, denying as he did the existence of devils, were a mere piece of jugglery, and he went (he says) as he might to a comedy, from no other motive than the desire of amusement. The exorcism had nearly terminated, when the possessed, turning towards him, or rather the demon who spoke by her mouth, began giving vent to the most horrible blasphemies against God, accusing Him of injustice, in that He had condemned so many millions of angels for one only sin, and yet showed mercy to the most wicked of men, who had committed the most dreadful crimes without number; having delivered out of his hands that wretched blasphemer and atheist, who had made a vow to our Lady of Liesse which he never performed, and was altogether undeserving of the Virgin's pity. This reproachful mention of his vow, of which he had never breathed a syllable to mortal being, fell upon his soul with a more startling force than the thunderbolt which had awakened a passing feeling of compunction within him, and, rushing

---

* M. Picoté, one of M. Olier's companions, was among those who were deputed by the king to inquire into the affair; he went with a mind rather prejudiced than otherwise against the reality of the possessions, but returned perfectly convinced. His opinion was shared by M. Meyster and M. de Foix, the former of whom examined the case at the instance of the Bishop of Saintes. See the work of P. Surin, entitled, *Triomphe de l'Amour divin sur les Puissances de l'Enfer*.

from the place, he sought a neighbouring chapel, and there, with his face to the earth, gave free course to his sorrow. Those who saw him thought he was ill, and would have raised him from the ground, but his countenance, all bathed in tears, showed the nature of his grief, and he was left alone. All night he lay on the floor of his chamber, bewailing his sins, and on the morrow he made a general confession of his whole life. The first act of his new existence was to repair to Liesse in fulfilment of his vow: he dismissed his servants, gave all he had about him to the poor, put on a beggar's dress, and made the whole journey bare-footed, and with head uncovered, asking alms by the way, and weeping unceasingly for his crimes. From Liesse he went, in the same manner, to La Sainte Baume, in Provence, to obtain through the intercession of the holy Magdalen, some portion of her spirit of penance, and her love of Jesus. Returning to Rennes, he persevered to the day of his death in the same rigorous self-humiliation, condemning himself never to raise his eyes from the ground, making eight or ten hours' prayer a day, and taking scarcely any food from Thursday at mid-day until Sunday at the same hour.

We have said that he had come to Paris to make the acquaintance of F. Bernard; the manner of their meeting is too characteristic to be omitted. We give the story as F. Bernard himself told it to M. du Ferrier. "As I was going," says he, "in the direction of the Carthusians, I saw a man coming towards me, covered with dust, with his cassock turned up, as sorry a looking figure as you can conceive; he stopped me, and asked if I could tell him where a certain M. Bernard lived, who went by the name of the poor priest. I inquired if he knew the man, and what he wanted with him. 'I am come,' said he, 'to make his acquaintance, for they tell me he is a good man, but a little crack-brained.' Feeling somewhat surprised at this observation, 'I do not know,' answered I, 'that you are much wiser than he is.' 'Perhaps,' continued he, 'you are yourself the very man I am seeking.' 'Yes,' replied I, 'the very man.' Upon which he seized me in his arms, saying, 'I am Quériolet; I am come all the way from Brittany to have the pleasure of seeing you.' I cordially returned his embrace, for I knew him well by reputation, as having been converted at Loudon by one possessed by the devil."

The third of these eccentric, but eminently holy men, was Adrien Bourdoise, of whom mention has been made before in this history. He was the founder of the Seminary of S. Nicolas du Chardonnet at Paris, and appears to have been raised up by God to perform the office of pioneer in the work of ecclesiastical reform. Consumed with grief at the scandals that everywhere prevailed, he lifted up his voice, like another John the Baptist,* and called on men to do penance ere the wrath of God fell upon them. Ignorant of fear, and utterly regardless of what was said or thought of him, he spared no one, whatever might be his station, but spoke the truth plainly and without disguise, in season and out of season, with a freedom and a bluntness, a power of sarcasm, and sometimes even with a practical facetiousness, which, while it irritated or moved to laughter, often succeeded in mitigating or repressing the evil he denounced, where a milder manner and a more polished address would have failed of effect. Zealous and single-minded himself, he was impatient of the want of these qualities in others, and such men were peculiarly obnoxious to his raillery and wit; but where he perceived genuine earnestness and a heartfelt love of God, it seemed as if he could not sufficiently express his admiration and sympathy, and all the hidden sweetness and kindliness of his nature were allowed to gush forth, with an overflowing abundance which would have astonished those who knew only the more obvious and less engaging, though not less estimable, portions of his character.

---

* His character is portrayed in the following distich :

" Hic fuit Elias more, et clamore Joannes,
Ore Nathan, curâ Paulus, amore Petrus."

A life of this remarkable man is still a desideratum. There is a short memoir of him in MS. (composed from a larger work, also in MS.), which M. Faillon, the historian of M. Olier, pronounces to be a masterpiece of biography.

The apparent severity and almost rudeness* of his speech and manner, particularly when he wished to try a man's worth, may be inferred from the following incident. Knowing the zeal and piety of M. Olier and his friends, he wished to be better acquainted with them, especially with a view to conferring together on the requirements of the clerical life. The mode he adopted for gaining his object was such as would have occurred to none but himself. One morning M. Olier, accompanied by M. de Foix and M. du Ferrier, went to S. Nicolas, the model parish-church of Paris, for the purpose of saying Mass. They waited on M. Bourdoise, who received them courteously; but when they mentioned the object of their visit, and asked permission to say Mass, he replied, "No, gentlemen, I am sorry to refuse you, but you must have more of the look and demeanour of ecclesiastics before I can let you approach my altars." The young priests, imagining that so holy a man had perceived some impropriety or defect in their manners and conduct, reproached themselves accordingly, and thanked him for his rebuke. This was just what he wanted; he continued the conversation, and soon their hearts were all in a glow from the affectionateness with which he spoke to them, and the warmth of the Divine love which animated all he said. It need not be added that all three said Mass that morning at S. Nicolas. From that day a firm friendship was established between M. Olier and M. Bourdoise; and if our abbé honoured the Superior of the Oratory as his spiritual father and guide, he now accepted the Rector of S. Nicolas as his master in the clerical life.

M. Bourdoise was not long in finding work to be done by M. Olier and his friends. In a little mission he had been giving at the château of the Presidente de Herse, mother of M. Vialar, one of M. Olier's associates, as also a relative of the latter, he had become acquainted with the spiritual destitution of the surrounding villages; and

---

* To wit, he one day reproached S. Vincent de Paul for his pusillanimity, and called him a *poule mouillée* (a chicken-hearted fellow).

hither he now sent our abbé and others, to evangelize the neighbourhood. They found an admirable coadjutrix in the mistress of the mansion, who, in her zeal for the reformation of the clerical body, had contributed largely towards the establishment of exercises for the candidates for orders, both at Chartres and at Paris. One day they had scarcely begun dinner, when M. Bourdoise put to them what appeared a whimsical question. "Gentlemen," said he to those who had just been preaching with so much fervour and zeal, "may I ask whether you have each made your sermon to-day?" "How can you question it?" was the reply. "I question it," he rejoined, "until the fact be proved. We have already had some dinner, and here is a crowd of poor people who have come twenty miles and more to hear you preach, and who have not a morsel of bread. Unless we give to them, they will faint by the way. Now then, gentlemen, let us make your sermon good; let us give them the rest of our dinner, and content ourselves with a little dessert." The proposal was adopted, and instantly put in execution, to the edification and, no doubt, entire satisfaction of the poor villagers.

Shortly after, M. Olier gave another mission at Illiers, a small town near Chartres, which was attended with unusual effects, not only among the poor and working classes, but also among the higher ranks. The family of a M. Bellier, one of the queen's officers, and otherwise well connected, afforded a striking instance of this. He had some property in the neighbourhood, and his family consisted of four sons and two daughters. So deep was the impression produced by M. Olier's sermons, that both daughters eventually entered the Order of the Visitation, and their two elder brothers also embraced the religious state. The third died young; the fourth, who was a most fervent Christian, died soon after marriage, and his widow consecrated herself to God in the Congregation of Providence.

It was while engaged in this mission that M. du Ferrier discovered one of those holy souls, thousands of whom, it may be believed, have lived and died in obscurity, and whose supereminent sanctity is known only to God and His angels. He was summoned to attend a poor blind woman who was lying dangerously ill. Her name was Françoise Fouquet, and she was fifty-two years of age. She made her confession, but in a manner so spiritual, with so keen a discernment of her faults and of her infidelities to grace, that he was filled with astonishment and admiration. Her compunction for what hardly amounted to a defect or an imperfection, affected him powerfully. He found, too, that she had a thorough knowledge of all those profound truths which had formed the subject of F. de Condren's Conferences; and all this joined with the most exalted virtues. She had become blind when twelve years old, at which time also she lost her mother. Her father, who was a vine-dresser, took another wife, who treated her unkindly, driving her from the house at dawn of day, when her father was gone to his work. The child went and sat under a tree, crying, and thinking of God; ready to receive her father when he returned in the evening. Yet she made no complaint, and to the day of his death her father never knew how cruelly she was treated. When he died, her mother-in-law turned her out of doors; on which she went, accompanied by a cousin, on a pilgrimage to some of the famous shrines of the country, praying God to restore her sight. But perceiving that it was His will that she should remain blind, she returned to Illiers, where she was able to earn a few pence by spinning, living the while on bread and water. The purity of her conscience may be estimated by two *faults* of which she accused herself in conversation with M. du Ferrier. The first was, that a neighbour having been crushed by a waggon, she had prayed and then touched him, and he was instantly healed; this, she thought, betokened presumptuousness and pride. The other that, on some mischievous person thrusting a piece of dung into her mouth, she had made a movement of repugnance, forgetful, as she said, of the gall and vinegar which her Saviour drank upon the cross. One thing there was which for a while perplexed M. du Ferrier, that when he asked her whether from her heart she renounced the world, and put aside all desire of remaining in it, she replied, "I never give it a thought." On his repeating his question in another form, and asking her whether she did not deem those miserable who loved this earthly life, full of so many occasions of sin, her reply was still the same: "Sir, I never give it a thought." A third time he said, "Françoise, let us renounce the world, and all that belong to it; and let us abandon ourselves entirely to our Lord, that he may separate us from it." And then came an answer which explained all: "Ah, sir, excuse me; I do not wish so much as to think of the enemy of my Saviour."

M. Olier was still in the full career of missionary zeal, when he received a missive which obliged him to repair at once to Paris. This was a royal nomination to the episcopal coadjutorship of Châlons sur Marne. The bishop of that see, Henri Clausse Marchaumont, was overwhelmed at the appalling condition to which the total loss of discipline had reduced his diocese, and had long desired the establishment of an ecclesiastical seminary. He had addressed himself with this view to M. Bourdoise, both personally and through his grand vicar. The latter wrote thus:—"The least of the ecclesiastics of Paris would here be worth their weight in gold. How many poor souls are perishing in these parts through the neglect of their pastors, who are ignorant, and more than ignorant, but whom it is impossible to remove from their benefices!" M. Bourdoise, however, was unable to supply the urgent need, and the bishop then turned his thoughts to M. Olier, as the man most capable of effecting a reform which his own advanced age did not permit him to undertake. Accordingly, he solicited the Cardinal de Richelieu to recommend M. Olier to the king as his coadjutor. That great minister, who, whatever his faults, had an earnest zeal for the honour of the Church and the good of the realm, not only readily acceded to the bishop's request, but urged the appointment with all the force of his authority. "Sire," he said to Louis XIII., " in recommending M. Olier, I feel that

I am proposing the man who, of all others, is the most fitted by his intelligence, piety, and prudence, to fill this important see." An eulogium so emphatic did but express the unanimous sentiment of all good men, and in the July of 1639 the nomination received the royal assent.

In the estimation of the public the matter was now concluded, and the canons and clergy of Puy hastened to felicitate him on his appointment. The intended bishop, however, was of quite another mind. F. de Condren's response was still the same: "God has other designs respecting you; they are not so brilliant or so honourable, but they are fraught with greater advantages to the Church." And this response was understood by M. Olier as a signification of his unworthiness. "The dignity of which you speak," he wrote, in reply to the clergy of Puy, "supposes great talents, which far exceed my capacity. I pray our Lord that He will give me grace to remain of the number of His least servants in the holy work of his missions." He therefore returned the brief to the cardinal with all suitable acknowledgments; but the cardinal declined to accept his refusal, and he was obliged to request a private conference, for the purpose of explaining the motives on which he was acting. A disinterestedness so rare, especially as a peerage was attached to the see in question, struck the minister with admiration, and he did not refrain from giving public testimony to the respect with which he regarded him.

Having failed to obtain M. Olier for his coadjutor, the Bishop of Châlons endeavoured at least to secure for his diocese the services of one who had taken an active part in the same labours of charity, and was known to possess a large share of his devotion and zeal. The prelate's choice fell on M. Vialar (of whom mention has been made in this chapter), to our abbé's extreme joy and satisfaction; feelings which, it is scarcely necessary to say, were not reciprocated by the members of M. Olier's own family, who were loud in their condemnation of what they deemed his obstinacy and folly. His mother especially set no bounds to her resentment, which became still more exasperated when, shortly after M. Vialar's nomination, and before he had even received the bulls, the Bishop of Châlons died, and he became the occupant of the see. But M. Olier, foreseeing the storm, had left his mother's mansion and gone to reside at S. Maur les Fossés,* in a house belonging to M. Brandon, where he and his friends were in the habit of staying in the intervals of their apostolic labours. It was now that, by F. de Condren's advice, they chose one of their number to be the head of their little community; the individual selected was M. Amelote, who, young as he was, for he had not yet attained his thirtysecond year, had acquired a certain influence over the rest by his greater knowledge and experience, and a judgment singularly matured, and it was under his direction that the succeeding missions were conducted.

The first was that of Amiens, the occasion of which was an accidental sermon preached by M. Meyster, which threw the whole town into a ferment. The bishop invited M. Olier to give a mission in the cathedral; he was so absorbed in the study of Holy Scripture, in which the Spirit of God favoured him with extraordinary lights, that he hesitated to accept the invitation; but acting under F. de Condren's advice, he proceeded to Amiens, accompanied by MM. de Foix, du Ferrier, de Bassancourt, and four others. It was a new and untried experiment, as, like the Vincentians and the Oratorians, they had hitherto confined their ministrations to villages and hamlets, and many grave and prudent persons strongly condemned the enterprise. But it was soon apparent that the blessing of God was with them, for their labours were attended with unprecedented success. The cathedral was crowded all through the day, and such multitudes besieged the confessionals, that it was ne-

---

* There was in the Abbey of S. Maur les Fossés a shrine of the Blessed Virgin, which was a frequented place of pilgrimage. It went by the name of Our Lady of Miracles, and such was the veneration in which it was held, that the monks of S. Maur never entered it except barefooted.

cessary to call in the aid of seventeen priests of the city.

Many notable conversions took place, the most extraordinary being that of a Swedish colonel, a Protestant, who was in command of a troop of horse in the town, composed of eight hundred men; extraordinary not only in itself, but in the effects it produced on others. M. Meyster learnt that he was lying dangerously ill, and went late one evening, accompanied by M. du Ferrier, to visit him. He found him in a room with his wife and fifteen or twenty of his men sitting round the fire. The missionaries were civilly received; but on M. Meyster telling the sick man that he had come for the purpose of offering him his services, he was met with the reply that he had no need of his instructions, that he was quite content with the religion in which he had been born, and wished to be left at peace. M. du Ferrier was greatly disheartened at this reply, but M. Meyster, asking for a light, produced a miniature in a case, and showing it to the Swede, inquired what he thought of it? The man answered that it was very beautiful. "It is the mother of our Lord Jesus Christ," said the priest; "will you not salute it?" The colonel did so in military fashion. Then, turning to his companion, and to a young and devout Catholic, who happened to be present, M. Meyster said, "Let us pray to the Blessed Virgin for his conversion;" and making all kneel down with him, he recited the Litany of Loreto. When it was ended he laid both his hands on the shoulder of the sick man, and said, "I am here to tell you from God that you must no longer delay your conversion." "Yes!" replied the man, "I wish to be converted, seeing it is the will of God." "But," resumed M. Meyster, "I mean that you should become a Catholic;" and, to the astonishment of all, the man continued, "I wish to be a Catholic, a Roman Catholic, with my wife and children, and to abandon the religion I have hitherto professed, and which I now believe to be false." M. Meyster received his abjuration on the spot, heard his confession, and gave him absolution. The next day the

Bishop of Amiens went and administered confirmation to him.

One remarkable circumstance remains to be told. Three days afterwards, M. Meyster was hearing confessions late at night, when (it being 11 o'clock) he was called away to take a little food, in order that he might not be prevented celebrating Mass the next morning. He was in the act of saying grace, when he suddenly stopped, threw on his cloak, and saying, "This is no time for eating, the colonel is dying," hastened out of the house. All was silent when he reached the sick man's lodging, and he was assured that there was no alteration for the worse. Proceeding, however, to his room, the Swede no sooner saw him than he cried, "Ah! sir, help me." M. Meyster begged him to join in spirit with the acts of faith, hope, and charity, which he himself repeated aloud, and gave him the last absolution. The man warmly expressed his gratitude, and, praying God to bless his benefactor, he expired. So quickly had all been dispatched, that M. Meyster, after reciting the prayers for the departed, had time to eat his supper before the clock struck twelve.

During the three days which elapsed after his conversion, the colonel had acted the part of an apostle to his men, and with such success that numbers were converted. The work thus began was concluded by M. Olier and his colleagues, and indeed by the men themselves, for they who had yielded to grace became missionaries to their comrades, and a strange, and an almost incredible spectacle was to be seen in the streets of Amiens. When the priests emerged from their lodgings in the early morning they found themselves surrounded by bands of soldiers, complaining that they were unable to get near the confessionals, around which penitents had been gathered, several ranks deep, two hours before daybreak. The missionaries explained that they must in justice take all comers in turn, and that they could not therefore show them any preference; on which, to excite their compassion, and as though to compel them to hear them, the men began telling their sins out aloud, and such as were

CH. VI.] ACCUSATIONS AGAINST THE MISSIONARIES. 93

Catholics numbered up the years that had elapsed since they had been at confession. "We may have to mount horse any day—any hour," they cried. "Are we to go to be killed before we have got absolution?" The people were so moved by their fervour, that they gave up their places to the soldiers, and they made their confession. Three days afterwards this very troop fell into an ambuscade, and were cut off to a man.

So great was the enthusiasm which these extraordinary conversions caused in the town, that the corporation of the city proposed sending the missionaries a present of wine and sweetmeats, the customary mark of honour shown to the governor of the province on occasion of his official entry. As M. Olier and his friends never received presents, and would have been puzzled how to dispose of six large pewter vessels full of wine, with the city arms thereon, to be presented by as many town-sergeants in their scarlet robes of office, they suggested that the whole should be carried to the public hospital instead. However, there were not wanting those who made the very success of the missionaries the occasion of a charge against them. Some monks of the place, jealous of the influence acquired by these secular priests, went to the governor, the Duke de Chaulne, and gravely represented that M. Meyster had obtained this ascendancy over the inhabitants only that he might hand over the town to the King of Spain, whose born subject he was. The governor was foolish enough to listen to these envious counsellors, and actually wrote to the Cardinal de Richelieu, apprising him of the threatened danger. The cardinal, however, was too sagacious to be so easily imposed upon, and after writing privately to the Intendant of Picardy, who was the brother-in-law of M. Brandon, to ascertain the truth of the matter, informed M. le Duc that he need not be under any alarm.

This mission, which lasted five months, was followed by another at Montdidier; and, after a few weeks' repose, instead of returning to Picardy, they went, at the invitation of the bishop, to Mantes, in the diocese of Chartres. This was in the month of July, 1640. The fruits were, as usual, most abundant; they succeeded in terminating amicably as many as five hundred law-suits; an event so astounding that certain of the inhabitants accused the missionaries before the Parliament of Paris of making the occupation of a lawyer a sin beyond the grace of absolution. To these wiseacres the Chancellor simply replied, that the Parliament of Paris had nothing to do with the sacrament of penance.

The labours of the missionaries were not confined to the laity, their zeal extended also to the clergy. Already they contemplated a prodigious work—the restoration of ecclesiastical discipline throughout the whole sacerdotal order. This appears from a letter addressed to them by the Archbishop of Rouen, in which, referring to a book they were about to publish for the instruction of the clergy, he proffers his advice as to the nature of its contents, and promises at their request to give the work his personal revision. It was probably with a view to this publication, that, after the mission at Mantes was concluded, M. Olier and his friends retired to a country place that belonged to one of them at Lorean, near Epernon, in the diocese of Chartres. Here they were visited by M. Bourdoise, who, ever consumed with the desire of communicating to other priests what he called the parochial spirit, began at once to give them a lesson on a subject of which, by their own confession, they had very little knowledge. Ever on the move, and engaged continually in giving missions up and down the country, they were but imperfectly acquainted with the ceremonies of the Church, the manner of performing the more solemn functions, and, in short, the whole art, as it may be said, of regulating a large parish church. M. Bourdoise, to his great surprise, found that they each said Mass and performed their other devotions in the chapel of the house, instead of repairing to the parish church, and he proposed that they should all go forthwith and solemnize High Mass in the face of the congregation, it being S. Matthew's day (September 21, 1640). With his characteristic energy, he instantly set every one his part, and Mass accordingly was said to the great edification of the people, and to the surprise of the chief actors themselves, who scarcely knew how they had been able to acquit themselves so well. Solemn vespers were improvised with equal rapidity and equal success. The lesson learnt that day was not forgotten; wherever they went the parish church was now their centre and their place of resort; the ceremonial of the Church was accurately studied, and every endeavour used to celebrate the Divine offices, not only with befitting decorum, but with all possible solemnity. The example became contagious: a taste, or rather a zeal for the beauty and decorum of God's house began to spread among the clergy, and soon the progress of the missionaries through the country might be traced as much by the order that reigned in the sanctuary, as by the devotion of the people. Delighted with the docility and earnestness of his disciples, M. Bourdoise invited them to frequent the church of S. Nicolas du Chardonnet whenever they were at Paris, and it was there that they perfected themselves in the ecclesiastical chant and ceremonies.

CHAPTER VII.

Trials of M. Olier, interior and exterior—Death of F. de Condren—Seminary of Chartres—Reform of La Regrippiére completed.

HITHERTO we have seen M. Olier in the full and vigorous exercise of all his natural powers, bodily and mental, favoured of God, and honoured among men. He had encountered obstacles and contradictions, but they seemed ever to give way before him. He had undergone many interior trials, but they were of short duration, and he came forth all the stronger for the contest. He had been sick and disabled, but he was restored speedily and as by miracle. Entire freedom from pain and inward affliction he seems never to have enjoyed, but his sufferings neither attracted attention nor incapacitated him for severe and prolonged exertion. Over his immediate friends and associates he exercised a powerful influence; as a missionary he had achieved extraordinary success; in short, he had acquired the highest reputation as well for his abilities as for his virtues. But in all this there was danger, and he knew it: the consideration with which he was regarded was a perpetual martyrdom to him, and he trembled lest he should yield to the solicitations of vainglory, by which he was unceasingly assailed.

It was during the illness he had in Auvergne, at the close of the mission of 1637, that his eyes (he says) began to be opened, and he was enabled to perceive how much of self-love mixed itself up with everything he did. The sight of what he was struck him with dismay, and he became possessed with an intense desire of being wholly united with God, so that he cared not what might befall him if only he could attain to this blessed state. In his solitary walks he would raise his eyes to heaven, and say continually, "O life divine! life divine! when shall I live only of God?" In July 1638, while in retreat, preparatory to going to Brittany, he was moved to make two petitions: first, that the vexations and annoyances he was then enduring in consequence of certain legal proceedings in which he was involved, as well as from other causes, might be exchanged for spiritual trials more beneficial to his soul; and, secondly, that the good opinion which men had of him might be turned into contempt. And now both of his requests were about to be granted: God would raise him to a still higher degree of sanctity; He would empty him entirely of self, and form within him the life of His dear Son; and to this end He subjected him to humiliations the most painful to pride and self-love. He withdrew from him not only those spiritual gifts for which he had been conspicuous, but the exercise of his natural powers and faculties. At times he lost the use of his bodily limbs; they would suddenly refuse to obey the motions of his will, as though God would show him by actual experience that we live and move only in Him. Sometimes he trembled and tottered as he walked, at others he was unable to put one foot before another; he could not lift his food to his mouth; he wondered (he says) to see others eating with such facility, and whatever he took seemed as if it were put into a lifeless body. His mind was at the same time affected with a similar torpidity: his memory and understanding failed him; often he knew neither what he said nor what was said to him; he felt (as he describes it) like a deaf man in a crowd, with a continual hubbub and confusion going on around him. He would have a clear perception of what he was about to express, and would have begun to put his thought into words, when in an instant it would pass from him, and he no longer recollected what he had had in his mind to say; and this not merely on subjects of high import, but in the commonest things, and while in easy converse with a friend. He seemed also to have forgotten the art of writing, and would be hours accomplishing three or four lines, and those (as he adds) all awry. He would suddenly forget where he was going, and the names of the persons he wished to see; he would lose his way in the streets, so that he was obliged to be always accompanied by a servant. His mother, seeing him in this miserable state, said, People would think he was an idiot or a fool; while he, on his part, offered himself to God to deprive him altogether of his senses, if such were His holy will.

This suspension of his natural powers interrupted also the exercise of his priestly ministrations. He was unable to preach: often, when directed to do so, he could find neither ideas nor language; if he attempted to expound a text of Scripture, he became so confused, and the terms he employed were so ill chosen, that he was obliged to desist. Yet, on one occasion (he says), as though God would not have him wholly discouraged, he delivered a discourse before a large audience with more than his usual facility. In the confessional he did not know what to say to his penitents, and in his misery could not refrain from deploring their ill fortune in having recourse to so incompetent a guide. And with all this was conjoined the greatest interior darkness and distress. He seemed to be abandoned by God, and his soul was filled with disquietude and fear. If he opened the Gospel, or any spiritual book, his eye was sure to light on some passage which spoke of the narrowness of the way of salvation, and the judgments of God on the wicked; while the name of Judas was like the stroke of a dagger to his heart. "Ah, sirs!" he once said to his colleagues, "you may think that the traitor is mentioned only four or five times in Holy Scripture, but his name occurs more than twenty times." He felt as if he were himself the Judas of the little company, and the thought was never absent from his mind. One day, when saying Mass at the high altar, having to read this hated name, he was seized with such an agitation that it was with difficulty he could proceed. He was harassed, moreover, with scruples of conscience, so that (as he declares) he was a torment to his confessor, his colleagues, and to everybody else. The name of God recalled to him only a cruel, arbitrary, inexorable being, whose pleasure it was to make his creatures suffer; while the mention of hell had a certain terrible satisfaction for him, as being the place to which he was destined for all eternity. Although he remained constant in prayer, he received not a single ray of light or comfort; he could not lift up his heart to God, and shrank from presenting himself before the tabernacle. The only devotion of which he was capable was that of the rosary, which he made a vow to recite for a year, in order to recover the presence of the Holy Spirit, of which he deemed himself deprived. He experienced also a sensible satisfaction in making a pilgrimage; but in all things else he felt as though his heart were dead within him: he seemed (as he says) to have sunk utterly back into his own nothingness. All the favours and consolations he had enjoyed were now to him but mere delusions; he believed that he was the object only of the hatred of God, and so dreadful was the thought that his whole appearance was altered, and his countenance became so pale and haggard that it was feared he was sinking under some fatal disorder. His sleep was disturbed with horrible dreams; he would awake in the night and think he saw devils at the foot of his bed, ready to drag him down to hell. The particular temptation with which he was assailed was, not to do evil, but to perform extraordinary acts and practise excessive mortifications, which might be the occasion to him of vainglory; and once he heard a voice accusing him of pride, in tones so terrible that he remained shuddering and trembling in all his limbs.

This depression of spirits, and loss of capacity, provoked animadversions of the most humiliating kind. It was supposed that he now bitterly regretted having refused the coadjutorship of Châlons, and that this was the cause of his melancholy and want of energy. The king, the Cardinal de Richelieu, as well as the bishops and others about the court, indulged in many a jest at his expense, and he became (he says) the laughingstock of the whole town. His colleagues shared the general opinion; they looked upon him as a vainglorious man, who wished to gain a character for disinterestedness, but had broken down in the attempt. M. Amelote, who was now (as has been said) the superior of the little community, wishing to try of what spirit he was, would laughingly ask him whether he had ordered his equipage yet, and what number of servants he intended to have in his train. These bantering questions, so little in harmony with the sentiments of compunction and self-reproach with which his soul was filled, jarred painfully on his feelings; and one day he replied, "Ah! father, such thoughts are far from me; I wish only for a hole in which to do penance for my sins." He was now convinced that there was an intention to exclude him from the society; in fact, M. Amelote had one day told him to do as he pleased, and go where he would, for they had nothing to say to him; and on another occasion had

was favoured with particular lights respecting the state of his soul. The truth, however, was that both M. Amelote and the rest wholly misapprehended M. Olier's character and conduct; they thought they perceived in him an arrogant and intractable temper, and believed that God had withdrawn His Spirit from him, and refused any longer to bless his ministrations. This apparent pride and haughtiness of manner was, indeed, not altogether imaginary; M. Olier was himself most painfully conscious of it, but it seemed as if his movements were not subject to his own control, and that, in spite of himself, he had at times the air of a man full of his own conceits. The result was that he was interdicted from preaching, and other similar employments, even to the hearing confessions, except in cases of absolute necessity, to all which he silently submitted, without seeking an explanation, or attempting to justify himself.

Such were the extraordinary trials to which this holy man was subjected for the space of two years; and if we look for a reason in the designs of Divine Providence, over and above his personal sanctification, we may find it in this: that it might be proved beyond all dispute that he who was to inaugurate the great work of ecclesiastical reform, was chosen for the office, not by men, but by God. M. Amelote had been preferred before him by his associates; M. Olier had become the object of suspicion and contempt; and yet he it was, and not M. Amelote, who was destined by God to be the founder and first superior of the seminary of S. Sulpice.

Even F. de Condren apparently fell in with the general opinion, and withdrew, or seemed to withdraw, from him his confidence. This to M. Olier was the greatest blow of all, for he no longer experienced the same consolations in his direction which he had hitherto had, and was left, as it were, in a state of complete abandonment. In this, too, he recognized the hand of God, who would have him cease from all dependence on creatures, however holy, and adhere to Him alone. And yet, for all his coldness and reserve, it would appear that this master of the spiritual life discerned in the state to which his pupil was reduced, only a further proof of God's love and favour towards him, and one of the stages in that course of perfection along which he was being led. In the very last interview which M. Olier had with him, he spoke much of the adoration of Jesus in the Blessed Sacrament, as being the peculiar devotion of priests, and that which he should labour most to propagate; bidding him pay particular honour to that angel of the Apocalypse who is described as casting on the earth the fire with which he had filled his censer from the heavenly altar. He spoke also of the singular graces with which God had gifted individual souls. M. Vincent (de Paul), he said, was remarkable for prudence, M. Amelote for wisdom, while his own peculiar gift he considered to be that of a childlike spirit; and, on M. Olier asking what was his particular grace, he answered that it was the same as his own; that (as M. Olier himself writes) God would have him conduct himself after the manner of a child, without care or deliberation, with all simplicity, casting himself into His arms, as into those of a father; desirous only of pleasing Him, loving Him, praising Him, seeking only His glory, and willing to be himself despised. F. de Condren added that he should take as his director the Infant Jesus: a suggestion the more remarkable that M. Olier, unknown to his spiritual guide, had begun to practise this particular devotion from the time that F. de Condren appeared to become estranged from him.

This estrangement had lasted two months, when F. de Condren was seized with his last illness. As yet he had not opened his lips on the subject that lay nearest his heart, but on the very day before he fell sick, he communicated his design to M. du Ferrier, and even then, as it appeared, more by accident than from premeditation. The young priest had gone to consult him as usual, when, in the course of conversation, the father repeated a remark he had before made, that there was a still greater work to be done than that in which he and his companions were at present engaged; and on M. du Ferrier inquiring what greater work there could be than that of converting sinners, he replied, "I will tell you." M. du Ferrier, however, fearing that he had asked the question from a motive of mere curiosity, would have had him be silent; but he said, "No, make yourself easy, it is not curiosity; it is an effect of the Providence of God, who would have me at length make known to you what He requires of you. The time is come." He then appointed an early hour on the following day for pursuing the conversation, and when they were alone he proceeded to show that the effects of the missions, great as they were at the time, were not as lasting as they otherwise might be, because of the lack of zealous pastors. It was useless (he said) to endeavour to change those who had been raised to the priesthood without due preparation; it was necessary to educate an entirely new race of ecclesiastics, and this could be effected only by means of seminaries, such as the Council of Trent had enjoined. M. du Ferrier pointed to the attempts that had been made at Toulouse, Bordeaux, and Rouen, but which had failed notwithstanding all the exertions of Cardinals de Joyeuse and de Sourdis. The father, however, in return showed him the reason of this failure, maintaining that the youths admitted into an ecclesiastical seminary ought to be of such an age that it was possible to judge of their character, and, after some trial, to determine whether they possessed the necessary qualifications. He entered at some length into the subject, and assured M. du Ferrier of the Divine assistance, and of entire success, if only the undertaking were commenced at once, and before the demon of discord had introduced dissensions into the clerical body. This he said with a prophetic eye for the evils with which the Jansenistic heresy was about to afflict the Church; and ended by counselling all who should be engaged in this work to avoid contentions and "strifes of words," and never to espouse any side but that of the Holy See.

Ten o'clock struck while he was speaking, and Brother Martin, his assistant, came to remind him that it was time to say Mass. He bade him wait awhile, and the brother retired. At eleven he came again, and the father said to him, "Brother, if you knew what I was about, you would not be so urgent; for I am engaged upon something even of greater consequence than that you would have me do." He continued discoursing till noon, when he said, "Brother Martin will be losing all patience; we must reserve the rest till to-morrow;" but when the morrow came, he was too unwell to receive visitors, and M. du Ferrier never saw him again. Fearing, however, that the father might die before he had concluded his instructions, he sent in a note to the priest who was in attendance upon him, begging him to entreat the sick man, if God should call him to Himself, to bequeath his spirit and his lights to some one who should be able to supply what he had left unsaid.

F. de Condren passed from this world on the Feast of the Epiphany, 1641, and that very night he appeared in vision to M. Olier, surrounded with glory, and told him that he left him the heir of his spirit and counsels, in conjunction with two others whom he named, one of whom was M. Amelote. On the night also of his burial he appeared to M. Meyster, who had an intention of leaving the society, bidding him abandon his design, for that he was appointed by God to take part in the establishment of a seminary which should be the source of the greatest benefits to the Church. M. Meyster communicated to M. du Ferrier all that the father had said to him, and which tallied exactly with the instructions he had himself received from him when alive, although M. Meyster had not heard a word previously on the subject. M. Olier, however, kept his own counsel; and it is only from the memoirs which he composed by order of his director, and solely for his inspection, that we incidentally learn the nature of the revelation that was made to him. All the time that the body of the father lay exposed in the church of the Oratory, and on the day of his funeral, M. Olier felt himself (as he says) more and more penetrated with that spirit of self-annihilation which was so conspicuous in the deceased, so that he seemed wholly absorbed therewith. His interior trials still endured, and no one among his associates suspected that the man so humiliated and so little regarded was he to whom they must look for the accomplishment of the great design now communicated to them, and in which they were destined severally to bear a part.

One principal end for which the French Oratory had been instituted was the education of ecclesiastics, but Providence had other designs; and, contrary to the mind and will of the founder, Cardinal de Berulle, it was employed almost exclusively in the conduct of missions, the performance of parochial duties, and, more than all, in the management of schools. So opposed was this last to the intention of the cardinal, that he would have had the Pope, in his bull of institution, expressly prohibit the fathers from connecting themselves with anything of a purely scholastic nature; but no such clause was introduced, and instead of establishing seminaries for priests, the French Oratorians undertook the direction of numerous schools. So far, indeed, were they from wishing to engage in what their founder intended to be their chief occupation, that they even allowed F. Eudes to leave them rather than second his designs in that direction. In this we cannot but discern a providential arrangement; for, after the death of F. de Condren, the Oratory (as is well known) became one of the strongholds of Jansenism, and had its members at that time had the education of the clergy in their hands, the greatest evils would have resulted to the whole Church of France. F. de Condren seemed to have a divine intimation of this; for it is very remarkable that, with the strong sense he entertained of the urgent need of ecclesiastical seminaries, he did not engage the members of his own community in the undertaking, but got together a separate company of priests whom he destined for the work. True it is that at one time (1637) he had a design of founding a seminary at the Abbey of Juilly, in connection with the Oratory, towards which M. Olier contributed; but the institution, in fact, never became anything more than a school.

The little band of priests, now informed as to their true vocation, resolved to abandon the field of missionary labour, and, retiring first to Loreau, then to Epernon, gave themselves up to prayer and instruction of the people, until Providence should open out a way for the execution of their design. It was now that M. Olier obtained at length some relaxation of his trials, from which, however, he was not entirely delivered until the end of the same year. It was in the cathedral church of Chartres that (to use his own expressions) he first began to breathe interiorly, and to recover that exterior cheerfulness which had been natural to him previous to his afflictions. His companions were astonished at the change, though they little suspected the cause. We have seen that he laboured under a continual dread that all his actions were defiled with a secret pride and self-love. He had been favoured with a most vivid perception of the malice of the sin of pride; how it robs God of His glory, and sacrilegiously despoils His altars of that in which He most delights—the adoration of the heart and will; and the sight had filled him with a horrible fear. But on the octave of Corpus Christi, having risen earlier than usual, and repaired to the cathedral, when the bells of all the churches of the city began to ring out in honour of the Sacramental Mystery, his mind, as by a sudden and divine illumination, apprehended the immense glory which God receives during that great festival, when Jesus is enthroned on a thousand altars, and is offered to His Eternal Father in union with the homage of all true believers throughout the world. His heart was inflamed with joy, and with the joy that he experienced came also the reflection that he, too, shared in this universal homage;—he, too, rendered praise and glory to God. The thought seemed to remove a heavy burden from his soul, and he found relief to his feelings of love and devotion in a gush of tears to which he had been long a stranger. From that moment his fears diminished, and gradually departed.

God also was pleased to grant him, in the person of M. Picoté,* who was a member of the community, a

---

* An amusing instance is related by M. du Ferrier of the simplicity of this good priest. Being one day on his road to Orleans, director in whom he could repose entire confidence, and from whence he experienced all the affection and sympathy of a father. This good priest (he says) seemed to be acquainted beforehand with the dispositions of his soul, as though God, who knows the secrets of the heart, had communicated them to him; and he was able to entrust to him the conduct of his affairs, temporal and spiritual, without the least reserve.

By the desire of M. de Valence, Bishop of Chartres, the little band of priests, eight in number, gave a mission to the inhabitants of the town, during which M. Olier preached four or five times on the glories of Mary, with all his accustomed power. So great was their success that the bishop invited them to take up their abode in the city, with a view of conducting the regular retreats provided for the candidates for orders. To this they gladly consented, under the idea that it would gradually lead to the establishment of an ecclesiastical seminary. Accordingly they engaged a house in the parish of Sainte-Foi, close to the cathedral, furnished it at their own expense, and took upon themselves the entire support of the candidates, as long as the exercises lasted. Their hope was that some of these might be induced to remain with them, in order to being more perfectly instructed in their priestly duties; but nothing of the kind followed. Notwithstanding their charity and zeal, and the edifying example of their lives, not a single individual

of which city he was a native, he was stopped in the Vale of Trois Croix by six mounted highwaymen, who, with the politeness which in that age characterized these gentry, begged he would present them with his purse. Suspicious of no evil design, M. Picoté no sooner heard the request than he replied, "Willingly, good sirs, and with all my heart." Then taking out his purse, in which there were five or six crowns, he emptied the contents into his hand, and presenting it to them, said, "I wish it was a better one, for your sakes." Half surprised, half indignant, the men asked him what he meant. "Why," said he, "I thought you asked me for a purse, and here is one at your service." The unaffected simplicity of the reply so delighted them, that, bursting out laughing, they said, "The joke is worth all your money; pray, sir, keep your purse; we have no wish to deprive you of it;" and so saying, they gallopped off, still laughing with all their might.

entered the house during the whole eight months they were at Chartres.

Left thus without occupation, these zealous men employed themselves as best they could in the several parishes of the city, until God should more clearly disclose His will to them. M. Olier devoted himself in particular to catechising the children, rewarding their proficiency by distributing among them little presents which Sister de Vauldray sent him for the purpose. The ill success, however, which had attended their efforts, began to produce an unsettled feeling among the associates, and it was soon apparent that the community had arrived at a crisis in its affairs. M. de Foix et M. du Ferrier, whom business had taken to Paris, were on the point of returning to Chartres, when M. Meyster, who at this juncture retired from the society, said to them, while at dinner, in a voice of great earnestness, "My dear friends, you are losing your time; you are not doing what God requires of you. He disapproves of your remaining at Chartres, and I am bidden to tell you so." He added that M. Amelote was called to other labours. His words had such effect upon them that, rising from table, they went at once to consult the Fathers of the Oratory, and, acting on the advice they received, resolved, instead of returning to Chartres, to proceed on a pilgrimage to Notre Dame des Ardilliers,* near Saumur in Anjou. It was at the same time agreed between them that they should not speak of the matter on the way, but should make it simply the subject of prayer, and leave the issue in the hands of God.

Meanwhile M. Olier arrived at Paris †, before the Feast

---

* This celebrated pilgrimage owed its origin to the following circumstance :—A peasant, while digging in a field, found a little image of Notre Dame de Pitié, by which many miracles were wrought. A chapel was built over the spot where it was found, which became much frequented by the faithful. This chapel was served from the year 1616 by the Fathers of the Oratory, to whom it belonged.

† It was about this time (according to his biographer) that, on the demise of the Bishop of Puy, the chapter begged the king to

of the Assumption, for the purpose of settling a difference
with the prior of his abbey, whom the monks had, in defiance of all right, just nominated to the office. While
there, he received a visit from the Abbess of Fontevrault,
who begged him to repair in person to La Regrippiére,
with a view to completing the reform he had so auspiciously commenced. Nothing could be more in accordance with his wishes, and he followed his two friends to
Saumur, with the hope of inducing them to accompany
him into Brittany. He was especially anxious to have
the co-operation of M. du Ferrier, as he relied upon his
assistance to effect a conversion in which he had himself
entirely failed. It was that of a nun whom he describes
as the haughtiest and most self-sufficient in the house,
and who had conceived a great aversion to him, either
because of his success with Sister de Vauldray, who had
been the leader of the opposition, or because (as he says)
she despised what she regarded as want of spirit in him.
His two friends consented, and they arrived at the convent late one October evening, where they were well received. M. Olier, however, was seized with one of his fits
of timidity, and said to his companions, "Three years
ago I had the courage to preach to these religious, and
now I protest to you I should not venture to open my
mouth." In the morning he rose early, and took for the
subject of his meditation those words of our Lord,
"They shall adore the Father in spirit and in truth," of
which his mind had been full the evening before, when
he was proceeding to the convent. The result was such
an accession of strength and light, that, when, on his way
to say Mass, the mother prioress requested him to preach,
he at once consented, and delivered himself with so much
unction and power that the hearts of all were touched.
They who did not yield to grace on that occasion were
brought to contrition by a second sermon on the following day, and made their confession with many sobs and
tears.

nominate M. Olier to the vacant see; in which they were warmly
seconded by the very persons who had been the authors of the
violent opposition he encountered during his mission in Auvergne.

CHAP. VII.] CONVERSION OF SISTER DE LA TROCHE. 109

M. Olier, however, was right in his conjecture that the presence of another priest was needed to effect the conversion of the nun to whom allusion has been made. On the second morning after their arrival, M. du Ferrier, who was about to depart for Clisson, was on his knees before the high altar, preparatory to saying Mass, when Sister de la Troche (such was the name of the nun), who had been watching him through the grate, sent the sacristan to beg him to offer the Holy Sacrifice for her intention. Acting on a sudden impulse, M. du Ferrier, who was naturally of an obliging disposition, refused, in a way which, on after-reflection, surprised and confounded him. The sacristan thinking he had not heard, or did not understand the request, repeated it; on which the priest replied, "I tell you I will do nothing of the kind." So stern a refusal, coming from a man whom she regarded as gifted with a divine discernment, struck the sister with a sort of terror: she thought she was lost beyond repentance, and throwing herself on the floor of her cell, shed a torrent of tears. She then begged one of the nuns who had been converted on the occasion of M. Olier's first visit, to procure her an interview with M. du Ferrier; but finding that he had departed for Clisson, she was seized with such a paroxysm of grief, that M. Olier despatched a messenger after him to bring him back to the convent. No sooner had M. du Ferrier returned, than the Sister de la Troche made a public confession of her pride and obstinacy, avowing to her shame that hitherto she had encouraged the rest of the religious in the violation of their engagements, but protesting that for the future her only desire was to lead a life of obedience, and to fulfil the obligations of her state in silence and recollection. The others who had still held out followed her example; all insubordination was now at an end, and perfect harmony was restored by a solemn act of reconciliation before the Blessed Sacrament. At the request of the abbess, to whom a report had been sent of all that had occurred, M. Olier and M. du Ferrier remained for a month at the convent, during which they instructed the nuns in the exercise of mental prayer, and in all the requirements of a community life.

This long-desired reform at length effected, the two priests retook their way to Chartres, whither they had been preceded by M. de Foix. In passing through Angers, M. Olier was entertained by M. Gui Lanier, abbé of Vaux, in Saintonge, a holy and zealous priest, to whose particular charge he committed the convent of La Regrippiére. From Angers he repaired to Tours, where, on the 11th of November, he had the satisfaction of assisting at the ceremonies observed in honour of the great S. Martin, whom he had always held in singular veneration for his heroic humility and self-abjection. During this journey he was favoured with a greater calm in his soul than he had enjoyed since the commencement of his interior trials. He met with a confessor to whom he could open himself without reserve, and from whom he received such helps and encouragements that all his doubts and obscurities vanished, and he beheld with a clear vision the road along which he was to walk. On reaching Chartres, he found the greatest differences of opinion prevailing among his associates, as to the course to be pursued, and it soon became evident to him that a dissolution of the community was impending. M. de Foix strongly urged the necessity of abandoning the establishment at Chartres, as having failed in the object for which it was designed, and to this opinion M. Olier himself inclined; but it was as strongly contested by others of the society. In the midst of these debates M. du Ferrier, after imploring the assistance of the Blessed Virgin in the subterranean chapel of Notre Dame de Chartres, went to consult the Mother Gabrielle, a Carmelitess, sister of F. de Condren. She was under the spiritual direction of M. Amelote, to whose judgment in the matter in question she would naturally defer, but this did not render M. du Ferrier, who placed the greatest reliance on her piety and prudence, less desirous to obtain the benefit of her advice. On learning what F. de Condren had said to him before his death, on the subject of which that great man had never uttered a word to M. Amelote, she replied without hesitation that if the latter decided on breaking up the establishment, M. du Ferrier might take it as a sign that it was the will of God that he should associate himself with M. de Foix and M. Olier in the endeavour to found an ecclesiastical seminary. The very next day M. Amelote pronounced in favour of a dissolution of the society, and from that moment M. du Ferrier became convinced that this ecclesiastic was destined to have no part in the work of which F. de Condren had spoken. The friends, however, continued to live together in perfect amity and concord, until the translation of the Bishop of Chartres to the archbishopric of Rheims determined them to quit the place.

CHAPTER VIII.

Seminary of Vaugirard—M. Olier's state of union with God.

MEANWHILE M. Picoté had gone to Vaugirard, a village in the close neighbourhood of Paris, to assist Marie Luillier, the lady of Villeneuve, who had the superintendence of an establishment, the members of which were engaged in the management of schools in country places. It had been commenced at the suggestion of S. Francis de Sales, who was her director, and with the active co-operation of S. Vincent de Paul; and from the difficulties and trials which the institution had encountered, its members had obtained the appellation of the Sisters of the Cross.[*] Madame de Villeneuve, like so many other devout persons, had long made the reformation of the clergy the subject of especial prayer; and hearing from M. Picoté an

[*] Through the exertions of M. Olier, the Sisters of the Cross were established in several towns where he had been engaged in giving missions, in order to perpetuate the benefits which had been derived from the ministrations of himself and his fellow-labourers.

account of what was passing, she said at once, " Perhaps our Lord would have you establish yourselves at Vaugirard." M. Picoté would have taken no notice of the remark, but she pursued the subject, representing the facilities and advantages which such a situation offered: its seclusion, and yet its close proximity to the capital; the assistance they would derive from the *curé*, M. Copin, who would willingly place the parish church at their disposal; while for herself, she would engage to give them all the aid in her power, even to their entire maintenance, if that were necessary. Her earnestness had its effect on M. Picoté, and, after recommending the matter to God, he wrote to his friends at Chartres, and in particular to M. de Foix. When his letter was read, there was but one opinion of its contents, and an immediate answer was returned, that the proposition was neither feasible nor reasonable. But on M. de Foix going to Paris, he was induced by M. Picoté to hear what Madame de Villeneuve had to say on the subject, and her representations, combined with those of M. Picoté, who was now a strenuous advocate of the plan, had the effect of bringing him entirely over to her views. As for M. Amelote, he regarded the whole scheme as a mere piece of extravagance; but considering that his friends had need of retirement and repose, he advised them to repair to Vaugirard for the good of their health. The jubilee was about to be observed in the parish, and as there was a lack of confessors, M. Picoté begged M. du Ferrier to come and help him, with the hope of enlisting his services also in the cause he had so much at heart. Madame de Villeneuve, moreover, availed herself of the influence of the Abbé de Pormorant, who, like herself, was devoted to the Christian instruction of youth; but nothing that was said to him had any effect on M. du Ferrier, until, while saying Mass in the church, at the moment he communicated, he found himself possessed with the conviction that Vaugirard was the place which God had chosen, and that he must abandon himself entirely to the divine will.

Their next endeavour was to gain over M. Olier, but

the attempt did not meet with the success expected. He was more entirely opposed to the proposed establishment than the others had been, and expressed himself accordingly. At the request, however, of M. Picoté, his director, he consented to recommend the matter to God, and in the beginning of December, 1641, retired for that purpose to Notre Dame des Vertus, near Paris, where M. Picoté continued to visit him. While in this retreat the Lord was pleased to speak to him in vision, after a manner of which he had hitherto had no experience. It was on the 5th or 6th of the same month that, being absorbed in prayer, he seemed to behold in spirit the Eternal Father, bearing in his arms a company of ecclesiastics, who were the objects of His tenderest care; and at the same moment there rose to his lips, with a significance he had never before realized, those words of David: *Qui regis Israel, intende; qui deducis velut ovem Joseph.** Abandoning himself without reserve to God, he supplicated an outpouring of His love on those who were to be united with Him in the fulfilment of His designs, and, as in reply to his petition, there came vividly before his mind the words of the Divine Son to His Eternal Father: *Mea omnia tua sunt, et tua mea sunt.*† He prayed for all with whom he had been associated at Chartres, and offered them one by one to God; and then an interior voice seemed to speak to him, and to tell him that some of these, and in particular M. Amelote, were destined for other spheres of labour. From that moment his destiny was clear before him.

By this time the community was entirely broken up, and its members were living separately at Paris. M. Olier, now assured of the Divine intentions, would have reassembled them for the purpose of laying the foundations of a future seminary; but the failure at Chartres discouraged them from making a similar attempt, and

---

* "Give ear, O Thou that rulest Israel; Thou that leadest Joseph like a sheep."—*Ps.* lxxix.

† "All My things are Thine, and Thine are Mine."—*John* xvii. 10.

especially in a mere village like Vaugirard. Besides, they had not recovered sufficient confidence in M. Olier since his state of trial, and were less disposed than ever to listen to his counsels. The result, therefore, was that, with the exception of M. de Foix and M. du Ferrier, all his old associates withdrew from him, some accompanying M. Amelote, who, while at Chartres, had resolved on quitting the society, to Caen, where he had been invited to give a mission. M. Olier, however, nothing discouraged, lost no time in procuring a house at Vaugirard, as near the church as possible, and then prepared to enter on his newly-allotted sphere by a second retreat at Notre Dame des Vertus. It was a peculiar satisfaction both to himself and to his two associates, that their future residence should be in a place especially dedicated to the Blessed Virgin; the church also possessed a miraculous image* of his beloved Patroness, before which it was his daily habit to pray, and he never left the sacred building without first saying a "Hail Mary" at its feet. With such expedition were all the arrangements completed that they were able to take possession of their new abode in the beginning of January, 1642. It was a mean-looking building, so small and inconvenient that, to make room for the ecclesiastics whom they hoped to receive, it was necessary to partition off a few cells in an adjoining dove-cot, and even the best apartment in the house scarcely deserved the name. They were but three in number, M. Picoté, who was engaged at the establishment of the Sisters of the Cross, not being in a condition to join them; and as they had exhausted their private resources in the expenses incurred at Chartres, they led a life of the strictest poverty. They had no servant, but performed all the offices of the house with their own hands, while for their daily food they were compelled to be dependent on the charity of Madame de Villeneuve,

---

* This image was broken to pieces at the Revolution, and tradition avers that the perpetrator of the sacrilege received a wound in the arm from a splinter of the wood, which long remained unhealed.

who (as we find from M. du Ferrier) used to send them soup and *bouilli* in a little kettle for their dinner, and a few scraps of roast mutton for their supper. Their occupations consisted in prayer, the reading of Holy Scripture, and study, and even a portion of the time set apart for recreation was spent in adoration before the Blessed Sacrament. Thus they waited, ignorant of God's intentions, but assured that He had special designs regarding them, and prepared simply to fulfil them, whatever they might be.

Nor was it long before God made known His will. Since the death of F. de Condren, they had had (properly speaking) no director, but a few days after taking up their abode at Vaugirard, they placed themselves under the spiritual guidance of Dom Grégoire Tarrisse, Superior-General of the Benedictines of the Congregation of S. Maur. He was a man of extraordinary virtue and sagacity, and, as such, held in the highest esteem by some of the greatest personages in France. Though indifferent to all merely human interests, it was under his auspices that the Abbey of S. Germain des Prés became celebrated for the many learned and accomplished writers who, in the several departments of science and art, exercised so powerful an influence in their day. And here, with M. Olier, we cannot but admire the watchful care which the good Providence of God exercises over those who simply surrender themselves into His keeping. When first he devoted himself to works of active charity, he was given for his director S. Vincent de Paul, Superior of the Priests of the Mission; then, when the time arrived that he should be more deeply instructed in all that concerned the interior life, he became a pupil in the school of F. de Condren, who, perhaps, of all men living had the profoundest knowledge of spiritual things; and now, when God would draw him nearer to Himself, and admit him to the sweetest caresses of His love, he was brought into close relation with this holy Benedictine, who was a very model of prayer, mortification, and detachment from the world. For his own particular director he had another eminent Benedictine, F. Bataille, Procureur-Général of the Order, of whom he says that he possessed greater lights for the regulation both of the interior and exterior life, and a more decided gift for advancing souls in the ways of perfection, than all others he ever knew. To these two men M. Olier was mainly indebted, under God, for the success with which he was enabled to communicate to others the spirit with which he was himself animated, and to surmount the formidable obstacles which his zeal encountered. From the first intimation they received of his design, and that of his associates, they exhorted them with the utmost confidence to persevere, in which also they were seconded by S. Vincent de Paul, and the celebrated Jesuits, FF. Hayneuve and Saint Jure.

But that which most clearly marked the divine approbation was the marvellous change which was produced in M. Olier himself. From the moment of his arrival at Vaugirard, not only was he entirely delivered from his afflicting trials, but he was visited with the most consoling proofs of God's love. He experienced that blessed and utterly supernatural effect of Christ's indwelling presence which is accorded only to a few most favoured souls, prepared for so transcendent a boon by first passing through a state of extraordinary humiliation, of which S. Paul speaks, when he says, "I live, now not I, but Christ liveth in me."—(*Gal.* ii. 20.) In M. Olier these words were literally fulfilled. His soul, nay, his very body, became the sensible habitation and organ of Jesus Christ moving in him and operating by him; so that he no longer spoke or acted as of himself, but only with the concurrence and by the disposal of Him who lived within him. His state, as he describes it, was now the precisely opposite of what it had been in the time of suffering. He felt the presence of the Spirit that ruled him, in the exercise of all his natural powers and faculties: not only in his speech and general bearing, but in his very gait and each particular gesture; so that they who beheld him were astonished at the composed, possessed demeanour of one whose movements had always displayed a certain precipitancy and absence of control. M. Tronson, in the work entitled "L'Esprit de M. Olier," thus writes: "The Spirit of our Lord rendered Itself such absolute master of his heart, and took such complete possession of his soul and all his faculties, that It no longer permitted him the slightest movement save in dependence on Itself and with Its concurrence. It showed Itself in his very eyes, his tongue, his hands, making him act, or preventing him from acting, according to Its pleasure." The Spirit of Jesus was the soul of his soul, and the informing, animating principle of his whole life. If he set himself to write, It dictated his words, and seemed even to guide his pen. And this presence and influence was abiding and continual. "If I leave It (he writes), It immediately follows me, and again takes possession of me the instant I give myself to It, whether at home or abroad, in action or in repose; whether alone or with others, this Divine Spirit is with me everywhere." *

He experienced the same marvellous change also in his mental powers and supernatural gifts. Instead of the darkness and confusion in which his soul had been involved, it was now filled with light; his thoughts were clear and distinct, his tongue unloosed; that distressing dryness from which he had suffered so much was succeeded by an influx of the sweetest spiritual joy, and his mind, no longer occupied with its own miseries, was able to raise itself to God with the utmost facility and the liveliest affection. "I remember" he writes, "that during my trials one consoling thought occurred to me, that if God should deign to make use of me in His service (an event of which I had no expectation), at least it would be plain who was the agent. My state of aban-

---

* This statement has nothing in common with the doctrine of the false mystics, as if it were meant that the soul, in such a state of union, loses its liberty of action, and consequently can no longer sin, even venially, and is incapable of falling from grace. In the case of M. Olier himself the extraordinary aids of the Holy Spirit, although habitual, were not always available, and were sometimes suddenly withdrawn. The true Catholic doctrine will be found explained at length in the *Catéchisme Spirituel* of F. Surin.

donment taught me that whatever good we possess is from God alone, and that the absence of it is all that is our own. What I now possess is not my own property, it does not belong to my soul; it is a grace, a mercy, for which I did not look, and of which I am utterly unworthy. Then I was devoid of all direction, interior, and I might almost say, exterior: now the goodness of God gives me all the counsel I can desire. If two things presented themselves for me to do, I had no power of deciding, there was nothing to determine my choice; now I am scarcely ever at a loss. I am guided interiorly like a child tended by a father of consummate wisdom and perfect goodness. This takes place in the depth of my soul by a divine operation inexpressibly delicate, and which the devil cannot counterfeit. Sometimes it is a movement, sometimes a voiceless word, making itself heard more distinctly than any utterance. For God, who is the Word, renders Himself more sensible to our souls than man can do by articulate speech. O Divine Substance, who art word, light, power, love; O Divine Being, be Thou praised, exalted, and blessed for ever!"

This supernatural assistance of the Holy Spirit became more constant from the day on which he made himself by solemn vow the servant of Jesus Christ, abandoning himself without recall to be at His entire disposal, with an utter dependence on His Spirit in mind and body, even to the smallest things. The first time he felt a desire to take this servitude upon him was during his state of suffering, and especially on the octave of the Epiphany, 1641, three days after the death of F. de Condren, who had made the same vow, though M. Olier was not aware of the fact. His confessor, however, had advised him to wait a year, and it was not until the January of 1642, shortly after his arrival at Vaugirard, and on the very day on which he took F. Tarrisse for his spiritual guide, that he made the irrevocable engagement. " From that moment," he writes, "I could undertake nothing, I could neither speak nor even think of God, save in dependence on the Spirit of my Master, who possessed me, and moved my soul to what He would." Such were the extraordinary ways by which it pleased the Holy Spirit to lead this favoured soul. God, who desired to pour down upon him the abundance of His graces, would have him on his part set no bounds to his generosity and devotion. He had chosen him for the high office of sanctifying those who were called to minister at His altars, and it was His will that he should have experience of the extraordinary operations of His love, in order that he might be able to bring others, each according to the measure of his grace, to a state of union with His dear Son, albeit after a simpler and more common manner.

The three solitaries of Vaugirard (as we may now call them), never for a moment doubting the designs of God, had no sooner entered their retreat, than they proceeded to consecrate themselves to His service and form themselves into a community. As the end which they proposed to themselves was to promote the glory of the Most Holy Trinity by means of the sacerdotal order, they desired to take as their only bond of union the ineffable love of the Three Divine Persons. In this they followed the counsels of F. de Condren, who had forbidden their binding themselves by any vow. In furtherance of their design they resolved to undertake a pilgrimage to Montmartre, and there solemnly consecrate themselves to the work to which they believed they had been called. The form of consecration, which was approved by F. Bataille, ran thus: " Three priests, feeling themselves called in the unity of the Spirit to the service of God and His Holy Church, to form for Him ministers who may worthily promote His glory, honour His Son Jesus Christ, and love His members, have resolved, in honour of the Divine Society of the Three Persons, indivisible by the unity of Their essence and Their holy love, to bind themselves by a sacred promise never to abandon or to depart from the design which it has pleased God to manifest to them, and even to confirm by numerous signs. If any one among them should deem himself called by the goodness of God to serve Him apart from the others, he shall be free to do so only with their mutual agreement and consent. This it is they desire to promise, in the presence of the three martyrs—S. Denis, S. Rusticus, and S. Eleutherius, devoting and consecrating themselves, in imitation of the same blessed martyrs, as living victims, to the honour of the Most Holy Trinity, the glory of Jesus Christ, and the exaltation of His Church."

It had been the constant prayer of M. Bourdoise that three priests might be given to the Church, who, in honour of the Three Divine Persons, would unite to raise the sacerdotal order in France from the degradation into which it had sunk, and now, unknown to himself, his prayer had been fulfilled. Hearing, however, that M. Olier and his two friends had established themselves at Vaugirard, he wrote to them in the following terms, "O that God would give us three faithful men, whose sole aim it should be to do His will, and in His own way! O that there were found three priests, so filled with love for the Church as to be willing to trust her in all those rules which have been dictated to her by the Holy Ghost, and to espouse her cause against the world and all its customs; three priests, who when the rules of the Church are put before them, do not reply, 'This is not the custom; we do otherwise. What would people say?—they would laugh at us. Let us leave things as we find them; we are not wiser than those who have gone before us.'" And then from that narrow house at Vaugirard, there came a reply after his own heart: "Come here, and you will find three such priests as you are looking for, if only you will teach them the things that the Holy Church has ruled. Nor custom, nor aught else, shall prevent those rules being faithfully obeyed, with the help of God's grace, which we entreat you to ask of Him for us."

Accordingly M. Bourdoise went to Vaugirard, and many, doubtless, were the pious witticisms in which he indulged, relative to the dovecot and its expected occupants as he shared the contents of Madame de Villeneuve's, "little kettle." The house and all its arrangements— no servants and an empty larder — with a plenteous allowance of prayer and meditation, must have been thoroughly to his taste. Good advice, too, we may be assured, was liberally bestowed, and that in the plainest and often not the most complimentary terms. "We admired the dealings of God with him," says M. du Ferrier, "in that off-hand bluffness which was natural to him, but we tried to conduct ourselves with a little more graciousness of manner." M. Bourdoise, however, was a thoroughly practical man, and the three weeks he spent with his friends were employed in giving them instructions in all that concerned the ecclesiastical regimen, down to the smallest minutiæ of chants, rubrics, and ceremonies, with explicit directions as to their attire, the wearing of their hair, and their demeanour and conversation generally. His zeal and his firmness continued to be of the utmost service to the young community; he put into their hands from time to time certain manuscript treatises which he had composed for the use of priests living in community, and never ceased to testify towards them on all occasions the sincerest friendship and esteem.

But the individual who most of all contributed to the establishment of the seminary of Vaugirard, was one who has been already mentioned, Marie de Gournay, widow of David Rousseau. "This poor woman," writes M. Olier, "though of low extraction, and of a condition in life which it is almost a disgrace to name, is nevertheless become the adviser of persons the most illustrious by birth and rank, and the guide of souls the most exalted in virtue. Even princesses have recourse to her counsels, and recommend their most important affairs to her prayers. The Duchess of Orleans, the Princess of Condé, the Duchesses of Aiguillon and of Elbeuf, the Marchioness of La Châtre, and many others, count it an honour to visit her; indeed, I have known a lady of the highest rank afraid of even going into her presence. Souls the most advanced in the ways of God seek lessons of perfection from her lips; men of the most apostolic spirit go to consult her before entering on any enterprise which they have in contemplation. F. Eudes, that famous preacher, the wonder of the age; Mademoiselle Manse, raised up by God to the aid of the infant Church of Canada; M. le Royer de la Dauversière, to whom that Church owed its first establishment; M. du Coudray, devoted to the missions of the Levant, and the defence of Christendom against the Turks; Dom Jacques, the Carthusian, the bold rebuker of vice in the wealthy and the powerful: when these, and so many others * of the most zealous servants of God, who at this day adorn the Church of France, are to be seen seeking counsel of this wise and holy woman, we might think we beheld the 'Virgin most prudent' once more directing the Church of her Divine Son, and guiding His Apostles after His ascension into heaven. Such is the influence she exerts over the hearts of men, that in a moment they are completely changed; there is none so holy but in conversing with her he derives fresh courage for God's service: persons the most eminent for their sanctity have experienced the most surprising effects, and all from a few simple common words. When consulted, her replies are short; she never enters into her reasons for the advice she gives; she does but say, 'God would have you do this or that.' In her would seem to be visibly displayed the absolute power of God; she has but to speak, and at a word all that she asks or wishes is done; and that without any of those exterior advantages of appearance, address, or manner, by which such influence is usually accompanied."

This holy widow was one among the very few who retained their high esteem for M. Olier at the time he was contemned by all the world; and when, after his retirement to Vaugirard, God restored to him all his former powers, she never rested until she had disabused the minds of his late associates, and once more collected them about him. She sought out each singly, and urged him to go and judge for himself whether M. Olier were

* She was also frequently consulted by F. de Condren, and shortly before his death urged him to set down in writing the instructions for the conduct of ecclesiastical seminaries which he had long had in his mind to put together, warning him at the same time that he had but a few days to live.

such as he had come to regard him. Several accordingly went, and when they saw and heard him, they could not disguise their astonishment. It was but a few weeks ago that they had seen him stand dumbfounded in the pulpit when desired to address the people, and now they heard him expounding the mysteries of the faith in language so sublime, and with so much authority and command, that it was with difficulty they recognized him as the same person, and said one to another, " O what a change is here! the hand of the Most High is manifest: never man spake more eloquently of the things of God!" Those among them especially who had been disciples of F. de Condren seemed to find again in this lately despised priest the lights, the wisdom, and the virtues of their holy master, and they could not refrain from loudly testifying their astonishment and delight even to M. Olier himself. "I am confounded," he writes, "when I think of it: that I, a vile worm of the earth, so mean and despicable that I wonder I dare make my appearance before the world, should be listened to with surprise and admiration by those to whom but yesterday I was the object of contempt and ridicule. But well may they be surprised, for I am amazed at myself, knowing as I do my ignorance and dulness, and so long assured as I have been, in the mercy of God, of my own blindness and nothingness. And yet it is true I have no difficulties on any subject; on the contrary, I receive the clearest lights respecting truths of which I had never so much as heard, and of which the greatest theologians amongst us are astonished they should have remained in ignorance, in spite of all their science. It is now that I behold accomplished the promise of the deceased father-general, that I should be one of the inheritors of his spirit. I cannot doubt it: things that I heard him formerly say, and which at the time I was incapable of comprehending, are now laid open before me with a clearness that exceeds the brightness of the sun."

Providence, too, in a marvellous way, gave Its approval to the new institution; and that so notably, that men were constrained to confess that God was there. Every day M. Olier saw visibly fulfilled before his eyes the intimation conveyed in those words which had been so forcibly presented to his mind during his retreat at Notre Dame des Vertus:—*Mea omnia tua sunt, et tua mea sunt.* His tongue seemed to possess a wonderfully persuasive power; nay, he no sooner even wished a thing than it was done. Conferring one day with his colleagues— and it was the first time that the subject had been mooted—on the need they had of a practical man of business, who could transact their affairs for them, at the very moment he was speaking, there came a rap at the door, and he beheld standing before him the very person whose help they needed, who had come to offer himself to the community, to assist them in any way they might require. " I declare," he says, " that never in my life was I more confounded or more amazed at the goodness of God than at that moment. I could not restrain my tears, and in spirit annihilated myself before the Divine mercy." Then, too, began to be realized those other words which had risen to his lips when he had beheld in vision the Eternal Father: *Qui regis Israel, intende; qui deducis velut ovem Joseph.* All the tenderest care and nurture which a parent could bestow upon his children were sensibly lavished upon him and his associates; their wants were supplied with a bountifulness and a loving solicitude that was even in advance and in excess of their requests or desires. All things seemed to work together for their good; the services they received from others, so far from being rendered grudgingly, and as of constraint, were offered from a motive of charity and out of the abundance of the heart; and they who lately had held aloof from him, now seemed to find their satisfaction in heaping kindnesses upon him. His father had left a lawsuit on his hands, which (as usual in such matters) appeared interminable. His opponents had refused all accommodation, when one day, to his surprise, they begged him to forego further proceedings, and yielded all his demands.

The three priests had been but a very short time at Vaugirard, when Cardinal de Richelieu, hearing of the new establishment, and surmising that its originators, with whose merits he was well acquainted, were among those to whom F. de Condren had alluded in conversation as destined to render great services to the Church, sent his niece, the Duchess of Aiguillon, to pay them a visit in his name. He had it in contemplation to lay the foundations of an episcopal seminary, and in his own mind had fixed upon M. Olier and his associates as the men whom he wished to have near him for the execution of his plans. He commissioned his niece, therefore, to express to them his regret that they should be so ill accommodated in their present dwelling, and to offer them his own château of Ruel, where they should be at liberty to live in as complete retirement as they pleased. So generous an offer was received with all the respect and gratitude it deserved; and had they not been resolved to rest on no other support but that of God alone, they might have recognized in this proposal of the great statesman a providential dispensation in their favour. But they desired to have no human patron, and begged the duchess to represent with all humility to the cardinal, that, having fixed upon the village of Vaugirard as the place where they could insure the greatest seclusion, they should find it difficult to follow their vocation in the house of a prime minister; and that the meanness of their dwelling rendered it only the more suitable to their purpose.

The cardinal, far from manifesting displeasure at such a reply,* sought only how to give them further proofs of

* In the Memoirs of M. du Ferrier we have an anecdote of this great man which may surprise those who know him only as the astute politician or iron-handed statesman. M. Meyster, after paying a visit to his friends at Vaugirard, went to see the cardinal, who for several years had desired to converse with so eminent a missionary. On this occasion he offered M. Meyster more than a million livres for the use of the missions, and, to his astonishment, met with a decided refusal. A circumstance so unexpected deeply moved him, and even filled him with alarm. "But, monsieur," he said, "has God revealed to you that I am reprobate, and that He will not accept anything at my hands? Tell me, I pray you, do you think that I cannot be saved in the position I occupy?" "My

his confidence and respect. Their character was now established at court, and many young ecclesiastics of merit were induced to join the community. The first who were received at Vaugirard were M. Louis Henri de Pardaillan de Gondrin, then in his twenty-third year, who two years later was promoted to the coadjutorship of Sens, and M. Gabriel de Thubières de Queylus, Abbé of Loc-Dieu. The next was one of whom we shall have frequent mention in this memoir, M. Antoine Raguier de Poussé. He was the intimate friend of M. de Gondrin, and the account which the latter gave of the sanctity of M. Olier and his great spiritual discernment, inspired him with a strong desire to see so extraordinary a man. Accordingly, he went to Vaugirard, and a few minutes' conversation with the servant of God sufficed to lead him to beg with all earnestness to be admitted among his disciples. To these were soon added M. Hurtevent, who died superior of the seminary of S. Irenæus at Lyons; M. de Cambiac, brother of M. du Ferrier; and several others.

How one of these was gained to the community we learn from M. Olier himself. They had need of an able theologian, and the matter had been made the subject of

---

lord," replied M. Meyster, "we have spoken on the subject several times with F. de Condren." "And what conclusion did you come to?" asked the cardinal. "We were agreed," was the reply, "that you had in your possession one means of making sure your salvation, and that was the power of upholding the rights of the Church, and procuring the nomination of good men to bishoprics." "I declare to you," said the cardinal, "that I am so entirely of this sentiment, that I never dream of selecting any but the most worthy and most capable men, without regard to the solicitations or the services of relatives. I know of how momentous a nature the matter is, and am convinced that a man would incur damnation who should nominate to a benefice out of consideration for friends, or on account of services rendered by relatives, as much as if he were to sell it to the highest bidder." And, in fact, to this great minister was due the alteration that was made in the briefs of nomination to bishoprics and abbeys. He cancelled the following words which before had been inserted: *Et pour reconnaître les bons et agreeables services rendus* ("And in acknowledgment of good and acceptable services rendered"). But see Note A.

their united prayers. Now it happened one day, when he and M. de Foix were on their way back from Paris, that they met an ecclesiastic of high repute for his theological science, who had been to see them at Vaugirard, and was returning. M. Olier, in his humility, stepped a little aside, to allow M. de Foix (who at that time was superior) to speak to one whom he knew to be a person of no ordinary ability. But M. de Foix obliged him to come forward; and, against his will, M. Olier found himself drawn little by little into the conversation. Then, abandoning himself (as he says) to the Spirit who ruled him, and uttering the words that were put into his mouth, he expressed himself with so much force and unction, that the ecclesiastic was moved in an extraordinary way. M. de Foix himself was equally astonished at his companion's eloquence, and the effect it produced. The result was, that the ecclesiastic in question, whose name is not mentioned, but who proved to be the very person of whom they stood most in need, joined the community, and for several years taught theology and philosophy to the inmates of the seminary.

About this time also the attractions of the same marvellous grace drew to the community another ecclesiastic, who, though not possessed of equal theological science, was remarkably well versed in the Sacred Scriptures, and had an extensive and accurate knowledge of all that related to the duties of the ministry. This was M. de Bassancourt, already known to the reader as one of M. Olier's early associates, and a man of considerable powers. After the dissolution of the community of Chartres he had accompanied M. Amelote on his mission into Normandy, and on his return to Paris lost no time in paying his friends a visit at Vaugirard. They had felt the want of him, at least they had a great wish that he should join them—for (says M. Olier) "we wanted only God"—but they had small hope of winning him, knowing how strongly he was attached to M. Amelote. Nothing, indeed, was further from his own thoughts. He went to see them simply for old affection's sake, and almost for the amusement of the thing, and began by rallying them in a good-natured humorous way on the wonderful reform they were about to effect in the clergy, settled down as they were, like so many hermits, in that obscure little village. But after he had listened a while to M. Olier, his manner completely changed, and he said, "My friends, I am convinced that I shall be more sure of finding our Blessed Lord among you, than in my mother's house. No, it is not among their relatives that ecclesiastics are visited by His Spirit. My choice is made: I pray you give me a cell, and let me stay with you." Then, aware that the house was full, and seeing the dovecot at the back, he begged them to let him occupy it. "You may do as you please," he said in his usual lively manner, "but go back to my mother I declare I will not: I sleep here to-night." They took him at his word, called a conference immediately, and then they told him he was their friend, their brother, and they could not deny him a request made with such a grace.

This resolution on the part of M. de Bassancourt created much sensation at Paris, where his family were held in high consideration, but the public attention was even more arrested by what next followed. M. Amelote himself paid a visit to Vaugirard and desired to be admitted into the community. This was the occasion of much embarrassment to the fathers. On the one hand they were reluctant to exclude an old associate of whose virtues and abilities they had so intimate a knowledge; but, on the other, they were convinced, from what both M. du Ferrier and M. Meyster had said, that he did not possess the requisite vocation. Such, therefore, was the answer they returned. M. Amelote, however, was not so easily repelled and renewed his solicitations with redoubled vigour, pressing his suit more particularly on M. Olier, who (as we shall see) shortly became superior. There was no one for whom the servant of God entertained a warmer admiration, nor had the words of F. de Condren lost any of their effect with him, when, on occasion of his appearing to him after his death, he told him that M. Amelote was one of the two persons whom together with himself he had left inheritors of his spirit.

But neither had he forgotten that interior voice which, in his retreat at Notre Dame des Vertus, had assured him that this ecclesiastic was destined to serve God elsewhere. Nothing, therefore, could shake his resolution. M. de Bassancourt was most urgent in his friend's behalf, offering to endow the seminary with an income of 4,000 livres if he were received among them. Mme. de Brienne, also, wife of the statesman of that name, persevered for three years in repeating the same request, even engaging the queen regent to use her influence in the matter; but all to no purpose. M. Olier was willing to endure any amount of obloquy rather than go against what he believed to be the will of God. There were not wanting ill-natured persons who did not scruple to aver that his opposition was founded on a mere dislike of having a rival in the community. M. Olier held his peace, never disclosing to any one except to his director, and that under obedience, the motives that determined him in his refusal; for he could not have done so without at the same time making known the other communications with which he had been favoured. His conduct was justified by the event. The institution in which M. Amelote was called to labour for the glory of God, was that of the Oratory, which he entered eight years later, and where he contributed more than any one to uphold the faith of the Church against the pestilential errors with which unhappily the greater part of that congregation became infected.*

M. de Bassancourt was followed by M. Houmain, more commonly known as M. de Sainte-Marie from the name

---

* F. Amelote, at the request of the French clergy, published a version of the New Testament in opposition to that of Mons, 100,000 copies of which were distributed by the order of Louis XIV. He also composed several treatises against the Jansenistic heresy, among others a "Defence of the Apostolical Constitutions," and a "Treatise on Grace," in support of the condemnation of the five propositions. His attachment to the faith, and the persecutions he underwent in its defence, endeared him still more to M. Olier, with whom, and with the community generally, he continued till the day of his death bound in the closest ties of friendship.

of his priory, an ecclesiastic of great merit and talents. He was of a good family, and being of a delicate constitution had been so daintily nurtured, that before joining M. Olier in the missions he was afraid of the slightest exposure to cold or damp. His room was matted and carpeted, and furnished with double hangings of cloth and paper. But no sooner had he embraced the laborious life to which God had called him, than his health seemed to undergo a complete transformation; he slept on the ground like the rest, and bade adieu for ever to all his indulgent ways. He had been a witness of all that M. Olier had endured during his time of trial, and on visiting him at Vaugirard, he was so moved by his words that he resolved not to leave him.

But not only did M. Olier exercise an extraordinary influence over those with whom he was brought into contact, he seemed to possess a supernatural insight into the secrets of men's hearts. Scarcely had they who came to consult him opened their lips, when he knew, as by a divine instinct, the nature of their requests and the state of their souls. One of the members of the community, yielding to the suggestions of others, had formed the design of quitting the society. Dissatisfied, however, with himself, he went to M. Olier and begged him to tell him his faults. In an instant the servant of God perceived what was in his mind, and laid open before him his intentions with such fulness of detail, that, struck with astonishment, the man went about among his brethren declaring that M. Olier had disclosed to him all the hidden thoughts of his heart. And so it was continually. He would feel himself moved to speak with peculiar earnestness on some particular subject, and an hour or two afterwards one of the community would come and tell him that the words he had uttered had gone home to his conscience with a force he could not resist. He would address himself to some of his young ecclesiastics when he had made his thanksgiving after Mass, and their souls would be set on fire with divine love, and they would be filled with an intense desire of offering themselves like so many living victims on the altar of God.

By the help of the light within him he would solve the deepest questions of theology: sometimes on the instant; at others, as though to remind him that the knowledge he had was not his own but the mere gift of God, he would be left awhile in darkness, and then, as with a sudden flash, the truth would dart into his mind, and all would be clear to him. "This" (he says) is my daily experience, whether in conversation or in hearing confessions. The clearness of the light varies with different persons; but to all I answer according to their respective needs, with no other preparation than that of renouncing my own spirit, waiting for whatever it may please God to give me for the good of His children."

The same thing happened in his public preaching. One day, in particular,—it was the Eve of the Annunciation, 1642,—he was desired to go and prepare the people for a becoming celebration of the feast. He went at once, but with his mind as if in a state of blank: he felt unable to utter a word. Twice he was on the point of saying as much; but, accustomed to this feeling of incompetency, he resigned himself with all simplicity into the hands of God. Immediately his mind was filled with light, and he spoke with so much power and fervour, that his auditors were deeply affected, and himself not least, at the sweet and holy things that fell from his lips as he discoursed of Jesus and Mary. Such was the effect of his exhortation, that the people came in crowds to confession and communion, and it was between one and two o'clock in the day before all had finished. His words also had often a wonderful application beyond his own knowledge or intention. Thus one Sunday, in the fervour of his address, he broke out with a panegyric on the sanctity of the great patriarch S. Francis. Now, it so happened that at that very moment, unknown to him, there came into the church a monk of the order who had gone back into the world. The poor culprit was covered with confusion, and following M. Olier into the sacristy, stood before him with eyes cast down and as if speechless with shame and remorse, so cut to the heart had he been by the impassioned words of the preacher, which seemed to have been directed at himself.

Another instance was still more remarkable, and is characteristic both of the man and of the times. It was the feast of S. James, and he was preaching on the Gospel for the day, inveighing, with his accustomed energy, against those who, like the mother of Zebedee's sons, seek to promote their offspring to high places in God's kingdom for the sake of the emoluments and dignities attaching thereto. "Verily," said he, "the altars of Jesus Christ would be deserted, and the churches left empty, were it not for the pride and self-love which urge so many to enter the ecclesiastical state." Then lifting up his voice, and carried, as it were, out of himself by the indignation which worldly vanity and ambition ever excited in his soul, he exclaimed: "Had this blessed Apostle been in my place, and were he standing at this moment in this pulpit, he would have preached against his own mother, and with his own lips have denounced the unhallowed request she had preferred in his behalf." In the midst of his harangue, there came into the church his cousin Madame Dolu de Dampierre, accompanied by her two sons. M. Olier saw her enter, but had no suspicion of the object of her visit, which was nothing else but to request him to use the influence he possessed at court to obtain preferment for her children. When the sermon was ended, the lady, nothing daunted by what she had heard,—in all probability perfectly unconscious of any application the discourse might have to herself, or regarding it as nothing more than one of those unmeaning oratorical displays which it had not unfrequently been her lot to witness in other places,—paid her intended visit, and preferred her request with all the confidence imaginable. The reader will not need to be told what kind of reception she met with from her relative; it is sufficient to say that she retired in tears, which, we may hope, had their source in true compunction and not in mere mortified pride.

The inmates of Madame Villeneuve's establishment, as well as the children under their care, were also the objects of his pastoral solicitude, and we read of his collecting both mistresses and scholars together, and making them an exhortation which produced the liveliest effects. He spoke to them of the Holy Spirit, experiencing (as he says) a peculiar delight in making Him known to souls. He adds that he scarcely ever preached on any subject without himself, in the course of his address, deriving light concerning it which he had not enjoyed before; and he instances a sermon he delivered on the feast of the Transfiguration, in which thoughts were suggested to him infinitely surpassing anything that had occurred to his mind in his previous meditations.

The community, which was composed at first but of three individuals, now numbered twenty members, and a larger dwelling was required. In nothing was the munificence of the Lord whom they served more conspicuously displayed than in what occurred in this matter of a habitation. M. Olier and his associates were not destined to be long imprisoned within the narrow, incommodious building which they had chosen on first coming to Vaugirard. They had been but a few weeks in the village when M. Copin, the *curé*, requested them to take charge of the parish for a fortnight during his absence at Paris, an absence, however, which was extended to a space of nine months. This circumstance not only placed a convenient house at their disposal, but was providentially ordered so as to afford them ample opportunity to acquire a thorough experimental knowledge of the duties of a parish priest. Their next piece of good fortune, however, was far more remarkable. Near the church stood a large house, with a spacious garden, surrounded by a high wall: finding that the tenant was seldom resident, they proposed that he should sub-let it to them. This, however, he declined to do; but insisted on their taking up their abode in it, all furnished as it was, merely stipulating that he should be permitted sometimes to come and say his rosary in the garden walks. The house belonged to a M. de Rochefort, lord of Souplainville and grand-vicar of the Archbishop of Auch; and as it was very commodious, and in all respects suitable to a large community, they made overtures to him for the purchase of it. Here, again, they were met with a refusal, the good man protesting he would not let them have it at any price, and begging them to accept it as a gift. This, however, they absolutely refused; and as he saw the uselessness of persisting, he affected acquiescence, and made over to them the house with all its appurtenances, which comprised several acres of vineyard and meadow-land, for the nominal sum of two thousand crowns, the land alone being fully worth the price. And then, when they proceeded to pay the purchase-money, he refused to accept it, declaring that, as he had bequeathed them the amount in his will, he preferred leaving it in their hands, without charging them interest.*

They had now, therefore, two establishments. Some of the community remained at the presbytery for the discharge of parochial duties, the rest took up their residence at the house of M. de Rochefort, where they conducted all their spiritual exercises with the strictest punctuality. In the afternoon there was a conference on Holy Scripture, at which M. Olier was usually the principal expounder. The profundity of his theological knowledge, and the extraordinary insight into the meaning of the Sacred Writings of which he now gave evidence, struck all who heard him with surprise and admiration; and they who but lately acted as his instructors, voluntarily placed themselves in the ranks of his disciples. In all this the humility of the servant of God only became the more conspicuous as his true position as head of the new community was more indisputably recognized. "My greatest joy," he wrote at this time,

* On the 18th of March, 1643, M. Olier and M. de Foix bought the house adjoining that of M. de Rochefort; and the two buildings united into one subsequently formed the little seminary of S. Sulpice, until the year 1759, when it was occupied by a community of poor scholars, called the Robertines. The lands were sold by M. Olier for 5,000 livres. At the Revolution the house was sold as national property, and in part demolished. M. Emery, however, superior of the Seminary of S. Sulpice, made great personal sacrifices in order to re-purchase it; and there at this day may be seen the chamber occupied by M. Olier, now converted into a chapel.

"is to see that every one is persuaded that what I say is not of myself, but of God only. I rejoice thereat, and I rejoice the more in perceiving that of all that is done among us nothing is ascribed to any one of us, but God is acknowledged as alone doing all things here. There is not one amongst us who can give the world occasion to say, 'He did this or that.' Blessed be God, who would alone be glorified in His own work!"

It was not long before M. de Foix insisted on resigning his office of superior, and M. Olier was with one voice elected in his room.

CHAPTER IX.

The spirit of the Seminary of Vaugirard—Removal to S. Sulpice.

IT may be supposed that an undertaking begun simply from supernatural motives and on supernatural grounds, would not command general confidence and respect, even among good men. Why (it was said) abandon the field of missionary labour, in which so much had incontestably been accomplished, for the sake of an uncertain and speculative good which experience had proved to be unattainable? Many also who at first had evinced a warm interest in the work, disapproved of M. Olier's measures, and augured ill of its success. Others, who were admirers of his zeal and abilities, and had expected great things from him, protested loudly against the infatuation which led him to bury his talents in retirement and obscurity. The grand-vicar of the archbishop of Paris, when M. Olier paid him a visit, gravely proposed that he should establish himself at Rome, and there inaugurate an institution which should extend itself throughout the Church. "S. Peter and S. Paul," said he, "did not remain shut up in Judea—they went to Rome; and thither also ought you to go. Yes, I repeat it, you must go to Rome: indeed you must. Now attend to what I have said." In such an address, voice and manner are everything, and the reader will be at no loss to supply them. "This speech," says M. Olier, "surprised me not a little, as coming from such a person, and delivered with so much assurance;" but it had no other effect.

At the bottom, however, of all these objections and counter-suggestions, lay the fact that every endeavour hitherto to found an ecclesiastical seminary in France had proved a failure. Eighty years had now elapsed since the Council of Trent enjoined the erection of seminaries for the education of the clergy; many provincial councils at different times had repeated the injunction; and yet nothing had been done. In some dioceses the chapters had refused to move in the matter; in others the injunction had simply been disregarded, or the question had been left pending. By dint of repeated remonstrance and entreaty, M. Bourdoise, Dr. Duval, and some others had succeeded, in 1629, in bringing the subject before the assembly of the clergy, and it was proposed to establish four general seminaries for the whole of France; but although the proposition met with a favourable reception, it appeared in the end so difficult of execution, that it was judged better to leave each bishop at liberty to provide for his own diocese in such way as seemed to him most advantageous. The question was what form should be given to the seminaries, and to whom the government should be confided. It had been the intention of the Council of Trent, as also of the provincial councils in which the subject had been discussed, that the candidates for the ecclesiastical state should be received into the seminaries at an early age; but whether the selection of subjects had been unfortunate, or those who undertook their direction were wanting in the necessary qualifications, the institutions had either become extinct or had degenerated into mere schools. S. Vincent de Paul, indeed, in the year 1636 had established a seminary at the Collége des Bons Enfants, but even he was forced to confess that owing to the youths being admitted before their character was sufficiently pronounced, the experiment had resulted in no permanent advantage to the Church. From the same high authority we learn that other attempts had met with no better success; that the seminaries of Bordeaux and Agen were deserted; and that the archbishop of Rouen had failed in realizing half a dozen vocations out of all the numerous young men on whom he had expended so much labour and care. To which may be added, that the seminary founded in the diocese of Limoges had not produced a single priest during the whole twenty years it had been in existence.

The Oratorians (as mentioned in a previous chapter) had been equally unsuccessful. The house called S. Magloire at Paris, which twenty-two years before had been erected into a diocesan seminary, had not fulfilled its object, and they had found themselves obliged to confine their exertions to giving lessons in theology to such of the pupils in their schools as were intended for the ecclesiastical state, and providing them with a retreat of ten days previous to ordination; which was all that bishops the most remarkable for their zeal were able to accomplish. Even M. Bourdoise, who for more than thirty years had devoted all his energies to supplying the crying need of the Church, had succeeded only in forming a community of parish priests at S. Nicolas du Chardonnet;* and when to these we add such prelates as S. Francis de Sales and Alain de Solminihac, each of whom had made the attempt and had failed, we cannot be surprised that on M. Olier and his associates com-

---

* M. Bourdoise, and the ecclesiastics associated with him, long remained without any fixed abode, and their poverty was so great that they wanted even the most ordinary pieces of furniture, making the shutters of their windows serve them for tables during the day. Cardinal de Retz employed them in instructing the younger clergy, saying Mass, managing schools, &c.; and several other prelates also commissioned M. Bourdoise to superintend the conduct of ecclesiastics belonging to their dioceses who were resident at Paris. The community of S. Nicolas du Chardonnet was incorporated in the year 1631, but it was not until 1644 that it was erected into a seminary.

mencing their establishment at Vaugirard, it was regarded as a mere chimerical undertaking.

The remarkable success, however, which attended the new institution speedily led to an entire change of opinion, and it began to be acknowledged on all hands, that if any one were able to carry into execution a work which hitherto had appeared impossible of accomplishment, M. Olier was the man. And, in fact, to him belongs of right the title of the founder of the first seminary ever erected in the land of his birth, if by founder be meant one who succeeds in establishing what he has erected.* In this was fulfilled the prediction of the Mother Agnes de Langeac, when (at their first interview) she assured him that God had destined him to lay the first foundation of ecclesiastical seminaries in France. True it is, that S. Vincent de Paul had made a beginning, but, by his own confession, that beginning had no permanent results. However, he was not to linger long in the rear: in this same year, 1642, with the approbation and assistance of Cardinal de Richelieu, who gave him a thousand crowns for the work, he made his first essay in establishing a greater seminary, by admitting twelve young men into the Collége des Bons Enfants. Shortly after, the same great statesman encouraged F. Bourgoing, general of the Oratory, to commence three seminaries of the same kind —one at Toulouse, a second at Rouen, and a third at Paris; but the first did not last more than a year, the second was not of much longer duration, and the third had scarcely been opened when the cardinal died, before he had provided the necessary funds for its support.

But to return to M. Olier, at Vaugirard. The foundations which it was his design to lay, were such as should be sunk deep in the interior man, and these were (in Scripture language) the putting off the old Adam and

---

* The Abbé Faillon is at the trouble of establishing this fact at some length, in refutation of those who have given the precedence, in point of time, to S. Vincent de Paul, M. Bourdoise, and others.

putting on Christ. It was at this time that, in obedience to his director F. Bataille, he began to set down in writing the particular graces which he received from God, and all the more notable circumstances of his life, so far as related to the progress of his sanctification. We are enabled, therefore, to give in his own words the instructions which, in conversation and otherwise, he imparted to his ecclesiastics. "Speaking one day" (he writes) "to our young associates on the necessity of crucifying the old man that the life of our Lord may be made manifest in us, I said, that in order to give Jesus Christ complete liberty to act within us, we must crucify the flesh by poverty, suffering, and mortification; that never would He humble Himself to us unless we mortified the spirit and the movements of our own pride. Whereupon one of them said to me relative to the subject of poverty, 'Is there, then, no difference between counsels and precepts? Wherein do they differ, if to renounce the goods of fortune, which appears to be only a counsel, is nevertheless necessary to us all?' God suggested to me this reply: 'In this matter of renunciation two things must be considered: interior detachment, and actual despoliation. The first is in suchwise necessary, that without some degree of interior detachment from earthly goods we cannot save our souls; according to those words of our Lord which are addressed, not to any individual in particular, but to every Christian: *Every one of you that doth not renounce all that he possesseth, cannot be my disciple.*'— (Luke xiv. 33). We must live in the midst of worldly goods, and even acquire them, as if we possessed them not, without allowing our affections to cling to them by any disorderly attachment of the heart. Whereas that which is of counsel, is actually to part with these same goods, because of the difficulty there is in not loving them when we possess them; as if our Lord said to us: 'I counsel you to part with your goods, in case you cannot possess them without loving them.' This is what appears in those words addressed to a certain young man who loved his possessions: *Go sell what thou hast, and give to the poor.*—(Matt. xix. 21). God commands even this exterior renunciation when there is evident peril of sin.

"A few days ago a question was put to me, to which I will here give the answer, as it does not seem to have come from myself. One of our young associates, experiencing some difficulty in giving up the habits of the world, and particularly in the matter of his hair, asked me why people had such an attachment to mere trifles. I replied on the moment, that it has its source in self-love, and in the great desire we have of pleasing the world, and possessing a share in its esteem and affection; one of the strongest and most deeply-rooted desires that actuate a man, who is made up of pride. Now, the hair having been given him for ornament, and conducing to a fair appearance, and consequently to making him well esteemed and agreeable in the eyes of the world and of himself—this is why we are so extremely attached thereto. When it is cut off we feel it keenly, as though we had been shorn of a portion of our self-love, and our pride had been maimed and mutilated; for one of our means of attracting the love and complacency of the world has, in fact, been destroyed. The pain we feel is a measure of the desire we have of making an appearance, and being esteemed and loved by creatures. This it is to which we must die, as I am constantly saying, seeking the love and esteem of no one, that we may do no wrong to our God, who alone ought to fill all minds and hearts."

M. Olier exhorted his followers to kill the old man,*

---

* A ludicrous story is told in connection with M. Olier's frequent repetition of this phrase. One day he was exhorting his followers with his usual energy, and often repeated the same expression: *Il faut faire mourir le vieil homme* ("We must put the old man to death"). The gardener's wife happened to be listening at the door, and thinking that "the old man" meant her husband, hastened in a state of great consternation to apprize her spouse of the fate that awaited him. Terrified at his wife's report, the old man resolved to quit the house that very day, and going to M. Olier, he said with a voice almost choked with fear, "Oh! sir, pray give me leave to go; my wife has told me everything; I wish to live a little longer; I know all your design." "What design?" asked M. Olier. "Oh! you know better than I can tell you." "But,

only that he might establish within them the life of Jesus Christ, the new man, created in justice and true holiness. This was the point to which all his addresses tended. With the affection of a father he applied himself to the removal of any doubts by which their minds were perplexed or disturbed, as well as to the mitigation in practice of the apparent rigour of his maxims; and always with eventual success. There was amongst them an ecclesiastic of excellent disposition, and an accomplished theologian; but he had come filled with his own ideas, and furnished with a system of piety devised by himself. His mind revolted at the pure spirituality proposed to him, and he combated it with all the appliances of his theological science. To punish him for his attachment to his own views, God permitted him suddenly to lose all recollection of the knowledge he possessed; and when he endeavoured to reason on any subject, he became bewildered and confused. Sensible, at last, of the miserable state to which his pride had reduced him, and unable to resist the force of truth, he confessed himself vanquished; and immediately God restored to him all that, in chastisement of his obstinacy, He had taken from him, and he became one of the humblest and most obedient in the community.

The very spirit of the seminary was that of union with Jesus Christ. "Explaining one day," writes M. Olier, "a number of questions which had been put to me on the necessity of uniting ourselves with our Lord in our actions, I said:—When we unite ourselves to Him by faith, that instant we are clothed with His intentions; He resides within us only to be entirely ours, to the end

my good friend, what do you mean?" "Why, did you not say that the old man must be put to death? I am old, it is true, but old age is no crime, and I am still able to support myself." Despite the evident terror and agitation of the poor gardener, it was impossible for M. Olier and his companions to refrain from laughing; but it was no easy matter to persuade him that the "old man" whose death M. Olier had so vehemently demanded, was nothing else but that corrupt nature which every one ought to endeavour to mortify in himself.

that His Father may be glorified by us; and our works, done by the movement of the Holy Spirit, become invested in His sight with a marvellous sanctity. What more easy than to say to God, at the beginning of all our actions, 'My God, I renounce my own disorderly intentions, and I give myself to Thee, to perform my actions in Thy intentions, which are infinitely adorable'? We may unite ourselves to the intentions He had in doing works similar to our own: as, for example, when He ate, drank, slept, conversed, prayed, and the rest. Although you know not what those intentions were, do not the less consent to all, and desire them such as they are in themselves, and as God knows them. The Eternal Father, seeing you would desire to have all the intentions of His Son, and that you would be glad to give expression to them in your interior, if you were capable, will regard your actions with great complacency. We may unite ourselves with the intentions of the Son of God even in actions which He never performed exteriorly on earth, for He offered them all beforehand for us. In forming His church, He designed to make it perform all its works to the glory of His Father; so that all Christians, without a single exception, are but the executors of the designs and intentions of Jesus Christ.

"To all my instructions," he adds, "I bring no other preparation but that of renouncing myself and my own knowledge, waiting for what God may please to give me for the good of His children; and this way of acting is so efficacious and so powerful, that I see them making far greater advances in three weeks than I made myself in eight or ten years, during which I was ignorant of the ways which it is necessary to follow in order to arrive purely at God. I pray our Lord to continue His graces both to them and to myself; but if they go on as they have begun, I cannot help persuading myself that they must become saints. I firmly believe that God regards the whole community with complacency, because of the purity with which it walks, and the zeal with which it labours in His service. I may even say, in passing, that, having the consciences of all in my keeping, I have been a considerable time without remarking in any one of them a single venial sin. There is no longer any question here of the things of the world, or of aught that may content the flesh, any more than if we were living the life of the saints after the resurrection."

The conversion of the Canadian Indians had long been an object of the deepest interest to M. Olier, and it was in this same memorable year (1642) that he first made the acquaintance of one who, by his prayers and personal exertions, contributed most effectually to the success of that holy enterprise. This was Claude Leglay, or, as he was always called, Brother Claude, a native of Lorraine; of whom it is sufficient to say, that his low estate and exalted sanctity, combined with the extraordinary influence which he exercised over the good and great, render him worthy of being classed in the same category with Marie de Gournay. His condition in life was that of an artisan, and he had come to Paris to escape the effects of the dreadful famine which was then desolating his country. Desirous only of serving God in lowliness and obscurity, his piety and virtues acquired him a reputation, and even a celebrity, which equalled, if it did not surpass, that of any of the most accomplished masters of the spiritual life. His knowledge of Divine things was truly marvellous in one who was not only illiterate, but compelled to labour for his daily maintenance, and could have been imparted to him only by the immediate teaching of the Holy Spirit. Persons distinguished both for their piety and rank in the world went to hear and to converse with him; and on Sundays and on other holidays, when he was not engaged in his work, a long line of carriages might be seen standing in the humble street in which he lived. Men who were reckoned the oracles of the day in religious matters were in the habit of consulting him, and in 1641, when M. Le Gauffre succeeded F. Bernard in the conduct of those works of charity to which the latter had devoted himself, Brother Claude was induced, after much entreaty, to take up his abode in the house of that good priest, for the purpose of assisting him in his labours. It was then that the more supernatural portion of his life began to develop itself. Although naturally of a lively disposition, he was inwardly so occupied with God as to be at times wholly withdrawn from this outer world. In the crowded streets of Paris he remained insensible to all the din and tumult around him; he neither saw nor heard aught of the thousands who were traversing his path in all directions; in short, he was as unconscious of their presence and proximity as if he had been crossing a lonely silent heath in utter darkness. He was jostled, struck, thrown to the ground, trampled on; in an instant he was on his feet again, and though often bruised, and even in appearance injured, he seemed to be protected and preserved from harm by an invisible hand. He had in him the very spirit of Elias in rebuking and withstanding evil, and a heart filled with an impatient desire to quit the world and go to God; "such," says M. Olier, "as the souls of the blessed might be supposed to have if they revisited their mortal bodies."

On the 16th of July, being the feast of our Lady of Mount Carmel, M. Olier went to say Mass at the church of the Carmelites. There was a gathering of the friends of the Canadian mission, and among them were several who were preparing to go to Montreal. Brother Claude was also present, and by a particular movement of the Holy Spirit (for he had no knowledge of M. Olier's vocation) he was led to pray all through the Mass for two things: first, that the priest then offering the Holy Sacrifice might attain to a perfect union with God; secondly, that he might become a great captain in the army of Christ, to marshal soldiers in His service. At the same time he conceived a strong personal affection for him, and meeting M. Olier in the afternoon of the same day, he declared that in him he had at length found the friend he had long been seeking. From that moment these two holy men remained bound to each other in the closest ties of union. In this circumstance M. Olier did but find another occasion of humbling himself, and confessing his own nothingness: "I see" he says, "with a clearness exceeding that of day, that there is something in me which is not myself; this it is that constrains these holy souls to come to me, and to speak words of benediction directed truly to our Lord."

A few months only had elapsed since the establishment of the seminary at Vaugirard, and the Providence of God, to which M. Olier and his companions had wholly surrendered themselves, was already opening a way to the fulfilment of their designs, under circumstances which set at complete defiance all human calculations. The parish of S. Sulpice was the most extensive in the metropolis, being a sort of city in itself, under the jurisdiction, civil and ecclesiastical, of the Abbé of S. Germain,[*] and had become a very hotbed of iniquity, to the contamination and scandal, not only of Paris, but of all France. The duchess of Aiguillon, who resided within its limits, horrified at the disorders which met her eyes at every turn, had prevailed on the priests of the conferences of S. Lazarus, to give a mission in one of its quarters. This had taken place in the preceding year; but though much good was effected in the immediate locality, it did but reveal more distinctly than ever the hideousness of the evil, and the hopelessness of providing an adequate remedy. At length the *curé*, M. Julien de Fiesque, determined in his despair to relinquish the benefice, whenever he could meet with a worthy successor. His thoughts adverted to M. Olier, with whom he was personally acquainted, and for whom he entertained a particular respect; many also had begun to speak of the new institution of Vaugirard, and of the devotion of its members; and he seemed to see in these men the only persons competent to carry out a reform, which, with all his endeavours, he had utterly failed even to commence. An opportunity soon presented itself of sounding their dispositions. Every year, on S. Mark's day, there was a procession of his parishioners to the

---

[*] It included the present parishes of S. Sulpice, S. Germain des Prés, l'Abbaye aux Bois, les Missions Etrangères, S. Thomas d'Aquin, and S. Valère, not to mention the parish of Gros Caillou, and the Hôtel des Invalides.

church of Vaugirard, and as the parish priest was still
absent it fell to the lot of the little community to preside
at the usual ceremonies. But if M. de Fiesque had conceived any hopes that his proposition would be favourably entertained, he must have been greatly disappointed,
for on the part both of M. Olier and the rest, he met
not only with a decided refusal to undertake the charge,
but with a positive reluctance to speak on the subject.
Circumstances, however, shortly after enabled him to
renew his overture. Vaugirard lying on the borders of
Paris, some of the parishioners of S. Sulpice came to
make their confession to M. Olier and his priests, and
M. du Ferrier was accordingly deputed to ascertain from
the *curé* whether he had any objection to their receiving
his people. M. de Fiesque gave his cordial consent:
"But why put them to the trouble," said he, "of going
so far?" and he then repeated his proposition, offering to
resign the parish to them, simply on the condition that
M. Olier should make over to him, in exchange, his
priory of Clisson in Brittany (of which he was himself a
native), and a pension of 1,400 livres. M. du Ferrier
could hardly listen to him with patience, but on returning
to Vaugirard, and reporting the conversation to M. Olier
and M. de Foix, the three discussed the subject amongst
themselves, and M. de Foix marked down with a pencil,
on the back of a letter, the reasons for and against the
undertaking, with the view of consulting their director,
F. Tarisse.

Early the next morning M. du Ferrier started for
Vendôme, where F. Tarisse was then holding a chapter
of his congregation. On his way he beheld a meteor,
which seemed to explode directly over S. Sulpice, and
though he knew it was but a natural phenomenon, it
recalled to his memory the words of our Lord to His
disciples: "I saw Satan like lightning falling from
heaven" (Luke x. 18), and he accepted it as a sign that
God would succour His Church, and defeat all the power
and malice of the devil. The reply of F. Tarisse was
direct and decisive: that the hand of Providence was
visible in the opportunity that now presented itself of

establishing a model seminary for the whole of France, and that the affair should be prosecuted without delay. He added that they might rely on receiving all the assistance his congregation could render, and this was not small; for the parish of S. Sulpice being dependent on the Benedictines, under the Holy See, and altogether exempt from the jurisdiction of the archbishop, the matter rested entirely with themselves, and there was no occasion to obtain the approval or sanction of that prelate or his council, a proceeding which might have been attended with difficulties and provoked opposition. On his return through Paris M. du Ferrier lost no time in calling on M. de Fiesque, and receiving from him a formal engagement to resign his parish into their hands. As Marie de Gournay (or Marie Rousseau, as she was indifferently called) resided near the church, it occurred to him to pay her a visit also, for the purpose of communicating to her the result of his mission; but to his astonishment he found her already in possession of all that had occurred. "This morning at 9 o'clock," said she, "you were with M. le Curé; he was the first to begin the subject;" and she related in detail everything that had passed. This circumstance as showing that the project had the favour of heaven, contributed not a little to disarm all further opposition on the part of M. Olier and his associates, and it was definitively determined to accept M. de Fiesque's proposal.

No sooner did it become known at Paris that the community of Vaugirard were about to undertake the charge of the parish of S. Sulpice, than the greatest dissatisfaction prevailed. So strong was the conviction that the reform of a parish so extensive and so depraved exceeded the powers of M. Olier and his associates, that even good men set about defeating the attempt at its outset. But here again the supernatural knowledge manifested by Marie de Gournay came to their relief. On the 22nd of May she received a Divine intimation that at that moment two ecclesiastics at the other end of

came to confer with her, and was met on his appearance with these words, uttered with her usual simplicity: "So, sir, a pretty business this, in which you are engaged: you want, then, to destroy the work of the Lord. Yesterday, between four and five you and such a one (mentioning his name) were busy enough at it. I saw how the devil, who is bent on upsetting the work, succeeded in warping your mind: but take care what you are about." These words produced so complete a change in the disposition of her visitor, that he went to Vaugirard, and himself pressed M. Olier and his community to take charge of the parish. Some even of their own immediate friends exhibited much indignation at their presumption and temerity, for such they regarded the attempt to grapple with an evil of so tremendous a magnitude; and M. Renar (of whom mention has been before made) proceeded to Vaugirard for the purpose of remonstrating with them. They listened to his protest, which was couched in no gentle terms, and thanked him for his counsel, but assured him that they had not acted without consulting the Divine will; adding that they deserved all the ill success and confusion which he predicted, but that they begged him to pray to God that they might have grace to profit by their discomfiture. "Ah!" exclaimed he, "that is just what I said: when they are warned of their imprudence, they will think they set all straight by making an act of humiliation; and yet good people will be despised, and piety itself decried, because these gentlemen are pleased to undertake what they will never be able to carry through." Marie Rousseau, however, bade them trust in God and persevere. When M. Olier first acceded to M. de Fiesque's proposal, it formed no part of his design to undertake the office of *curé*, and he urged several of his colleagues to accept the charge, but they one after another declined. On consulting Marie, she at once, and without hesitation, declared that he was himself to be *curé* of S. Sulpice; that such was the will of God, and that no opposition could prevent it. She bade him, therefore, abandon himself courageously to the Divine pleasure, and not be discouraged, even if all his friends and associates were to desert and forsake him. S. Vincent de Paul and M. Bourdoise gave him similar counsel, and at length F. Bataille ordered him, under obedience, to accept the office.

No longer doubting the Divine will, the servant of God cast himself at the feet of his heavenly Patroness, and begged her to aid him in bearing the burden; and now there was no indecision or distrust. Was it objected that so small a body of priests would be unable to cope with so gigantic an evil, he answered that God who had inspired himself and his little band with the courage to undertake the work, was able to impart the same grace to others also, and that if with twelve Apostles He had subdued the world, He would not fail, even by their ministry alone, to win to Himself this single parish, if such were His holy will. Was he warned of the injury to health which so heavy a charge would entail, his reply was simply that to do God's will we must sacrifice even life itself, and that there could be no greater happiness than to die in the exercise of charity.; moreover, a profound conviction now possessed him that at length the designs of Providence which had long ago, and all through his life, been intimated to him with more or less distinctness, were about to receive their consummation. He called to mind the dream which had left so indelible an impression on his memory, when, nine or ten years before, he had seen Pope S. Gregory the Great on a lofty throne, with S. Ambrose seated below him; while below again were seats for priests, with a vacant place immediately beneath the latter saint, and below all, and, as it seemed, even far below, were ranged a number of Carthusian monks; and now he understood its import in its full significance, and it was shown him that the reform of a parish so notorious for vice as that in which he was called to labour, would be an example and a model for similar reforms, not only in Paris, but throughout the realm. At the same time, as appears from the writings he has left us, there was unfolded before him the whole scheme of his vocation, involving as it did these three great objects:—

1. The instruction and reformation of the people, high and low.

2. The introduction of the highest Christian maxims into the schools of the Sorbonne, by means of those seminarists who should proceed to the doctorate.

3. The formation of young ecclesiastics for all the functions of the sacred ministry.

It was on June 25th, during the octave of Corpus Christi, that the agreement for the transfer of the parish was finally concluded, of which, however, M. Olier was not to have actual possession until the arrangement had been sanctioned by the Holy See. But so assured was he of the Divine will that, with the approval of his director, F. Bataille, he had already hired a house adjoining the presbytery, where he was preparing to receive the ecclesiastics who had been admitted at Vaugirard. On July 31st he had an interview with the Abbé of S. Germain, Henri de Bourbon,* who welcomed him with every demonstration of regard; and on the same day he made a solemn protestation of perpetual devotion to the service of the parish in the name of all his colleagues, which was afterwards ratified severally by each.†

---

* It is worthy of note in how many instances men such as this Abbé of S. Germain were constrained, as it were, to co-operate in the reform of those very abuses of which they were themselves the most flagrant examples. Henri de Bourbon, Marquis de Verneuil, was a natural son of Henry IV.; though he had never received holy orders, he was Bishop of Metz, and held six or seven rich abbeys besides that of S. Germain, the revenues of which he squandered in luxurious living at Paris, even at a time when the people of his diocese were dying by thousands of famine. In 1678 he married.—See Bedford's "Life of S. Vincent de Paul," p. 127-8.

† This act seems to have been accepted by the Divine Goodness, for from M. Olier's days to our own, the *curés* of S. Sulpice have always been members of the community. And so essential to the spirit and object of the institute has this connection between the seminary and the parish been considered, that in 1802, when the house was taken down, M. Emery, the superior, preferred purchasing, at his own expense, a building within the limits of the parish to accepting a more commodious habitation, which was

It was with infinite disgust that M. Olier's relatives learnt that, after refusing a bishopric, and consequently a peerage, he had actually accepted this country parish, for so they regarded one of the *faubourgs*, or suburbs of Paris. That a scion of their house, who might have appeared at court with all the pomp and circumstance of a prelate of the Church, should be seen walking the streets of the capital in the garb of a humble *curé*, appeared to them a studied personal affront. They felt themselves positively aggrieved and outraged by conduct so unseemly, and his mother, accompanied by his eldest brother, went to Vaugirard for the purpose of formally remonstrating with him on the disgrace he was bringing on himself and his family. Finding all their expostulations unavailing, Madame Olier, in her indignation, forbade her son ever setting foot again inside her doors. That son, though deeply wounded, so far from imputing blame, sought even to excuse the unkindness with which he had been treated. "I cannot bring myself to tell you," he said, writing to F. Bataille, "what I have suffered from my mother and my eldest brother; and yet I will say nothing to their prejudice, for they only do what they think is right. They are far more free from guilt than I am in my most ordinary actions. I believe them to be quite innocent in this matter; they think I am doing something unbecoming a man of my birth." His second brother alone seemed capable of appreciating his conduct, for, thanks to M. Olier's counsels and assistance, he had unlearnt and now estimated at their due value the false maxims of the world.*

To prepare himself for entering on the duties of the pastoral office, M. Olier made a retreat,† under the

---

offered him on peculiarly advantageous terms in another quarter of the town.

* M. Olier had the happiness of leading his eldest brother to repentance, and of disposing him for death. François Olier died in the month of March, 1644.

† A summary of his meditations during this retreat, as committed to writing by himself, will be found appended to this chapter. They exemplify, in a remarkable manner, the spirit with which he was

direction of F. Bataille, in which he was inspired with an extraordinary love of crosses and humiliations, and with an intense desire to suffer a thousand deaths, if thereby he might promote the glory of God and the sanctification of souls; regarding himself, in his sacerdotal office, as another Jesus Christ, sent by the Eternal Father to make the continual sacrifice of himself for the good of his flock. It was at the same time revealed to him that grievous trials awaited him in his new position. He was still in retreat when information was brought him that M. de Fiesque, wishing to avoid all explanations with his parishioners, had suddenly resolved on quitting S. Sulpice before the Feast of the Assumption. Without further preparation, therefore, M. Picoté and M. du Ferrier took up their abode in the presbytery, the removal being conducted with so much haste, that they had not even time to lay in provisions. This was on Saturday, the 9th of August, and the next day M. Olier was to enter on his ministrations. The Saturday was spent by him in paying visits of respect to some of the ladies in the parish, but previous to setting out he went to present himself before his heavenly Patroness, and beg her permission and protection. "It seemed to me," he says, "as if she wished me to look upon those I visited simply as her representatives; and this is what I sensibly experienced. I paid no regard to creatures, my mind being occupied with the thought of the Blessed Virgin, and of her alone, all the time I was addressing them." Another proof also was afforded him, as he says, of the Divine goodness. The Duchess of Aiguillon offered to go, with the Princess of Condé and other ladies, to call upon his mother, and by their personal civilities and attentions endeavour to appease her anger, and make amends to her for the loss of honour which she conceived she had incurred by the conduct of her son.

He had hoped that F. Tarisse would have been present

animated in undertaking the pastoral charge, and which he succeeded in infusing into the members of his community.

CHAP. IX.]   INAUGURATION AT S. SULPICE.   153

in person at his inauguration, and given him formal possession of the church, but as it was not the habit of that holy man to take part in any public ceremony, he was represented by two of his religious. When they led him to the altar, and he stooped to kiss it, he seemed (as he says) to become at that moment the spouse of his Church; he felt as though he were charged with the sins of the whole flock, and bound henceforth to share its sufferings and woes, to be its advocate and protector, and to have only one object and one will, that of procuring it all imaginable blessings. "Ah! my God," he exclaims, " what a grace to choose me from the midst of sinners, from the dregs of humanity, and the mud and filth of my sins, to exalt me to this high, holy, and divine dignity of pastor and spouse of the Church. To Thee alone does this dignity and title of right belong: how blind is the world, how depraved, miserable, and ignorant, which judges so unworthily of the true glories of God, when in its blindness and stupidity it thinks that a cure of souls is nothing, that it lowers the dignity of a man of good birth, and believes, miserable that it is, that an origin which dates from Adam, mere birth, accompanied with imaginary goods, riches, and honours, is something worthy of esteem." One of the first acts of his ministry was to officiate at the marriage of his second brother's daughter with one of his parishioners, and at the marriage feast he gave the newly-wedded couple instructions on the duties of their state; thus changing (as he says) the tasteless water of earthly pleasures into the good wine of the word. He seemed to receive a particular grace for the occasion, the influence of which was felt by all present, the husband testifying to the joy of his soul in words suggested by the Gospel: "You have given us a delicious draught, far better than the first; you have kept the good wine to the last."

On the Feast of the Assumption took place that event which was to be the source of untold blessings to the Church of France, the establishment of the seminary and community of S. Sulpice. Early in the morning the ecclesiastics of Vaugirard took up their abode in the residence prepared for them, and later in the day High Mass was celebrated, at which, by F. Bataille's express desire, M. Olier, surrounded by his clergy, offered the Holy Sacrifice, and afterwards conducted the procession in honour of the Queen of Heaven. All through the Mass, and especially at the moment of communion, he had so intimate a sense of the presence of our Lord, that his soul (as he says) swooned and grew faint with the excesses of Divine love: " I had no longer either strength or feeling, and the thought of the Most Holy Virgin throned in glory served but to increase the flames, and to kindle still more those consuming heats." He preached the same day, taking for his text the first words of our Lord's Sermon on the Mount; *Beati pauperes spiritu, quoniam ipsorum est regnum cœlorum* (Matt. v. 3). "To-day," he began, "this prophecy of our Lord Jesus receives its great fulfilment, whereon we behold exalted into heaven her who was the humblest of creatures on earth." His heavenly mistress seemed to rejoice in making him a sharer in her glory on this her day of exaltation: swept away for ever from the memories of men were the humiliations by which the servant of God had been tried in the day of his abasement, and they who had despised and mocked at him now came and did him reverence. Persons high in rank and station, several even of his own relatives, whose influence might prove of the greatest advantage to the cause of religion, were forward in testifying their admiration and respect. The members of his own immediate family were filled with amazement, when they perceived how one who fled from honours and the notice of the great was pursued with praises and applause, when they heard themselves congratulated on possessing such a relative, and beheld men and women of the highest consideration hastening to offer him their services or place themselves under his direction. He meanwhile, though he blessed the goodness of God in thus removing obstacles from before him, and giving him that support and authority which he needed in the execution of his arduous office, nevertheless estimated all these tokens or promises of success at their true value; and when, on the 27th of August, the Feast of the Translation of S. Sulpice,* he preached before a crowded audience, among whom were many doctors of the Sorbonne and other ecclesiastics, on the greatness of the sacerdotal office and the duties of the pastoral charge, and men celebrated for their theological science thronged about him to express the satisfaction with which they had listened to his address, so far from showing contentment at the effect he had produced, we find him saying, in that record of his life to which such constant reference has been made, "It seems to me that as yet I have not preached in the full light of God, and in the energy of His pure word, as by His mercy I did heretofore. I hope that Jesus Christ, my Master, will one day bestow this grace upon me, and I have a confidence that He will."

So far, however, God had blessed his efforts; he had won himself a high position in the esteem of those who were most capable of furthering the interests of the seminary, and recommending it in the most influential quarters.

Summary of M. Olier's Meditations during his Retreat, preparatory to undertaking the Pastoral Charge.

"On the 4th of August, being the Feast of S. Dominic, my director gave me for my subject of meditation, the importance of succouring souls, and the zeal I ought to have for their salvation, after the example which the Son of God left to all the pastors of His Church. Addressing myself, then, to prayer, I saw that this great love of our Lord for souls, had its source in that which He bears His Father. That the glory of His Father is His great and only desire, and that seeing souls who might glorify Him eternally, He loved them from this motive; He willingly left the bosom of His

---

* The translation of the relics of S. Sulpice took place on the 27th of August, 1518, and owing to the numerous miraculous cures which continued to be wrought at the shrine, that day was observed by the people with greater solemnity and devotion than the feast of the saint, which occurred in winter. In M. Olier's own days, the iron bedsteads were still to be seen, in the vaults of the church, on which the sick were laid to pass the night before the saint's relics.

Father, He quitted His own proper glory, and humbled Himself even to conversing with men, not disdaining to partake of their poverty. That to render them capable of honouring and glorifying God His Father, He endured so many labours, watchings, and sufferings, and in the end the ignominious death of the cross. That, as this death would open heaven to a multitude of souls, who should render to God an immortal glory, He would for this end have given a hundred thousand lives, and have suffered a hundred thousand deaths. Nay, more, that His death appearing to Him as nothing in comparison with this glory, no pains, no sufferings were sufficient to satisfy the immense desire He felt of procuring it.

"Whilst I was occupied with these thoughts, it pleased the goodness of Jesus, my only Master, to communicate to me something of these sentiments, so that I felt my heart all on fire, and experienced the most ardent desires to give my God a thousand lives, and a hundred thousand millions of lives, if that were possible, to procure some accession to His glory. This divine communication, which came to me quite suddenly, lasted almost the whole time of my prayer; there was no circumstance in the life or death of my Master, which, as I contemplated it, I did not desire closely to imitate, and which I did not resolve to practise, with the approbation of my director. My Saviour not only desired to die a thousand times for His Church, He desired also to give Himself to her as food, which He accomplishes daily in the Most Holy Sacrament. Of this desire, likewise, His goodness made me partaker. If I have not the happiness of shedding my blood for the Church, I will be, at least, her living victim, to serve for her nourishment; I must possess nothing which is not hers,—above all, my worldly goods, which must be devoted to the support of the poor of this great parish. It shall be my desire, moreover, after having given the day to labour, to spend the night also in prayer before the Most Holy Sacrament. I entreat my director not to deny me this favour, for which I have sighed so long—at least, to grant me the boon sometimes. I desire to imitate in this the piety of my good Master towards His Father, and to be like those lamps whose lot I have so often envied, that my life may be consumed for the glory of God, and of Jesus Christ His Son.

"This morning, when preparing to say Mass, I felt in my heart an ardent desire to be in as many places as there are Hosts in all the world, that everywhere I might glorify God: this also is the disposition of my Jesus, the Host (or Victim) of God. As I was about to offer the Holy Sacrifice in honour of the great S. Dominic, who, by means of his order has been, as it were, dispersed and multiplied throughout the world for so many ages, as often as there have been good religious in his community, which is as a vessel of fire to burn and consume heresies, and rekindle fervour in the hearts of the faithful, I besought God that He would bestow on all parishes, and on every place where my Master reposes in the tabernacle, good pastors who should be ever vigilant in guarding and honouring this divine and adorable treasure, and should know how to dispense it in

CHAP. IX.] MEDITATIONS DURING RETREAT. 157

a manner worthy of its infinite sanctity. O Lord Jesus, true Pastor of the universal Church, apply a speedy remedy to her needs; raise up men who may renew the divine order of S. Peter, the order of pastors, with as much love and zeal as S. Dominic established his order in Thy Church. Inflame with the fire of Thy love and of Thy devotion others, again, who may carry and spread it through all the world. Were I not so wretched, and so proud, were I not a very sink of filth and corruption, how willingly would I offer myself to Thee to be employed in any way that might please Thee for the good of Thy Church; how heartily would I offer and devote myself, even as at this moment I do, as a worthless vessel to be put to any use, and to become whatsoever Thou willest! I am Thine without reserve. I am Thy slave, O my Jesus! I have vowed to Thee an absolute servitude, and what I have done is irrevocable; and now I give myself up anew and for ever, not reserving to myself any right to revoke the offering which I make of myself to Thee. Dispose of me according to Thy good pleasure, as an absolute lord and master disposes of his servant and his slave. Of myself I can can do nothing. Thou only, O Lord, who art almighty, canst produce anything out of my wretched nothingness.

"On the second day of my retreat I had for the subject of my meditation this truth: The pastor of souls must be a Jesus Christ on earth. Our Lord showed me that I must produce fruit in souls by example; that they are not to be ruled by commanding, but by touching hearts by means of all the apostolic virtues, and, above all, by sweetness and humility; that being, as I am, the greatest sinner, I must be the most humble of all my flock; being burdened, moreover, with the innumerable sins of all this people. This good Master disposed me yesterday, during the reading at supper, to this last thought of which I speak, drawing my mind to dwell on the command which God gave S. Peter, the universal pastor of the Church, —to eat of all the creeping things contained in that mysterious sheet. Whence He taught me that, participating in the sins of the whole Church, I ought to do penance for her, and weep for her sins as for my own, seeing that I am her spouse; for the spouse shares the debts as well as the goods and possessions of her consort. It is also said that this holy apostle wept continually, not only for his own sins, but likewise for the sins of his spouse; for whom he implored pardon, giving her at the same time an example of penance, that she might imitate him in weeping for her own sins: the true and lawful wife ever shares the sentiments of her husband.

"I learnt also that our Lord, seeing Himself loaded with the sins of the whole world, refused all consolations during His mortal life: never once was He seen to laugh; and not even the society of His holy Mother could divert Him from this abiding sorrow. He went on His way as though the impetuous torrents of our sins were perpetually rushing in upon Him, and overwhelming Him; He wept without ceasing in His Heart, doing penance for His people, and imploring pardon continually for them in His prayers. For although these were not the only affections in which His soul was engaged, but He was filled also with the love and praises of His Father, and with gratitude for the blessings granted to man, yet the spectacle of our sins was ever before His eyes, and this kept Him continually plunged in affliction. As I entertained myself with these thoughts, it pleased the goodness of my Master to communicate to me this interior disposition, and I seemed to be wholly possessed with it, feeling experimentally, not only this species of sadness, but also the deep humility in which I ought to live, and the lowly sentiments that ought to accompany that state; in fine, it seemed to me that I ought to be prepared in mind to suffer with the most perfect sweetness every conceivable outrage of which I might be made the object.

"The third day of my retreat, continuing my meditation on the imitation of our Lord, of whom I was to be the living representative before the eyes of the faithful, I perceived that I ought to imitate His modesty. Now this modesty has for its principle the respect due to God, and proceeds from the Holy Spirit, who, when He has possession of the body as well as of the soul, composes and keeps it in a state of perfect recollection, thereby inspiring all beholders with piety, and darting forth as many arrows of the love of God as there are hearts susceptible of the movements of charity. It must not be mundane in its nature, or the effect of self-complacency: this is the affected modesty of the old man; on the contrary, it must be a virtue of the new man, an exterior composure, which has its source in that of Jesus Christ Himself, who, dwelling in us, diffuses it over our whole person, regulating our exterior after the pattern of His own—our very gait, our manner of speaking, eating, and all else—this is what is called Christian modesty. The excellence of this virtue appears in the powerful results which it produces, as in winning hearts and leading them to God: in a word, all those admirable effects of which S. Paul speaks (2 Cor. x. 1) when he beseeches the faithful "by the modesty of Christ," so mighty in its influence over the minds of men.

"To-day I was taught that in the mystery of the Transfiguration, which we celebrated yesterday, our Lord spoke of His cross to show that He came principally with this object, to preach it to men, and that, moreover, as an excellent Master, He came to teach us the practice of it. This is why it is written in the Gospel of the day, *Loquebatur excessum*—here is the teaching of the cross; *quem completurus erat in Jerusalem*—here is the confirmation of the teaching by example. Yesterday, in my prayer, I beheld our Lord trodden under foot, struck, thrown to the ground by the Jews, and I beheld myself in the same condition, treated in like manner by the world. At the same time I contemplated the interior disposition of our Lord, whilst He was enduring all these afflictions and sufferings. It was all ineffable sweetness and patience, a continual saying to Himself that He well merited this treatment, seeing He had taken the sins of all upon Himself; I saw that he had laden Himself, not only with the sins which men have committed against God, but with all those of which they have been guilty towards their neighbour, as robbery, treason, all the infidelities which thieves, servants, and subjects can commit against men, masters, and kings. Now, as a thief, or a faithless servant, taken in the very act, is maltreated and loaded with insults and ignominies, I learnt that our Lord, having loaded Himself with all these kinds of sins, was pleased to bear the penalty and the just chastisement of them with equal sweetness and patience, and that so I also ought to resolve to bear all kinds of ignominies and insults, seeing that I was taking on myself the sins of all my flock, and to abandon myself as a victim into the hands of Divine Justice, to receive on my own person the chastisements destined for them.

"I cannot refrain from manifesting the love which our Lord gave me for His cross during my prayer, and the great joy He caused me to experience in assuring me that in my ministry at S. Sulpice, on which I am about to enter, I should have a large share in it. This assurance quite transported me with joy, and constrained me to offer myself to His love with ardent aspirations and words like those of S. Andrew: *O bona Crux, diu desiderata!* (O good Cross, so long desired). To confirm me in the promise of this grace, it pleased God to renew before my mind the vision of a cross which He had already shown me, and which I am to carry when it is His will to lay it on my shoulders. I believe it is approaching, for I have heard that there is a certain person who is violently incensed against me, and threatens to publish libels against us, of which our director, it would appear, has already had some secret anticipation. This morning, when I was engaged in fervent prayer, and was meditating on self-abandonment to crosses and sufferings, word was brought me that the Curé of S. Sulpice had retracted his promise concerning the transfer of his parish; then, without experiencing any movement of discontent, I said to the bearer of these tidings, 'This news is very welcome, blessed be God for all things.' The goodness of my Master is thus pleased to put me in dispositions the most fitting to receive such crosses as on that particular day He has designed for me. The news, however, proved to be false.

"Ah! Lord, now that I see myself charged with the sins of all this people, said to be the most depraved in the whole world, if in Thy mercy Thou wouldst inspire me with those sentiments of humility, confusion, and self-annihilation which I ought to have by reason of this burden, O my Saviour, I would imitate Thee in Thy deep humiliation. Alas! ought I not to take great shame to myself, that, being Thy representative in the Church, I should truly have nothing in me that represents and reflects Thy virtues? On Friday, August 8th, in my morning prayer, I had so clear a perception of my own nothingness, and so intimate a conviction of it, that I said to my Master, that but for my hope that He would Himself support for me the burden about to be laid on me, I should fly to the ends of the earth rather than accept it, having in myself only nothingness, blindness, ignorance, weakness, and an utter incapacity to do Him any service. It seemed to me that our Lord had inspired me with an utter horror of worldly honour; I earnestly implored Him to give me death rather than the praise of men, which I can in no wise accept; for my Saviour lived and died in the midst of confusion and contempt. Moreover, all my desire being to procure the glory of my Master, I cannot experience a greater pain than in receiving honour, seeing it is a good which belongs only to my God. Alas! O my God, to Thee be all honour and glory, and to me all confusion. If I could steal from Thee all the ignominy Thou endurest, and could restore to Thee all the honour of which Thou art robbed, I should be content. Vouchsafe, then, to be honoured by my confusion, seeing it is Thy pleasure to employ me for Thy greater glory, and that Thou desirest to ground it on my humiliation as a parish priest, a charge now fallen into contempt with all the functions belonging to it; in fine, on the ignominy which has always been promised to me in this condition.'

"I am not astonished at the love which ought to be felt for the Church, and for the meanest of creatures, so far as such creature is a portion of that august body; for, what more admirable than the Church? Rather, I am unable to conceive how it is that one does not die of love for the faithful, seeing that each shall be one day a component part of the Church triumphant, which shall praise the greatness of God to all eternity. While I was full of these thoughts, they brought me a poor child, begging me to bestow some alms upon it. I do not know what I did not feel ready to do for it, regarding it as a member of that Church so admirable and so divine, that kingdom so perfect, that throne so magnificent of the adorable Majesty of God. O Goodness! what shall we not be willing to do for Thee? How readily would I shed my blood for Thy love,—yea, and if it were mine, the blood of all creatures!"

CHAPTER X.

Frightful state of the Parish of S. Sulpice—M. Olier establishes a Community of Parochial Clergy.

M. OLIER was now to solve before the eyes of all France a twofold problem: viz., how to establish a seminary for the training of ecclesiastics, and to unite with that seminary a community of priests who should perform all the ordinary functions of parochial clergy. With this twofold task, hitherto found impracticable, was combined another from which the stoutest hearts might well have shrunk back appalled, that of reforming the most vicious parish in the whole city of Paris. The faubourg S. Germain, which constituted the largest portion of S. Sulpice, was notorious at the time for the number of professed atheists and libertines who had made it their abode. In the previous century it had become the stronghold of the Calvinists; it was there they had erected their first conventicle, and had made their first public and most daring demonstrations. Hither they had continued to resort from all sides during the contest that desolated France, and such was the success of their proselytising efforts, that this quarter of the town had acquired the name of the Little Geneva. The effect had been to undermine and destroy the faith of the people, to inspire them with a contempt for all religion, and an inveterate hatred for the priesthood, and to make them regard whatever was expended in the support of the clergy and the decoration of the churches as so much which might have gone towards maintaining themselves in idleness and debauchery. The most horrible impieties and blasphemies were openly promulgated, and a belief in the essential doctrines of Catholicism, and even in the first principles of natural religion, rejected with scorn and derision. Christianity, in short, had come to be generally regarded as an invention of the governing powers, and its ministers as impostors or the mere agents of tyranny.

This monstrous impiety, with an inconsistency not uncommon, was associated with the most revolting superstition, and a systematic practice of magic. Books on the diabolic art were publicly sold at the very doors of the church, and shortly after M. Olier entered on the duties of the parish, the bailly of the suburb, being in pursuit of three persons accused of sorcery, and mistaking one house for another, found an altar dedicated to the evil spirit, with these words inscribed upon it: "*Gratias tibi, Lucifer; gratias tibi, Beelzebub; gratias* *tibi, Azareel."** The altar was a sort of travesty of that consecrated to Catholic worship; the candles were black, the ornaments about it were all in keeping with its infernal object, and the book of prayers, as if in mockery of the Missal, consisted of diabolical incantations. The bailly took possession of the book, but the affair was not prosecuted further on account of the numbers and position of those who were implicated. So prevalent also at this time had become the study of astrology, that F. de Condren had thought it necessary to make himself acquainted with all the mysteries of that false science, in order more effectually to disabuse the minds of those who were addicted to it, and at the request of Cardinal de Richelieu had even published a treatise to expose its folly and wickedness.

But though impiety and superstition abounded to so fatal an extent, these were but secret and partial evils as compared with the violence, the riot, the debauchery, the general lawlessness for which this unhappy parish had gained so infamous a notoriety. The long-continued civil wars, and the scandals of a dissolute court under preceding reigns, had rendered Paris one of the most demoralized cities in the whole world; while the insufficient protection afforded to life and property by the municipal authorities, had left the inhabitants a prey to bands of robbers and marauders, who traversed the streets at nightfall and set both laws and police at defiance. So intolerable at length had these outrages become, that the citizens were empowered to act in their own defence, and sallying out to the aid of the armed patrol, succeeded in dispersing the gangs of ruffianly plunderers. Compelled thus to seek a retreat from the vengeance of the laws, these miscreants took refuge in the faubourg S. Germain, where they were sure of finding perfect security. Pursuit was no longer possible; for the whole parish enjoyed an immunity from the control of the magistracy of the city, being (as it has been said)

---

* "Thanks to thee, Lucifer; thanks to thee, Beelzebub; thanks to thee, Azareel."

subjected to the peculiar jurisdiction of the abbé of S. Germain, by whom justice was feebly administered and most inadequately enforced. Moreover, the fair* which was held in this quarter, and which lasted two whole months in the year, conduced beyond all calculation towards fomenting the disorders. Vendors flocked thither from all parts of the country to display their wares; thieves, mountebanks, strollers, jugglers,—every panderer to vanity and crime was there to ply his trade or exhibit his dexterity; booths were set up in the public streets; the people assembled in crowds, especially in the evenings, when the concourse was greatest, and the whole region became one wild scene of revelry and carousal, riot, frolic, and sin. Brawls, too, and assassinations were frequent; and such was the rage for duelling, which in the midst of so much license could be practised with the utmost facility and impunity, that when M. Olier first took possession of the parish, seventeen persons were mortally wounded in one week.

The picture would be very incomplete without some mention of the condition of the clergy and of their ministrations. Amidst all this vast and lawless population, there was but one church, no larger than would have been suitable for some country village; and yet, small as it was, it was far too spacious for the congregation that frequented it. The interior was dirty and ill-kept; the pavement of the floor broken and uneven; the high altar naked and desolate; the very walls destitute of all ornament; and there was not even a sacristy, properly so called, to which the clergy could retire. In the celebration of the Divine Mysteries no order or punctuality was observed; the priests vested before the altar, and a bell, suspended at the entrance of each chapel, was rung to warn the faithful that Mass was beginning. The guilds were so numerous, and their meetings were held so frequently, that the clergy who had to attend their

---

* The reader will not have forgotten that it was from the fair of S. Germain M. Olier and his young companions were returning when they were accosted by Marie de Gournay.

frivolous ceremonies, were unable to devote the necessary time to the duties of the parish. The burial-ground, which was close to the building, but unenclosed, was the favourite haunt of idlers and drunkards, while—will the fact be credited?—a tavern was kept in the very vaults of the church, to which even communicants were in the habit of resorting before returning to their homes. But the scandal did not end here. The clergy themselves, instead of endeavouring to stem the tide of corruption, were foremost in setting an evil example to their people; and we learn from M. Bourdoise—in these express terms —that often, after offering the Tremendous Sacrifice, they spent the remainder of the day in this tavern in the vaults, eating and drinking to excess. When such were the priests who served the altar, we cannot wonder that the officials about the church—the organist, the ringers, and the rest—were models neither of morality nor of temperance. The suburb, in short, was a sink of iniquity, and its church was become a den of thieves. "To name to you the faubourg S. Germain," wrote M. Olier to a certain bishop, "is to express in one word all the monstrous vices that prey upon humanity."

And this, then, was the soil which the servant of God was called to cultivate, and these were his fellow-labourers! Not that it need be presumed that all the clergy of the parish had become so utterly depraved and so lost to all sense of shame as the above description would imply—indeed, the contrary incidentally appears,—but few there were among them who retained the true sacerdotal spirit, or who had any but a low professional view of the obligations of their sacred calling. His first efforts, therefore, were directed to raising these men out of the depth of degradation, or at least rousing them from the state of apathy, into which they had fallen, by placing before them a higher and a holier standard; and to this end he would fain have led them to adopt a community life. But here, as may be well imagined, he encountered the most determined opposition, and there was cause to apprehend that, if he persisted in the attempt, an insurmountable wall of separation would be raised between the old established clergy and the ecclesiastics who had come with him from Vaugirard. He did not, however, relax his endeavours on that account, but, committing himself to God, summoned all his priests together, and urged the proposition upon them in an address, the substance of which he has left us in his writings.

He spoke of the irksomeness of a priest's existence when leading a solitary life in the world: the teasing distractions, from which it is impossible for him to escape, and which haunt and hang about him even in the performance of his most sacred duties; the time, the thought, the care he must expend on the mere bodily wants of food, lodging, and clothing; and, on the other hand, of the advantages to those who are specially set apart for God's service of associating with each other, as contrasted with the evils of mixing in secular society. He then descanted on the principle of association in general, whether in cities or in families—that it has the approval and sanction of Heaven, and is, as it were, an image of the Indivisible Unity of the Three Divine Persons; that in the beginning of creation God formed the community of angels, consisting of three hierarchies, themselves also a figure of the same ineffable mystery, and of the order and communication subsisting therein;—how from one to another the flame of love is incessantly darted, flashing to and fro, and kindling with mutually engendered heat and fervour, as they cry continually, Holy, Holy, Holy. "Now the priests of God" (he continued) "are His visible angels, whom He invites to combine in serving and honouring Him. He would have them mutually inflame each other with Divine love, speaking one to the other of His perfections, admiring His goodness, adoring His greatness, and uniting to render praises to His infinite sanctity. Then, since God desires to be honoured by societies, let us not refuse Him this glory: *Venite, exultemus Domino, jubilemus Deo salutari nostro* [*]; and altogether, all with one heart, one voice, one mouth, offer

[*] "Come, let us praise the Lord with joy, let us joyfully sing to God our Saviour."—*Ps.* xciv. 1.

to the Divine Majesty our jubilations, our praises, and our homage."

This discourse produced the desired effect on some few of his auditors, but the greater part, including the oldest and best qualified of M. de Fiesque's former colleagues, refused to acquiesce in the plan proposed. They claimed also nearly the whole of the parochial fees; so that M. Olier, who, on accepting the cure, had resolved to resign his abbey of Pébrac and his priory of Bazainville, would have found himself destitute of wherewithal to support his community, had he put his design into execution. Nevertheless he would have made the sacrifice but for the remonstrances of his directors, who represented the need he had of the revenues of these benefices, in order to carry out the reform of the parish with the help of his associates.

The opposition he encountered in nowise diminished his affectionate solicitude for those who were its authors; on the contrary, it seemed to operate as a motive for lavishing on them every mark of confidence and respect. His generous faith and love of mortification conspired to make him regard as his best friends those who gave him occasions of suffering; and we read in his Memoirs that he offered on their behalf to God all the pains he endured in a severe illness, with which he was at this time afflicted, and expressed his readiness to undergo much greater evils for their sakes. So far, too, was he from showing a preference or giving a precedence to the members of his community, that he maintained all in their former rank and offices, and, for fear that they might be led to go elsewhere and fall into worse disorders, he increased the stipends of every one of them. He strove, in turn, to win their regard and confidence by every manner of kindness and attention in his power; always paying them honour, as the oldest of his clergy, inviting them to his table, consulting them on the management of the parish, and informing himself as to their circumstances, so that all might be properly provided with clothing, lodging, and furniture, as well as supplied with whatever was needful in case of illness.

Foiled in his endeavours to persuade the parochial clergy to live with him in community, he sought to recruit his establishment by an addition of fresh members, and, as usual, had recourse to the powerful assistance of the Blessed Virgin; begging her to gather about him a company of ecclesiastics who, in a spirit of entire disinterestedness and detachment from the world, would be content to regard the community, not as the vestibule to honours and preferment, but as a school of sacerdotal science and virtue, where they might labour solely for the glory of God. His prayer received a speedy and an effectual answer; for the community, which was composed at first of the twenty ecclesiastics who had removed from Vaugirard, of seven or eight others who had since joined them, and of four of the parochial clergy of S. Sulpice, soon numbered fifty members, all men conspicuous for their zeal and fervour. M. du Ferrier was made superior of the community; to M. de Foix was committed the general superintendence of all that concerned the relief of the poor; while M. de Bassancourt regulated the service of the altar, and whatever was connected with the order and beauty of Divine worship: all acting as M. Olier's representatives, and under his direction and control.

Their life was now ordered according to the strictest rules of discipline. To take away every occasion of scandal, on which the dissolute or unfriendly might seize, it was forbidden to give admission to females under any pretext whatever; all the fees that might be received in the ordinary course of their ministry were to be thrown into a common fund, and each was to be content with what was sufficient to provide him with food and clothing. M. Olier particularly enjoined that no fee should be charged for administering the Holy Viaticum, and, that on no account should money be accepted in the tribunal of penance, an abuse which prevailed in certain parishes, both at Paris and elsewhere. In fine, he presented a powerful example in his own person of that simplicity of life and love of poverty by which he wished his community to be distinguished; appropriating nothing to himself of all the proceeds of his benefice, but applying one portion of them to the relief of the poor, another to the maintenance of his clergy, and a third to the support of the community: thus (as he says) giving to those who were in want, and supplying those who wanted not, with means for giving to our Lord, whether in His Church or in His poorer members. His dress, like that of the rest, was such as became the priest, but always of the simplest kind, his habit being of common serge, and his under garments of materials still coarser; neither would he ever permit his surplices to be trimmed with lace, as had become the general custom.

He would have no distinction observed between one priest and another: all were equally to employ themselves in the various functions of the ministry, each in his order performing those offices which, in the eyes of the world, were esteemed the least honourable. No one, for instance, was to be dispensed from carrying the cross at funerals, accompanying the priest when called to administer extreme unction, or walking before the Blessed Sacrament with the bell when borne to the sick and dying. The last-mentioned office was always to be performed by one in priest's orders, who was to see that the bystanders bent their knee in adoration, and if any neglected this mark of homage, he was then and there to admonish them of their duty; a practice which was continued without interruption until the Revolution. Ecclesiastics, whether beneficed or otherwise, who with the permission of their bishops came into residence for a while, to be more perfectly instructed in their pastoral duties, were subjected to the same discipline. The wills of all were to be in entire submission to the will of the superior, who (to use M. Olier's forcible metaphor) was to hold them at his disposal like so many arrows in a quiver, either to remain by his side, or to be sent hither and thither at his pleasure. They were to yield a ready obedience, not only to the *curé* himself, but to all who shared his authority—to the superior of the community, the sacristan, the master of ceremonies, and the very doorkeeper, in all things that concerned their respective offices and were in accordance with the rules. Even bishops, who might wish to go into retreat, or to have the benefit of a quiet habitation when affairs detained them at Paris, were obliged to conform to all the regulations of the house; as, for instance, in being present at morning prayer, and observing the canonical hours. And such was the regularity and order that prevailed, that they who were prevented from attending by other avocations, were careful to make up the arrears of the exercises they had been compelled to omit, as soon as they found themselves at liberty. This fidelity M. Olier assured them was the surest means of maintaining a spirit of recollection and union with God in the midst of occupations, however multifarious and distracting; and without this spirit of recollection and of union there could be no fruit, whether in preaching, hearing confessions, holding spiritual conferences, or performing any of the other duties of their ministry. His instructions on all these points, as well as on union amongst themselves, charity towards the poor, sweetness and patience with their parishioners, love of humiliations, and zeal for the salvation of souls, formed a volume of considerable size.

The parish, which M. Olier looked upon as God's estate, which he was set to cultivate, he divided into eight departments, dedicated to the Blessed Virgin under the titles of her respective festivals. Each of these eight divisions he assigned to as many priests, who had the especial charge of the inhabitants within its limits, associating with them ten or twelve others as their coadjutors. A list of the several households, with a statement of their necessities, spiritual and temporal, was to be kept by the priests of each quarter, and all necessary alterations entered every three months. They were to make themselves personally acquainted with the poor and ignorant, to seek out those who neglected the sacraments, or gave occasion of scandal by their immorality, and apply a remedy to all such disorders. For this end also he appointed in each street some person of piety whose duty it was to give information as to any haunts of vice and iniquity, in order to their suppression. From these lists he compiled a general survey of the whole parish, as recommended by Pope Paul V., under the title of *De statu animarum*, a form of which was drawn up by S. Charles Borromeo and inserted among the "Acts of the Church of Milan." So careful was he to provide for the needs of the sick and dying, that he strictly charged the priests of each district to see that all who were in danger of death were visited every day, and that those whose state was precarious were not left for two days together without spiritual assistance. Besides these priests of the districts, there were others whose special duty it was to administer the sacraments of the Holy Eucharist and Extreme Unction; others were appointed to baptize and solemnize marriages; others to bury the dead; or, again, to be in readiness to give advice to the people, and receive their confessions at any hour of the day. In short, each had his particular office assigned to him, and a complete system was thus organized, which might be made to bear with most powerful effect on all the wants of so vast a parish.

Even the time of recreation was made subservient to the purpose of mutual edification and instruction. After dinner it was the practice to propose to the superior any questions arising out of cases of difficulty which had occurred in the parish, whether bearing on some point of morality, or controversy with heretics, or the conduct of souls. If the superior were in doubt as to the solution, he commissioned some doctor of the community to go to the Sorbonne and obtain a reply, which he was to communicate to the assembled members at supper-time. These conferences were of the greatest service to all, being equivalent (says M. du Ferrier) to a vast amount of study. One principal advantage, however, was that they conduced more than anything else to establish in the community a thorough unity of spirit on all that concerned the direction of souls. M. Olier, in concert with the rest, drew up a series of maxims or general principles, which might serve as the basis and touchstone of all their decisions, and to which individually they should be bound to conform. Among these were two which bore directly on one of the greatest practical evils of the time. It was laid down as a rule, from which no one should be at liberty to depart, that absolution should be refused to such as remained in a proximate occasion of sin, and that in the case of habitual sinners absolution should be deferred for eight or fifteen days.* These regulations were rendered necessary by the lax morality then in vogue among the professors of casuistry, and by the dangerous facility with which many confessors administered the sacrament of penance. This abuse had led to another no less pernicious,—an excessive severity, calculated to drive souls to despair. M. Olier would have his priests observe the true and salutary mean between the two extremes, and gave them for their guidance the "Instructions of S. Charles Borromeo to the Confessors of his Diocese," included among the "Acts of the Church of Milan," which, under his directions, were now published for the first time in France. The edition was dedicated to the doctors of the Sorbonne, and was productive of untold benefits to the Church. The "Instructions" became the standard book of authority in the seminaries, and, eventually, among the whole body of the clergy, who, in 1657, caused them to be printed at their own expense.

One rule M. Olier had prescribed to himself, to which he ever faithfully adhered, that in all things he should set the example to his ecclesiastics. To this end he lived with them in common, took part in the same exercises, and was ever among them as one of themselves. Like a good pastor and a true superior, he was ready to sacrifice his goods, his health, his life, for those of whom he had the direction and the charge. Mindful of the vow of perpetual servitude he had made to his parish, he regarded his people as the rightful masters of his time, his person, and all that he possessed, to make such use of them as their needs required; and absolute and all-embracing as such an engagement was, it never caused him the least disquietude, proof incontestable that it had the approval of God. Convinced, also, that in his two-

* See Note B.

fold character of pastor and superior he could not present before others too high a standard, he made, in addition, a formal vow of doing from that moment whatever he believed to be the most perfect. This heroic determination, which made itself felt in all his actions, enkindled a corresponding degree of zeal and fervour in the members of his community; and though (in obedience to the light he had received in his retreat) he never addressed any of them in terms of command, nevertheless he obtained from them the most generous sacrifices by the sole ascendancy of his example. Were it question of visiting the sick, hearing confessions, preaching the word of God, he was always ready to take the place of his colleagues, and spare them fatigue and trouble. It was his desire that the priests who had come with him from Vaugirard, and, in particular, M. du Ferrier, whom he had made superior of the community, should display a similar spirit; and in this he was not disappointed, as the following instances may show. One night the porter informed M. du Ferrier that a sick person required the immediate attendance of a priest; after learning the particulars of the case, which the porter was instructed always to obtain, he sent him to one of the community whom he deemed most fitted for the office, with a request that he would go forthwith and visit the sick man. The priest, however, feeling himself somewhat indisposed, begged to be excused at so late an hour; upon which, without further delay, M. du Ferrier went himself. The next morning, when the priest heard that the superior had discharged the office he had himself declined, he was extremely distressed, and the more so when, on going to express his regret at what had happened, he was met only with an apology that he should have been disturbed at a time when he was not quite well. When the same thing had occurred seven or eight times in other cases, such a spirit of generous emulation was aroused in the community, that every summons, whether to attend the sick, or perform any other ministerial duty, was obeyed with the utmost alacrity, and no one, for any consideration whatever, would have suffered another to supply his place.

A few months after the establishment of the community, one of the members, M. Corbel, who, of his own choice, had undertaken the task of awakening the inmates in the morning, was sent by M. Olier to Pébrac. Nevertheless, everything went on as usual, and it never occurred to any to inquire who it was that knocked at their door and placed a light in their room, until one day, at recreation, they began to speculate among themselves who it could be, and as one after another denied all cognizance of the matter, they discovered that it was the superior himself who, for five or six weeks, had volunteered to perform the troublesome office. This little incident had a most powerful effect in quickening the zeal of the community, and stimulating them to still greater efforts of self-denial.

In all that he undertook M. Olier had regard, not only to the reformation of his own people, but also to the good of the Church at large; and his joy and thankfulness may well be imagined when, only fifteen days after his installation at S. Sulpice, he received a visit from an ecclesiastic who had been deputed by the parochial clergy of the metropolis to assure him of their sympathy and confidence, and to beg him to attend their monthly conferences. They at the same time requested that he would make them acquainted with the rules he had adopted, that they might profit by them in the management of their own parishes. He was now only in his thirty-fifth year, and it was with surprise and confusion, inspired by the sense he entertained of his own ignorance and unworthiness, that he found himself consulted by persons of greater age and experience than himself, some even holding the most responsible offices in the state, on affairs of the highest moment. Thus in this present year (1643), several of the bishops most conspicuous for their activity and zeal sought his advice on the subject of establishing seminaries in their dioceses; and after the death of Louis XIII., the Queen Regent resolved that no ecclesiastic should be nominated to the episcopate who had not passed some years in the seminary of S. Vincent de Paul or in that of S. Sulpice.

CHAPTER XI.

M. Olier's reforms at S. Sulpice—His coadjutors.

THE state of the parish was so radically corrupt, that to effect any solid reformation, it was necessary to commence the work of reconstruction from the very foundations. Children and parents, young and old, were equally ignorant of the rudiments of Christian doctrine; many, it would appear, not even knowing the words of the Creed. M. Olier, therefore, began by instituting a series of catechetical instructions in twelve different localities besides the parish church. These catechisings, with the exception of those which were given at S. Sulpice, and which he undertook himself, were entrusted to the seminarists, two being appointed to each locality. Of these, one was called the *clerk*, and acted as the other's assistant; going through the streets with a bell, to call the children to the classes, and seeking them in the houses of their parents. Other ecclesiastics visited the various schools in the parish, to ascertain that none of the youth within its limits were deprived of Christian teaching. A sight so novel in that neglected quarter as that of young men in surplices, many of them known to belong to the best families in France, gathering poor children together for instruction, produced the liveliest sensation among the people; and crowds were drawn by curiosity to see and hear what was going forward. This was a result which M. Olier had directly contemplated, and care was taken to conduct the catechisings in such a way that they should be profitable to persons of all ages. The success surpassed all expectation; in a few weeks his clergy had as many as 4,000 children under their immediate personal care, who became in their turn missionaries and catechists to their friends and relatives. Every week, also, instructions were given preparatory to first communion; and he moreover required, what at that time was an innovation on existing practice, that all who were candidates for the sacrament of Confirmation should pass an examination before being admitted to that rite.

Priests were specially selected to hear the general confessions of the younger members of the flock; nor, in spite of his numerous avocations, did he disdain himself to receive any who chose to come to him. On the contrary, they experienced in him all the tender affectionateness of a mother; his manner towards children (as before observed) was characterized not so much by a gentle condescension, as by a sort of loving humility, which inspired confidence while it touched the heart; and he strove to trace on their tender souls the first lineaments of the new man, as modelled before their eyes in the Infant Jesus, subject to His parents, and advancing daily in wisdom and in grace. At the same time he knew how to mingle severity with sweetness, and did not fail to reprove their faults when reproof was needed; yet all with a tact and a delicacy to which their young minds were peculiarly sensitive. A slight incident which has chanced to remain on record may serve to illustrate this. He was kneeling one day before the Blessed Sacrament, when a little girl of the higher classes came to make a request of him. There was something in her dress and manner which struck him as savouring too much of the fashionable world, and he gently remarked upon it at the moment. The better, however, to cure her of her affectation, he continued for some time after to call her *mademoiselle* when speaking to her, instead of *my child*, as he had been used to do. The little girl was sensible of the change, and one day begged him, with tears in her eyes, to call her by the old endearing name. "When you have the manners of a Christian child," he answered, "then I shall be as affectionate as ever."

There was not a single class among his people which did not find itself the object of his particular care. Thus, in addition to the exhortations contained in the sermons which were common to all, he desired that the servants of the parish should receive separate instructions adapted to their condition and circumstances. Three times a week during Lent he assembled the pages and footmen, who were very numerous in the faubourg S. Germain; and not content with making an announcement from every pulpit in the parish, he directed the priests of each district to distribute handbills from house to house, that neither masters nor servants might remain in ignorance of their duty. On three other days he summoned all the beggars together, and taught them in detail all the mysteries of the faith, and the means by which they might sanctify their state of life, and receive with profit to their souls the sacraments of Penance and the Holy Eucharist. On every such occasion there was a distribution of alms, according to the attention and proficiency displayed by each; the numbers collected amounting commonly to 300 or 400, sometimes even more. Nor were the aged poor forgotten: the old men of the parish had special instructions provided for them every Friday; and, to encourage them to attend, every one received relief in proportion to his needs and merits. In addition to all these, he provided what was called a general catechism, intended for all sorts of persons. This was given at the church, and that none might be kept away by a feeling of shame, the language employed was always of a higher order; without derogating, however, from that plainness and simplicity which is suited to all capacities. And even yet his zeal and charity were not exhausted. He directed his ecclesiastics to visit from time to time those families who hitherto had lived in ignorance of the truths of salvation, and who were withheld, by motives of human respect, from attending the public teaching. He had a number of broad sheets printed, embellished with some device or picture, explanatory of the chief doctrines of the faith and the necessary duties of a Christian, with forms of prayer for night and morning, and a mode of sanctifying the common actions of the day by offering them all to God. These familiar instructions he recommended fathers and mothers to hang up in some conspicuous place in their houses, and to use them every day for themselves and their families. Lastly, he established a series of short and simple discourses for workpeople, which were delivered in the early morning; and again, at the end of the day, some profitable reading, accompanied by a verbal commentary; a custom which, ere long, was adopted in all the parishes of the city.

But, besides making provision for the poor and ignorant, his care was particularly directed to those who occupied the position of teachers, many of whom were themselves in need of instruction. Schoolmasters and schoolmistresses were examined as to their proficiency, and trained for the due discharge of their important office. Availing himself also of the powers which the laws accorded him, he assembled the midwives of his parish, in order to ascertain that they were sufficiently acquainted with the form of administering baptism; at the same time he urged upon them the duty of fulfilling their calling in such a way as should best conduce to the spiritual profit of those whom they assisted. He gave them forms of prayer which they could recite either with or for the objects of their care, and taught them how to suggest to the poor women modes of lifting up their hearts to God, making acts of contrition, accepting their pains as the chastisement of sin, and bearing them with willingness, as being more pleasing to the Divine justice than any voluntary mortifications, however severe.

Another object of his solicitude, and one which was recommended to him by the peculiar circumstances of his parish, was the conversion of Protestants. It abounded (as has been said) in Calvinists; the Lutherans, also, had congregated here in great numbers. The latter sectaries were prohibited by the laws from holding their conventicles within the realm; M. Olier, however, might have left them in peace, but for an abominable sacrilege they were in the habit of committing. While adhering to their own heresy, and blasphemously impugning the Catholic faith, they made a practice of receiving communion clandestinely at the church of S. Sulpice. Justly indignant at so outrageous an insult to the Adorable

Mystery of the altar, M. Olier endeavoured, in the first instance, to arrest the evil by obtaining an exact register of the houses they occupied, with a view to acquiring a personal knowledge of the inmates. This plan, however, proving of no avail, as they were able to baffle inquiry by continually changing their residence, he determined to seek the assistance of the secular power; and having first solicited the protection of the Duke of Orleans, the king's brother, he proceeded with the bailly of the suburb and two guards, provided by the duke, to a house which had been designated to him. Here, as he expected, he found 300 or 400 persons assembled, whom he immediately dispersed. The Lutherans attempted to continue their meetings elsewhere; but, unable to evade M. Olier's untiring vigilance, they were compelled at length to evacuate the parish.

But the weapons with which he desired to combat against heresy were not carnal, but spiritual: continuance in prayer, a tender and extraordinary charity, and the force of a persuasive eloquence, addressed to the mind and conscience of those whom he sought to win. To remove the obstacles to their conversion, he instituted public and private conferences, which were blessed with remarkable success; but here, too, the humility which marked whatever he did was as conspicuous as his zeal. Writing to S. Vincent de Paul, he begs him, for the love of God, to send him one of his priests, to confer with a Huguenot, who had urged objections to which he had found himself, owing to his great ignorance, unable to reply, and generally to instruct him in the mode of dealing with heretics. To assist him in his arduous task, he also engaged the services of the ablest controversialist of the day. This was the celebrated Father Véron, whose logical subtlety and caustic irony rendered him the scourge and dread of the teachers of error. He had been made *curé* of Charenton, where the Calvinists had their largest conventicle, for the express purpose of being a perpetual thorn in the side of these obnoxious sectaries; and his success, so far as confounding his opponents was concerned, was, even by the confession of those opponents themselves, as complete as he could have desired. M. du Ferrier gives us a specimen of his method. "You would reform us," he would say, "on the sole authority of Scripture: well, we are ready to hear you. We believe, for example, that Jesus Christ is really and substantially present in the Eucharist; you believe He is there only by faith, and not in reality, and you are bound on your own principles to prove this to us by a formal text of Scripture. Produce it then, and we will believe you." The Protestant minister would quote the words: "It is the spirit that quickeneth: the flesh profiteth nothing" (John vi. 64). F. Véron, repeating the words after him, would say, "This is not to the purpose: I ask you for a passage which says, 'The Body of Jesus Christ is not in the Eucharist;' the text you have quoted does not say this. If the Protestant added what follows: "The words that I have spoken to you are spirit and life," he repeated his demand for a passage which said, "The Body of Jesus Christ is not under the species of bread;" showing them that they could not produce a text which expressly denied the Catholic doctrine. If his opponent brought forward those words of S. Peter (Acts iii. 21), "Jesus Christ, whom heaven must receive until the times of the restitution of all things," and argued thence that He could not be present in the Holy Eucharist, he replied, "I ask you for a passage which says that Jesus Christ is not there, and you give me only reasonings and conclusions. Confess that you have no direct passage to quote: we will come to reasonings and conclusions presently." He thus compelled them to admit that they could produce no direct and formal text of Scripture, and this provoked them greatly. He then came to deductions and conclusions. "You say that your faith is grounded, not on reasoning, but on Scripture only: now show me a passage which says that, if Jesus Christ must remain in heaven until He comes to judge the world, He is not therefore in the Eucharist. In matters of faith we do not rest, as you truly say, on arguments and syllogisms: we Catholics also believe that Jesus Christ is, and will remain, in heaven, at the right hand of the Father, but we do not the less believe that He is in the Eucharist, really and corporally, but after an incomprehensible manner."

This eminent theologian was now invited by M. Olier to give a course of controversial lectures at S. Sulpice, and to hold public disputations with the Protestants. His opponents were silenced, but they were not convinced. He even succeeded in obtaining from his auditors, Protestants as well as Catholics, a formal declaration of his victory, signed by public notaries, which was printed and placarded about the streets; but the Protestants remained Protestants still: they were not converted. His method was perfect: his syllogisms were unassailable; in the sphere of argument he was triumphant, and his opponents, by their silence, acknowledged their defeat; but M. Olier desired, not their defeat, but their salvation, and the end he sought remained unfulfilled.

Providence, however, brought to his aid two men whose manner and whose method were wholly different: simple and illiterate, but wonderful adepts in a science wholly divine, and which had God alone as its author, they seemed to fulfil to the letter that saying of M. Olier's while at Vaugirard: "God will rather create a new race of beings than leave His work without effect." The first of these extraordinary men was Jean Clement, by trade a cutler. In early youth his mind had been perverted by associating with the children of Casaubon, the celebrated critic; and on the family removing to England, he repaired to La Rochelle, at that time the stronghold of the Calvinists, for the purpose of joining their sect. Having no acquaintance in the town, he addressed himself to an elderly man whom he saw labouring in a blacksmith's shop, and acquainted him with his design. To his surprise the old man replied, "Ah, my child, take heed what you do. Perhaps you may fall into the same state of misery in which I now am; for I know that I am doomed to hell for having quitted the Roman Church. I was a priest and a monk, and I cannot escape from the religion you are about to adopt, because I have a wife and four children dependent upon me." He then bade the youth stay neither to eat nor to drink, but to leave the place at once, before God had wholly abandoned him. Filled with horror, Clement asked him whither he should go, and the old man directed him to proceed at once to the *curé* of Estrée, six miles distant, who would instruct him and put him in the way of salvation. This advice he followed, remained ten days with the good priest of Estrée, and on returning to Paris devoted himself to the conversion of heretics, earning his livelihood at the same time by working at his trade.

His practice was to take up a position within the enclosure, or in the vaults of the church, after Father Véron had descended from the pulpit, and letting the Protestants first adduce their texts of Scripture, and urge their objections, he would explain the passages they had quoted, and show that when rightly understood they were not opposed to the faith of Catholics; and then, in turn, propounding the true doctrine, he would support it by Scriptural proofs, so aptly chosen, and enforced with so much simplicity and sweetness, yet with such marvellous clearness and force, that numbers of those who had only been irritated and confounded by the arguments of the learned doctor, were convinced and converted. He knew almost the whole of the Bible in French by heart, an accomplishment which gave him great influence with the Protestants; nor was his acquaintance with Catholic doctrine less extraordinary than his familiarity with Holy Scripture and his insight into the meaning of the sacred text. Indeed, such was the ability he displayed in the difficult art of controversy, that (as M. du Ferrier says in his Memoirs) the priests of the community would often leave the dispute in his hands, when by a few words he would dissipate doubts which long hours of discussion had failed to remove. So great was his success that (as we learn from the same authority) in one year he made on an average six converts a day. These conversions were sometimes accompanied, in the case of very ignorant persons, with circumstances which showed that the grace of God gave an efficacy to his words indefinitely surpassing any persuasive power they might naturally possess; and

M. du Ferrier (who, on F. Véron's falling ill, succeeded that theologian in the office of preaching to Protestants), records his conviction that disputation has incalculably less to do with the conversion of souls than many are apt to suppose; for that he found on inquiry that the reasons that had weighed most with the persons he had addressed were such as had formed no part of his argument.

The other gifted individual was Beaumais, a draper. Like Clement, he was on the point of abandoning the faith for the purpose of marrying a Protestant, who made his apostacy the condition of her consent to the union, when remorse of conscience took him to Clement, who not only delivered him from the distressing doubts to which his mind was a prey, but induced him to join with him in combating heresy and teaching the truth. By a wonderful effect of Divine grace he received an infused knowledge both of the true sense of Holy Scripture and of the right interpretation of the Fathers, wholly independent of any instruction or study; and at M. Olier's desire he established himself in the faubourg S. Germain,* where his exertions were crowned with astonishing success. His powers of disputation were allowed to surpass those of the ablest doctors of the University of Paris, and no one could be compared with him, uneducated as he was, for the facility and completeness with which he refuted the objections and exposed the inconsistencies of the Protestant teachers. His labours were not confined to this single parish, for he visited in turn the towns most infected with heresy, and succeeded in reclaiming large numbers of Calvinists to the faith of the Church.

* Beaumais, like Clement, did not quit his business as long as he remained at Paris. The clergy allowed him a pension of 400 livres, and he dined every Sunday with the community of S. Sulpice. That Clement continued to work at his trade, is proved by the fact that in the year 1649 he was chosen by the associated artisans of Paris to be their spokesman before the king and queen. In his harangue, which was published, he speaks of himself as living by the labour of his hands. He died in 1654, with the universal reputation of sanctity.

By these two striking examples God would doubtless prove to the clergy of France the little efficiency of educational polish, theological knowledge, or dialectic skill when unaccompanied with those high moral qualifications and those supernatural virtues — humility, patience, sweetness, love—which He requires in the preachers of His word. This it was that made Adrien Bourdoise so indignantly exclaim, "The world is sick enough, but the clergy is not less so: frivolity, impurity, immodesty are everywhere paramount. The majority of our priests stand with their arms folded; and God is forced to raise up laymen—cutlers and haberdashers—to do the work of these lazy ecclesiastics. Seldom nowadays do we meet with a man who is well-born, learned, and, at the same time, a devoted servant of God. Whence is it that God makes use of M. Beaumais the draper, and M. Clement the cutler, both laymen, as His instruments for the conversion of such numbers of heretics and bad Catholics at Paris, but that He finds not bachelors, licentiates, or doctors, filled with His Spirit, whom He can employ for the purpose? It is the heaviest reproach, the bitterest affront, He can offer the clergy of an age so devoid of humility. Long live the draper and the cutler! '*Non multi sapientes, non multi potentes, non multi nobiles*'." (1 Cor. i. 26.) Even if it be admitted that there was something of rhetorical exaggeration * in this vehement protest, attributable to the ardent zeal of this fearless man, it may at least be taken as indicative of the extent and the enormity of the evil against which it was directed.

The proselytising efforts of the Calvinists had been (as already said) only too successful in the parish of S. Sulpice in drawing away many from the faith; and they laboured no less assiduously to deter their unhappy victims from recanting their errors on their death-beds. Cases of the latter kind were of such frequent occurrence, that it became necessary to have recourse to the

* And yet in Abelly's "Life of S. Vincent de Paul," we find two bishops using language (when writing to the Saint) even still more condemnatory of the lives of the clergy in their dioceses.

most determined measures to defeat the artifices and even violence employed by these heretics. For instance, a young man, who had been recovered to the Church, fell ill, and, intimidated by the opposition of his friends, refused to receive M. Olier's ministrations, when, on hearing of his condition, he hastened to visit him. Recommending him to the Mother of mercy, this good pastor ceased not to beg her intercession; and his prayer was heard. The sick man was seized with so vehement a desire to see a priest that, finding all his entreaties and expostulations useless, he protested that, weak as he was, he would drag himself to the window, and there, until his voice failed him, he would cry to the passers-by for assistance; nay, that if necessary, he would precipitate himself into the street below rather than die without confession. This threat compelled his relatives to send for a priest, but thenceforward they refused him all aid in his sickness; and, had not M. Olier caused him to be removed to a place of safety, he could only have purchased the necessaries of life by renewed apostacy. No wonder, therefore, that on hearing that the Calvinist minister Aubertin, who was dying, desired to make his abjuration, but was forcibly prevented by his relatives, M. Olier should call in the aid of the civil power to gain admission to his bedside. He went accordingly, accompanied by the bailly of the faubourg, as well as by a strong party of the parishioners, who had collected for the protection of their pastor. The report, however, proved to be unfounded, the man protesting with his last breath that he died in the belief he had ever professed. M. Olier at once withdrew, and having succeeded, not, however, without some difficulty, in persuading the people to disperse, went immediately to the Church, and, throwing himself before the altar, gave free vent to the sorrow that filled his soul. We shall have no difficulty in conceiving the use that was made of this display of zeal by the sectaries, who accused M. Olier of violating the terms of the edict of Nantes, which forbade that Protestants should be disturbed on their sick beds by the forced ministrations of the Catholic priesthood.

He was doomed to meet with a similar affliction in the case of one of his female parishioners, who had seceded from the Church, and who, in spite of all his exhortations and the prayers of many devout souls, persisted in her errors to the last. To console him in his bitter grief, one of his priests suggested that as he had employed every means in his power to effect her conversion, he had nothing wherewith to reproach himself. "Ah! my child," he said, "cease—cease to speak to me thus: you know not the value of a soul. It might glorify God eternally, and its loss is irreparable. The thought is frightful!" and he sought refuge, as was his wont, in prayer before the tabernacle. This distressing circumstance seemed to add even greater vigilance to his zeal, and he neglected no means in order to discover if any of his flock frequented the meetings of the Huguenots, or evinced an inclination towards their errors, never failing to visit them in person, or to depute one of his priests to visit them in his stead, and displaying towards them the utmost kindness and solicitude. Nor were these precautions the effect of an indiscreet zeal: they were necessitated by the secret and unscrupulous machinations of the sectaries, who were indefatigable in their endeavours to recruit their diminished numbers by the accession of every bad and ignorant Catholic whom they could persuade to make even a nominal profession of Protestantism. The charity of this good pastor, however, was no less fruitful in devices both to rescue his people from the snares of heresy and unbelief, and to warn them against the fatal seductions of vice. As an antidote to the number of irreligious and immoral publications which were widely disseminated, M. Olier established a book-stall close to the gates of the church, where, as it will be remembered, the vendors of charms and amulets, and books of superstition and magic had been in the habit of plying their iniquitous trade. Every work exhibited for sale was previously examined, to ascertain that it contained nothing contrary to faith or morals.

But it was in the church and its precincts that the

multitude began first to perceive the complete revolution that had been effected in the management of affairs. Where but a few weeks before everything testified to the state of ruin and desolation into which religion had fallen, the order and beauty that now prevailed struck beholders with astonishment. The altars had been reconstructed and richly adorned, the floor had been repaired, the sacristy, but lately so forlorn, was now duly furnished and decorated, while a second was set apart for the use of the priests in saying the daily Masses. So scanty had become the vessels for the altar, that when M. Olier entered on the *curé*, the church possessed only three chalices for the service of that large parish; but he never rested until out of his own resources, or through the bounty of his richer parishioners, he had repaired what he regarded a scandal to religion and an offence to the Divine Majesty; so that in a few years no church in the whole metropolis was more richly provided with all that was necessary for the worthy celebration of the Holy Mysteries. Instead of the bells which had been suspended over the entrance to each chapel, and which rang at irregular intervals, as the celebrant happened to be ready, a single bell had been placed at the sacristy door; and every day, at every quarter of an hour, from six o'clock in the morning till twelve at noon, that bell gave warning to the faithful that a priest was proceeding to offer the Adorable Sacrifice. For the future the sacristan and the master of the ceremonies were both to be ecclesiastics, and no official was permitted to enter the church unless he was vested in surplice or gown. The singers, however, who had not received the tonsure, were prohibited from wearing the surplice. No laymen, on any pretext whatever, were admitted into the sanctuary or choir, with the exception of the princes or princesses of the blood, when they were present in state at any extraordinary solemnity. Two doorkeepers had been appointed, whose business it was to disperse the crowd of beggars who gathered round the entrance, to the annoyance of the congregation, many of whom, to avoid their importunity, had been driven to frequent the chapels of the different communities in the suburbs. No one employed in the sacristy was allowed to ask for presents at baptisms. The organist, who in the choice of his pieces had observed neither times nor seasons, was provided with a book of regulations in accordance with the Roman practice, as then in use. The ringers also received a set of instructions; the sexton also, who hitherto had been left to his own devices, was subjected to supervision and control; nor did M. Olier disdain to see to the ordering of the parish clock, on which depended the punctual performance of all the offices of the church. Need it be added that an end had been put to the tavern in the vaults, where, as M. de Bassancourt with affected gravity informs M. Bourdoise, "our communicants used to go to take a little draught, and eat a bit of blessed bread, in the excess of their devotion!"

One sublime and beautiful thought M. Olier had, which it was now his delight to see realized. It was that while the greater part of the priests of his community were dispersed about the parish, engaged in labouring for the salvation of souls, the rest should be assembled in the choir of the church, offering to God, in the name of clergy and people, the sacrifice of homage and praise. This was M. Olier's great idea, which he expressed at length in some considerations* which he drew up for the benefit of his ecclesiastics; that in "reciting the divine office they act in the name of the Church, or rather in that of Jesus Christ Himself, who is pleased to make use of their mouths and hearts to give praise to the Majesty of His Father by His Spirit dwelling in them." Henceforth, therefore, the Canonical Hours were publicly recited by the priests of S. Sulpice, an endowment being provided by M. Olier for their perpetual observance; in all which his exertions were powerfully seconded by the zeal and piety of M. de Bassancourt,

* An extract from these considerations is appended to this chapter.

who for the first seven years after the establishment of the community conducted the religious services of the seminary.

We have been witnesses of M. Olier's missionary zeal, his love of souls, his tenderness to sinners, his care of the poor, his labours, and his sacrifices; and all this in the service of those of whom he had not the personal charge; but now it is his own flock to which he is called to minister, and of which he must one day render an account to the Chief Shepherd. The profligacy, the obduracy, the ignorance, the worldliness, the indifference of the thousands by whom he was surrounded, filled his soul with a most poignant anguish, and he would have willingly sacrificed his life to rescue and save them. It was the one continual subject of his prayers as he knelt before the tabernacle, pouring out his heart to God with sighs and tears and inward moanings; and in his discourses to the people it was his ever-recurring theme. "'*Continuus dolor cordi meo.*' It is the one abiding grief of my heart," he cried, "to behold the little esteem in which the only real and solid goods are held by men. Alas! the world is for ever chasing vain phantoms, striving to plunge deeper and deeper in vanity and lies, and no man thinks of his eternal salvation. '*Non est qui recogitet in corde; non est qui faciat bonum, non est usque ad unum.*' See how the courts of princes and the ante-rooms of statesmen are crowded with greedy and ambitious applicants! Behold the multitudes that throng the marts of commerce and all the public places of this vast city! Why all this restless activity and excitement? To fulfil the desires of the flesh. I say it weeping, with S. Paul, *flens dico*,—All these men who live only for their pleasures, are the enemies of the Cross and of the Life of Jesus Christ, who condemns this accursed self-seeking, the end of which is the ruin and perdition of souls: they make their belly their God; they labour only for their everlasting destruction. O great Saint, who art the patron of this parish, thou didst not walk by these ways in the days of thy pilgrimage: thou who now reignest with God in the holy Sion, be present with us; grant me something of the spirit with which thou wert so abundantly replenished; grant to me, great Saint, that I may draw the hearts of this people to an imitation of thy virtues, to a death unto sin and the love of holiness; assist me with thy spirit and thy zeal."

His only preparation for preaching was humble and fervent prayer before the Blessed Sacrament; and when he spoke it was as uniting himself to Jesus Christ, the true light of man, and surrendering himself entirely to the impressions of His grace. On one only occasion, when he knew that the Queen Regent* and other great personages were to be present, did he deviate from his usual practice, thinking to do more honour to the sacred ministry; but he experienced so much sterility and constraint in thought and feeling, and so much difficulty in expressing himself, that he never renewed the attempt; being assured that God would have him renounce his own intellectual lights, and abandon himself without reserve to the movements of His Spirit.† As he preached, a beauty not his own seemed to pervade his features; his voice, naturally sweet and powerful, assumed a richer and more ravishing tone, and to his whole appearance there was added a nobility and a majesty that had something in it celestial and divine. The emotions kindled in his breast were at times so

---

* Anne of Austria, who held M. Olier in the highest esteem, wished him to undertake the direction of the Abbey of Val de Grace, the first stone of which was laid in the April of 1645, by Louis XIV., still a child; and to this end proposed that he should exchange the parish of S. Sulpice for that of S. Jacques du Haut Pas, in which the abbey was situated. M. Olier would have been disposed to entertain the question, but for the assurance of Marie Rousseau, that such a change would lead to the ruin of the seminary. The queen would then have had him nominate one of his ecclesiastics, but from this he was deterred by the consideration that the abbey was in the close vicinity of S. Magloire, where the Oratorians had their establishment, with which it might be deemed to interfere. For the same reason he declined the office of superior of the Filles Penitentes of S. Magloire, lately reformed.

† A similar instance is recorded of S. Vincent Ferrer. See "The Spiritual Doctrine" of F. Louis Lallemant, p. 165.

overpowering, that he was fain to pause in his discourse; his voice would fail him, and he would be compelled to leave the pulpit. The effect on his audience was of a corresponding intensity; it was not rare to see men and women suddenly burst into tears and throw themselves on their knees, imploring the mercy of God; and after the sermon was ended, the confessionals would be surrounded with persons who, touched by the grace of contrition for their sins, desired to make their peace with God, and lead the rest of their lives in His faith and fear.

Nor was this evangelical fervour confined to the interior of the church. One day, as he was passing through the streets, he came upon a crowd of people, who were amusing themselves with the immodest jests and antics of a merry-andrew. Fired with holy indignation at the shameless language that met his ear, and emulating the zeal of the Apostle when, as he walked the streets of Athens, he beheld the city wholly given to idolatry, he stopped at a few paces from the throng, and lifting up his voice, began to speak of the things of God and of eternity. At first a few bystanders gathered round him; but curiosity even got the better of present amusement, and gradually the whole laughter-loving multitude had left their saucy favourite, and were hearkening with strange emotions to one who spoke to them of justice and chastity and judgment to come. It was indeed a scene to excite men's wonder: the influence exerted by an earnest man over a giddy fickle crowd; but to this succeeded a prodigy of grace; the poor buffoon, deserted by his hearers, drew near in turn: —he listened, and was converted.

Allusion has been made to the various guilds or confraternities of artisans and workmen, and the onerous yet often frivolous duties imposed by them on the clergy. These companies were recognized by the laws, and had their peculiar privileges and customs. Instituted originally with the laudable object of uniting in the bonds of fraternal amity, and by the common obligations of religion, members of the same trade or handicraft, whom motives of self-interest might naturally render jealous and distrustful of each other, they had degenerated into mere associations for periodical feasting and carousing; in other words, intemperance and debauchery. The principal occasions on which they assembled were the festivals of their patron saints, particularly that of S. Martin, which ancient piety had set apart as times of special devotion, but which popular license had converted into days of Bacchanalian riot, and profaned by a number of heathenish superstitions and extravagances. These abuses had become so consecrated by long, immemorial custom, that the people indulged in the worst excesses, apparently, without shame or remorse; and the Protestants, with a disingenuousness—examples of which are unhappily too prevalent in our own time and country—had the hardihood to declare, even from their pulpits, that such were the "devotions" authorized by the Church for the observance of these sacred times. All these abominations M. Olier now laboured to suppress. He called the different confraternities together, and instructed them in the proper modes of solemnizing these privileged days. His kindness, his sincerity, his genuine earnestness, produced a powerful effect on the rough but passionate natures of the men he addressed; and from many his appeal met at once with an effectual response. These he prepared for a general confession, and afterwards for communion. A large number of the brothers renounced their profane practices, and banished every emblem of their once cherished superstitions from their houses. To give the more authority to his acts, he obtained from the doctors of the Sorbonne a formal condemnation of the usages in question, which he caused to be printed, and copies of it distributed among the members of the companies. He directed the confessor of the community to direct his especial attention to the brothers and their families; visiting them repeatedly, particularly at times of sickness and distress, reconciling differences, and exhorting them to the practice of all their Christian duties. These visits were often made by himself in person; and there was scarcely an attic or a hovel—for the parish extended far into the country—to which his charity did not take him. The people soon learnt to regard him, not as a prying servant of the governing powers, or one who presumed on his social position to intrude into their dwellings, but as an affectionate and anxious father, a true pastor of souls, whose only desire was to promote their welfare, temporal and eternal. So great was the influence he obtained over all sorts of men, that even the public notaries entered into an agreement among themselves not to transact any legal business, except in cases of necessity, on Sundays and holidays.

An activity so zealous and unceasing on the part of M. Olier and his associates, and the consequent revival of piety among the people, produced all the effects and presented all the appearances of a continual mission. So great, at length, became the number of penitents, that before the end of the first year it became necessary to procure the co-operation of additional confessors. The priests of the community were occupied on Sundays and festivals from five in the morning till one o'clock in the day, and again in the afternoon till late in the evening; and this, at the time of the greater solemnities, continued several days together. In the first Lent, that of 1643, M. Olier found himself compelled to call in the assistance of certain doctors of the Sorbonne, and to beg the superiors of the several religious communities in the parish to send some of their subjects to his aid. Fearing, however, that all these doctors and religious, the latter members of different orders, should not follow the same system of spiritual direction, he assembled them three days previously, and set before them in detail the principles and express instructions of S. Charles; a precaution which was productive of the happiest results. If M. Olier had any predilection for any particular religious, it was in favour of the Dominicans and Jesuits, who had each a noviciate in his parish, and whose doctrine (he says) was as pure as their piety was exemplary. "If" (he adds) "the Divine mercy lavishes such abundant graces on this parish, and effects every day fresh conversions, they are the fruit of the prayers of these two holy communities."

The church was soon so densely crowded, that it became necessary to concert measures for the construction of a more spacious building; but as this would be a work of time, and, in fact, was not completed for several years, all that was accomplished at present was, to enlarge the approaches by demolishing several houses in the vicinity. Yet even then, the multitudes that filled the precincts were so great, that, during Lent, the carriage of the Queen Regent was detained for nearly ten minutes at the corner of the Rue du Petit Bourbon before it could be extricated from the throng.

Extract from M. Olier's Considerations on the Canonical Hours.

"Matins and Lauds, which are said at night, denote the praises of heaven rendered to God by the Saints and Angels in glory; and so we may consider the other Hours, which are said in the daytime, as the prayers of this life: viz., from Prime, at six o'clock in the morning, till Vespers, at six o'clock in the evening.

"The Christian life, which is a life divine, is the life of heaven begun upon earth. Hence the four Little Hours, which comprehend the whole day, are composed of a single psalm, in imitation of heaven, where there will be but one psalm, and one song of praise. This single psalm is divided into four Hours, representing the universality of the supplicating Church; and these four Hours are said at intervals of three hours, and in each three psalms are recited, or, rather, three divisions of the same psalm. And here we must observe the wonderful care of the Church at once to honour and remind us of the sacred mystery of the Most Holy Trinity; for, at intervals of three hours, we find three psalms, all which three make up but one, as the Three Divine Persons are one only God.

"The beautiful distribution of this psalm throughout the day aptly denotes the establishment of the divine life of the Christian religion in us, which is an imitation of Paradise; where there is one never-ending song of praise, in which each moment is occupied in giving glory to God. This is why we chant that great and divine psalm of David: *Beati immaculati in via,* wherein we see the hidden life of God within us entirely unfolded; and this psalm extends through all the Little Hours, to show that every hour we ought to ask of God that we may thus live, and be filled unceasingly with that divine life, in order that we may live in Him every moment of our life upon earth.

At six o'clock the day closes, and we begin to reckon the hours of the night. Hence these prayers, according to the intention of the Church, are chanted in the evening, about six o'clock, which is the time at which the evening star called Vesper begins to appear: hence the name Vespers. Then we begin to chant the praises of God and of Jesus Christ, ascended into His glory, which is the beginning of all the glory of the Blessed. Compline signifies the completion of the prayers of men and of this present life in Jesus Christ, who by the close of His Life and by His Death merited for us the happiness and the glory of the life to come. Hence all the psalms of Compline speak only of our Lord suffering, who in heaven, where He is exalted in the fulness of His glory, continues the memorial of His state of passion, as being the subject of His glory, and of the beatitude which is the recompense He would set before men. The Hour of Compline is not, properly speaking, reckoned among the separate Hours; it is, in fact, part of Vespers, of which it forms the complement (*completorium*), that is to say, the termination and completion of the prayers.

"The whole Christian year is designed to honour Jesus Christ in His mysteries, or in His saints, and throughout all this time you will find only one single day set apart for honouring the sacred mystery of the Most Holy Trinity, and even that without an octave, although one more solemn would be due to it than for all the other mysteries conjoined. And even on that day commemoration is made of the Sunday, which is not done on the Easter or the Pentecostal festival. If there be only this one day specially set apart to honour the Most Holy Trinity, it is in order to show that the worship we render thereto cannot as yet take full possession of our souls, but that this perfect adoration must await our entrance into heaven, where, being wholly consummated in Jesus Christ, after having long adored and contemplated Him on earth, we shall be, like Him, an everlasting sacrifice of praise to the glory of God. Meanwhile God the Father allows Himself to be, as it were, forgotten in the world, as if He desired to receive homage only in His Son. This great God, in acknowledgment of the love which His dear Son has testified for Him by His death, would make Him partaker of all His glory, and even, as it were, hide Himself in Him, so as only to receive glory through Him.

"Jesus Christ, indeed, manifests in Himself all the perfections of His Father; His might, His knowledge, His love, and all His fulness: *In quo inhabitat omnis plenitudo divinitatis corporaliter*. He is the perfect image of the life of God, as God; having received all the life of His father to preserve it, and distribute it to all the saints. This is why, after Jesus Christ, the saints are set forth as images of the perfection of God and of His divine life; and why we have every day brought before us the holy martyrs, and their heroic and divine acts, which show forth the perfections of God in them. Thus we have a S. Martin cutting his mantle in two for a poor man, which shows the charity of God; a S. Paulinus selling himself for his brethren, which shows also the love of Jesus Christ; a S. Agnes, in the midst of torments, displaying the might of God in her feebleness and in her bodily weakness; and so, too, in S. Alexis, hidden under the disguise of a beggar at the steps of his father's door, and become the sport of the domestics, we see the humility of Jesus Christ suffering abasement in the world and despised by His servants. In a word, everything we behold in the Church is but a picture of the beauties and perfections of God in their exalted sublimity."

CHAPTER XII.

M. Olier's reforms continued.

OF all the measures adopted by M. Olier for the reformation of his parish, that on which he most relied was, an increased devotion to Jesus in the Sacrament of His Love and to His blessed Mother. "When God" (he wrote) "would revive the piety of His people, it is not through the instrumentality of preaching or of miracles; these are the means He uses for the first establishment of His Church; but by renewed devotion to the Most Holy Sacrament of the Altar. The design of the Son of God in coming upon earth, was to communicate to men His divine life, in order to render them like unto Himself. This transformation He begins in Baptism, and advances in Confirmation; but he brings it to perfection in the Holy Eucharist, that divine food which really communicates to us His own life and feelings, gives us a participation in His adorable interior, and makes us one with Himself: *Qui manducat meam carnem, in me manet et ego in eo.* He has taken up His abode in the Blessed Sacrament that He may continue His mission even to the end of the world, and form in the remotest corners of the earth adorers of His Father, who may worship Him in spirit and in truth. It is there that He becomes the source of a divine life, the inexhaustible fountain, the boundless ocean, out of the fulness of which we are sanctified. By the Most Holy Sacrament He would fill priests with His Spirit and His grace, and convert souls by their means .... The priest who is assiduous in honouring It, invoking It, and supplicating It for his people, will sooner or later obtain their conversion. It is impossible but that being assiduous in prayer, and remaining thus before the Most Holy Sacrament, he must communicate in the sentiments, the fervour, and the efficacy of our Lord, to touch, enlighten, and convert the souls of his people. For the power of Jesus risen, who now dwelleth in the Church with a zeal all on fire for the glory of His Father, must produce these effects."

At the time he committed these thoughts to paper the devotion to the Blessed Sacrament, and the piety which nourishes itself with the Bread of Life, seemed to have died out in the parish of S. Sulpice. Few communicated, and that but seldom; while the very idea of visiting Jesus present on the altar was to all appearance lost among the people. From the moment he entered into possession, he made this pious practice the subject of his continual exhortations; but he did more: he enforced his teaching by example. He was constantly to be seen upon his knees before the tabernacle; he never left the presbytery but he first paid a visit of adoration, and again when he returned; it was observed, also, that he chose by preference those streets in which there were churches, and where, therefore, he could perform a passing act of homage. His ecclesiastics were so emulous of his piety, that from morning till night there was no lack of worshippers;[*] he would have them resort to this devotion as a relief and recreation in their toils, and their one engrossing occupation in old age: here they were to find their peace and repose in their declining years. He invited all his parishioners to join the confraternity of the Blessed Sacrament, and with such success, that ere long he had the happiness of seeing a perpetual adoration established, in which the noblest born did not disdain to be

---

[*] It was probably for the sake of edification to the parish that he never sought permission to have the Blessed Sacrament reserved in the chapel of the seminary; nor did the community enjoy this privilege until the year 1698.

seen kneeling side by side with the meanest of the poor. At first it was observed only in the afternoon; it was then commenced in the early part of the day, and at last was continued through the night. Every Thursday he assembled the associates in the church, and renewed their fervour by an earnest exhortation. Having remarked that several persons, and especially some of the greater people, were remiss in their devotion, he rebuked them for their negligence, showing how unbecoming it was to leave their Sovereign Lord without worshippers at such times as He was pleased to invite them to His presence. The Princess of Condé,* who was among his auditors, and had been absent on a late occasion, desirous of repairing any scandal she might have given by her apparent indevotion, stood up, and said with a touching simplicity, "I was absent, sir, on Saturday, having gone to pay my court to the Queen." M. Olier, who had no regard to rank or birth where duty was concerned, replied, " You would have done better, madam, had you come here to pay your court to the King of kings." The princess, however, had a legitimate excuse. Louis XIII. was just dead, and the queen, who, during the first forty days of public mourning, was obliged by court etiquette to remain in her own apartments, with flambeaux burning, had begged her to come and take her out privately for an airing. On being made aware of the circumstance, M. Olier felt that some reparation was due for the public rebuke he had administered, and, making her very presence there the occasion of a commendation, bade his hearers take pattern by the piety and humility of one of her exalted station, who came in the crowd like any ordinary person, and sat with the rest on her little straw chair. This princess, who was under M. Olier's spiritual direction, did much, both by example and direct influence, for the promotion of piety among the ladies of the parish, and especially in this matter of devotion to the Blessed Sacrament.

* Charlotte Marguerite, daughter of the Constable Henri de Montmorenci, and mother of the great Condé.

One of M. Olier's first acts on coming to S. Sulpice had been to establish a solemn Benediction of the Most Holy Sacrament, with a procession and exposition, on the first Sundays and Thursdays in each month. This most beautiful devotion was at that time of much rarer observance in France than it has since become; and it was objected by many persons of piety (M. Bourdoise among the number), that a more frequent celebration would so familiarize people's minds with the tremendous mystery, as to lead to irreverence and desecration. But M. Olier contended—and the authoritative sanction of the Church, as well as the general experience of the faithful, has confirmed his judgment—that the dispensations of grace vary in such matters with the needs of the age; and that, as in these latter days the blasphemy of heresy has especially assailed the august sacrament of the altar, so it was the will of God that reparation should be made by a more open, more frequent, and (so to say) more triumphant display of homage and adoration; moreover, that the elevation of the sacerdotal order was inseparably associated with this increased devotion to the Blessed Sacrament, of which priests were the consecrated ministers and guardians. He was careful, however, to provide against the apprehended evil consequences, by surrounding the celebration with every circumstance that could tend to exalt it in the eyes of the people.* Every first Thursday in the month there was solemn High Mass, with a procession; and the exposition was announced by three peals of bells. It was ordered also that there should never be less than thirty-eight ecclesiastics present, four of whom should bear the canopy, four be vested in copes or dalmatics, while the rest should carry lighted torches in their hands; two thurifers, moreover, preceding, who were to incense continually as the procession advanced.

* As a proof of the care he took in this matter, it is mentioned that when a person of some consideration in the parish offered to found a solemn Mass of the Blessed Sacrament, with Benediction, to be celebrated every Thursday throughout the year, he refused his consent, for fear of diminishing rather than stimulating the devotion of the people.

For the perpetual observance of this edifying practice, the Duchess of Aiguillon established a special endowment; and a similar fund was contributed by a pious family in the parish, for the solemnization of the Forty Hours' Adoration, during the three days immediately preceding the season of Lent.. M. Olier also instituted an annual exposition of the Blessed Sacrament on the feast of Epiphany, and that of S. Martin, both in reparation and as a corrective of the disorders that prevailed on those particular days. Unable, amidst his numerous avocations, to satisfy the ardour of his devotion, he kept two tapers continually burning on the altar, to represent his own consuming love; and provided at his personal expense the torches which were borne before the Blessed Sacrament, when carried to the sick. Such devotion. and liberality could not fail to be contagious. Accordingly, we find, that although, when M. Olier took possession, there was but a single lamp in the church, there were soon to be seen no less than seven, all of silver, before the high altar alone, the gifts of the parishioners; one, however, being the contribution of M. Olier himself. The days which had been devoted to riot or mere amusement, began to be observed religiously: soon the people came in crowds to the holy offices, and endeavoured by their piety and fervour to make reparation for their former profanities.

Communions at S. Sulpice (as has been said) had become both few and rare; a circumstance attributable, not only to the tepidity and indifference which is sure to follow where pastors are themselves wanting in zeal and devotion, but to that insidious and most detestable heresy which was now fast gaining ground in France, and which, under the pretence of aspiring after a higher spirituality and doing greater honour to the Sacrament of the Altar, prevented thirsting, perishing souls from approaching the fount of life and sanctity. Jansenism was doing its utmost, by exaggerating the qualifications required for a right reception of the Holy Eucharist, to make unfrequent communion a mark of piety, as it was the badge of its own pernicious sect. Against this odious hypocrisy the teaching of M. Olier and his community was one continued protest. Equally free, on the one hand, from a severe rigorism, and, on the other, from a too indulgent laxity, he sought to inspire his people with a reverent, but tender devotion to Jesus in His Sacrament of Love, and to instruct them in the necessary dispositions for worthily partaking of the Bread of Angels. To accomplish this in the most solid and effectual manner, he expended the greatest care in preparing children and young persons for their first communion; and to train them from their earliest years in the practice of frequently approaching this heavenly banquet, he established a monthly general communion, which was the source of incalculable blessings to his flock. With this most salutary of all devotions was conjoined that which is its offspring and its complement, a most tender and confiding love of Mary, whose power and prerogatives were also covertly assailed, if not openly decried, by the Jansenistic party. On entering the parish he had solemnly placed it under the patronage and protection of the Blessed Virgin; and in all public processions, her banner was displayed together with that of S. Sulpice. It was his desire that on the first Saturday of each month the younger members of his flock should renew their consecration to their holy Mother; and to this end he established a Mass and procession, at which all the children in the schools assisted. But it was on the day of their first communion, that he, who had ever loved to bestow that which was best and dearest on his heavenly Patroness, rejoiced in making her the offering of hearts, then most worthy of her favour; hearts which her Divine Son had just deigned personally to visit, and had replenished with the Spirit of His grace. In the seminary of S. Sulpice is a painting representing M. Olier kneeling before an altar with a youth of noble aspect, whom he is consecrating to the holy Mother of God. This was Anne Auger Granry, page to the Duke of Orleans. He made his first communion when he was twelve years old, and having through divine grace preserved his innocence unstained, he came in his fifteenth year to make a retreat at the seminary. Surrounded by all the temptations of the court, and now arrived at a most critical period of his life, the one desire of his heart was that he might sooner die than live to offend God by one mortal sin; and scarcely had he entered on his retreat when he was taken ill, and in a very few days expired. M. de Bretonvilliers, who acted as his confessor, was so assured of his being in a state of bliss, that he would have contented himself with saying two or three Masses for him; but on M. Olier declaring that the youth still needed his prayers, he procured several Masses to be offered in his behalf, until the holy pastor learnt by divine revelation that the justice of God was satisfied. "This morning," he said, "when offering the Adorable Sacrifice, I beheld his soul, resplendent with light, ascending into heaven."

Next to Jesus really present on the altars of the Church the servant of God loved the poor, who are His images and representatives. On arriving at any town, his first visit was to the Blessed Sacrament, his second to the hospital or the asylum of the poor. He had bound himself by vow to be their servant to the end of his days, and faithfully did he perform it when he became pastor of S. Sulpice. Crowds of miserable objects, the fetid odour from whose garments tainted the very air, might be seen surrounding the doors of the presbytery, where they ever met with a ready, cordial welcome. Not content with receiving them with a sweet and gentle kindness, he invited them to come to him, he went out to seek them, he gathered them about him, and lavished on them every mark of the tenderest affection. The bashful poor were specially the objects of his solicitude, and of these the first list presented to him contained no less than 1,500 names. To inquire into the circumstances and relieve the necessities of all who claimed his bounty, he needed an assistant of peculiar talents and experience; and such a one was provided him in the person of Jean Blondeau, better known in his own day as Brother John of the Cross. He had himself belonged to the tribe of beggars until he was taken into the service of Father Bernard, and the way he obtained the name by which he was popularly known is too characteristic to be omitted. Great as was their mutual respect, servant and master seem to have been a peculiar trial to each other: their dispositions and humours were always clashing; and so troublesome and vexatious did the "poor priest" find his adopted beggar, that he reckoned him among the extraordinary *crosses* which God was pleased to lay upon him. The principal subject of Brother John's complaints was singular enough. "When I am serving his Mass," said he, "he remains rapt in an ecstacy three hours together; and all the time I am wanted elsewhere, for he has nobody but me to wait upon him. When I have prepared his meal, and go to tell him it is ready, I find him in an ecstacy again, and I have no means of getting him out of it. It is perfectly unendurable!" F. Bernard, however, retained him in his service as long as he lived, and when he was gone, the good brother, who had a real veneration for the virtues of his master, never ceased reproaching himself for all the trouble he had given him. "He has turned out a great saint," he would say, with tears in his eyes; "and what fills me with confusion is, that, instead of imitating his example, I contributed to his sanctification by all I made him suffer."

Accompanied by Brother John, M. Olier visited in person all the poor of his vast parish, listening patiently to their complaints and distributing alms. For the sick he provided nurses and medical attendants; for the orphans a home; for distressed females employment; and he charged certain of the parishioners in whom he could confide, to watch over their conduct, and supply their wants out of funds which he placed at their disposal. The number of beggars whom he relieved with food and clothing alone amounted to several hundreds; and so continual was the drain upon his resources, that they were often quite exhausted. One friend, however, he had who never failed him, and who, he used to declare, would never be wanting to those who loved and cared for the poor, the Blessed Virgin. To the purses which were hung up in the presbytery to receive alms for their relief, he had attached an image of this compassionate Mother; and although they were always being emptied, they were as continually refilled when the moment of need was come. "She it is" (he would say to his priests, pointing to the image) "on whom I rely to take care of the poor: I leave the whole management to her; I tell her my wants, and she in her goodness provides for them."

One of his first acts was to reorganize the Confraternity of Charity, which had been established at S. Sulpice ten years before by S. Vincent de Paul, but had become well-nigh extinct. The association was composed of the ladies of the parish, many of them high in rank, who met every week at the presbytery after hearing Mass. Some contributed a fixed sum every month; others provided victuals; others again visited the sick at their own homes. Of these devoted women the most remarkable was Mme. Leschassier, of the illustrious family of Miron, who, though delicately and even luxuriously brought up, was in the daily practice of making the beds of the poor creatures and washing their linen with her own hands. One day that her daughter, whose humility and charity were worthy of such a mother, saw her preparing to comb the head of a little girl more than usually dirty and revolting, she drew the child towards her that she might perform the office instead. But Mme. Leschassier, perceiving her object, said, "No, my dear; that is not fair; you must not take the best to yourself." Acting under M. Olier's direction, this young lady refused several advantageous offers of marriage, and devoted her whole life to works of charity.

It was found, however, that the aid thus rendered was uncertain and precarious at the best, particularly as many of the ladies, unable to give the constant and regular attention which was needed, were in the habit of hiring young women, or sending their servants, to supply their place. M. Olier, therefore, called in the aid of the Sisters of Charity, lately founded by Mme. Legras*, under the

---

* Readers who are acquainted with the volumes of the "Popular Library" already published must be sufficiently familiar with

direction of S. Vincent de Paul. But it was to his own ecclesiastics that he principally looked to minister to the necessities of the suffering poor, to whom, as the dearest and most cherished members of the body of Christ, he would have them consider nothing less than a father's care was due. To obviate, however, any evils that might arise from mixing up together the temporal and the spiritual, no confessor was allowed to give alms to his penitents. If the poor, when they entered the tribunal of penance, began to complain of their bodily wants and sufferings, the priest was instructed to say, "Do you wish to confess your sins, or to receive alms? If I hear your confession, I cannot give you anything."

Deeply touched as was the heart of this good pastor by the poverty and distress of so many of his flock, there was one misery which caused it a far more bitter pang. The parish abounded in houses of infamy, to the ruin of the peace and happiness of families, and the eternal destruction of innumerable souls. To cope with this monstrous evil, there needed the zeal and the courage, and, we may add, the charity of an apostle; and none of the three were wanting in the *curé* of S. Sulpice. Again and again he urged upon his parishioners the strict obligation under which they lay not to receive as their tenants persons of notoriously profligate lives; and when this did not suffice, he denounced the vengeance of Heaven on all who knowingly lent themselves to this iniquity, enforcing his threats by the most terrible examples. He proceeded in person to demand the assistance of the magistrates, boldly declaring that, as the guardians of the public morals, they would have to answer at the judgment-seat of God for the disorders, which, through pusillanimity or supineness, they failed to suppress. A number of abandoned women having established themselves in one of the most frequented streets near the church, where their shameless conduct was a scandal to the whole neighbourhood, he inveighed from the pulpit with so much vehe-

this charitable lady, as she fills a prominent place in no less than three.

mence against the toleration of the foul enormity, that the bailly of the *faubourg*, using the authority he possessed, expelled the offenders from the parish, and even changed the appellation of the street with the hope of obliterating the very memory of the disgrace that attached to the locality. This act the magistrate followed up by enforcing the severest punishment allowed by the law, which was that of imprisonment for fifteen days, on bread and water, and adopting other vigorous measures. But M. Olier, meanwhile, was labouring to turn the vengeance of the law to the spiritual profit of its unhappy victims. He strove to provide them on their release with the means of obtaining an honest livelihood; he sent some of the most virtuous among his parishioners to visit them in prison, and endeavour by kindness and sympathy to rescue them from the gulf of misery into which they had fallen; and he induced charitable persons to afford the poor creatures an asylum at his personal expense, where they could be duly instructed and reconciled to God. Uniting himself interiorly to the sentiments of our Blessed Lord, when He conversed with the woman of Samaria, he would himself undertake their reformation, blending in such measure as an enlightened prudence suggested, or rather as the Spirit of God dictated to him at the time, severity with sweetness, and not unfrequently by a word or two of calm persuasion allaying the fiercest bursts of passion, or subduing the most obstinate temper.

On its being observed to him one day by a person of piety, that all the trouble he took was simply thrown away, for that every day's experience showed that those on whom so much zeal was expended, on returning to the world betook themselves again to a life of sin, he answered, "No, the labour we undergo for God is never lost. True it is that our efforts do not always meet with success; but success is not altogether the end we have in view: there is another on which we may infallibly reckon; and that is our own spiritual advancement, an increase of personal merit, greater glory in heaven, and the highest honour to which a creature can aspire on earth, that of working for God. Besides, have *all* fallen who appeared to be reclaimed?" and on receiving an admission to the contrary, he added, "Then you ought to rest content. If your life served only to save one single soul, could it be better employed, seeing that the Son of God would have given His own life to save that soul, had it been the only one in the whole world?" The better, however, to secure the fruits of his labours, he entrusted his penitents to the care of the community which bore the well-known name of the *Madeleine*, and would himself have founded a similar institution in his own parish, but for the opposition he encountered from the persons on whose assistance he most relied, and who represented that such a foundation would be prejudicial to the establishments already in existence. In this, therefore, he had only the merit of the desire, without succeeding in his enterprise, and at the same time gave occasion to admire his exemplary patience and conformity to the will of God. When told that he must abandon his charitable project, he replied, "Ah, well, blessed be God! He is master; His holy will be done in all things."

After seven years of incessant toil, he had the consolation of seeing his parish almost entirely delivered from that open exhibition of profligacy which had been its foulest blot; but it was not without the endurance of great personal suffering and the infliction of much voluntary mortification. The sins and disorders of his people filled his heart with an abiding sorrow, and embittered every moment of his life. "I cannot understand," he would say, "how it is possible to love God, and not to grieve over the loss of souls." Often he would shut himself up in the church, and pass the whole night in prayer before the altar, imploring the Divine mercy for his flock; or he would lie on the floor of his chamber, giving vent to the anguish of his soul in audible sighs and groans; or, again, he would rise from his bed after two or three hours' sleep, and remain in prayer till morning. To this perseverance in supplication, he added the severest bodily austerities, punishing his flesh with pointed iron girdles, and disciplines so sharp and merciless, that the room in which he scourged himself would be found sprinkled with his blood. A charity so supernatural and heroic drew down extraordinary blessings on his people, and obtained the gift of repentance even for many inveterate sinners. One remarkable instance is related of his hearing for the first time of a certain notorious evil-liver, and saying Mass for his conversion; when, on the very same day, the man, suddenly seized with compunction, went to M. Olier, made his peace with God, and led ever after a good and exemplary life. Such, too, was the grace that accompanied his ministrations that, as we learn on the authority of M. de Bretonvilliers, out of all the numbers who were under his direction, or for whose conversion he had laboured, there were only two who died without giving signs of true contrition. The first was the Calvinist mentioned in the preceding chapter; the second was a girl twenty-two years of age, of abandoned character, who, struck down by a mortal illness, was brought in a few days to the brink of the grave. In spite of all his endeavours, his prayers, and his penances, and the prayers and exertions of the priests whom he called to his aid, she persisted in her obduracy, and died like one possessed by the devil, howling and blaspheming; her last act—horrible to say—being to spit on the crucifix which was held to her lips! So awful an event produced the deepest sensation in the parish, and the wretched creature was buried in unconsecrated ground, deprived in her death of all the rites of the Church, which in the closing moments of her life she had rejected and profaned. The loss of this soul seemed to strike the holy pastor with a sort of consternation; and for long after, his countenance and whole appearance gave tokens of the anguish that rent his heart.

The zeal of this great servant of God was no less conspicuously displayed in his unwearied efforts to preserve young and innocent girls from the arts of the seducer. If he became aware that there were any in danger of falling into sin, through the poverty or ill conduct of their parents, or their own inexperience and indiscretion, he never rested until he had relieved their necessities, or removed them to a place of security. And here he found a powerful coadjutor in the celebrated Madame Pollalion,* whose life was devoted to this and similar works of mercy. The numbers which are said to have been saved from destruction by their united exertions sufficiently prove the frightful prevalence of the evil against which they had to contend. Not content with interposing where his assistance was asked, he was indefatigable in detecting and defeating the machinations of the profligate and vicious. Learning one day that a miserable woman had agreed for a sum of money to deliver up her step-daughter to a wealthy libertine, and that the iniquitous bargain was to be concluded at a certain house which had been indicated to him, he obtained privately the protection of a guard, which he stationed at a convenient spot; then, going in company of Madame Pollalion to the house, he boldly confronted the infamous woman and her accomplice, and exposed their nefarious design in the presence of the intended victim, who, thus apprized of the plot contrived for her ruin, threw herself into the arms of Madame Pollalion, and begged to be conveyed to a place of safety. But when a soul's salvation was at stake M. Olier was reckless of danger, and would brave any insult or outrage to effect his charitable object. He was in his chamber one winter's evening when, hearing a tumult outside, and being told that it was occasioned by a party of soldiers who were carrying off a young girl, in an instant, without consulting his own safety, he rushed into the street and pursued the ravishers, who, astounded at the courage and resolution of one unarmed man, gave up their prey into his hands. On another occasion he followed a gang of ruffians as far as Montrouge for a similar purpose and with similar success. His wish was to establish a house of refuge, under the care of a religious community, where young females whose chastity was imperilled might receive the protection they

* A sketch of the life of this admirable woman is given in "The Heroines of Charity," published in this series.

needed, and be Christianly and virtuously brought up. Failing health, however, prevented the execution of this among many other charitable plans which he had devised, but was unable to carry into effect.

Finding that many were living as man and wife in the parish who had never been married, or that their marriages had not been validly solemnized, he employed the necessary measures for supplying whatever was defective, taking care, however, not to publish to the world the shame that had attached to their position, or the nullity of the previous contract. To prevent as far as possible similar abuses for the future, he drew up a paper of instructions, which he caused to be distributed among the people; and required that persons, before entering into the marriage state, should evince a sufficient knowledge of the principal articles of the faith, and approach the Holy Sacraments. From this obligation none were exempted, whatever their rank or station in life. The mother attended with her daughter, the intended bridegroom came alone; and M. du Ferrier says of himself, that finding that one of his penitents who was among the first lords about court, did not know his catechism, he directed him to learn it, and the young nobleman repeated his lesson with all the humility of a child. M. Olier solemnly admonished all fathers and mothers of families, as they would answer before God for their children's souls, to keep strict watch over their morals, himself suggesting the precautions to be taken against contamination, and assisting the poor to observe them. Unable to procure the discontinuance of the fair which, as already observed, was held for two months together in the *faubourg* S. Germain, he laboured to suppress its greatest enormities; as, for instance, the exhibition and exposure for sale of immodest pictures, and other incentives to impurity. Nor was he content with a mere official inspection, but conducted the inquiry in person, or by means of ecclesiastics appointed for the purpose; and when their interference was productive of no effect, he had recourse to the civil authorities, from whom, to their honour be it recorded, he always received prompt and efficient aid.

An incident which made some noise at the time may here be related. The head of a troop of strolling players, who were performing during the fair, fell dangerously ill, and desired to receive the last sacraments. The priest who attended him felt himself justified in giving him absolution, but refused to bring him the Holy Viaticum, on account of his profession, to which, as being dangerous to morals, a particular scandal attached. As the man grew worse, his friends came late at night to the presbytery, and begged again and again that their dying comrade might be permitted to receive communion; but M. Olier was inexorable. His refusal, which was conveyed in terms of the most earnest charity, had such an effect on one of the party, that two days afterwards, from motives of conscience, he retired from the stage altogether; and, to M. Olier's joy and consolation, the sick man himself, acknowledging his unworthiness to receive the boon he had solicited, solemnly engaged from that moment to renounce his profession for ever—a promise which, on recovering his health, he faithfully performed. The occurrence created considerable sensation in Paris, and the matter was discussed at the monthly meeting of the clergy, who unanimously approved the conduct of the ecclesiastic in question. Nevertheless, he deemed it advisable to advert to the circumstance from the pulpit, entering fully into the reasons which justified the course he had taken. It so happened that the manager of a company of actors, who styled himself *comedian* to the Duke of Orleans, was present at this discourse, and, offended at the same designation being applied to a mere strolling player, he went to the presbytery and made a formal remonstrance. He met with a most courteous reception, and was patiently listened to while he enlarged on the dignity of his profession, as compared with that of an itinerant buffoon who performed before a rabble in a booth; but all that was urged in return made no impression upon him, and he was about to retire with a profusion of compliments expressive of the high esteem in which he held so zealous a body of ecclesiastics, when, on his politely declaring that his services would ever be at their command, the ecclesiastic to whom he addressed himself took him at his word, and said that there was one thing he could do, by which he would infinitely oblige them. The actor again protested his readiness to do anything in his power. "Then," answered the other, "promise me that you will recite the Litany of the Blessed Virgin every day on your knees." The actor willingly consented, little thinking to what he was engaging himself; for in a few days he returned to the presbytery a changed man, declaring that he had once for all abandoned the stage, and was now in the service of M. de Fontenay Mareuil, who was proceeding as ambassador to Rome.

The great reputation which M. Olier now enjoyed, the order that reigned in his parish, and the general edification afforded by his community, brought him into close relations with all who, in his day, were remarkable for their virtues and zeal. It was in the year 1644 that he contracted an intimate and lasting friendship with M. Cretenet, who, though a surgeon by profession, and a married man, exercised an extraordinary influence in reanimating the devotion of the clergy, and became the founder of the Missionaries of S. Joseph. Such was the respect which M. Olier entertained for this good man, that in his frequent visits to the presbytery, he bade his ecclesiastics take him as their model. But a still more notable personage, and one whose name will always remain associated with that of M. Olier and the community of S. Sulpice, was Father Yvan, founder of the nuns of Notre Dame de la Miséricorde, whose acquaintance he made in the same year. Burning with zeal for the conversion of sinners, and gifted with extraordinary lights in the direction of souls, this celebrated man, now considerably advanced in years, led a life of severe austerity, which seemed to affect his whole manner and conversation. There was a certain roughness in his exterior and plainness in his speech which to men of the world must have borne the appearance of insufferable rudeness. He had a way of testing people's merits by taking them to task for some fault which he thought, or affected to think, he had observed in their conduct, and he subjected M. Olier to this ordeal the first time he saw him. Joining the community in the refectory, where the servant of God was taking his simple repast with the rest, F. Yvan kept his eyes fixed upon him, and after observing him awhile he said, as with an air of disappointment and disgust, "I am astonished at your want of self-denial; you eat your dinner with all the avidity of a glutton;" and he continued for some time in the same strain with the utmost freedom, adding whatever he thought most likely to irritate and provoke. M. Olier listened with all placidity and patience, and when the old man had said his worst, he thanked him unaffectedly for the charity which had led him to rebuke him so frankly for his faults, and promised, with God's help, to profit by his advice; "for, father," said he, "it is seldom one meets with friends who do not flatter, but speak the truth in love." While he was uttering these words, F. Yvan watched him narrowly, to judge by his features whether his speech expressed the genuine emotions of his heart; then, no longer withholding his admiration, he enthusiastically declared that M. Olier, while taking his ordinary repast, practised a mortification as real as the austerest anchorite; and such was the opinion which from that moment he entertained of his sanctity, that he was wont to say, "M. Olier is truly a saint: he is dead; nature is extinct in him." M. Olier, on his part, appreciated no less highly the virtues of his eccentric friend, and begged him to aid him by his counsels and co-operation in the establishment of the seminary. F. Yvan had come to Paris to claim some property that had been bequeathed to his institute, but seeing that a lawsuit was inevitable he relinquished his rights, and having thus effectually rid himself of worldly distractions, devoted all his energies to the seminary and parish of S. Sulpice.

M. Olier was emphatically the friend of the clergy; and in nothing was his charity more singularly displayed than in the kindness and liberality with which he received all, whether ecclesiastics or laymen, who came to make a spiritual retreat under his direction. The care and attention he paid them extended to every particular; and it was one of his invariable rules that their maintenance should be provided for at the sole expense of the community, although voluntary offerings were not refused. Many devout and holy men resorted to him for counsel; among others may be mentioned M. Jean Poincheval, who lived and died at Paris in the odour of sanctity, and of whom it is recorded that he scarcely ever left his chamber except to go to the altar or the confessional, or to visit the curé of S. Sulpice. Were any ecclesiastic aggrieved by the rich and powerful, M. Olier stood boldly forward in his defence, and never ceased his exertions until redress had been obtained. The curé of Arcueil, a man of the highest integrity, had been insulted, and indeed assaulted, at the very door of the church, in the presence of his flock, by the *seigneur* of the place. The Parliament of Paris took up the affair, but the parishioners, dreading the great man's vengeance, dared not make any formal deposition, and nothing would have been done had not M. Olier addressed an energetic appeal to all the bishops with whom he had any personal acquaintance, as well as to S. Vincent de Paul, who had been appointed a member of the Council of Conscience,[*] calling upon them to lay the matter before the Queen Regent, and in the name of religion and justice demand satisfaction for the outrage. It was but one instance, he declared, among many, in which, as was notorious, the *noblesse* presumed upon the impunity which their crimes enjoyed, to oppress and maltreat an unoffending priesthood. The general assembly of the clergy also, acting at his instance, presented an earnest remonstrance in the same influential quarter, and with such success, that the *seigneur* of the village was compelled to make public reparation for his violence.

[*] This council was instituted by Anne of Austria with the object of assisting the crown in the nomination of properly-qualified ecclesiastics to the highest offices in the Church. It consisted only of four members,—Cardinal Mazarin, the Chancellor Seguier, the Grand Penitentiary Charton, and Vincent de Paul.

CHAPTER XIII.

Attempt to expel M. Olier from S. Sulpice—Erection of the Seminary into a Community.

A GREAT work was doing, and great successes had been wrought, and a whole army as it were of auxiliaries had gathered about him, and he enjoyed the countenance and support of many in high places; but never for a moment was M. Olier deceived. He knew (for God had told him) that a heavy persecution awaited him, and that, ere three years had run their course, he should be driven with ignominy from his parish; but he knew also that, whatever might be his personal sufferings, the trial would serve only to bring about the accomplishment of his designs. Even thus far his path had been anything but smooth, or free from contradictions, and a host of foes beset him on every side. To establish the seminary on a firm foundation, it was necessary that it should be erected into a community, and the Abbé of S. Germain, who had conceived a prejudice against the projected institution, refused his consent. His zeal, too, had raised up many adversaries among the great and powerful, who openly or covertly threw obstacles in his way. Several of the old clergy also, who had never forgiven him for disturbing their self-indulgent ease, caballed against him; the churchwardens, some of whom were of the highest rank,[*] thwarted and opposed him; many of the civil magistrates resented his interference and the constraint he had laid upon them by obliging them to fulfil duties to which they were wholly disinclined; finally, and above all, the libertines of the parish, who were bent on his destruction, only awaited an opportunity to wreak their

[*] For instance, Gaston, Duke of Orleans, and the Princes Henri and Louis de Condé.

meditated vengeance. But in the midst of these alarms he possessed his soul in peace, convinced that to indulge his natural fears and misgivings, and speculate on what would become of him if his enemies were triumphant, was displeasing to God, who would have him look simply to the present, and repose in confidence on His Providence for the disposition of the future. So, like his Divine Master, he continued to fulfil the mission with which he was intrusted, embracing willingly in his heart all the shame and suffering which he knew was fast coming upon him.

It had become necessary to erect additional buildings for the increasing number of seminarists, and it was with difficulty he could obtain from the Abbé of S. Germain and the churchwardens permission to construct three tenements in the garden of the presbytery at his own entire expense, even on the condition that they should form part of the domain and afford accommodation to the lay persons employed about the church. The works were already in progress when, on Monday, March 22nd, 1645, going as was his wont to lay his plans before his august patroness in the Cathedral of Notre Dame, and obtain her approval, he was rapt in an ecstacy, and beheld the Blessed Mother of God standing before him and bearing in her hands the model of an edifice much larger in extent than that which he was intending to construct. Obedient to the heavenly vision, he immediately stopped the works, and waited until Providence should enable him to obtain a site where he might raise a building which should remain in his own possession, and for which he might have all possible security that it would be devoted for ever to the purpose for which he destined it. Such a site presented itself in a piece of ground belonging to one of his friends, M. Méliand, procureur-général of the Parliament of Paris, and situated in the Rue du Vieux Colombier, in close proximity to the church of S. Sulpice. It was a large inclosed garden, containing three tenements, to which he at once transferred a number of students, both from Vaugirard and from the presbytery, until the larger building which he contemplated could be erected. The purchase was completed May 27th in the same year by M. Olier in conjunction with M. de Poussé and M. Damien, at their sole personal expense; the sum paid being 75,000 livres.

No sooner was it known that he had relinquished the design agreed upon, and was meditating a more extensive undertaking, than he was assailed with a storm of ridicule and reproaches; but his reply was always the same: "He who has begun the work will in His own time bring it to a conclusion; we must not distrust the mercy of God." Seeing, however, how implacable was the hatred of his enemies, and not knowing to what extremities their violence might carry them, he, on the 2nd of May, being the feast of S. Athanasius, repaired with M. de Poussé and M. Damien to Montmartre; and there, in the presence of F. Bataille, they renewed the solemn engagement which they had before made, never to abandon the work of the Seminary, and at the same time made an entire surrender to God, for His sole use and service, both of the ground and of the buildings they had purchased, renouncing all right and ownership in them, although of necessity retaining the nominal possession of them. Yet with all his unwavering confidence in God, and despite the supernatural peace which reigned undisturbed in the depths of his soul, he was not insensible to the unceasing opposition he encountered, and feelings of sadness would at times weigh heavily on his soul. On the 25th of May especially, being the Feast of the Ascension, he was thus cast down and dispirited, when an interior voice said to him,—"Thy work shall stand." "Not mine, Lord," he answered; "the work is wholly Thine;" but the words, as he says, filled his heart with light and joy, and he knew that God accepted him as the servant of those whom by His grace He should bring into the Seminary.

The three years of promised quiet had now all but expired; already in the month of January, two devout persons had foretold to M. de Bretonvilliers the approaching persecution, and from time to time M. Olier would himself speak to his more intimate associates of some great trial which was in store for them, bidding them hold themselves prepared, and beg fervently the assistance of God's Holy Spirit that they might be able to bear the cross He was about to lay upon them. So far, therefore, from losing confidence when the storm burst, they did but see in it a fulfilment of his words, and were the more encouraged to believe that the blessing of Heaven rested on him. The first rising of the tempest showed itself in a quarter whence it was least of all expected. The relatives of the former curé, irritated at seeing a stranger in possession of a benefice to which they considered that one of their own number had a prior claim, sought to have M. Olier expelled from the parish; but finding all their efforts fruitless, they endeavoured to make M. de Fiesque himself a party to their design. They represented to him that the abbey he had received in exchange was of far less value than he had a right to expect; that his simplicity had been imposed upon, and that his honour no less than his interest demanded that he should be reinstated. These representations were loudly seconded by such of the old clergy as disliked the reforms introduced by M. Olier; they assured M. de Fiesque that since his removal nothing but disorder and confusion had prevailed, and that in relinquishing his parish he had deserted and ruined his flock. The poor man, who was naturally both weak and credulous, thus beset by false friends, fell readily into the trap; and utterly forgetting that the exchange had been effected, not only at his own repeated instances, but on the very terms he had been the first to propose, allowed himself to be cajoled into a belief that he had been deceived and ill treated. There were circumstances, too, at the time which unhappily lent a colour to his complaints. The Abbey of Clisson, which originally belonged to the Benedictines of S. Jovin, had in the year 1626 been converted into a simple benefice by an arrangement between M. Olier's father and the monks, and from that date had been occupied by four secular priests, who performed all the offices of the church. The monks, however, now wished to rescind, or rather to ignore the arrangement to which they had been parties nearly twenty years before, and in vindication of their pretended rights, had sent two of their body to take possession of the abbey under the titles respectively of sub-prior and sacristan. They had further deputed a chaplain to reside within the walls, as though the benefice were vacant; and all this without opposition or even protest on the part of M. de Fiesque. Their next step was to obtain the royal authorization for their acts; and the judges who were commissioned to inquire into the case had ruled that the abbey was to all intents and purposes a conventual establishment; relying for their conclusion merely on the fact that such had been its ancient constitution, as was evident from the very disposition of the buildings. Accordingly they seized the revenues in the name of the religious, and pronounced them to be entitled to all arrears of rents since the date of the alleged secularization. It was at this juncture that M. de Fiesque was induced to publish his formal case of grievance against M. Olier, in which he set forth that he had been surprised into an act of resignation which in law as well as in equity was null and void, and had been fraudulently put in possession of a benefice in place thereof, from which he had been ejected by the monks of S. Jovin, with the express warrant of the crown.

It may be conceived with what undisguised joy and exultation a charge so gross and scandalous was received by M. Olier's enemies, who felt that they could now proceed against him with some show of justice, and even of legality. By the side of M. de Fiesque's friends and abettors arose another faction, indefinitely more violent in its character, and bent on far more desperate measures. It was composed of libertines and profligates of both sexes, who, infuriated by the perseverance with which this good pastor pursued them to their most secret haunts, were determined to be satisfied with nothing short of his expulsion, and that of his whole community. Their numbers were swelled by a multitude of grooms and lackeys, a race notorious for their disorderly conduct and ready for any outrage. In less than a week

CHAP. XIII.] ATTACK ON THE PRESBYTERY.

both parties were fully prepared, and it only remained that they should join forces, and appeal to the passions of the mob, to excite a popular commotion which may be said to have served as a prelude to the barricades of the Fronde, and the civil war that followed.

It was early on the morning of the 8th of June, 1645, being Thursday in Whitsun week, that M. du Four, a gentleman attached to the household of the Duke of Orleans, came to apprize M. Olier of the formidable conspiracy which was being organized against him, tidings which were speedily confirmed by another person, who assured him that an immediate attack was threatened, and that if he remained in the presbytery it would be at the certain peril of his life. The only use he made of this warning was to prepare himself, not to avert, but to meet the approaching trial. He repaired to the church as usual in his surplice, and said Mass, offering himself in union with the Adorable Victim to drink the bitter draught for which he had so long thirsted. It was about eight o'clock when he returned, and he had scarcely entered the house when it was besieged by a furious crowd, shouting that they had come to expel the intruder and restore the rightful pastor. M. de Bretonvilliers, who presented himself at the window, was struck on the head by a paving-stone, which, however only slightly injured him; and before the doors either of the church or of the presbytery could be secured, some of the foremost of the rabble had made good their entrance, and were busy pillaging or destroying whatever fell in their way. At the first sounds of the tumult below, M. Olier had thrown himself on his knees, and was repeating the words of his Lord,—" If it be possible, let this chalice pass from me: nevertheless, not as I will, but as Thou wilt,"—when a party of ruffians, headed (with shame be it recorded) by one of the former clergy of the parish, burst into his chamber, seized him violently, dragged him downstairs, showering upon him kicks and blows, and bore him, or rather threw him, out into the midst of the excited multitude, who received him with yells of derision.

Holding a loaded pistol to his head, his assailants now carried him through the neighbouring streets, his surplice and cassock hanging about him in tatters, amidst the hootings of the mob, who continued to heap upon him every manner of insult and outrage. S. Vincent de Paul, informed of what was occurring, hurried to the spot, and, regardless of the danger he incurred, strove to penetrate through the crowd to the rescue of his friend. He was no sooner recognized by the rabble than, forgetting the inestimable services his charity had rendered to the poor of the capital, and seeing in him only the adviser and supporter of their obnoxious pastor, they refused to let him pass, and assailed him with menaces and blows, while he, good, generous man, offered to all their violence the opposition only of a most enduring patience, and continued crying, with that imperturbable good humour which never deserted him,—" Strike S. Lazarus as hard as you please, but spare S. Sulpice." At length those who had hold of M. Olier, fearing to lose their share of the plunder, left him in the hands of the populace, when a number of his friends, who had mingled with the crowd, took advantage of the movement to draw more closely about him, and affecting to treat him as a public criminal, contrived to screen him from the blows that were levelled at him, and to convey him in safety to the palace of the Luxembourg. Meanwhile the rioters were carrying off or destroying the furniture of the house, laying hands on any money or valuables they could find, appropriating even the provisions of the community, and when they had sufficiently gratified their vengeance and their cupidity abandoned the place to the fury of the mob. Some, however, who amidst all the frantic excitement had not forgotten the original cause of offence, set about walling up two openings in the inclosure of the garden, which had been made to facilitate the conveyance of materials for the intended building; and as there was no mortar at hand, they supplied its place by staving in the heads of some casks of wine and making a mixture of earth and plaster.

In the Luxembourg, the man of God was received with

all the respect and consideration due to his exalted virtues. The Maréchale d'Estampes entertained him in her own apartments, and lavished on him every attention which his situation demanded. M. de Bretonvilliers, who hastened to join his friend, in a state of the greatest anxiety and alarm, was amazed at finding him as calm and self-possessed as if nothing had happened. But that which impressed him most was his extraordinary humility and charity. While others were reprobating the conduct of his enemies in no qualified terms, M. Olier, on the contrary, spoke of them with so much moderation and affection, and suggested so many excuses for the violence with which they had treated him, that M. de Bretonvilliers could not forbear bidding him, in a whisper, be more cautious what he said, lest in his wish to exculpate others he should make himself out to be the guilty party. But the man of God merely smiled, and continued to speak lightly of the whole matter, and to impute the best intentions to all who were concerned. "Ah! wretched man that I am," he said, "it is I who by my infidelity throw all these hinderances in the way of God's work: my unworthiness is the sole cause of them all."

The parish was now left without a pastor, and the presbytery remained in the possession of the mob. For the next two days the services of the church were interrupted, and even the Viaticum was carried to the sick without any ceremony or other outward demonstration, for fear of outrage. M. Olier now, in conjunction with the churchwardens and certain of the more influential parishioners, preferred a formal petition to the Council of State to be restored to his *cure*. The Abbé of S. Germain supported the application, but it was coldly received by the Council, many of the members of which were incensed against M. Olier, whom they regarded as the cause of the tumult, while others threw the whole blame on S. Vincent de Paul, whom, because the priests of S. Sulpice were popularly called Missionaries, they erroneously supposed to be M. Olier's superior. Fearing, moreover, that the authority of the Regent might be compromised in public estimation if its judgment failed in allaying the excitement, the Council, on the day after the events just related, referred the whole matter to the decision of the Parliament. And now commenced a species of contest, which, viewed in the light of our modern ideas, must appear passing strange. As soon as it was known that the determination of the affair was left to Parliament, the enemies of M. Olier began to convass the judges to his prejudice; and Prince Henri de Condé himself went down to the assembly, and inveighed with so much violence against him, that it was feared his harangue would have an ill effect upon those who were most disposed to look simply to the justice of the case. On the other hand, the Princesse de Condé interested herself with equal zeal and warmth in his behalf, and, accompanied by the Duchesse d'Aiguillon and other ladies of rank, visited all the judges in succession, and pleaded his cause as earnestly as if he had been one of her own relatives. To crown all, the Queen Regent went in person to solicit the favour of Parliament for the pastor of S. Sulpice.

All these proceedings were viewed by M. Olier with the same reference to the supernatural in which he loved to regard every event of his life. "In the person of the Prince, who stands in the place of the King, God (said he) would manifest His anger against me; while in those who defend my cause, I seem to see the most Holy Virgin, the advocate of sinners, who has made them partakers of her charity and pity. S. Anne, again, to whom I have been in the habit of confiding my temporal affairs, displays her goodness towards me in the person of the Queen. But for the pleadings of these ladies with my judges, who represent the justice of God, there would have been no peace for me." According to the practice of the time, he went to lay the facts of his case before those who were to decide upon them, and as he passed Nòtre Dame on his way to the Parliament, he begged his companion to allow him a few minutes, as usual, for prayer. Then, throwing himself on his knees before the shrine of Our Lady, he remained two hours immovable, absorbed in devotion. To be eager about the success of affairs, and to trust to the influence or the assistance of men, he regarded as an infidelity to God, and more likely than otherwise to ruin even a good cause; and he was used to say, that in times of particular anxiety and trial we ought to be the more diligent in prayer, not only to obtain the strength and courage we need, but also to prevent our having recourse to creatures, and throwing ourselves upon them; seeing that nature, when deprived of heavenly consolations, is so prone to seek for such as are merely human. A friend, who wished to recommend him to the favour of one of the chief magistrates, asked him in what terms he should speak of those who were bringing the falsest charges against him. "Say," he replied, "that I am under the deepest obligations to them;" and on the other refusing to take such an answer, as being contrary to the truth, he repeated, "the deepest obligations;" adding, "for they help me in gaining Paradise."

The Parliament assembled on Saturday, and happily for M. Olier, one of the judges most opposed to him, and whose influence it was feared would gain many others over to his opinion, withdrew the same day into the country, under the idea that M. Olier would follow him, with the hope of disarming his opposition. But this shortsighted stroke of policy, which was intended to humble the servant of God, served only to secure his triumph. In the absence of this important personage, the Parliament ordered that M. de Fiesque should appear before them in person, that instant measures should be taken to seize the ringleaders in the late outrage, four individuals being designated by name, one of whom was the ecclesiastic before mentioned, and that unless they surrendered in three days, their goods should be confiscated. It was at the same time ordered that, without prejudicing the rights of either claimant, things should be restored to the state in which they were previous to the outbreak; that, consequently, M. Olier should be reinstated in the presbytery, and those who were in occupation should forthwith depart. The order was at once executed, and two functionaries of the law put M. Olier and his priests in possession of both the house and the church, taking, at the same time, what they conceived to be adequate measures to insure the public tranquillity, and the safety of the pastor and his community.

Scarcely had these proceedings been concluded when the tumult recommenced with even greater violence than before. The house was again besieged by an armed multitude, gathered from the lowest quarters, and exasperated to the utmost fury by the tidings that the object of their hatred had been brought back in triumph, and that their own leaders were marked out for the vengeance of the law. Baffled in their efforts to force in the doors, which this time were strongly secured and defended from the inside, they heaped up faggots against them and sought to set them on fire; but failing in this attempt also, their next endeavours were directed to gaining an entrance through the adjoining garden. But here again they were met by an insuperable obstacle in the result of their own labours on occasion of the former riot, when they had industriously closed up two apertures in the wall by which an easy access might now have been obtained. The struggle continued for three hours, and the little garrison, hard pressed and well-nigh exhausted, was on the point of yielding, when, just as a body of the assailants had all but succeeded in setting fire to the building, a company of the royal guards appeared on the spot, sent by the queen, whom M. Picoté, at the risk of his life, had hastened to inform of the pressing danger. At the first sound of the drums, the rioters took to flight, and thus, to the joy of M. Olier and his colleagues, all effusion of blood was spared. The Parliament, apprized of what was passing, held an extraordinary meeting, and officers of justice were at once dispatched with orders to seize all persons whom they should find collected in the streets, a proclamation to the same effect was read in the public places, and a detachment of soldiers left at the presbytery for the protection of the clergy.

Throughout the whole contest, M. Olier would not

permit his ecclesiastics to employ any other weapons of defence than that of prayer; and even when the peril was greatest, his calmness and equanimity remained unaltered. "The cross," said he, "ought never to deprive us of our peace, for it is the cross that gave peace to the world." The next day, which was Trinity Sunday, he appeared in the pulpit, and preached to the people with his usual dignity, affection, and zeal; in eloquence he seemed even to surpass himself. There was nothing either in voice or manner to indicate what humiliations he had endured, or through what dangers he had passed, since he last addressed them. And yet an incident occurred which, slight as it was in itself, might have disturbed a man of stronger nerves, aware, as he was, of the excitement that prevailed. For some time past it had been the practice to have the blessing of the water before the first High Mass on the Sunday, in order that the second might follow immediately, without unnecessary delay. While he was preaching, an old woman stood up in her place, and with a quavering, tremulous voice, began to accuse him of depriving the people of their holy water; then, emboldened by the silence that ensued, she proceeded to give her opinion freely on other changes he had made, and having administered, as she thought, a fitting rebuke to her pastor, she looked about her for applause, and sat down again. M. Olier let her have her talk out without interrupting her, and when he saw she was fairly settled in her place, he said quietly, "Ah, well, my good friend, we will think about it." He then resumed his discourse as though nothing had happened. His colleagues would fain have dissuaded him from venturing outside the doors, for fear of endangering his life: but this good

who were deeply alarmed when they were made aware of his absence. He found the sick person in a state of unconsciousness, but in spite of the representations of her friends, who assured him she was not in a condition to communicate, he sent to the church to have the Blessed Sacrament brought forthwith. Then, taking in his hands the Body of his Lord, he, in accents which expressed the fervour and confidence of his faith, bade the fever leave her, and permit her to receive the Holy Eucharist; and, turning to the sufferer, he asked her whether she desired to communicate. To the astonishment of all, the apparently dying woman returned to consciousness, replied in the affirmative, and communicated; and so pleasing to God were His servant's faith and courage, that they seemed to have obtained the cure of the sick woman, for she immediately rallied, and was soon perfectly restored to health.

M. Olier's enemies were far from being discouraged by the resistance they had encountered, and on Trinity Sunday all Paris was astonished by a public demonstration, such as probably it had never before witnessed. This was no other than a procession of the abandoned women of the *faubourg* S. Germain and the neighbourhood, three hundred in number, going to demand of the house of Orleans the expulsion of the pastor of S. Sulpice, as an intermeddler in the people's affairs, and a disturber of the public peace. They had tricked themselves out in their gayest attire, and thought they should be able to pass for ladies of distinction, whose presence must command respect. The *ruse*, as may be supposed, was too gross to succeed, but it served to exhibit the true character of M. Olier's opponents, and the audacious extremities to which they were prepared to go. Nothing disconcerted, however, by the contempt and indignation which the attempt had excited at the Luxembourg and among all respectable citizens, the miserable creatures resolved to try their influence with the Parliament. On the Monday there was to be a *Te Deum* at Nôtre Dame, on occasion of the taking of Roses in Spain, by the Count du Plessis-Praslin, and all the members of the Parliament, with the king and the royal princes, were to assist at it. On entering the hall of the palace, the magistrates found it well-nigh filled with a strange assemblage of women and others, who received them with clamours and menaces. Indignant at the insult offered to them in the very sanctuary of justice, they ordered the hall to be cleared, and issued a decree on the spot, denouncing the authors of this fresh outrage, interdicting all public gatherings, and prohibiting all persons, at the peril of their lives, from coming to the hall of assembly in a larger number than four together, under any pretext whatever. At the same time, all who had been concerned in the late demonstration were ordered to retire at once to their homes, under penalty of being treated as enemies of the state without form of trial; and all officers of justice were directed to inflict summary punishment on such as violated the terms of this decree.

Measures so determined and severe had the effect of preventing any disturbance by day, but as more than one attack was made on the presbytery during the night, it was found necessary to obtain the protection of an armed patrol until all fear of danger was removed. The feast of Corpus Christi was now approaching, and M. Olier, fearing that if he carried the Blessed Sacrament through the streets, the malcontents might be provoked to the perpetration of some sacrilegious outrage, delegated the office to the Apostolic nuncio, Mgr. Bagni, Archbishop of Athens, himself bearing the humble part of an assistant. For better security, however, the procession was escorted by a guard of soldiers. The irritation caused by the late events was not speedily abated. His more moderate opponents, who condemned the violence of the mob, bore their defeat before the Parliament with evident displeasure, and still hoped that by continual vexations they might oblige him to resign his *cure*. With such, ridicule was the favourite weapon; and a certain prince, whose name is not given, had the ill grace to offer M. Olier a public insult; the only effect of which was to fill his heart with gratitude towards one who had furnished him with an occasion of imitating his Master's patience when mocked by Herod and his court. Towards his personal enemies he manifested not merely a kindly forbearance but a most tender charity. Hearing that M. de Fiesque was on the point of being arrested at the instance of a powerful person whom he had offended, he hastened to intercede in his favour, and with such success that all further proceedings were stayed. So far, too, from pressing the execution of the parliamentary decrees against the authors of the tumult, he sought to obtain the liberation of those who were in custody; and on being remonstrated with for such mistaken leniency, he replied: "Jesus Christ forgave His murderers, and prayed for them; and these, thanks be to God, have not proceeded thus far: what they did to me was nothing. Grant that they bore me some ill will, yet, after all, are they not my children? God gave them to me, and by the help of His grace I will try to have towards them the heart of a father. David would have no evil done to his son, although he sought his kingdom and his life; and these had no such intention towards me. Ah! if their salvation depended on the sacrifice of my life, and God enabled me to retain the desire of their eternal good which I now feel, they would all be sure of attaining to the joys of Paradise." Learning that one of his most violent assailants had been thrown into prison he went to visit him, and though the man received him with the utmost scorn and insolence, he continued to treat him as though he were his dearest friend; and at length, by repeated solicitations, obtained for him the royal pardon. He continued to evince the same interest in him after he was set free, and when increasing infirmities prevented his paying him any personal attention he charged M. de Bretonvilliers to show him every kindness. So, too, he gratified the charitable feelings of his heart by assisting another of his worst enemies during his last illness, and disposing him for a holy death. In short, so many and so striking were the instances of the care and affection he bestowed on those who had borne a prominent part in the persecution against him, that it became a common saying in the parish, that if you wanted to receive any favour from M. Olier, the surest way to obtain it was to do him an injury.

Although, after a while, the agitation in men's minds began sensibly to subside, many of M. Olier's friends, seeing the determination of his opponents, and alarmed for his personal safety, endeavoured to persuade him to leave the parish. They represented to him the difficulties he would have to encounter, and the impossibility of establishing his seminary without the consent of the authorities and in defiance of his numerous opponents. He replied, " We ought never to abandon God's work on account of opposition; on the contrary, opposition ought to increase our courage. If we care for contradictions, we shall never do anything for God. Is not the cross inseparable from all the works of which He is the author? In no other way did Jesus Christ establish His Church, and in no other way can we hope to effect anything. Let the world and the devil fret as they may: cannot He who has hitherto vanquished them continue still to triumph over them? I have undertaken this work only for His glory, and I will abandon it only when I know that such is His will." The queen engaged S. Vincent de Paul to compose the difference with the former curé, but even his sweetness and moderation could not conquer M. de Fiesque's obstinacy. There seemed no hope of accommodation, when Mgr. de Corneillan, Bishop of Rodez, pressed M. Olier to accept his see, which it was his wish, with the queen's express approval, to resign in his favour. Everything seemed to render such a step desirable, and his friends redoubled their solicitations. His reply was still the same, that the very difficulties on which they grounded their appeal were only a stronger reason for his remaining bound to his church; that even to be overwhelmed by the weight of a burden which the Divine Goodness lays upon us, is to die a glorious death, seeing that we perish in doing the will of God. His friends then insisted on the greater means which, as a bishop, he would have at his command for promoting the glory of God; to which he replied in these most admirable words: "Not the service we may render our neighbour, nor the excellence of the works we perform, nor even the sight of the good we may do in the Church, ought to be the rule of our conduct; but simply the will of God, to which we ought to adhere solely and unalterably. Though I should be certain of working miracles; though I should see at my disposal the means of undertaking the greatest works for the Church, and the utmost facility of succeeding; though even in performing them I should make myself the greatest of all the saints,—I would never undertake them except so far as it was the will of God. And if I were assured of His will, I would not apply myself to them for the sake either of the greatness of the works themselves or of the glory to be reaped in heaven, which are not the most perfect rules of our conduct, but because it was the will of my Master, which alone I wish ever to do."

The will of God: and might it not be the will of God that he should resign the charge of S. Sulpice? Might not God have put it in the heart of M. de Corneillan to relinquish his see in his favour? To know the will of God, it had ever been his wont to submit implicitly to the judgment of superiors, even when that judgment was directly opposed to his own assurances of the will of Heaven. He resolved, accordingly, to refer the matter simply and absolutely to the decision of the abbé of S. Germain. Going to him, therefore, he said, that if his services were agreeable to him, he would continue to devote them to the salvation of the flock with which he was intrusted, and would think no more of the bishopric of Rodez; but that if, on the contrary, he did not deem him a fitting person to have the charge of the parish of S. Sulpice, he would at once withdraw; his sole object being to fulfil the designs of Providence, and this he should be doing by submitting to his judgment as his superior. Hitherto (as we have seen) the abbé had been opposed to M. Olier's projects, but Henri de Bourbon, with all his faults, was open to generous impulses, and a disinterestedness so genuine filled him with admiration. He begged M. Olier, very earnestly, not to think of resigning, promised him his protection, and engaged to assist him to the utmost in establishing his seminary. A result so unexpected struck M. Olier's friends with astonishment, and they could not but admire the Providence of God, which had made the persecution which was designed for his overthrow, the very means of accomplishing the great work he had at heart. The difficulties they had made so much of had vanished in a moment, and the confidence of God's servant was justified in the sight of all the world.

About the same time, the dispute with M. de Fiesque was definitively concluded, yet not without prolonged negotiations, and then not so much through the force of justice as by the generosity with which M. Olier returned good for evil. M. de Fiesque, before all things, insisted on his resuming the priory of Clisson; he next demanded, not a pension of 1,000 crowns, as in 1642, but a clear income of 10,000 livres, as an indemnification for the alleged wrong that had been done him. M. Olier's friends would have dissuaded him from acceding to a proposal so unreasonable, which was tantamount to a demand for the whole revenue of his *cure*. But he replied, " If Jesus Christ bids us give our cloak to him who asks us for our coat, why should we not deprive ourselves of something for one who makes an excessive and unreasonable demand? Besides, money ought to weigh as nothing with us where the interests of Jesus are concerned." The proposal, therefore, was accepted, and the contract signed July 20th, 1645; and now arose a contest of generosity among his friends, who should strip themselves of their benefices to provide M. de Fiesque with the stipulated income. But that gentleman was not to be easily satisfied; several benefices were resigned in his favour, and at last the offer of the well-endowed priory of Gondon appeared to have contented him. It was made without the knowledge of its owner, M. Barrault, nephew of the archbishop of Arles, who, on being told of the arrangement that had been made, was overjoyed at the confidence reposed in him, and reckoned it amongst the truest tokens of regard which his friends could have shown him. It was two years, however, before the affair was finally concluded.

It was now also that the affair of the Abbey of Pébrac was finally settled. Two years before, M. Olier had endeavoured to re-establish the primitive rule, and for this purpose had sent M. Corbeil, one of the community, who was deeply versed in the direction of souls, to take the habit as a novice, and prepare the inmates for the contemplated reform; but his efforts had proved utterly fruitless. M. Olier then resolved to cede the abbey to S. Vincent de Paul, that it might become a residence for his Missionary Priests, who should labour in Auvergne, and the neighbouring parts; and he had commenced negotiations with the religious which promised success, when this plan likewise was entirely frustrated by the opposition of the prior, who affected to be actuated by a desire to embrace the reform of S. Geneviève, but who, when it came to the point, proposed conditions in every way so extraordinary* that the authorities refused to sanction the arrangement. M. Corbeil had consequently returned; and M. Olier now exchanged the abbey for that of Cercanceau, in the diocese of Sens, a benefice of less value, with the object of making some compensation to Mgr. Vialar, Bishop of Châlons, for the sacrifices that prelate had made in his behalf in the matter of M. de Fiesque. It was his hope that Mgr. Vialar would be able to introduce the reforms of S. Geneviève, which in fact was accomplished three years later. To this end M. Olier enlarged its revenues, and raised the number of the monks from eighteen, to which his father had reduced it, to twenty-one, as fixed by the ancient constitutions. The servant of God ever considered that in the troubles that had come upon him at S. Sulpice he was bearing the chastisement of his father's fault, committed

---

* As, for instance, that each of the monks should have a key of the church and of the cloister, with the liberty of going in and out at pleasure, subject to no control.

inadvertently, and by the advice of indifferent casuists, in procuring him the preferment on conditions not strictly canonical.*

The humiliations that had befallen him were not of a nature to soften his proud mother's heart, and her vexation found its usual vent in taunts and reproaches. Yet he was not the less assiduous in visiting her from time to time, and the modest expression of his countenance, when in her presence, was a sufficient indication, remarks M. de Bretonvilliers, of the filial respect which he entertained for her—a respect all the more sincere and deep as it had a religious root, for in honouring his mother he felt that he was showing reverence, not merely to an earthly parent, but to the Majesty of the Eternal God. It was his delight to speak to her of our Blessed Lord, and he sought every opportunity to turn her thoughts to the saving of her soul. As this is the last occasion on which her name is mentioned, it will be interesting to the reader to learn that she was attended on her deathbed by her saintly son, although at the time he was himself afflicted with the malady which soon terminated his life, and in a state that required the most considerate care.

At length, on the 23rd of October, 1645, M. Olier had the satisfaction of seeing the Seminary of S. Sulpice erected into an ecclesiastical community, M. de Poussé and M. Damien being associated with himself in the formal act of association.

---

* "The memory of M. Olier," writes the Abbé Faillon, "is still held in benediction by the inhabitants of Pébrac. They show the chamber in the abbey which was occupied by the servant of God, and which has been converted into an oratory. On a little turret, at the entrance of the courtyard, his arms are still to be seen, a circumstance which would seem to indicate that it, or at least some portion of the edifice adjoining, was erected by him. This was probably anterior to the establishment of Vaugirard; for from that time he ceased to use the arms of his family, and substituted in their place the monograms of Jesus, Mary, and Joseph."

CHAPTER XIV.

M. Olier's influence in the world.

M. OLIER resumed the labours of his parish with renewed energies of mind and body, and the humiliations he had so recently undergone seemed to enhance the general respect, or rather veneration, with which he was regarded. The piety of the people responded to the zeal of the pastor. His sermons found an echo in the hearts of his hearers, and were productive of extraordinary fruits; all the offices of devotion were largely attended, and the number of penitents increased with such rapidity, that it became necessary to obtain the services of additional priests. The church could not contain the multitudes that sought admittance, and on Sundays and festivals especially the building was so densely crowded that many of the parishioners were unable to reach their places, and permission was given to the Count and Countess of Brienne, and other persons of consideration, to enter by a private door, which was constructed for the purpose.

We have seen that from his first entrance on his *cure*, he had in contemplation to erect a new parish church; and on the Feast of the Assumption, 1645, he convened a meeting, at which he laid before his people the plan of a building three times larger than the existing structure. Hopeless as it might appear that so vast a design should ever be realized, he was not deterred by any consideration of the difficulties to be encountered in raising the necessary funds; and instead of regulating the cost of the building by the amount already collected, he fixed his estimate of the expenses at such a sum as in his judgment the charity of the parishioners ought ultimately to furnish. The plan was accepted and endorsed, and on Tuesday, February, 20th, 1646, the first stone of the new edifice was laid by the Queen Regent, after it had been blessed by M. Alain de Solminihac, now Bishop of Cahors, with all the accustomed formalities. The Regent, on inspecting the plan, desired that one of the chapels behind the high altar, nearest to that of the Blessed Virgin, should be dedicated to her patroness, S. Anne; and another, in the name of the young king, to S. Louis. The Duke of Orleans, and the Prince of Condé, made similar requests—an example that was followed by other noble families of the *faubourg;* the former also promised an annual donation of 10,000 livres until the building should be completed. M. Olier, however, did not rely on the favour or the munificence of the great; and an incident that occurred soon after the works had commenced, he took as a warning not to reckon on the support or promises of men for the success of an undertaking intended for God's glory alone. The workmen had dug a well to obtain water, and he was proceeding to ascertain its depth, when a pole on which he set his foot moved away, and rolled over to the opposite side, carrying him with it, to the astonishment of those who were present, and who expected to see him precipitated into the pit. Instead of manifesting any alarm at the danger he had so narrowly escaped, he seemed to be occupied with this one consideration:—" So deceitful is the dependence on creatures; he who puts his trust in them will find only weakness and frailty." His intention, after laying the foundations of the choir, was to complete the construction of Our Lady's chapel, but owing to the troubles of the Fronde he was able to finish only the walls, and those of the choir, which in the year of his death were raised to the height at which they remain at the present day. The building, which was interrupted for many years, was resumed in 1718, by M. Languet de Gergy,* M. Olier's

---

* This worthy pastor was a man of extraordinary charity. In 1725, during a time of great scarcity, he sold his furniture, his paintings, and a quantity of rare and valuable objects, which he had been at great pains to collect, and gave the proceeds for the relief of the suffering poor. From that time his only possessions were

sixth successor, by whom it was completed in 1745, just a century from the date of the attempt to expel the servant of God from the parish.

Aware that the new parish church would not be completed for many years, M. Olier exerted himself to procure the erection of a chapel of ease, which was dedicated to S. Anne, and solemnly consecrated on the Feast of the Purification, 1648. At the same time the approval of the Abbé of S. Germain was obtained for creating a new parish, under the title of S. Maur, in the Pré-aux-Clercs, which was served by the Priests of the Community of S. Sulpice.

Never was pastor more devoted to the interests of his flock. There is nothing, perhaps, of which an active-minded, hard-worked man is naturally more jealous than his time; yet M. Olier was always at the disposal of others. With all his multifarious avocations, he was always accessible to those who sought his counsel or assistance; and such was his sweetness and kindliness of disposition, that he could not bear to deny himself even to those who seemed to wish to converse with him solely for their own gratification. He received all comers with a certain respect, blended with humility, never betrayed any movement of impatience at being detained from his other occupations, and was never the first to terminate the interview. Sometimes when, towards the end of the day, his colleagues observed that he was exhausted with fatigue, they would suggest that he should admit no more visitors until the morrow; but he would answer, " Our time is not our own; it belongs to Jesus Christ. We ought to employ every moment of it as He directs; and since He permits these persons to come to us now, so far from not admitting them, we ought, in a spirit of submission to His adorable providence, to receive them with joy and affection." A

---

three *couverts* of silver, two straw chairs, and a bed of coarse serge, which was left him as a loan, to prevent his giving it away; carpets he had none. He also sent large sums to Marseilles, when in 1720 the plague was ravaging that city. The Abbé Languet was Mme. de Maintenon's confessor.

charity so self-sacrificing was accompanied with a sensible blessing; for many who were leading a sinful, worldly life, and who visited him simply from motives of courtesy, were converted and gained to God, although the conversation apparently had been confined to ordinary subjects. The influence he thus acquired was very great, and he used it to induce persons engaged in the world and moving in its highest circles to lead, nevertheless, a devout and interior life. Under his direction, numbers of public men, holding judicial and other civil appointments, as well as many ladies of the first distinction, practised daily meditation, spiritual reading, and other devotional exercises, without, therefore, neglecting any of their social or official duties; while others, of all classes, who had more leisure at their command, he encouraged to adopt a fixed rule of life, and assigned them particular hours in each day for mental prayer, visiting the Blessed Sacrament, assisting the sick poor, and similar works of charity.

But his influence was shown most conspicuously in a society of gentlemen united, not only for mutual encouragement and edification, but with the professed design of labouring for the conversion of those with whom they associated in the world. It was composed of about a hundred persons of the highest rank, and professedly of those only who had acquired considerable military distinction, and who were still employed in the army or about the court. Previous to enrolling themselves, they went through all the exercises of a retreat, and bound themselves to make public disavowal, as far as discretion allowed, of the false maxims of the world, contrary to the precepts of the Gospel, while continuing outwardly to lead an ordinary life, free from all marks of singularity, and to fulfil all the obligations incidental to their position in society. One principal object at which they aimed, was to abolish duelling, and to discountenance the practice of profane swearing, so common among men of their calling. They were distinguished by a particular devotion to the mystery of the Passion, by which name the Company was designated, as pledging them to be as ready to bear reproach, and peril their lives in resisting sin, as men of the world are forward to shed their blood in the vindication of what they term their honour. They engaged also not to go on a campaign or on a journey without first imploring the assistance of the Blessed Virgin in her own church of Notre Dame, nor to omit offering her their thanksgivings on their return.

Of these associates, one of the most celebrated was the young Baron de Renty, who, at F. de Condren's death, had taken M. Olier for his director. To a fearless, generous spirit, and a frank and manly bearing, he united, in an eminent degree, all the devotion and fervour of a sincere and humble Christian. He was one of those men of high principle, genuine piety, and mortified life, whom God seems to have raised up at this time to quicken the smouldering zeal of His clergy; and such was the respect and confidence he inspired, that he acted the part of spiritual director to many ecclesiastics as well as laymen. His personal sacrifices and exertions in behalf of the poor were extraordinary, and there was scarcely an institution, whether of charity or of religion, in which he did not take an active part. Another of the associates was Antoine de Salignac, Marquis de la Motte Fénelon, distinguished for his bravery. At the age of sixteen, on learning that his brother had been killed by a cannon-ball at the siege of Catelet, he went to request Louis XIII. to promote him to his company; and on the king's objecting to his youth, he replied, "Sire, I shall have the more time to serve your Majesty." To an intrepid and, indeed, headstrong courage, he united a charity and a kindness of heart as chivalrous as it was religious, exposing himself to the most murderous fire in order to rescue his wounded soldiers, lifting them on his shoulders, and bearing them to the trenches, that they might receive the last sacraments. But all his fine qualities were tarnished by a passion for duelling, the practice of which he defended with an energy and a sophistry which it was alike difficult to combat. On his begging M. Olier to undertake the direction of his conscience, the servant of God replied, "What can I do for a man who has not the resolution to renounce duelling?"—"Why, what harm is there in it?" said the young soldier. "Can a gentleman put up with an insult without resenting it?"—"Well," answered M. Olier, "since you do not feel the evil of the practice, pray to God to enlighten you; and promise me that when you are convinced of the contrary, you will set your face against duelling, and labour to convert duellists." The marquis pledged his word, and at the end of his next campaign returned a different man. By M. Olier's advice, he retired awhile from active service, refusing several important posts offered to him by the Regent, and devoted himself to the interests of his soul. He married Catherine de Monberon, a lady remarkable for her piety, who died at the age of twenty-seven, in the odour of sanctity. A third associate, equally celebrated for his personal courage, and, it must be added, his forwardness to display it in "single combat"—for such was the title of honour bestowed on duelling—was Abraham de Fabert, subsequently marshal of France. He had seen twenty-five years of military service, had been present at fifty-nine successful sieges, and had obtained universal renown by the prodigies of valour he had performed, when he yielded to the power of divine grace, and became one of M. Olier's most energetic coadjutors. Nor must mention be omitted of M. du Four, to whom allusion was made in the last chapter, and who was employed in any affairs in which tact and discretion were particularly required.

That ardent spirits such as these should range themselves under the direction of the pastor of S. Sulpice, was a proof alike of his ascendancy of character and of their devotion and earnestness. An amusing anecdote is related, which may serve to illustrate both; we have it on the authority of one of the parties concerned. He was driving one day to call on M. Olier, when, on the Pont Neuf, he met a friend, and invited him to join him. After the other had taken his seat, and the carriage-door was closed, he told him, laughingly, he was taking him to that good priest he had once promised to go and see. His friend was loud in his remonstrances, and tried to open the door; but he ordered the coachman to drive the faster, and defeated all his attempts at escape. Finding resistance useless, the other gradually submitted, and his captor succeeded in conducting him to M. Olier's room. The owner, however, was absent, being engaged in hearing the confession of another officer, and they employed their time in turning over some of the pious books that lay on the table. When M. Olier came in, he imagined that the stranger, who received him with much respect, wished to go to confession, and accordingly, making a sign to him to lead the way, proceeded forthwith to his private oratory. On entering, he fell on his knees, and the young soldier, taken by surprise, followed his example. M. Olier then seated himself, and commenced the usual form, perfectly unconscious of his visitor's embarrassment, who saw that he was expected to make his confession, whether he would or not. Retreat there was none, and, indeed, having got so far, there seemed nothing for him but to go on; so he began his '*confiteor*,' as if he had come for no other purpose in the world. His companion, meanwhile, sat wondering with himself at the whole proceeding: why he was excluded from the interview, and why it lasted so long. At length the two reappeared, looking extremely well satisfied at the result of their conference, and the young men shortly after took their leave. When they were alone, the one began complaining to the other of not having been allowed to have a share in the conversation; on which his friend informed him of all that had occurred, declaring that he had felt himself under the influence of an attraction which he was powerless to resist, and blessing God for the extraordinary grace with which he had been favoured. The narrator adds that he could not resist telling M. Olier shortly afterwards the truth of the matter, who was much amused at the blunder he had made, and did not fail to rally his penitent on what he called his singular adventure.

It was observed, indeed, that the servant of God had

a peculiar gift for winning the confidence of military men, and exercising a permanent influence over them. At the meetings of the associates he spoke to them as a father might speak to his sons, answering their questions and solving their doubts, and encouraging them to practise the maxims of Christian perfection with a manly courage and zeal. One day that he was exhorting them to make God their end in everything, one of them remarked on the extreme difficulty and virtual impossibility of adhering to this rule when mixing with those whose conversation and habits of life were merely worldly, even when they were not positively vicious. "This," replied M. Olier, "is the very reason why they who live in the world should be the more closely united to God, that they may remain uncontaminated in the midst of sinners. Besides," he added, "it is not our bodily presence that makes us belong to the world, but an attachment and an affection for its miserable vanities: let us never cease begging God to give us a contempt for them."

This association was eminently successful in checking and bringing into obloquy the frightful mania for duelling which then prevailed. To what an excess this vicious passion was carried may be estimated by the account which M. du Ferrier gives of the deathbed of M. de la Rogue Saint-Chamarant. He was a very brave man, and proud of his courage; a Christian, too, after a fashion; but in this one particular so obstinate and so infatuated, that on M. du Ferrier wishing to make him promise never to fight a duel again, he consented, but added the proviso that a friend whom he named did not ask him to act as his second. It was in vain to represent to him the insult he was offering to God by preferring to His laws the wishes of a friend,—a friend, too, by the way, who had himself unconditionally renounced the unlawful practice: on what he deemed a point of honour he was perfectly inflexible, and to perish in its vindication was to him the only death worthy of a gentleman. Soon after, he was seized with a mortal illness. The priest who attended him, hearing him groaning as he lay upon his bed, asked him the cause of his sorrow, with the view of suggesting religious consolation, and received this startling reply: "Alas! that La Rogue Saint-Chamarant, who has proved his courage on so many occasions, should die thus in his bed;" and in these sentiments he expired.

Hitherto, all means that had been tried to arrest this sanguinary frenzy had proved but of slight avail. The rigours of the law and the censures of the Church were alike disregarded. M. Olier had denounced from the pulpit the severest ecclesiastical penalties against duellists and their abettors, and several persons who had perished in these detestable encounters had, by his orders, been deprived, as the canons directed, of Christian burial. On the 11th of June, 1650, the vicar-general of the Abbé of S. Germain, in compliance with M. Olier's request, forbade all the priests of the *faubourg* to give absolution to duellists, except in danger of death, and then only on their engaging, in the event of recovery, to abjure the practice. In ordinary cases they could be absolved only by applying to himself or to the penitentiary of the abbey; and in default of absolution, they could neither receive the Holy Eucharist, nor be interred in consecrated ground. The facility with which confessors had granted absolution contributed much to aggravate the evil; but M. Olier laid strict injunctions on the priests of the community to question their penitents directly on the subject, and to withhold absolution until they had promised never to fight a duel; and this regulation was approved and confirmed by the assembled clergy of Paris. But although these measures effected much, they were not sufficient to disabuse men's minds of the fatal maxims which had been so long accredited in society, and it was only by opposing the principle of Christian fidelity to that of worldly honour that M. Olier at length succeeded in giving an effectual blow to a vice which was not only practised, but lauded, by the noblest and most chivalrous of the age. On Whitsunday, 1651, the associates assembled in the chapel of the seminary, and there, in the presence of a large concourse of distinguished witnesses, he received their public declaration and protest, which they afterwards severally signed, that they would never either give or accept a challenge under any circumstances, or on any pretext whatever.

Such a protestation, as proceeding from men whose valour was as unimpeachable as their honour, excited the liveliest astonishment, and the great Condé, whose mind was filled with ideas of worldly glory, could not help saying to the Marquis de Fénelon, that if he had not been so assured of his courage, he should positively have been dismayed at seeing him "the first to break the ice." But astonishment soon gave way to admiration. The marquis refused a challenge, with a noble intrepidity which was applauded by the whole court. His example gradually wrought a change in the public mind, and emboldened many a man to despise a worldly prejudice to which he had long been held in bondage. M. Olier's declaration against duelling began to be formally approved in quarters apparently the least likely to be influenced by such means. The marshals of France issued a manifesto, calling upon the gentlemen of the realm to adopt that declaration in all particulars, and the most illustrious persons in the kingdom hastened to give in their adhesion to it. But, warned by past experience of the inefficiency of all such measures, so long as the laws in force against duelling were partially administered, or were altogether evaded by pardons and private dispensations obtained from the crown—a practice which had extensively prevailed, not only under preceding reigns, but during the regency of Anne of Austria—M. Olier laboured to procure a new and more stringent edict from the king. Louis XIV. was on the point of declaring his majority, and on the 7th of September, 1651, the servant of God had the satisfaction of seeing him inaugurate his assumption of the reins of government by issuing an ordinance of the severest import against blasphemy and duelling, the two crying evils of the time. The principal clauses of the edict against duelling were proposed by the association of gentlemen already mentioned; and indeed to them, and to M. Olier, under whose direction they acted, are due the honour and the merit of this most salutary measure. Therein Louis, after recapitulating the enactments against duelling, solemnly swore and engaged, on the faith and the word of a king, henceforward to exempt no person from capital punishment, for any cause or consideration whatever, all remissions and abrogations by royal letters, close or patent, notwithstanding; forbidding all lords and princes of the realm to intercede for such offenders, under pain of his personal displeasure, and protesting that no plea of connection with the princes of the blood, whether by marriage or consanguinity, should be permitted to avail against this his decree.

The severity of this edict, and the impartiality with which it was carried into execution, drew down upon the Marquis de Fénelon a storm of obloquy, the violence of which might have made a less heroic virtue quail. Every calumny which malignity could devise was propagated against him, and his name became a very by-word of contempt in a world of which he had so lately been one of the brightest ornaments; but he remembered the words which he had so often heard from the lips of M. Olier—" If God loves you, He will humble you; and in exalting the work He will abase the workman;" and, like a bold soldier of the cross, he held on his way undaunted. This persecution continued until the campaign of 1667, in which, for the sake of watching over the conduct of his only son, who followed the profession of arms, he served as a simple volunteer. In this character, his military genius and capacity, no less than his gallantry and prowess, won for him such high consideration from the generals and the whole army, as well as from the king, that his revilers were at length silenced and their calumnies forgotten amid the universal admiration and applause. On peace being concluded, he conducted his son and four hundred other young soldiers to assist the Venetians in the defence of Candia against the Turks. Louis, who guessed his motive, said to him, " Now, tell me the truth; you are undertaking this enterprise to withdraw your son from the temptations of the court?" "It is so, sire," replied the marquis; "and when I think what those temptations are, Candia does not seem to me far enough." Every morning he prepared his companions for the struggle of the day by acts of devotion, and fought at their head in every *sortie* that was made. His son falling mortally wounded, he ordered him to be borne to his tent, himself continuing at his post; and after the action he assisted at his deathbed and received his last sigh.*

This association of military men continued, long after M. Olier's decease, to frequent the seminary of S. Sulpice for the purposes of devotion, and the blessing that accrued to them from his influence and instruction seemed to descend to their children. It would occupy too much space to relate in detail the measures he adopted to win the sons of the nobility to the love and service of God: from the single example that has been given, an idea may be formed of the extent and versatility of his resources, and of the measure of success to which he attained. The subject, however, has carried us beyond the date at which we had in due course arrived, and we must here retrace our steps.

Among the letters of M. Olier which have been preserved are many addressed to ladies of the highest rank, who were equally the objects of his charity and zeal. As an illustration of the sentiments with which he sought to inspire them, may be quoted some of the instructions he gave to the Princess of Condé, who was one of his penitents. On the death of her husband, Henri de Bourbon, which took place December 26th, 1646, she begged M. Olier to draw up a rule of life for her, and he sent her a sort of familiar treatise on the right use to be

---

* When he was dying, the young man said to his father: "I confess that I felt an extreme repugnance to this expedition: it took me away from the pleasures of Paris and of the court; I did not see how it could further my fortunes; I regarded it as an ill-judged enterprise, in which I was sacrificed to devotion; but what caused me greatest pain was a belief that I should never return. I had an abiding conviction that I could not save my soul in the world, and that God would have me die in this expedition, in order to save me in spite of myself. Miserable wretch that I was, I dreaded so great a blessing; but now I know its value, and I thank God, and die content."

made of wordly grandeur. "In creating man," he said, "God designed to represent in him an image of His own greatness; and after man fell from his high estate by sin, God still preserved a vestige of his original splendour in the persons of the great. Jesus Christ, who came to restore all things, sanctified both conditions: that of lowliness, which is common to the larger portion of men, by His own life of poverty and suffering; and that of greatness by His life of glory, inasmuch as since His Resurrection He is the King of the princes and lords of earth. I am not of the opinion of those who, mistaking the meaning of our Lord's words, affirm that the condition of the great is an abomination before God. True it is that the abuse of a state so august and sacred becomes an abomination in the sight of God, when men presume to appropriate to themselves the honour and glory with which they are surrounded, and would make themselves pass for gods on the earth. But looking at greatness in itself, and, above all, as it has been repaired in Jesus Christ, I find nothing more beautiful, more lovely, or more holy; for if Christians ought to behold in the great the glory and the royalty of Jesus Christ, and to honour Him in their persons, so the great ought to be clothed with holiness, sweetness, graciousness, and all the perfections of God, whose majesty they represent by their state. Remember then, madam, that you are upon earth a sharer in the Divinity, who is pleased to reside in you, not only to manifest His majesty before the eyes of men, but to receive their homage and load them with His benefits. I beseech you, therefore, to receive nothing save in the name of God, and for God, whose representative you are; and to take care that all the respect that is paid you stop not at yourself but pass on to Him. Do the same also when you give. Do not desire that men should have regard to you, but that God alone be acknowledged as the source of your gifts. When you see yourself surrounded by your court, remember that in this you ought to be the image of God, surrounded by His angels and His saints. Say often to God, 'It is for Thee, O Lord, and for what I have received from

Thee, that this assemblage pays me honour; and, as I cannot take aught thereof to myself without robbery, let this whole court render homage to Thy greatness, and Thy poor creature be annihilated before Thee.' Your retinue must be to you the image of the majesty of the glory of God. You must desire it in God and for God, and not in yourself and for vanity. If you pay a visit to the king or queen, do so with the intention of the principalities of heaven, who render the homage of their greatness to the majesty of God. If you visit a person of rank inferior to your own, honour in him a participator of the greatness of God, who desires to be honoured in him; and when you visit those who are of still lower degree, go with the disposition of God Himself visiting His lowly ones, condescending with kindness, sweetness, and charity, in order to assist and console them and do them a service. At the same time receive on God's behalf the honour they show you, so that, referring to Him what they may not think of giving Him, you may do your own duty and theirs together."

Never did man show more respect for the great, and never was man more zealous that the great should show honour to God. In all the ceremonies of the Church he made it a rule that the clergy should take precedence of the parishioners, however exalted their rank, even though they were princes of the blood. In his sermons he would speak of any acts of irreverence which he saw committed, and would himself move through the congregation to see that proper decorum was observed. Ladies of quality at that day had an absurd custom of wearing long trains, and they appeared with them at church. M. Olier set himself against the abuse with so resolute a zeal, that he succeeded in entirely abolishing it. He directed his priests to refuse communion to any who came unbecomingly attired; and observing one day a fine lady approaching to make her offering of blessed bread (as was the custom on great festivals) immodestly dressed, and attended by a footman, he rebuked her before all the people, and refused to accept her offering or to admit her into the sanctuary. Unless, however, it was a case of open scandal, he was careful to make his corrections in private, and never unnecessarily drew attention to the offenders. Sometimes his reproof was conveyed in the shape of a delicate hint. Perceiving one day, at a conference he was giving to the members of the Confraternity of the Blessed Sacrament, one of the queen's maids of honour, whose dress ill accorded with strict rules of propriety, he quietly sent her a pin, with a request that she would use it to fasten the scarf she had on her neck. The young lady received the admonition in the spirit in which it was given, and complied with a simplicity no less edifying than was the zeal of her pastor.

One of the most remarkable among M. Olier's spiritual daughters was Madame de Rantzau, wife of the celebrated marshal of that name. Both were natives of Holstein, and Lutherans in religion. She was a very active partisan of her sect, and her husband, looking upon her as a mere child, for she was then only in her nineteenth year, amused himself by pressing her with Catholic arguments, which she in her turn was most earnest in refuting. At length she began to feel the real force of what he said, but for two years she combated her doubts, until she was led to consult the Curé of S. Germain l'Auxerrois, when, after a fortnight's prayer and fasting, she obtained the light she needed, and was received into the bosom of the Church. Her husband at the time was absent with the army, and on his return laboured to reason her out of her childish folly,—for such he deemed it. Soon, however, discovering that she had acted not from ignorance, but from real and deep conviction, he bade her live as a true and sincere Catholic, for that he was satisfied of her prudence and good faith. Madame de Rantzau redoubled her prayers and her penances for her husband's conversion, and at length had the happiness of seeing the desire of her heart fulfilled. At the seige of Bourbourg he fell, as he supposed, mortally wounded, and immediately sent for a priest, and begged to be reconciled to the Church. He recovered, however, from his wound, and made open profession of the faith until the day of his death. Upon her conversion Madame de Rantzau had applied for spiritual guidance to M. Olier, who placed her under the care of an experienced director. This ecclesiastic was in the habit of hearing her confession in one of the side chapels; but finding him one day seated in a more public part of the church, she sent her page with a request that he would come to her at the usual place. He replied, that if she wished to make her confession, she must come to him. This accordingly she did, and, with the help of her servant, passed before the rest, and stationed herself close to the confessional. When she had finished her confession, the priest rebuked her for her arrogance in taking precedence of the others who were waiting their turn, and bade her observe more humility for the future. She went away in tears, but far from taking offence at the correction, she made a practice ever after of moving along upon her knees behind the rest, and although she had a cushion with her which she appeared to use, it was observed that she scrupulously knelt upon the ground. By the advice of her director, she never mixed in any of the gay society of the capital, except at her husband's express desire, but devoted herself to the instruction of her servants, the greater part of whom were Lutherans; and with such success, that in less than two years sixty* of them had abjured their errors. She was, indeed, endued with a peculiar grace for the conversion of Protestants, and with the assistance of Madame de Treuille, the wife of an officer, and Madame de la Rochejacquelein, was instrumental in bringing great numbers to the faith. At her husband's death she entered a house of the Annonciades Celestes,† being attracted to it by the

---

* It was the custom at that day for noblemen to retain a large number of servants. It is related of Madame de la Plesse, widow of the Marquis de Laval, that she had as many as a hundred attendants, and that she allowed none of them to be idle, employing them nearly all in her extensive works of charity.

† There were several orders designated by the name of Annonciades, all established in honour of the mystery of the Annunciation, or the Incarnation. The third, that of the *Annonciades*

strictness of the enclosure; but by a special dispensation of the Pope, who was unwilling that the gift she possessed should remain hidden and useless, she was allowed to converse with any German Protestants who desired to see her. After spending ten years in the house at Paris she founded a convent of her order at Hildesheim, where she died in the strict observance of her rule at the age of eighty.

Of the Duchess d'Aiguillon we have already spoken, and indeed her virtues and her charities are too well known to need description. M. du Ferrier, however, relates a little incident which, better perhaps than any elaborate eulogy, will give us a true idea of her fervent piety. "One night," he writes, "I went into the church of S. Sulpice, after taking my repast at half-past eleven o'clock, as was my custom. I was kneeling before the Blessed Sacrament, when I heard the door of the church open; but I took no notice, knowing that in so large a parish it was often necessary to administer the Sacraments to the sick at night. Soon afterwards some one came and knelt down very gently behind me. When I had finished my prayers, I rose from my knees, and found that it was the Duchess d'Aiguillon, all alone. I expressed my surprise at seeing her there at such an hour, for it was now one o'clock, and asked her the reason. She told me that she had been engaged all day, and that being on her way back from the Palais Royal (where the court then was), she wished to make her prayer, not having found time for it during the day; and that, as she would be more retired and collected than at home, she had begged the ringer to open the church for her. I admired her piety, and withdrew, leaving her at her devotions." We might search in vain for an incident like this among all the numerous memoirs from which modern readers take their only idea of the Paris of that day; yet what a glimpse does it give us into the interior

or filles bleues, was founded by a pious widow of Genoa, Maria Victoria Fornaro, who died in 1617. It was an order austerity, and the nuns were strictly enclosed.

of that hidden world of sanctity which underlay the gay and vicious surface of Parisian society!

M. Olier never ceased to combat with all his energies a maxim then, as now, very prevalent even among professedly religious people, that a life of perfection is only for priests, or such as are bound by vows. He regarded it as one of the most cunning devices of the devil to ensnare and destroy men's souls, and we have seen how he strove to defeat his malice by the numerous confraternities and associations which he established for persons living in the world. He possessed, however, a wonderful power of discrimination in the matter of vocations; and as he judged that one person ought to marry, and another to enter religion, so he would counsel a third to lead a life of celibacy in the world. One instance of the last kind caused a great sensation at the time. The Marquis de Portes, maternal uncle of the Duke of Montmorency who was beheaded in the reign of Louis XIII., died, leaving an only daughter, Marie Félice de Budos. When she was but ten years of age, she had made a vow of perpetual virginity; and her mother, who had taken as her second husband the Duke de St. Simon, when she learnt the fact, wished to make her go into a convent, in the hope that she would leave to her the disposition of her property. Finding, however, that she was determined to continue in the world, and devote herself to the service of the poor, she treated the matter as a mere girlish fancy, and when her daughter attained her sixteenth year, endeavoured, through the influence of a number of casuists whom she collected together, to induce her to look upon her vow as null and void. Mademoiselle de Portes, however, remained firm in her resolution, and her mother thought to bring her to submission by keeping her strictly confined to the house. The Duchess de Montmorency, who had retired to the Convent of the Visitation, at Moulins, feeling herself bound in her quality of cousin as well as of godmother, to protect her young relative against so unjust a persecution, entreated M. Olier to lend his assistance. He succeeded in communicating by letter with Mademoiselle de Portes, in spite of the vigilance with which she was guarded, and recommended to her the course she should persue. She followed his advice, and the result was a decisive victory. Her mother called in the aid of another conclave of doctors, but scarcely had they taken their seats, and begun gravely to discuss the question, whether a vow taken at so early an age was not void in itself, from default of a sufficient intention, when Mademoiselle de Portes, throwing herself on her knees before them all, uttered these words with a loud voice,—" O my God, if the vow which I made be not binding on me by reason of the tender age at which I made it, I renew it this day for my whole life." An act so unexpected broke up the conference, and the doctors at once retired, declaring there was no longer any room for doubt. The Duchess de St. Simon now protested that she would never see her daughter again, and Mademoiselle de Portes accordingly repaired to the Convent of the Visitation. Perceiving, however, that she had no vocation for a religious life, but that God had inspired her from her earliest years with a desire to consecrate herself to His service in the relief of the poor and the conversion of heretics, M. Olier decided that she ought to follow the attractions of Divine grace, and remain in the world. She therefore quitted Moulins, and went to labour in the Cevennes, where she also founded a Convent of the Visitation, to which she was in the habit of retiring whenever she needed a calm retreat from the harassing toils to which she had devoted her life. She died in 1702.

From the moment M. Olier first entertained the idea of undertaking the pastoral charge of S. Sulpice, he had resolved on the establishment of a house in which females could go through all the exercises of a retreat, an advantage which hitherto had been denied them. The person on whom he relied to preside over such an institution was the saintly Marie Rousseau. This design he now carried into effect by founding a community which became known as that of the Sisters of Christian Instruction. At first only women of the lower ranks were admitted to these retreats, but afterwards the higher classes enjoyed the same privilege. Here he opened schools for the children of the poor, which were managed by Mdlle. Leschassier, of whom mention was made in a previous chapter; here also he assembled a number of widows and young women who, after being duly instructed and trained for the work, were employed as schoolmistresses, and what in modern language would be called "district visitors." The result of these exertions was, that no less than fifteen similar schools were subsequently established in the parish of S. Sulpice, conducted by different communities. This was an object he had long had at heart. Convinced that if a school is to be a nursery of Christian youth, the teachers must labour at their calling in the spirit of apostles, and not as mercenaries, he wished to see communities established which should be devoted to the work of instructing the poorer classes; and he encouraged his young ecclesiastics to enrol themselves in an association[*] of prayer, which M. Bourdoise originated, for obtaining a race of educators such as the needs of the Church demanded. At the head of the house in question was placed Marie Rousseau, who was thus enabled to devote her whole energies to the accomplishment of the reforms for which she had prayed so long, and laboured so much. Thirty-four years of her

* This association was formed in 1649, and placed under the patronage of S. Joseph. The impetus given to religious education by M. Olier had the most important results in after-years. The Venerable De la Salle, founder of the Christian Brothers, entertained so profound a respect for this great man, that he always spoke of him as his father. His first establishment was at Vaugirard, and his desire was to affiliate his community to that of S. Sulpice, for which purpose he removed it into the parish; but the two objects were found to be incompatible, and he was compelled to abandon his design. The Venerable Grignon de Montfort was himself a Sulpitian, and his spirit still survives in the Sœurs de la Sagesse, a community which is among the most widely extended of any in France, especially in the west. M. Démia, again, who was in the habit of invoking M. Olier as a saint, on leaving the seminary devoted himself to the religious instruction of the poor. He instituted a society of schoolmasters, and another of schoolmistresses, the latter of which is known as that of the Sœurs de S. Charles; its field of labour is principally in the south.

life were spent in this work of piety and charity; she died August 4th, 1680, and was buried in one of the vaults of the church of S. Sulpice, directly under the Lady Chapel. "This testimony" (writes M. du Ferrier), "I can render to her virtue: although her life was altogether extraordinary, it was entirely free from singularity. I beheld in her a great humility, and an undeviating fidelity to her rule of life, never having observed in her the least symptom of self-seeking. To the end she continued to be *full of good works.*" *

It has been said that the sermons, and the numerous offices of the church were largely attended by all classes. M. Olier succeeded also in inspiring a special devotion for pilgrimages, and especially for that of Notre Dame des Vertus,† near S. Denis, which was performed every year on Whit Tuesday by the parishioners and seminarists of S. Sulpice, persons of the highest condition also taking part in it, to the great edification of the people. This

---

* Her successor was Marie Françoise du Plessis le Picard. At the death of her husband, M. de Paris, she went to the chapel of Notre Dame de Lorette at Issy, and there, despoiling herself of all her worldly ornaments, dedicated herself unreservedly to Mary. From that moment she wore nothing but the coarsest garments under her ordinary dress, and led a life of the greatest austerity.

† This pilgrimage owes its origin to a miraculous image of the Blessed Virgin, which, in 1338, attracted an immense concourse of people to the spot. During the spring of that year there was a great dearth of water; but on the second Tuesday in the month of May, a young girl, going to decorate the image with flowers, was surprised to observe it all bathed in moisture, notwithstanding the heat and dryness of the season. On the people assembling at the tidings, there fell an abundant supply of rain, which was followed by a number of miracles, and among the rest, by the restoration to life of two children, which took place under circumstances which precluded the possibility of fraud or collusion. Hence the shrine acquired the name of Notre Dame des Vertus ("Our Lady of Virtues"). It was here that M. Olier (as related in chapter viii.) received those remarkable favours from heaven, previous to the establishment of the Seminary of Vaugirard. From 1646 to 1689 the seminarists of S. Sulpice were in the habit of going thither in a body every Whit-Tuesday, when High Mass was performed at three o'clock in the morning. After the procession was discontinued, the seminarists still retained a particular devotion to the place.

general renewal of piety was accompanied with a corresponding increase of reverence for the priestly character and office, and the clergy were able to go at all hours into the loneliest quarters without fear of injury or insult. The very thieves and street-robbers treated them with respect; and M. du Ferrier relates how, being surrounded one night by a gang of these men, he had the courage to harangue them on the infamy of their lives, and with such effect that they offered themselves as an escort to protect him on his way home, and promised to abandon their evil courses. On the occasion, also, of a tumult caused by an obnoxious tax, when a violent mob were trying to break into the church, in order to sound the tocsin and summon the people to arms, he affected to believe that they were Huguenots who had come with the intention of profaning the building, and offering outrage to the Blessed Sacrament. On their protesting they were Catholics,—" What! " he cried, " do you believe that our Lord Jesus Christ dwells in the tabernacle in the holy ciborium?" " We do," they replied. " Then, my dear friends," said he, " how do you dare to force open His gates, when you would not venture to burst into the chamber of the king, if you knew he was within?" The men felt the force of the rebuke, and by this simple appeal to their faith in the Tremendous Mystery of the altar, he succeeded in quieting their minds, and turning them from their purpose.

CHAPTER XV.

Pilgrimages and Journeys.

NEARLY five years had elapsed since M. Olier first entered on the reform of his vast parish, and his health had at length begun to suffer from his unceasing exertions. As yet he had refused himself any relaxation, and to the expostulations of his friends, and especially of M. de Bretonvilliers, who warned him of the injury he was inflicting on himself, he would reply, "My child, this is neither the time nor the place for taking one's ease: our Lord would not have us find consolation on earth. Let us wait for a blessed eternity, and then we shall enjoy God only." Even when he yielded to their entreaties, and went for a few days into the country, he allowed himself no recreation. Prayer, Mass, writing letters, and sometimes reading, would occupy the whole morning; and if in the afternoon he submitted so far as to take a short walk, he was back again at his prayers and occupations till supper time. If he were reminded that he had come into the country for repose, he would answer, "Our Lord gives me grace to find my repose in these things more than in aught else." The autumn of 1647, however, found him in such a state of debility that, on the physicians assuring him that unless he had complete rest and change of air he would be compelled to resign his parish, he deemed it his duty to obey their injunctions.

It had long been his desire to visit Annecy, there to venerate the tomb of the holy Bishop of Geneva, and return him thanks for the recovery of his health some years before, which he attributed to the intercession of the saint. France was at this time full of holy places and holy relics, and, it may be added, of holy living persons, and M. Olier so ordered his route as to enable him to see a great number of all three. His journey was thus one continued pilgrimage. His first destination was the Abbey of Clairvaux, and he stopped on his way at Châtillon-sur-Seine, celebrated for its shrine of Our Lady, at which the great S. Bernard had received extraordinary graces. It was evening when he reached the place, but he went at once to the church, and remained some time before the miraculous image of Mary. The next morning he said Mass at her altar, where it seemed to the ecclesiastics who accompanied him that he was favoured with some signal consolation, for his countenance was radiant with joy, and his conversation more than usually inflamed with the ardour of divine love. On arriving within two miles of Clairvaux he dismounted from his horse, and, with his companions, walked the rest of the way in silence and prayer. The scene was one that invited to contemplation, being a thick, embowering wood, such as usually shut in the ancient monasteries. It was the eve of the Nativity of the Blessed Virgin, and he remained two days at the abbey, during which he was so absorbed in devotion that it was difficult to draw his attention to external things. He said Mass in the old conventual chapel, visited every spot in and around the monastery which recalled any circumstance in the life of the holy founder, and knelt for several hours in the narrow cell of the saint. From Clairvaux he repaired to Dijon, where he spent ten days with the Carthusian monks of that city, and thence moved on to Citeaux. Here his first act, as everywhere, was to adore Jesus in His Sacramental Presence, and to pray that he might have some part in those heavenly benedictions which of old He had been pleased to pour down upon the great order which had its birth in this spot, and which had been the source of untold graces to France. As though to assure him that his prayer had been heard, the abbot of the monastery, who was also superior general of the order, granted him and the whole seminary of S. Sulpice the privilege of a share in all the prayers and good works of the religious.

His next place of sojourn was Beaune, where, in the

Carmelite convent of that town, dwelt one of the most favoured souls of that age, Sister Margaret of the Holy Sacrament,* who had received a special call from God to promote an increase of devotion to the Sacred Infancy of His Son. M. de Renty was also very zealous in propagating this devotion, and though Sister Margaret lived in the closest seclusion, and for thirteen years had never spoken to any secular person, he succeeded in obtaining access to her, and had ever since kept up a correspondence with the inmates of the convent. It was his particular desire, and that of other devout servants of God at Paris, that M. Olier should see this holy nun, as they trusted to his spiritual discernment to test the reality of her gifts, and believed that both she and the community in general would derive much benefit from his counsels. M. de Renty had accordingly written to apprize them of the proposed visit. Sister Margaret had no knowledge, personal or otherwise, of M. Olier, but she had received a divine intimation that God was about to unite her, through the devotion of the Infant Jesus, in the closest spiritual relations with one who should act as her guide in the way of perfection. After visiting the church and the hospital, M. Olier repaired to the convent, and she no sooner beheld the holy man than, moved by a feeling of profound veneration, she threw herself at his feet, adoring (as she said) the Divine Infant in the person of His servant. Of the conversation that followed no record has been preserved; but when they had parted, the holy nun sent him a little picture on which she had written these words: "My Reverend Father, the Infant Jesus, who is our bond, our life, our all, will consummate and make perfect the grace He has wrought in us this day." M. Olier, on his part, gave her the crucifix of the Mother Agnes, which, however, was returned to him on the death of the nun, and he continued to direct her by letter as long as she lived. All the inmates of the house consulted him, and it was observed by the mother prioress that, exemplary as was the fervour and devotion which before

---

* Declared "Venerable" by the Holy See.

prevailed in the house, it became sensibly deepened from the date of this memorable visit. It would seem as though, by the knowledge M. Olier thus obtained of the secret virtues and extraordinary devotions of this chosen soul, God intended to make known to the world the perfections of her sanctity. It was through his report of her supernatural gifts that F. Amelote was led to write her life, and nowhere were the merits of this saintly woman held in higher consideration than in the seminary of S. Sulpice. It was in consequence also of this visit, and of the relations that followed from it, that the community has ever had a peculiar devotion to the Sacred Infancy. M. Olier engaged twelve of his most zealous ecclesiastics to recite the office; the 25th of each month was especially dedicated to It; and the illustrious Fénelon, then a priest of S. Sulpice, composed the well-known Litany of the Infant Jesus, which used to be sung in the parish church after vespers.

Quitting Beaune, M. Olier went to venerate the body of S. Claude, which had been preserved incorrupt from the end of the seventh century in the town which had grown up around his monastery, and had taken the name of the saint. On their way, the party found themselves on a dangerous mountain path, which ran along the edge of a precipitous ravine, down which the torrents went dashing and roaring into the depths below. Night came on, and they were obliged to dismount and lead their horses, treading warily every step they took; a heavy rain also began to descend, which rendered the pathway slippery, and drenched them to the skin. To their dismay, the guide now confessed that he had lost his road, and did not know how to regain it. In this extremity, M. Olier, who alone preserved his usual calmness, said, "My children, let us set ourselves to pray, and beg our Lord to vouchsafe Himself to be our guide. He has told us that He is 'the way;' let us follow Him, then, and we shall regain our road. Let us commend ourselves to the Holy Virgin, and to the great S. Claude whom we are visiting." They remained thus for a quarter of an hour, when the guide, as though he had suddenly recovered his recollection, exclaimed, "Now I know the way to go;" and so, following him through the darkness, they at length reached the confines of a village called Condé. The inhabitants, seeing five horsemen arriving thus at night, were distrustful of their intentions, and at first refused to let them enter. M. Olier, however, speedily induced them to relent; but whether their suspicions were not entirely dispelled, or that they had no better accommodation to offer, the only lodging they provided for the travellers was a hovel in which they kept their cattle, and all the food they gave them was some coarse bread and water. To M. Olier this hard fare seemed to be a source of real enjoyment: he conversed with the peasants with so much cheerfulness and affectionateness, and his manner, as he spoke to them of the things of God, was at once so familiar and so touching, that their hearts were quite won. When he took his departure the next morning, many of them burst into tears, and so unwilling were they to part with him, that they accompanied him on his way, and by the good Providence of God were the means of preventing one of the party losing his life in attempting to cross the river near a dangerous fall. On reaching S. Claude, the pilgrims venerated the holy body so wonderfully preserved;* and so great were the interior consolations which M. Olier experienced, that he says they surpassed

---

* The fact of this preservation is incontestable. The body of the saint lay in a silver shrine, adorned with precious stones. Three times a day the feet were exposed to the veneration of the faithful, who were permitted to approach and kiss them.—(Butler's "Lives of the Saints," June 6th.) In the year 1785 it was transferred to another shrine, in which it could be seen entire; but on the 19th of June, 1794, during the frenzy of the Revolution, these precious remains, which for eleven centuries had been the object of so much religious veneration in France, were torn from their resting-place, and after being dragged through the streets were burned, in the very town which bore the name of the saint. Heaven, however, avenged the horrible sacrilege; for on the very same day five years afterwards, the whole town was reduced to ashes by a conflagration which broke out at midday, and which to all human seeming might have been extinguished by the use of such ordinary means as were

in sweetness all the heavenly favours he had ever before received. It was painful to him to be disturbed when one of the priests of the place came to show him the other treasures of the church; but on being conducted to the chapel of the Blessed Sacrament, and finding himself alone with Him whom his soul loved, the thought came into his heart that while venerating the relics of the saints, he and his community must look for everything from the Spirit of Jesus and from the Adorable Mystery of the Altar, whence the saints themselves derived all their sanctity.

He at length reached the term of his pilgrimage, and on arriving at Annecy went immediately to the tomb of S. Francis de Sales. Many years had elapsed since he beheld the holy prelate, and then he had seen him only with the eyes of a child; but his whole aspect and appearance were as present to him as though it had been but yesterday, and he had drunk so deeply of his spirit, and the contemplation of his character and virtues had engraven his lineaments so ineffaceably on his heart, that he approached him with all the confidence of one who was going to seek counsel and instruction from a spiritual father. The three days he remained at Annecy were spent almost entirely in prayer: not, however, at the tomb of S. Francis, but before the Blessed Sacrament; for, as before at S. Claude, he was conscious of a secret communication which told him that it was in the Sacramental Presence of his Lord he would experience the most powerful effects of the intercession of the saint. Indeed, when he would address himself to the holy bishop, and beg him to give him a portion of that love for Jesus with which his blessed soul was burning, he found him, as it seemed, deaf to his prayers. This apparent indifference on the part of one who while on earth (as he says) was kindness and sweetness itself, and who,

---

at hand. The only house spared by the flames was that of a devout Christian named Calais, whose wife had carefully preserved a rosary which had been taken from the body. An arm of the saint is still to be seen in a silver reliquary.

now that he was perfected and confirmed in grace, and enjoyed the vision of God, must love Him with a more intense charity, could proceed, he knew, from no other motive but that of his spiritual advantage; and then the penetrating conviction entered his soul, that the lesson which the saint intended to teach him was this: that he did not love God purely for His own sake, but was too much attached to His gifts of grace: hence a want of repose, simplicity, and enlargement of heart; that henceforward God would have him love Him purely for Himself and in Himself; love Him in His Spirit, which is Charity; and embrace all his brethren in Jesus Christ, desiring for all the plenitude of His gifts. And this perfection God had decreed to give him only through the Sacred Mystery of the Altar.* In the Visitation Convent of this town there was an aged nun, who had been under the direction of S. Francis de Sales, had formed one of S. Jane Frances de Chantal's community, and had been head of a house at Bourges. She was

---

* The last degree of self-renunciation at which a soul arrives is when it gives up its attachment to those interior gifts and communications of God which are its joy and delight, and into which a kind of spiritual sensuality is apt to creep,—and consents to serve Him for the pure love of Him alone, and, so to say, at its own expense. Of this self-spoliation, M. Olier was to be a shining example. The great Pattern and Model of this high perfection is Jesus self-annihilated in the Blessed Sacrament, where He lies in a kind of mystical death. The Holy Spirit, who was leading His servant to this point of sublime perfection, directed him, therefore, to the school in which he was to acquire it. The Blessed Sacrament is the common centre of devotion to all Christians, and not one of the saints but has been distinguished for it; but a modern spiritual writer has shown that, over and above this, there may be what he calls a "special devotion" to the great Mystery of the Altar. God has His own ordained ways of guiding each individual soul to the perfection for which He designs it, and His graces are attached to the employment of the appointed means. They are strewn along a particular path, and no other. In this sense we must understand the above and similar passages, and not as implying, for instance, a disparagement of any degree of devotion to the saints. On the contrary, it was plainly through the intercession of S. Francis, to whom M. Olier was so devout, that he obtained the grace of direction on this occasion.

remarkable for her humility and simplicity of spirit; and as a test of the perfection with which she had mortified all feeling of human respect, her superiors called her into the parlour, and bade her sing before the stranger priest. She immediately complied, with no musical voice, as may be imagined, and continued singing till a sign was made to her to cease. On her withdrawing M. Olier, struck with admiration, exclaimed that an act of submission so heroic, was a more convincing evidence of sanctity than fifty miracles.

The object of his journey was now accomplished, but instead of returning the way he came, he resolved on visiting the holy places of Provence. The road from Annecy to Grenoble brought him within sight of Geneva, and he could not behold the unhappy city without an expression of grief: "Let us pass on, my children," he said, "and not tarry in a place where men will not have Jesus, our Divine Master and Teacher, to reign over them." He spent five days at Grenoble, where he again saw the Mother de Bressand, who had left Nantes to become superior of the convent in this town. It was here also that he made the personal acquaintance of Marie de Valernot, lady of Herculais, whose life was a miracle of prayer. She rose usually at three, and gave four or five hours to prayer; she then heard Mass, made her spiritual reading, and continued her devotions till dinner-time. A quarter of an hour after this repast, she retired again to her oratory, where she remained till supper, after which she again betook herself to prayer, occupying thus several hours; sometimes, indeed, she spent the whole night communing with God. The little nourishment she took, and the little sleep she allowed herself, made it difficult to understand how she could support life; but that which was still more marvellous, was her perfect self-abnegation. One day her husband, wishing to give his friends an example of her obedience and equanimity of spirit, called her, at a time when he knew she was engaged at her devotions, to take part in some game they were playing. She complied on the instant, and exhibited so much cheerfulness and liveliness in her manner, that a stranger might have imagined that none of the party took a warmer interest in the diversion; for, with all her dislike of the world, she had a great dread of making piety contemptible by any too apparent singularity.*

Finding himself in the neighbourhood of the Grande Chartreuse, he passed two days in a spot rendered holy by the presence of S. Bruno, and thence repaired to the abbey of S. Antoine de Vienne, where he venerated the relics of the great solitary of the East.† At Valence he once more conferred with Marie Teissonnière, and thence passed on to Avignon, visiting on his way the Mother Françoise de Mazelli, founder and first superior of the Convent of the Visitation at Pont S. Esprit, a woman of extraordinary sanctity and virtue, who (as it is said in her life) "received him as an angel sent by God, and made known to him with all simplicity the secrets of her soul." M. Olier next paid his devotions (for the second time) at what were called pre-eminently "the holy places of Provence," La Sainte Baume, Marseilles, and Tarascon, where, according to immemorial tradition,‡ S. Mary Magdalen, S. Lazarus, and S. Martha had lived and died. At Aix he visited the convent of Notre Dame de Misericorde, founded by F. Yvan, with the aid of the celebrated Mother Madeleine de la Trinité, who, although only the daughter of a common soldier, had gained such a reputation for sanctity and prudence, that the governor of the province and others in high station were accustomed to avail themselves of her advice. With the utmost simplicity she detailed to M. Olier the singular

---

* Madame d'Herculais died in 1654, aged 35.

† The body of S. Anthony, which, when the Saracens took possession of Egypt, had been conveyed to Constantinople, was transferred, about the year 980, to the church of the Priory of la Motte S. Didier, in Dauphiné, which subsequently became the head house of the order of the Antonines.

‡ These ancient traditions have been recently investigated, and their authenticity established by M. Olier's biographer, the Abbé Faillon, in his work entitled *L'Apostolat de S. Lazare, &c., d'après des monuments inédits*.

graces with which God had favoured her; and strongly impressed with the conviction that such high graces could be safe only under the guardianship of the deepest humility, he was moved to desire that that virtue should be rendered more perfect in her by a voluntary resignation of her office. His sole reply, therefore, to her recital, was a counsel that instead of ruling the house she had helped to found, she should descend to the level of the lowest of her subjects. The Mother Madeleine at once complied, only bewailing her imperfections, and declaring that she had not yet even begun to serve God in abasement and fear. The morning after her conference with M. Olier, she said to him, "Sir, we ought to speak little, love well, and do much." To which he replied, "Mother Madeleine, we ought to speak little, love well, and do *nothing;*" meaning that she must be content henceforth to obey. To the great grief of her religious she accordingly resigned her charge, as, indeed, she had long desired to do, but had been prevented by F. Yvan, who felt the need of her counsel and administrative talents. We shall hear of her hereafter at Paris, where she established another house of the order.

Returning to Avignon, he took occasion to deliver some letters with which he had been entrusted for the superioress of the Convent of the Visitation in that city, of whose sanctity, and indeed of whose very name, he was ignorant. On first beholding each other, they felt themselves (as we read in the life of the holy mother) elevated to God in so extraordinary a manner that neither was able to utter a word. Their only converse was silence, and their union was in spirit, not in speech. "Truly," as M. Olier himself writes on another occasion, "it is a thing altogether incomprehensible to the human mind, this divine operation of the Holy Ghost in souls." The next morning he said Mass at the convent, at which the Mother de S. Michel communicated; and then (as her life quaintly expresses it), "after having discoursed together after the manner of angels, they were able to speak in the language of men." Each conceived for the other a deep veneration; and, seeing the confidence which their superioress reposed in the holy man, the nuns begged him to induce her to moderate her extraordinary austerities. But he bade them not disquiet themselves, for that He who had hitherto enabled her to maintain so mortified a life was pleased that she should continue it, and would direct and support her as He had hitherto done.

Our limits will not permit more than a passing allusion to the most remarkable of those holy persons with whom M. Olier conferred during this journey. They may be taken as representatives of that very high order of sanctity which was to be found in many a nook and corner throughout the land, as well as in the great city of Paris, and between which and the ordinary standard of Christian goodness many gradations existed, of which history has recorded little and the world knows nothing.

From Avignon he moved on to Montpellier, taking Nîmes in his way, and thence to Clermont-Lodève, and Rodez, where several of his ecclesiastics were labouring for the reformation of the clergy of those dioceses, and so returned to Paris, after visiting the tomb of S. Martial at Limoges. This journey, which lasted three months, so far from interrupting his union with God, seemed even to increase his recollection and fervour. M. de Bretonvilliers, who accompanied him on various occasions and travelled with him as many as 3,600 miles, affirms that he never saw him look at any object from a mere motive of curiosity, although it were such as might well have engaged the attention of the passing stranger. And this not as if he were putting a forced constraint upon himself, but as one acting with an habitual modesty and self-control, who lived ever in the presence of God, to whom all his senses had been consecrated. One of the party, seeing a noble castle in the distance, and remarking on its beauty, "Ah, well," said he, "and what is this beauty? a great pile of stones one upon another: what a crash there will be at the end of the world, when it will be all destroyed!" However wearied he might be, he never dispensed himself from saying Mass, and would often rise at an early hour, and incur considerable fatigue, in order to reach some church where he could satisfy his devotion. If he saw a spire in the distance he would beg the company to recite with him the *Tantum Ergo*, in adoration of the Blessed Sacrament: "When I see a place where my Master reposes," he writes, "I experience a feeling of unutterable joy. I say to myself, 'Thou art there, my All; mayest Thou be adored by the angels for ever!'" On entering a village he would salute its angel-guardians, and commend himself to their prayers; and, if he were going to minister in the place, he would put himself entirely at their disposal, and beg them to obtain for him the gift of touching the people's hearts. He prayed almost literally "without ceasing." In order not to create delay he would make his hour's meditation on horseback; then he would say office, and perform all his usual exercises of devotion. His recreation was to speak of holy things and such as tended to edification. While at Mâcon, miscounting the strokes of the clock, he rose half an hour after he had lain down, and on discovering his error, instead of returning to rest, he spent the remainder of the night in prayer; and this he did on several other occasions. So constant, indeed, was his application to God, that at one of the inns on the way the servants, finding him always on his knees when they went into his room, said that there was one of the party who did nothing but pray.

His liberality was unfailing. In several convents where the religious were very poor, he gave abundant alms. At Mont Ferrand in Auvergne, seeing a debtor being led to prison, he was moved with compassion, and finding that his only crime was his poverty, he paid his debt and set him free. If he met with a beggar on the way, after giving him an alms, he would speak to him of God and of his salvation with all the affection of a father. Going once by water he took two poor people into his company, and during the passage both fed and catechized them with the tenderest charity. On another occasion he made a poor peasant woman get into the carriage with all her bundles, and as her only anxiety was to overtake her husband who was on before, he took occasion from the circumstance to make a most sweet discourse to his companions on the love of the Church for her Divine Spouse. Once, indeed, his charity was abused by an impostor, who lay by the roadside, pretending to be sick and destitute; but this good Samaritan did not fail to remind his friends that the merit of almsgiving is wholly in the disposition of the giver, and not in the worthiness of the receiver.

His humility was as admirable as his charity. He would make himself the servant of all, and it was impossible to prevent him; awaking his companions in a morning, carrying behind him on his horse such things as they wanted, anticipating all their wishes, and rendering them every service in his power. On the way to S. Claude, the horse of one of the party casting a shoe, he made the rider take his own in its place, and having covered the animal's hoof with a thick glove, he walked by its side for nearly three miles, and arrived at the next village bathed in perspiration. This spirit of condescension made him consult M. de Bretonvilliers on all occasions, little as well as great; and when that ecclesiastic complained of the deference he paid him, and asked him why he sought the advice of a man who had much greater need of his guidance, he replied, "My dear child, act with simplicity, and tell me frankly what you think; for, if I were alone with John (one of the servants), I should ask his advice, and should do simply what he told me. If possible, let us never do our own will, even in little things." For this reason he recommended that on a journey one of the company should be chosen as leader, who should be to the rest in the place of God, and be obeyed in everything with an entire submission. On arriving at an inn he would choose the worst apartment, and if there was a bed in it which seemed to be intended for a servant, he would take it for himself. On the way to Laon, being desirous of venerating a relic of S. Lawrence, which was preserved in the Premonstranensian Abbey of S. Martin, he rang several times at the bell, and when no porter made his appearance, he regarded it as a sign that he was unworthy to enter, and knelt down before the door, begging pardon of God and honouring at a distance what for his sins he was forbidden, as he deemed, to approach more nearly.

We may include in this chapter the particulars of another journey which he made in the following year, when his zeal impelled him to visit his priory of Clisson, in order to correct some abuses which had arisen. First, however, he repaired to the Franciscan monastery at Meulan, where, on the 4th of October, 1648, the feast of the holy patriarch, he commenced a retreat of ten days, by making a general confession of his whole life, both as a satisfaction for his sins, and to renew the confusion which (as he said) a sinner ought to feel for his sins, even when they have been remitted. From Meulan he passed on to Chartres, the scene to him of so many spiritual favours, and there, for several days, he might be seen kneeling, immoveable, from six o'clock in the morning till midday, and again from two o'clock in the afternoon till six, to the edification of all who were witnesses of his recollection and devotion. He also visited, for the second time, the church of Notre Dame des Ardilliers, near Saumur. It was on his way from this place that he gave an instance of his extraordinary humility and sweetness which reminds us of S. Francis Xavier. Mindful of his vow of making himself the servant of all, he was in the habit, when on travel, of acting as his own groom. While thus engaged, a gentleman entered the stable, and in the darkness mistook him for one of the men about the place, and bade him rub down his horse. M. Olier at once complied, only too well pleased to have an opportunity of doing a kindness. The gentleman's surprise may be imagined, when, returning shortly after, he found that the person he had taken for the ostler was, in fact, a priest; and his confusion was the more increased when he learned who it was that had performed such an office for him. But M. Olier took the whole matter so easily, and showed such unaffected pleasure at having rendered him a service, that the other knew not which most to admire,—the humility with which the man of

God had obeyed his orders, or the simplicity with which he received his apologies and his thanks.

He profited by his stay at Clisson to make a second pilgrimage to Notre Dame de Toute Joie, and after successfully accomplishing the reform of his priory, he took his way to Vannes, for the purpose of praying at the tomb of S. Vincent Ferrer, the Apostle of Brittany in the 15th century, whose body was exposed for the veneration of the faithful. Nor did he fail to satisfy his devotion to S. Anne by visiting her image at Auray,* which had lately become renowned for the number of miracles wrought before it, and which attracted a vast concourse of pilgrims. Through the intercession of this most powerful saint he besought of God the gift of silence, as well amid the contradictions he suffered from the world, as amid the favours he received from heaven, and also grace to act always in accordance with the Divine intentions and by the movement of the Holy Spirit. Returning to Nantes, he visited, for the last time, the convent of La Régrippière,† and had the happiness of finding it a model of regularity and fervour. Great was the joy of the nuns at beholding once more the holy priest to whom, under God, they owed the recovery of their vocation, and all hastened to profit by his instructions for their greater perfection in the religious life.

During this journey also he visited all the places sacred to the great S. Martin, to whom (as before related) he had a particular devotion. He beheld the grotto of

---

* On the 7th of March, 1625, a peasant named Yves Nicolasic found in the earth an antique figure, which was supposed to be that of S. Anne. The report brought great crowds to the spot, and the consequence was an extraordinary devotion to the Mother of our Lady throughout the whole province. A new image was wrought out of the old one, and became the object of veneration to thousands of pilgrims. This image was burnt at the Revolution, but a fragment was preserved and inserted in the foot of that which is still venerated under the name of S. Anne d'Auray.

† The convent shared the fate of so many other religious houses at the Revolution; but the memory of M. Olier, and of the reforms he accomplished, long lingered in the neighbourhood.

Marmoutiers, which the saint had converted into an oratory, and made the pilgrimage of Candes, where he died. But it was at Tours, and in the great church of that town dedicated to the holy prelate,* that he experienced the most powerful emotions; for there were preserved such of his precious relics as had escaped the sacrilegious fury of the Calvinists, when, in 1562, carrying fire and sword through the province, they did not spare the tomb of one whose resplendent virtues the whole Christian world had for so many centuries held in veneration. His soul thrilled with a secret awe, blended with a most consoling sweetness, a complex feeling, such as is said to have taken possession of the saint himself when he set foot in a basilica where reposed the bones of martyrs, and which became still more intense when he was shown the spot where the heretics had burnt the holy body. For hours he knelt before the tomb, so absorbed in his devotions that he never seemed to know how time was passing. One evening, supper being ready, the man of God was nowhere to be found. On inquiry, however, it was ascertained by his friends that in the afternoon he had been seen entering the church of S. Martin. The doors, which had been closed, were opened, and before the tomb of the saint knelt the object of their search, in the attitude of one who had lost all outward consciousness. He had knelt thus for seven hours unmoved; and even then, as though, like his Heavenly Master, he had meat to eat of which his friends knew nothing, he could not be induced to take his ordinary repast that night.

There was a reason why at this particular time M. Olier sought the special assistance of S. Martin. The patience and meekness of that prelate had been sorely tried by the insubordinate conduct of his deacon, whose sanctification, however, was at length effected through the admirable example of the saint. A like affliction

---

* This church no longer exists; but the devotion, of which it was formerly the scene, has been transferred to the cathedral, where some relics of the saint are still venerated.

M. Olier was now suffering from the irregular conduct of the ecclesiastics of his community. For several months, under the pretext of their other numerous occupations, almost all had dispensed themselves from the observance of the usual morning prayers, as well as from other exercises. The absence of M. du Ferrier at Rodez had given occasion to these disorders, and even when that ecclesiastic returned, as ill-health prevented him from being present at all the devotions of the house, their irregularity still continued. Convinced that nothing but his own personal example would correct the evil, M. du Ferrier began to rise at half-past four, and, ill as he was, repaired to the chapel of the community, where he found some five or six persons assembled. After dinner, the rest would have fain persuaded him that this strict observance would shorten his days; but the next morning he made his appearance as before. The third morning found not a single ecclesiastic missing, and, what was most remarkable, from that day M. du Ferrier's health, which had been ailing for three years, was perfectly restored, to the amazement of the whole community.

One effect of these journeys, or, rather, pilgrimages—for such they were in their spirit and object,—was a marked increase of zeal, devotion, and general spirituality among the clergy wherever he went. The mere sight of him kneeling before the tabernacle had more influence than many sermons; but neither were sermons wanting, for he preached in several places, though more, perhaps, was effected by private conversations and conferences. His appearance in any town seemed to be a call on the parish priests to arise and sanctify themselves, and his sojourn among them had to not a few all the advantages of a spiritual retreat. The like may be said of many a convent also, in which the extraordinary renewal of fervour among the inmates dated from the hour when M. Olier set foot within its walls.

In the summer of 1648, an event occurred in the parish of S. Sulpice, which wrung the heart of its pastor with the bitterest anguish. On the night of the 28th of July, some thieves broke into the church for the purpose of stealing the silver plate belonging to the confraternity of street-porters. It so happened, however, that the candlesticks and cross had been lent for the feast of S. Anne to the brethren of the new parish, and had not been returned. The robbers, not seeing these objects in their usual place, did not stay to examine the contents of the chest, but turned it upside down, by which means they did not perceive a chalice and other vessels which lay between the chasubles, and which, if discovered, might have satisfied their cupidity. Disappointed, therefore, of the expected booty, they forced open the tabernacle on the altar of the Blessed Virgin, and taking out the ciborium, emptied the Sacred Hosts on the elbow of one of the confessionals. But even while perpetrating their sacrilegious crime, the wretched men seem to have retained some feeling of reverential dread, for a few of the particles still adhering to the vessel, they did not dare to carry them away, but shook them out by striking the ciborium on the side of the confessional, the wood of which the next morning bore the marks of the edges; and some of them falling on the ground, they had left them lying where they fell.

Horror and consternation seized the inhabitants when news of the outrage spread through the *faubourg*. As with one consent, all diversions ceased, crowds flocked to the churches, to testify their grief, and to make such reparation as piety suggested for the dishonour that had been shown to their dear Lord in the Sacrament of His Love: one only thought seemed to pervade all classes, —that of penance and satisfaction to the Divine Justice for a crime of which each accused himself as the guilty cause. The Baroness de Neuvillette condemned herself to eat the coarsest bread, and drink only water for the rest of her days, in order to appease the anger of God;*

---

* At the end of five or six weeks, she became so ill that her confessor forbade her continuing her penance. This lady, during her married life, had been the acknowledged leader of fashion; her sole ambition was to excel all others in the sumptuousness and elegance of her table, her equipage, and her dress. But on the death of her husband she felt herself called to give herself wholly to God, and through

and when, on the following Sunday, one of the priests of the community recounted to the people all the circumstances of the sacrilege, the whole congregation were melted to tears, and sobs and wailings filled the church. But the chief mourner and the chief penitent—need it be said?—was the holy pastor himself; and nothing less would satisfy him than a public reparation, proportioned —if such a term be applicable—to the magnitude of the crime. With the consent of the Abbé of S. Germain he announced from the pulpit the order of the observances, proclaiming a three days' fast, to commence the following day.

Accordingly on Monday, August 3rd, 1648, as the bells gave forth their lugubrious sound, the people, all in mourning garb, assembled in the church of S. Sulpice; thence they walked in procession, chanting psalms as they went, to the abbey of S. Germain, where a Mass was said " for the remission of sins." The gloom of the day added to the universal sadness; the very heavens seemed to weep, for the rain continued to fall in torrents, and, owing to insufficient drainage in those times, so flooded the streets that the penitential crowd, among which were ladies of the highest rank, had to wend its way through streams of water. On Thursday, and the two succeeding days, the Blessed Sacrament was exposed with unexampled splendour. The whole court contributed whatever there was most magnificent and rare for the august ceremony; tapestry, and pictures, crystal

---

the prayers and counsels of M. de Renty she found courage to obey the call, and consecrated the remainder of her life to works of charity and devotion. To break at once with the world, and mortify in herself all remains of pride and human respect, she inflicted on herself a sort of public humiliation, going to visit a lady of her acquaintance in the Luxembourg, attired in a robe of patchwork. She had no sooner made her appearance at the palace-gates, than she was surrounded by a tribe of children, who followed her to the grand staircase crying out, "The Queen! the Queen! the Queen of Tatters!" A still greater affront awaited her in the presence of the fine lady she came to visit, but she was enabled not only to despise the world, but to despise being despised by it, and she conquered it in conquering herself.

vases, candelabra, and lustres of gold and silver. The Marchioness de Palaiseau presented a canopy [worth 20,000 livres, and though it was declined because of the certain damage it must sustain from the smoke of more than 300 burning tapers, she persevered in her entreaties that what had been made for vanity should be sacrificed to the glory of Jesus Christ. Her offer was therefore accepted; and, as though to reward her piety and devotion, at the end of three days' ceremony it was found not to have received the slightest tarnish. The whole length of the nave was covered with cloth of gold; the choir was hung with red velvet, on which columns were wrought in bold relief, ornamented with capitals, embroidered alternately with gold and silver, and all so skilfully designed, that it might have been taken as actually elaborated out of the precious metals; while in the midst of golden candlesticks, and vases, darting flashes of light, raised high upon a pyramidal throne, and surmounted with a crown glittering with jewels, appeared the Object of all this honour and glory; the Object, too, of the unceasing adoration of a countless throng that day and night filled the church to overflowing.

On the first and second days of the exposition two of the most celebrated preachers of the capital addressed the assembled multitudes; on the third the shops were shut, and all servile work was suspended; the whole clergy of the parish, secular and regular,* carrying lighted torches, accompanied in procession the Blessed Sacra-

---

* A circumstance is related in connection with this procession, which affords a curious instance of the jealousy with which the Benedictines of S. Germain maintained their prescriptive rights. M. Olier, absorbed in his devotions, inadvertently strayed from his place behind the monks, and walked among their ranks. Now, the parish of S. Sulpice (as was said above) was under the jurisdiction of the abbey, and for fear that this act of its *curé* should be taken in after time as a precedent against their authority and liberties, they obliged M. Olier to make a formal declaration in writing, to the effect that in intruding himself among them "in the aforesaid procession, contrary to all custom, right, and reason," he meant to assert no manner of precedency or encroachment on their privileges. This declaration was inserted among the archives of the abbey.

ment, which was borne by the Papal Nuncio. The queen-regent followed the canopy, together with all the princes and princesses of the blood, and a large proportion of the court, all wearing mourning; the people followed in immense crowds. The duchess of Orleans had caused a magnificent altar to be erected at the entrance to the Luxembourg; and the ceremony was concluded by a solemn act of reparation, pronounced by M. Olier with so much fervour, and with such an abundance of tears, that none of the assistants could refrain from weeping. From the day on which the horrible crime was committed no Mass had been said at Our Lady's altar; it was left stripped of its ornaments, with its broken tabernacle exposed to view. M. Olier now replaced it with another, richly adorned, and to perpetuate for ever in the parish the memory of the event, he surrounded the spot on which the sacred particles had been scattered with a balustrade, and inscribed upon a marble tablet, in letters of gold, the principal circumstances of the sacrilege and its reparation. Before this tablet he hung a silver lamp, which was to be kept burning day and night; and to offer to Jesus Christ a homage still more worthy of the love He bears us, he directed that on the first Sunday in August in every year, the Blessed Sacrament should be solemnly exposed in reparation for all the insults offered to Him in the Holy Eucharist. But even yet his devotion was not satisfied: it was now that he established the perpetual adoration of which mention was before made, and for which he had long been preparing his people. He chose twelve of his flock, the most devout to the Sacramental Mystery, who should unite themselves in spirit to the twelve Apostles, the first and chief adorers of an Incarnate God; and these again he bade associate with themselves twelve other worshippers, who thus with them should represent the four-and-twenty ancients of the Apocalypse, who fall down continually before the throne of the Lamb. Each had his hour assigned him, and the whole day was thus divided among them. Into this association others were admitted from time to time, who shared the devotion of the chosen brethren, and supplied for those who, through illness, or other pressing necessity, were unable to attend. In fine, a detailed account of all the circumstances of this reparation was circulated through the provinces, which had a powerful effect in producing a more tender devotion to the Blessed Sacrament, and a deeper awe and reverence towards that tremendous mystery.

Three months after the ceremony above described one of the perpetrators of the deed was discovered in the person of a soldier of the guards. Information was given by the individual in whose house he lodged, which led to his quarters being searched, and the ciborium of S. Sulpice, together with other property similarly obtained, was found hidden among his goods. The Parliament of Paris condemned him to provide funds for a lamp to burn perpetually before the tabernacle in the Lady Chapel, in addition to that which was already there; to make a public act of reparation before the doors of the church; and lastly, to suffer the punishment of death for the sacrilegious robbery; which sentence was accordingly carried into execution on the 16th of June, 1649. M. Olier himself attended the unhappy man in prison, and accompanied him to the scaffold.

CHAPTER XVI.

The Troubles of the Fronde.

It was almost immediately after the sacrilege related in the preceding chapter that the troubles of the Fronde began, which desolated Paris and convulsed all France with civil war. The sedition broke out on the 26th of August, 1648, and the populace of the capital, instigated by the Parliament, everywhere rose to arms. Yet in the midst of this general confusion, it was observed that the *Faubourg* S. Germain preserved its usual tranquillity;

not a single barricade was raised; and good men attributed the circumstance to the prayers of M. Olier, and the influence of his teaching. During the lull that followed, and while both parties were preparing for the coming struggle, when the court had retired to S. Germain-en-Laye, and the Prince of Condé was approaching to besiege the city, M. Olier offered himself continually as a victim to the Divine Justice: he multiplied his penances, he was to be seen ever on his knees in prayer, and his countenance and whole demeanour evinced such poignant grief, that M. de Bretonvilliers says the sight of him affected him more than any sermon he had ever heard. He never ceased calling on the people to repent and make their peace with God, and, instead of accusing each other as the authors of the evils that were hanging over them, to condemn themselves for their sins, which deserved still heavier punishment. With this intention he had public prayers said in the church, and directed such of his ecclesiastics as were labouring in the provinces, to unite with him in deprecating the anger of God.

When the troops of the Prince of Condé began to ravage the country, and provisions in consequence became scarce in the city, M. Olier assembled his parishioners, and arranged a plan of relief for the suffering poor. On inquiry being instituted, no less than 1,400 or 1,500 families were found to be reduced to the last necessity, but the system of visitation he organized, and, above all, his own charity and zeal, were equal to the occasion, and with the help of M. Gibily, a priest of the community, whom he associated with Brother John of the Cross, he succeeded in providing both spiritual and temporal aid for such as were in need. The tenderness of his charity was eminently displayed towards the sick, the number of whom was very great, especially in 1652: it was the sympathy of friend for friend, or the love of a parent for his child. His liberality was as inexhaustible as his charity. The necessities of the people increased daily, and at every round he made he commonly expended as much as 2,000 livres. When his purse was emptied he would give whatever he happened to have about him, as a handkerchief, or a book, or anything that could be sold to buy bread. Application being made to him one day for a certain sum in behalf of a destitute family, he replied that it was not enough, and bestowed three times as much as had been asked. He supplied the poor with victuals, clothes, and tools, and when a more than usually cold winter came to aggravate the general misery, he provided them with necessary fuel. So unalterable was his confidence in God, that when the distress was at its height he continued to exhibit the same composure and cheerfulness of spirit. It so happened, indeed, that at the time the extremity was greatest his resources were least, for the rich people of his parish, to whom he had been used to look for assistance, had either followed the court or sought safety in flight; but even thus his charity was at no loss for an expedient. He sold all his private property, and distributed the proceeds among such as were most in want; and when these funds were exhausted, he resolved on going in person to S. Germain-en-Laye, in quest of alms.

The adventure was a very perilous one. On the one hand, the environs were overrun with soldiers, mostly Poles and Germans, who robbed and maltreated, and not unfrequently murdered those who fell into their power; and on the other, if his design became known in the city, he might incur the suspicion of being in correspondence with the court. The danger was thus twofold; but this good pastor made no account of his life, so that at any risk he could relieve his famishing people. Taking one of his friends, M. de Grandval, into his counsels, he induced him to convey him in his carriage to the furthest limits of the *faubourg;* then, watching his opportunity, he quietly alighted, and accompanied by M. le Royer de la Dauversière, the pious layman of whom mention has before been made, succeeded in gaining the open country unobserved. The cold was intense, the snow lay deep on the ground, in places reaching even higher than the knees, and entirely obliterating the by-paths they had to traverse. The Seine, too, had overflowed its banks;

but, protected by the hand of God, they escaped the many straggling parties of soldiers they saw about, crossed the bridges, all of which were guarded, passed through the encampment unquestioned, and after much fatigue, reached their destination in safety. His friends at the court were not insensible to the tale of woe he brought them. The Princess of Condé, in particular, whose son was in command of the besieging forces, gave substantial proofs of her compassionate charity; and M. Olier and his companion became the bearers of a large sum of money, with which they returned unnoticed, as though they had been rendered invisible, through the midst of both guards and plunderers. When asked on his return how he had been able to make his way undetected, he replied,—" I do not know; all I know is that charity inspires courage." The alms thus obtained, together with other sums with which Providence supplied him, enabled him to support a vast number of destitute persons, until the close of what is known in history as "the first war of Paris." He also obtained permission for the poor to eat flesh-meat every day during Lent, Friday excepted, provided it were given them in the way of alms.

During the continuance of hostilities, he assembled his people every evening before the Blessed Sacrament, to implore the Divine mercy, opening the door of the tabernacle the more to excite their devotion, and would himself pass whole nights before the altar, clothed in sackcloth. At length, on Holy Thursday, April 1st, 1649, articles of peace were signed between the court and the parliament, and on the Monday following, a solemn *Te Deum* was sung in thanksgiving for the event. During three days, also, the shrine of S. Germain was exposed for the veneration of the faithful, a boon which had not been accorded for seventy years.

But though peace was restored to the capital, the distress of the people still continued, and the servant of God found himself charged with the maintenance of several hundred persons, who were unable to procure the means of subsistence. Yet this was the time he chose for the execution of a design which he had long meditated, and which presents us with an instance of his confidence in God which may well excite our admiration: he resigned his abbey of Cercanceau, and his two priories of Clisson and Bazainville, thus leaving himself entirely dependent on his *cure* of S. Sulpice. Among other motives which he assigned for the act, were the advantage he had experienced in relying solely on the good Providence of God, who, in a season of great public calamity, had abundantly supplied him with the means of maintaining so many destitute families. At the same time he begged pardon of his brethren for the bad example he had given them in retaining his benefices so long. His relatives would fain have had him resign in favour of a nephew, at least in the case of one piece of preferment, but he firmly refused, and recommended to the Pope three persons wholly unconnected with himself, whom he believed to be best fitted to succeed him.

Civil war, however, had brought in its train evils far more afflicting to the servant of God than those of poverty and destitution, which, after all, could but hurt the body: these were a great relaxation of morals and an increased indifference to religion, and M. Olier at once sought to apply a remedy with all his accustomed energy. As exhortations and warnings, whether public or private, were by many disregarded, he proceeded, with the authority of the Prior of S. Germain, to execute, against all who lived in a state of concubinage, the provisions of the Council of Trent, which ordered sentence of excommunication to be pronounced against such as, after three consecutive monitions, should persist in their evil courses, with the penalty of being refused burial in consecrated ground; which refusal was to extend likewise to those who, without legitimate excuse, should neglect to make their Easter communion. To these were superadded such punishments as the laws enjoined. But measures of severity, however necessary, were little in accordance with the tender compassionateness of this good pastor's heart, and he procured for his parish the benefit of a general mission, conducted by one who, for his extraordinary abilities as a preacher, was called the wonder of his age, Father Eudes, founder of the congregation which bore his name. The mission was announced to begin on the feast of the Purification, 1650, but owing to the Seine bursting its banks, the father and the twelve ecclesiastics who accompanied him were unable to reach S. Sulpice in time, and M. Olier himself preached the opening sermon. On their arrival they took up their abode in the presbytery; and their labours, which were continued during the whole of Lent, not only accomplished the immediate object M. Olier had at heart, but were productive of two other results, both of which he had directly contemplated, viz., a renewal of fervour among the priests of his community, and the establishment of a Company of Charity for the relief of the bashful poor.

To the miseries caused by the late siege of the capital, was now added a great dearth of provisions, consequent upon the destructive inundations which occurred in different parts of France. The sufferings of the people, as we learn from the accounts of the time, were dreadful in the extreme. In S. Sulpice alone, there were several hundred families which had not wherewithal to live; parents lay stretched on wretched pallets, or on the bare floor, with two or three children dead or dying of starvation by their side; others who (to use the touching phrase) had seen better days, were discovered, in rags which scarcely covered their nakedness, cowering in attics or in cellars, unable to stir out in the face of day, even to hear Mass. In the quarter of the Incurables persons were found who had not tasted food for days together. Some contrived to support life with a little bran sbaked in water in which a morsel of cod-fish had been boiled, or with such carrion as they had been able to pick up in the roads or outside the city walls. Infants died at the breast from lack of nourishment. In fine, some in a fit of frenzy and despair, produced by hunger and the sight of those they loved perishing around them, attempted self-destruction, by suspending themselves from the rafters of their rooms. For the removal of this frightful destitution, and the prevention of similar distress, he determined to organize a permanent system of relief; and he looked to that renewal of piety which a mission would produce for the means to carry his design into effect. The result corresponded with his expectations. But in this, as ever, he acted with deliberation; and, above all, with entire submission to the will of God. After long-continued prayer, he communicated his design in the first instance to a chosen few, and having secured their zealous co-operation, he called a general meeting of the parishioners, on Easter Monday, 1651. It was attended by persons of all classes ; and after representing in detail the miseries of those whom modesty or shame deterred from obtruding their sufferings on their neighbours' sight, he reminded them that alms-giving had its particular as well as its general obligations, and bade them, at such a time of extreme necessity, retrench their superfluities, and deprive themselves of what, under ordinary circumstances, they might innocently retain ; exhorting those who had nothing else to bestow to give their time, and what was more acceptable even than alms, their personal care and active sympathy. God so blessed his words that a large sum of money was contributed on the spot, and among all who were present, there was not one but promised his assistance according to his ability.

He now divided the parish into districts, putting four persons in charge of each, whose business it should be to inform themselves of the abode, condition, and circumstances of those who were the objects of their solicitude. As a great number of these poor people were unwilling to make personal application for relief, he set up a box at the entrance of the presbytery into which they could convey their requests in writing. The greatest care was taken that none but deserving persons were recipients of this bounty, from which professional beggars also were rigidly excluded. M. Olier discouraged the giving of money in these cases, and the Company accordingly established a depôt, from which not only food and clothing, but furniture, tools, and articles of every description were provided. On the last Sunday in every month a meeting of all the members was held, at which each gave in his account, and at the beginning of winter a general visitation of the whole parish was made, and again at its close. Schools were at the same time opened for the children of the poor who were thus relieved, which were inspected at short intervals by those who had the charge of the several districts; an ecclesiastic also went at regular times to give them religious instruction. A catechism was published, under M. Olier's direction, for their especial use, in which the chief points of doctrine were expounded in simple and familiar terms, and short forms of prayer added for all the common actions of each day. This Company* became the model of similar associations in other parishes, and was the first of those brotherhoods of Christian charity for which the city of Paris has been so honourably distinguished. Its members were also charged with the support of an orphanage, which M. Olier had commenced in the year 1648 for boys who, at a fitting age, were apprenticed to different trades. Two of his parishioners, brothers, afterwards presented him with a house in the Rue de Grenelle for female orphans, who were superintended and instructed gratuitously by charitable women residing with them; but the distance from S. Sulpice proving inconvenient, they were subsequently transferred to the Rue du Petit Bourbon, by Mme. de l'Esturgeon, who generously gave her own house for their reception. This establishment existed at the time of the Revolution.

There was yet another association which deserves especial mention. This was the Council of Charity, composed of persons versed in the law and affairs of business, who lent their assistance in preventing litigation among the humble classes, and in conducting the causes of those who were unhappily compelled to seek legal redress. For this charitable work Providence assigned him a most valuable coadjutor in the person of one of the priests of

* It was indulgenced by the Holy See, March 7th, 1654, under the title *pauperum infirmorum verecundorum*.

his community, Antoine Jacmé de Gaches, a man of great piety and austerity of life, who had been a member of the provincial magistracy, and whose acquaintance he had made during his missions in Auvergne and Velay. As acute as he was prudent, he was endowed with a remarkable gift of persuasion, and by his aid many differences were amicably adjusted to the satisfaction of both parties, which otherwise might have entailed ruinous legal proceedings.

But for the admirable organization, the details of which have been given in this and preceding chapters, it might scarcely be credited that, in the midst of his other numerous occupations, this extraordinary man could have provided for the many pressing necessities, spiritual and temporal, of so vast a population. An enumeration of the several charitable meetings held in the course of each month may serve to show the systematic character of all his arrangements, and the immense amount of actual hard work that was performed under his direction. The meetings of the first and third Sundays were on behalf of the newly converted, on which days also the Council of Charity held its sittings; the second and fourth were devoted to the bashful poor; the first Saturday and the 25th day of each month to the children in the schools; the first Thursday to the sick poor; the first Saturday, again, to the crippled, the blind, paralytic, and others. The second Thursday was set apart for supplying poor children with proper nourishment, and providing nurses for those whose own mothers were unable to bring them up. Lastly, on certain days, particular priests of the community were employed in procuring the liberation of prisoners; while, on others, the ladies of the parish superintended the work of finding situations for young women out of place.

This account of M. Olier's charitable labours has carried us beyond the date at which the narrative had properly arrived, and to which we here return. On the 18th of January, 1650, the Prince of Condé, whose influence with the army alarmed the court, was arrested by the orders of Cardinal Mazarin, and with his brother, the Prince of Conti, and his brother-in-law, the Duke of Longueville, conveyed to the fortress of Vincennes. The princess, his mother, retired with her daughter-in-law to Chantilly, whither M. Olier, compassionating her sorrow and desolation, went, in the capacity of her director, to support and console her. Some of the persons, however, who were about her, jealous of the confidence she reposed in him, had laboured to excite suspicions to his prejudice which, in her then embittered state of feeling, she was but too well disposed to entertain, and he consequently found himself very coldly received. Nothing disconcerted by a change so unexpected, he discharged his spiritual office with that consummate prudence which never failed him; and on his return to Paris, so far from complaining of the little regard that had been shown him, he made it matter of thankfulness to God, who (as he wrote to a friend) would teach His poor servants how little they ought to depend on creatures, and so constrain them the more to put their whole trust in Him alone.

Apprehensive that her presence in the capital would lead to some popular movement in behalf of the princes, whose party was gaining strength every day, the court stationed troops to prevent her leaving Chantilly; but, in spite of these precautions, she succeeded, on the night of the 16th of April, in eluding the vigilance of the guards, and the next day presented herself before the Parliament, and by her tears and supplications endeavoured to move the assembly in favour of her son. The counter influence of the Duke of Orleans, however, was exerted with such effect that she was obliged to leave the city, to the great regret of the inhabitants of S. Sulpice, and especially of the poor, of whom (as we have had occasion to see) she was the munificent benefactress. But in her exile she did not forget she was one of M. Olier's parishioners. On the 20th of May she sent some rich ornaments of crimson velvet, embroidered with gold and silver, for the decoration of the church; and a letter, which he wrote in acknowledgment of this act of devotion, led to a renewal of those confidential relations which had been the source of so much profit to her. A day was near at hand when she would need, if ever, his assistance and prayers. Her son, instead of being released, was transferred to a place of greater security; and sick and well nigh broken-hearted the unhappy princess obtained permission to retire to Châtillon-sur-Loing, a village twelve miles from Montargis, where, sensible that her end was approaching, she sent for M. Olier, to prepare her soul for its final passage. Here, in fact, she expired, on the 2nd of December, in the holiest dispositions.

The princess had died in disgrace with the court, her sons were in prison, and the other members of her family had been ordered to retire to their estates; but, like the clergy generally, who, while interceding for the liberation of the princes, held themselves aloof from either political party, M. Olier preserved a noble independence, and celebrated a solemn *requiem* Mass for the repose of her soul, in the presence of his whole community and a large assemblage of the people. The court, to its honour be it recorded, far from showing resentment, respected the motives of this worthy pastor; and on Christmas Day the young monarch came in state to hear Mass at S. Sulpice, and was received at the entrance of the church by M. Olier himself, who delivered an appropriate harangue. He afterwards assisted at Vespers. Louis XIV., even in his worst days and in spite of his personal immorality, exhibited a religious disposition, but in his early youth he seems to have given marks of genuine piety. It was the anniversary of his first communion, which he had made the previous year, and which he desired thus to commemorate; and it is with a melancholy interest we read that on this occasion he edified all the congregation by his unaffected modesty and devotion.

The popularity of the Prince of Condé was every day increasing, while the hatred of the citizens against Cardinal Mazarin became proportionably deep and violent. In the February of 1651 the party opposed to the court received a powerful accession in the person of the Duke of Orleans, and Mazarin was compelled to fly from Paris in disguise. The princes were liberated from confinement, and made their triumphal entrance into the capital amidst the acclamations of the multitude; the court itself went out to meet them at S. Denis, and escorted them to the Palais Royal, where they were admitted to an audience of the young king and his mother. But the reconciliation thus ostentatiously paraded was in reality only apparent; and the queen mother, deprived of the support of her favourite minister, and obliged to entrust the conduct of affairs to persons for whom she entertained neither esteem nor confidence —aware, too, of the unconcealed hostility of nearly all the parliaments in the kingdom, the ceaseless caballings of the nobles, and the universal exasperation of the people against her—sent for M. Olier to obtain his counsel and assistance. Something of the nature of the advice he gave her may be gathered from a letter still extant which he addressed to her, and in which, with a holy freedom, he represented the dishonour that had been done to God, and the evils that had accrued to the Church and to religion, by the unworthy conduct of the cardinal,* who had disposed of the highest ecclesiastical dignities, and especially bishoprics, to persons whose only qualification was the having rendered some service to the state. This unscrupulous minister, though bound to act in conjunction with the Council of Conscience, had eluded the obligation, on the pretext of other and more urgent business, and, in fact, had made the appointments by his sole authority. The queen took the remonstrance in good part, acknowledged her error, and promised for the future not to dispose of a single bishopric without first privately consulting S. Vincent de Paul, an engagement to which she conscientiously adhered.

The rupture between Condé and the court was not slow in declaring itself. The prince quitted Paris, and betaking himself to Bordeaux, began to levy troops

---

* Cardinal Mazarin, it should be observed, although he had received the clerical tonsure, was not in holy orders.

against his sovereign. In this emergency, Anne of Austria, regarding her son, who was still but fourteen years of age, as unfit to hold the helm of government, although his majority had been declared, took immediate measures for the cardinal's recall. This was the signal for the renewal of civil strife, to which history has given the name of "the second war of Paris." In December, the parliament set a price on Mazarin's head, and the coalition against him soon became general throughout the realm; he succeeded, however, in penetrating as far as Poitiers, where the court then was, at the head of six thousand men. The duke of Orleans, entering into a league with Condé, sent troops to dispute the cardinal's farther advance; their propositions for his dismissal were rejected by the court, and war with all its horrors again approached the capital. The dearth of provisions became an actual famine, and M. Olier, seeing all his resources exhausted, applied to the queen for succour, which was liberally granted. But there was another and a new cause of affliction which pressed heavily on the pastor's heart. The Calvinists, taking advantage of the intestine divisions, began to excite commotions; every day the situation of affairs became more alarming, and M. Olier wrote to the queen-mother, adjuring her in the name of religion and of the public weal, to yield to the counsels of her best and sagest advisers, by sacrificing her private preferences, and once more obliging Cardinal Mazarin to leave the kingdom. Had she adopted the advice contained in this letter, which was a model of that bold but respectful liberty which churchmen ought to use in addressing princes, she would have spared her people many terrible woes. Unhappily, she was induced to temporize, until she found herself compelled perforce to an act which at this juncture she might have accorded with a prudent and gracious condescension. Into the details of the lamentable struggle that followed we need not enter: Condé and Turenne, the two greatest captains of the age, encountered each other under the walls of Paris, and in the sight of Louis and Mazarin; the contest was long and furious; at length victory was

U

declaring itself on the side of Turenne, whose forces were far superior in number to those of his adversary, when, by the orders of Mdlle. de Montpensier, the daughter of the Duke of Orleans—it was even said that it was her own hand applied the match—the guns of the Bastille suddenly opened their fire upon the royal troops, the gate of S. Antoine was unclosed, and Condé made good his entrance into the city, his soldiers sweeping through the streets out into the Pré aux Clercs, and pillaging all the villages for ten miles round. Owing to dissensions between the princes and the parliament, the citizens also were divided, the lowest of the rabble taking part with Orleans and Condé; the Hôtel de Ville was attacked, many of the magistracy fell victims to the popular fury, the city was in the possession of an armed mob, numbers of the inhabitants were massacred, others sought refuge in the royal camp. It was not until the following October that peace was restored, and the king re-entered Paris.

From these scenes of blood and violence, it is a relief to turn once more to the exertions made by one good man to remedy the frightful evils of the time. The measures adopted by M. Olier for the relief of his suffering people have in substance been already recounted, but there are still two charitable institutions of which no mention has been made. One day, in the course of his pastoral visits, he was accosted by a country girl, who besought his charity. She had come to Paris for protection from the violence of the soldiery, and to obtain the means of subsistence. Touched with compassion at her desolate condition, one, too, fraught with so much peril, he resolved on the instant to open an asylum for young females similarly circumstanced. Those to whom he communicated his design, represented to him in vain the difficulty of accomplishing such a task at such a time, and the great expense it would entail. He answered simply, "The purse of Jesus Christ is inexhaustible to all that put their trust in Him: we have only to begin, He will help us." Accordingly he hired a house, and directed Brother John of the Cross to furnish it forthwith. There he lodged, clothed, and fed no less than two hundred poor country girls, as long as the troubles lasted; and not confining his solicitude to their temporal necessities, he provided them with the benefit of a regular retreat, during which they were instructed in their religious duties, and prepared for confession and communion. But there were other hapless fugitives, whom the dread of a lawless soldiery had driven from their peaceful seclusion to a crowded capital. These were nuns from several of the convents in the environs of the city and the adjoining districts, great numbers of whom, homeless and friendless, were to be seen wandering through the streets, and asking alms of the passers by. For these, the objects of the tenderest pity of every Catholic heart, the pure spouses of Jesus Christ, he also opened an asylum, in a large and commodious house provided with a garden. There all such as pleased to enter kept strict enclosure, fulfilling all the requirements of a community-life; and although they belonged to seven or eight different orders, they all conformed to one rule, under a superioress who was invested by the Prior of S. Germain with the necessary powers. Their temporary association was inaugurated with a course of spiritual exercises, M. Olier assigning them preachers and directors from among the priests of his community, and a chaplain to say Mass for them every day. For four months these poor religious were indebted to the *curé* of S. Sulpice for the means, not only of living according to the spirit of their holy vocation, but of advancing in perfection; and when peace was concluded, they received from the same fatherly hands whatever was requisite for enabling them to return each to her proper convent.

During the disasters of the civil war, the queen-mother had requested M. Picoté, whom she held in the highest respect, to vow in her name some work of piety which he should deem best suited to satisfy the Divine justice; and as the one thought which most touched and grieved his heart was that of the profanation of churches and holy places, and, above all of the Blessed Sacrament, he came to the resolution of establishing a religious house especially dedicated to the adoration of the Most Holy, and the reparation of the outrages of which It was the object. There is every reason to believe that M. Olier was a party to this act of devotion; this, at least, is certain, that he drew up for this princess the form of a vow to the archangel S. Michael, protector of France, in which she engaged to erect an altar to his honour, where, on the first Tuesday in every month, High Mass should be celebrated, at which she would herself assist whenever affairs of state permitted. This vow remained unknown, but that which M. Picoté had made in her name was soon noised abroad, and to it was very generally attributed the favourable change which took place at this crisis in the position of the adverse parties. Peace was no sooner restored than the royal vow was faithfully fulfilled. Some Benedictine nuns, who had fled to Paris for safety, were established in a house in the Rue Perou, where, under the government of Catherine de Bar, better known as the Venerable Mother Mechtilde of the Holy Sacrament, they took the name of Filles du Saint Sacrement, and commenced their perpetual adoration. The queen herself assisted at the ceremony of their installation, bearing a lighted taper, and was the first to make an act of public reparation to Jesus in the Sacrament of His Love. This new institution contributed greatly to an increase of devotion to the Mystery of the Altar in the parish of S. Sulpice, as also to the Blessed Virgin, under whose particular patronage the religious placed themselves.

In connection with this subject may here be mentioned another instance of M. Olier's charitable exertions. It was at the close of the first war of Paris that Mother Madeleine de la Trinité succeeded, with his aid, in founding a house of her order at Paris. The duchess d'Aiguillon had provided the necessary funds for the purpose, but despairing of obtaining the permission of the Cardinal Archbishop of Aix* for the nuns to leave

---

* He was the brother of Cardinal Mazarin, and though the royal

that city, she had bestowed the money upon the Carmelite convent, and on arriving in the great city they found themselves dependent on the bounty of Mme. de Bouteville, a parishioner of S. Sulpice. This pious lady gave up to them two rooms in her own house; but it was the very eve of the civil war: the queen, who had interested herself in their behalf, left Paris, and amidst the alarms and anxieties of the time, Mme. de Bouteville, who had an only son in the royal army, overlooked the necessities of her guests, and for three months Mother Madeleine and her religious were often without bread to eat. Every day they went to S. Sulpice to hear Mass, and from five o'clock till noon they might be seen upon their knees at prayer. M. Olier, who had himself recommended them to Mme. de Bouteville's hospitality, concluded that, as a matter of course, they were suitably cared for, and it was not until one of his priests visited them and beheld with his own eyes their destitute condition, that he became aware of their sufferings, when he caused them to be removed to the house of his brother, the *grand audiencier*, who was absent with the court, and made adequate provision for their support. In the midst of her greatest privations, Mother Madeleine gave testimony of a confidence in God that was truly heroic. At the very time that herself and her nuns were in want of the mere necessaries of life, she had the charity to go in quest of alms for the relief of another distressed community. An act so purely supernatural might well

authority had been put in requisition in order to obtain his consent, he persisted in withholding it, and assured the nuns that nothing should ever induce him to recede from his resolution. They reminded him that it was not in the power of creatures to thwart the designs of God, and that if God were so minded He would take him to Himself, and so end his opposition. To which the archbishop rejoined with a smile, "Thank God, I am in good health, and still a young man. If you are not to establish yourselves at Paris till I am dead, I hope it will be some time first." Shortly after he left for Rome, and M. Olier again availed himself of the same powerful influence in the hope of obtaining from the grand vicar the necessary authorization. On the very day the despatch arrived, tidings reached Aix that the archbishop was dead.

receive a supernatural reward; we may therefore give the readier credence to a circumstance which we find recorded in the annals of the house, viz., that a piece of money, which was placed under an image of the Blessed Virgin, continued to be miraculously multiplied, according to their needs. Peace being temporarily restored, the duchess d'Aiguillon came to their aid, and after overcoming many obstacles apparently insurmountable, the nuns of Notre Dame de Misericorde were established in community on the 3rd of November, 1649, M. Olier, at the desire of F. Yvan, undertaking the office of their director.

The duke of Orleans, by the part he had taken against the king, and by his refusal to sue for pardon, had irreparably ruined his fortunes, and was banished for life to his castle of Blois. His reverses were productive of the happiest effects in disenchanting his mind of the world and its illusions, a result to which, under God, the influence and counsels of M. Olier not a little contributed. He had in his household one Mme. de Saujeon, a lady of great piety and mental refinement, whose family had long been attached to that of Orleans, and from whose society the duke derived much spiritual advantage. A malevolent world chose to throw discredit on the relations subsisting between them, and in 1649 a certain Abbé de la Croix-Christ, a declared favourer of the Jansenistic tenets, persuaded her suddenly to leave the ducal mansion and betake herself to the Carmelite convent, with a view of entering the order. But through the counter-exertions of M. Olier and other ecclesiastics of S. Sulpice, who judged that she could effect much good by remaining in the world, she was induced to return, and, in time, even the most censorious were obliged to confess that she used her influence with the duke in a manner which did credit both to herself and to her advisers. The prince had been addicted to profane swearing to such a degree, that F. de Condren, who was his confessor, told him, at the time he was presumptive heir to the crown, that God would sooner work a miracle than allow either himself or his issue to ascend the throne of

France. But his manners in this, as in other matters, became entirely reformed, a change the merit of which his daughter, who had no liking for Mme. de Saujeon, ascribes mainly to that lady. "I must say" (she says in her Memoirs) "that she contributed greatly to make Monsieur think of his salvation. He went regularly every day to Mass; he was never absent from the High Mass of his parish, or from Vespers, or from other public devotions. He would not tolerate swearing in his house; he corrected himself of this bad habit; and I have great hope that God will have mercy on him." Mme. de Motteville bears similar testimony: "He submitted piously to the Divine Will; he became devout,—his life was exemplary; he had his hours of seclusion and prayer; he left off gambling; and never did prince take more pleasure in retirement than he."

Mme. de Saujeon accompanied the duke and his family to Blois, where, aided by the powerful co-operation of M. Olier, she continued to carry on the good work she had begun at Paris.* That zealous servant of God urged upon him the duty of repairing the evils of the civil war he had excited, by devoting a sum of money annually to restoring the churches of Languedoc, which had been destroyed by the Calvinists, supplying vessels for the altar in the place of those which had been plundered, and relieving the multitudes whom he had been so instrumental in impoverishing. With these admonitions

---

* Mme. de Saujeon subsequently took part in the establishment of a house at Paris, for the reception of ladies who wished to go through the exercises of a retreat. This institution had been projected by M. Olier, but it was not founded until after his death. With that spiritual discernment which was so remarkable in him, he perceived that Mme. de Saujeon, with all her excellences, was not the person to be the superior of a house, and had expressly forbidden her appointment to the office, which was accordingly conferred on Mme. Tronson, mother of the celebrated Sulpitian, a lady of rare piety and virtue, who had been for years under his direction. At her death, however, Mme. de Saujeon was chosen as her successor, and exhibited so imperious a spirit as to lend to the greatest disunion. Her influence at court at length succeeded in procuring the suppression of the community.

the duke cordially complied, charging himself also with the establishment of a community of priests at Blois, a design, however, which was eventually frustrated by the opposition of the Jansenistic party.

CHAPTER XVII.

The Seminary of S. Sulpice—Its establishment and interior spirit.

HITHERTO we have regarded M. Olier simply in his capacity of pastor; he is now to be presented to us in the character by which he is most widely known, and which constitutes his chief title to the gratitude of his countrymen, and to the veneration of all Catholics—that of founder and first superior of the seminary of S. Sulpice. This was the office to which he had been specially destined by God, and for which he had been prepared by many singular favours and many extraordinary trials.

On first taking possession of his parish he had lodged his ecclesiastical students in two houses which he hired adjoining the presbytery. In one of these he placed such as were already priests, in the other such as were in the inferior orders; but as their number rapidly increased, he was obliged to have little cells constructed in the lofts and outhouses, where, owing to the slightness of the partitions, the inmates suffered much, both from heat in summer and from cold in winter. Accordingly in the year 1645, he purchased a site (as related in a former chapter) close to the church on which to erect a commodious seminary. Owing, however, to a number of obstructing causes, the chief of which were the breaking out of civil war, and the consequent want of means, the building was not commenced until the year 1649. It was during the short period of repose which the capital enjoyed that he went, accompanied by M. de

Bretonvilliers, to lay his pressing needs before his heavenly patroness in the Church of Notre Dame. As they knelt together in prayer, he was favoured with a vision of the blessed Mother of God, who appeared to him holding in her hands the model of a building, which she presented to him. Knowing, however, that he did not possess wherewithal to undertake the work, he prayed her to entrust it to his companion kneeling at his side; but she gave him to understand that it was himself she had chosen for its execution. Then nothing doubting but that he should enjoy her powerful aid, he at once determined on fulfilling her behests, undeterred alike by his total want of funds, and by the taunts of those who ridiculed the notion of a man who had no money undertaking to build on so vast a scale. For himself, he trusted simply in God and in His holy Mother, and placed no reliance on human succour. A lady of rank, who had promised him a considerable sum, changed her mind, and withdrew her offer. Instead of evincing any disappointment, he did but express his joy at being obliged to have recourse solely to Jesus and Mary:—"To Them," said he, "the house belongs, and They will provide whatever is necessary for its construction." He refused on one occasion 60,000 livres, and on another 80,000 livres, because the donation was coupled with a condition which fell short, in his judgment, of the greatest perfection, and so was contrary to the vow which he had made always to choose the most perfect way. An instance also is recorded of his refusing a sum of money which was brought him, and begging the donor first to pray to God that he might learn His will.

The first stone of the seminary was solemnly laid by M. Olier himself, in the name of Her whom he loved to style Queen of the Clergy, on the octave of her Nativity; and the effects of her patronage were speedily shown in the contributions which now began to flow in from various quarters. The architect whom he employed was Jacques Le Mercier, the same who had continued the Louvre, and had erected the Palais Royal, and the Church of the Sorbonne. As the building was to be consecrated to the Divine service, M. Olier would have the greatest care taken that all the materials should be the best of their kind; he would have everything solid and substantial, but of the utmost simplicity, without superfluous ornament or display; and finding that without his knowledge the entablature had begun to be adorned with fretwork, he ordered the decoration to be discontinued on the side that faced the street, without regard to the beauty or uniformity of the appearance. The building of the Seminary afforded work for a vast number of people, who, deprived of employment by the disorders of the times, would have been the terror of the city; and so rapid was the progress made, that by the Feast of the Assumption, 1650, the edifice was well-nigh completed. It consisted of a massive square, enclosing a noble court, and pierced with numerous windows; and such was the solidity of the whole structure,* that during the 150 years it remained standing, no repairs were needed, not even in the roof. The chapel, which by M. Olier's desire was finished before the rest of the building, was consecrated in the November of the same year, the first Mass being celebrated by the Papal Nuncio, who, on the Feast of the Assumption, 1651, solemnly

---

* The Seminary of S. Sulpice eventually consisted of four establishments, communicating with each other. Besides the *Grand Séminaire*, so called, there was another, erected by M. Brenier, which bore the name of the *Petit Séminaire*, from the buildings being smaller and the terms lower. A third, which was founded in 1677 by M. Boucher, a doctor of the Sorbonne, was known as the *Petite Communauté des Pauvres Écoliers*, and subsequently as the *Robertins*, from M. Robert, one of its superiors, who endowed it largely. The fourth, being devoted to the teaching of philosophy, was called *des Philosophes*. All four had their country houses; the Grand Séminaire at Issy, as at the present day; the Petit Séminaire at Vaugirard, where the Robertins also had M. Olier's house, near the church; the Philosophers again at Issy, at a place now called the *Solitude*. The building erected by M. Olier was taken down in 1802, in order to throw open the *Place de S. Sulpice*, and a new seminary constructed on the site which had been occupied by the three other establishments, a portion of the garden of the Grand Séminaire, the community of the *Sœurs de l'Instruction*, and other adjoining houses.

blessed the Seminary itself. But the servant of God had already made a formal dedication of the new institution to the Queen of Heaven. In the cathedral church of Chartres, where, as we have seen, he had received such singular intimations of the Divine will, he offered the Holy Sacrifice at her altar, having with him the keys of the all but completed building, and there he prayed the Blessed Virgin to take possession of the house which she had herself designed, and to bestow upon it her patronage and protection. At the same time he presented her image with a costly robe of silk embroidered with gold, which his biographer says is still preserved among the treasures of the church; and in order to bequeath to the seminary a perpetual devotion to Our Lady of Chartres, he obtained for it the privilege of being associated with the chapter of the cathedral, and so being admitted to a community of prayer and spiritual graces.* He would never allow any one to apply to him the title of founder. "You know," he would say, "that it is Jesus in His holy Mother who is the founder and the owner of this house." To this end he placed in the centre of the court a statue of its heavenly patroness, who was represented seated, with the Divine Child standing on her knees, and placing a crown upon her head; and everywhere about the house might be seen the monogram of Mary, not only on every door and window, but on all the furniture, ironwork, and linen. But it was in the chapel especially that his devotion found its greatest gratification. If he was pleased to have the rest of the building a model of plainness and simplicity, here he would have the utmost magnificence displayed. The most skilful artists were employed in its embellishment, and with such success that, when completed, the chapel of S. Sulpice was reckoned among the finest ornaments of the city. That which attracted most admiration was the celebrated composition of Le Brun with which the ceiling was covered, and which was executed after a design

---

* The custom of visiting Notre Dame de Chartres has continued in the Seminary to the present day.

furnished by M. Olier himself. It was descriptive of the triumph of the Blessed Virgin, crowned by the Eternal Father amidst the jubilations of the whole court of heaven, and proclaimed Mother of God by the great council of Ephesus; the spaces between the painting and the cornice being filled with medallions representing the several titles by which she is invoked in her Litanies.

But this devotional beauty and adornment, combined with so much architectural modesty, solidity, and plainness, did but express the dominant idea and interior life and spirit of the institute; and these we have now to consider. The Seminary, it must be borne in mind, was the one great object of M. Olier's mission in the world, the true end of his vocation. To this all his previous life was but the preparation and the prelude. The plan which had been shown him by the Blessed Virgin he did not take merely as the model of the material building which it was the Divine Will he should construct, but he understood the heavenly vision as importing that the spiritual edifice was to be raised according to a pattern which God had designed, and which F. Condren had so often obscurely intimated to his disciples. "When God," said M. Olier, "would renew in these days the fervour of primitive Christianity, He would employ the same means as He made use of at the first. It was by Jesus Christ that He made Himself known to men; and as it was not the design of the Eternal Father to manifest His Son visibly to all the earth, He multiplied and disseminated Him in the Apostles, who, filled with His Spirit, His virtues, and His power, bore Him with them everywhere throughout the world, displaying exteriorly in their persons His patience, His humility, His sweetness, His charity, and all His virtues. To correspond, then, with the design of God, we must inspire our youth with the sentiments and virtues of Jesus Christ, and He must live in each as really as in the Apostle who said, "*I live, now not I; but Christ liveth in me.*" Such, then, is the fundamental idea on which the Seminary of S. Sulpice rested, devotion to the Interior Life of our Lord,—a devotion established and perpetuated by the institution of a festival so designated, which was celebrated annually, and, during a large portion of the year, even weekly. The object of this festival was to honour with a special devotion the interior dispositions with which our Lord accompanied His mysteries, and all the actions of His life; as, for instance, His sentiments of piety towards His Father, of charity towards men, self-annihilation in His own regard, horror for the world and for sin; and the fruit to be derived from this devotion was an abundant participation in these dispositions, according to the admonition of S. Paul,—" *Let this mind be in you, which was also in Christ Jesus.*" To reproduce this interior life in the hearts of the seminarists was M. Olier's one unceasing object, as being the peculiar vocation of all Christians, and especially of priests. "Then only," he said, "are men worthy of these august titles, when it can be affirmed of them,—It is thus Jesus Christ spoke; it is thus Jesus Christ acted; it is thus Jesus Christ suffered." And this has ever been the primary teaching of S. Sulpice. "We are for ever repeating," writes M. Leschassier, "those words of S. Ambrose,— '*Omnia Christus est nobis : signaculum in fronte, ut semper confiteamur ; signaculum in corde, ut semper diligamus; signaculum in brachio, ut semper operemur.*'* How widely should we have departed from the spirit of our fathers, if we abandoned the holy practice signified by these three expressions: *Per Christum, cum Christo, in Christo.*"

Next to the devotion to the interior life of Jesus, M. Olier laid as the second foundation of his Seminary devotion to the interior life of Mary, a festival in honour of which was also observed every year. It had for its principal object the interior dispositions of this incomparable creature in all her actions, and the treasure of graces with which she was enriched. "Jesus Christ,"

---

* "Christ is all things to us: a seal on the forehead, that we may ever confess; a seal in the heart, that we may ever love; a seal on the arm, that we may ever work."

he writes, "who promised to live in holy souls, communicated His life to no one with such plenitude as to His holy Mother. The communication which He makes to the whole body of the Church is far inferior to it. Mary is as a sacrament by which He distributes His blessings and His graces; and it is to this abundant source that the clergy must resort, to imbibe the life of Jesus Christ. S. John beheld all this: he represents the most Holy Virgin as a woman clothed with the sun, having on her head a crown of twelve stars, emblem of the apostles, and the moon under her feet; teaching us thereby that, wholly filled and penetrated with Jesus Christ, figured by the sun, she fills in her turn all the apostles and the Church, and gives them all that they have of light and splendour. She is shown, also, with the dragon under her feet; and this is to denote that all the apostles, the disciples, the priests, and the other ministers of the hierarchy of the Church, even to the exorcists, hold and receive from Jesus Christ, in Her, the power to trample the serpent under foot, and crush his head. According to this design, it pleased God that, although His holy Mother was not present at the Last Supper, inasmuch as she was not to receive the visible priesthood, according to the order of Melchisedech, nevertheless she should be present in the *cenaculum* on Whit Sunday, there to receive the apostolic grace and spirit; that is to say, the spirit of zeal for the glory of God and the salvation of men.; thereby teaching the Church that it could never be renewed, save in the company of Mary, and by participating in her spirit."

To keep this great and beautiful truth ever before the minds, and, as it were, before the very eyes of the students, he placed in the chapel a large painting by Le Brun, representing the Queen of the Clergy receiving the plenitude of the Holy Spirit on the day of Pentecost, which from her is distributed among the apostles and the assembled faithful. His wish was to have had ten other pictures executed by the same artist, the design for which he communicated to him in writing, all intended to exhibit the Mother of God as the channel and instrument of all graces in the Church; but one only was completed, that of the Visitation, in which mystery the Blessed Virgin exercised her apostolate in behalf of S. John the Baptist and S. Elizabeth.

This doctrine was not, indeed, peculiar to the founder of S. Sulpice. Bossuet and Bourdaloue regard it but as the consequence of the mystery of the Incarnation itself. "God," says the former, "having been pleased to give us Jesus Christ once, and by the Most Holy Virgin, this order changes no more. Having once received by her the universal principle of grace, we also receive, through her instrumentality, the different applications of grace in all the various states which go to make up the Christian life." "Mary," says Bourdaloue, "is the coadjutrix of God in the order of our salvation; and as salvation began by her, and by her consent to the word of God, it is by her and through her co-operation that it must be consummated." "This consequence, it is true, was not deduced," as the Abbé Faillon observes, "by the early Fathers generally, though some of them perceived it, but it is the property of Christian truths to receive their development successively, according to the wants of the Church in different ages and the designs of Providence; and God seems to have reserved the exposition of this doctrine principally for the age of theologians and doctors, who wrote with greater precision and with more of method than did the Fathers."* But the great promulgators of the doctrine in these latter times were the men whom God raised up to be the reformers of the clergy. Cardinal de Berulle and F. Condren revived it in the Oratory, and thence M. Olier, F. Eudes, and many others received it, to dissemi-

* "In fact," he continues, "S. John Damascene, who gave a new form to theology, and whose decisions are received by the Greeks with the same respect as those of S. Thomas by the Latins, S. Thomas himself, Albert the Great, his master, S. Bonaventure, S. Anselm, Peter de Blois, S. Antonine, Gerson, S. Bernardin of Siena, and a vast number of other doctors, teach simply and positively, as a matter on which all are agreed, that Mary is the channel of all graces."

nate it in their turn. "If the wisdom of God," wrote M. Olier, "was not pleased in the beginning to make known, by the holy fathers, to the whole body of the faithful the transcendent communications which Jesus makes to His Virgin Mother, and the intimate union which He has with her, and for which she is called throughout the Church *Electa ut sol* (elect as the sun), it is but meet that we should apply ourselves to the holy verities which Providence vouchsafes to manifest in the progress of time. The Seminary of S. Sulpice, entering into the design of God, devotes and dedicates itself to preserve with honour this glorious treasure, and to exhibit in the sanctity of its manners this hidden life. The end it proposes to itself is to derive from this exhaustless fount of divine life whatever gifts, graces, and virtues it is able to acquire; and this also it is which ought strongly to move all ecclesiastics to nourish themselves with the interior life of Jesus in Mary, in order to correspond with the intentions of our Blessed Lord, who in disclosing to us anything of His riches, does so only to make us sharers of them."

All from Jesus through Mary; all therefore to Jesus through Mary: this may be said to be the formulary which represents the distinctive idea or fundamental principle of the Seminary of S. Sulpice; and in nothing is it more conspicuously displayed than in the devotions which M. Olier originated, or to which he was instinctively attracted. This made him select S. John the Evangelist as one of its special patrons; for on whom could his choice have more appropriately fallen than on him who lay on Jesus's breast, and into whose heart Jesus when dying instilled the filial love He bore His holy Mother? "The love of Jesus and of Mary," said F. de Condren, "was so holy a love, that something of it was to be bequeathed to the Church; and to preserve it S. John was put in the place of Christ, when He said to His blessed Mother, 'Behold thy son:' *thy* son, not another. Mary thus received him as her own son, and this son survived her. S. John, on his part, forgetting self to take the place of Jesus, continued to render to Mary the same duties, and to serve her with the same filial love which Jesus showed her. Fain would I renew in souls this grace, this first odour of heaven, this singular benediction, which was given at the beginning; but as I am not worthy of the office, I beg our Lord to pour down His Spirit abundantly on others, who may accomplish so blessed a work." M. Olier was one of those in whom it may be truly said this prayer was granted. "As the most holy Virgin," says the man of God, in his panegyric of S. John, "though filled with the plenitude of the sacerdotal spirit, had not the sacerdotal character, and therefore could not exercise in her own person the functions of the priesthood, the Saviour gave her S. John on Calvary, not only that he might be a son to her in His place, but that by the Holy Mysteries which he celebrated for her and for her intentions he might supply her with the means of satisfying the ardent desires of her heart for the establishment of the Church; as also console her for the absence of her Son by the happiness she enjoyed of feeding on Him daily. This is why God does not leave the holy Virgin S. Joseph for her guardian, or any secular person, who had not been ordained priest of the new law; he does not even leave her any woman for her guardian, as might have seemed more fitting in the eyes of the world; but he leaves her one who is both virgin and priest, a man who is pure as an angel, and superior to the angels by his office of *sacrificer* of Jesus Christ, an office with which he was invested that he might offer upon the altar the continuation of the sacrifice of the cross, for the intentions of the most holy Virgin."

This pious practice of offering Masses for the intentions of the blessed Mother of God was one much observed by the French Oratory, and was particularly dear to Cardinal de Berulle and F. de Condren, both of whom were favoured with extraordinary lights from Heaven. M. Olier had made a vow to say Mass every Saturday for her intentions, and this vow he faithfully performed; but on founding the seminary he directed that three Masses should be offered every day, the whole fruit of which he would have put into the hands of Mary; considered, in the first, as queen of the Church triumphant; in the second, as queen and advocate of the Church militant; in the third, as queen and consoler of the Church suffering; and in a book, in which he marked down the several intentions with which Mass might be said, he recommended his priests to offer the Holy Sacrifice on Saturdays for the intentions of the Blessed Virgin.

So devout a client of Mary could never, we may be sure, separate from this Queen of Virgins the chaste spouse whom Heaven had given her. Another patron of the seminary, therefore, was S. Joseph, whose extraordinary vocation has so close an affinity to that of priests. He would have his clergy also cultivate a particular devotion to the holy Apostles, as being, after Jesus Christ, the foundations of the Church; and it was always the custom at S. Sulpice to celebrate High Mass upon their festivals. It was his wish, moreover, that there should ever be twelve individuals in the seminary who should charge themselves with the duty of rendering special honour to the twelve Apostles; venerating in them the abundance of their Apostolic grace, blessing God for having chosen them to be the preachers of His Gospel to the world, and, above all, imploring of Him a participation of their spirit for the universal Church, and in particular for all the ecclesiastics of the house. From a like motive of piety he called the twelve principal apartments in the seminary by their names.

Nor were these the only members of the heavenly court whose patronage M. Olier sought. Seeing the prediction of the Venerable Mother Agnes fulfilled before his eyes, he was moved to put in execution a desire he had long entertained of associating himself with the great order of S. Dominic. To this end he was admitted a member of the third order towards the close of the year 1651, with several other priests of his community, in the chapel of the seminary. There is good reason for believing that he attached himself also to the third order of S. Francis of Assisi, as well as to that of

S. Francis of Paula; at least both are equally ambitious of claiming him for a brother. His devotion to S. Martin of Tours has already been mentioned, and in the December of 1653 he obtained from the chapter of the church a formal association for himself and his successors, and for all the ecclesiastics of the seminary, in their prayers, Masses, and good works. And even yet his holy greed was not satisfied. To honour the great Apostle of France, S. Denis, and to inspire his company with a continual devotion to the saint, he effected a similar association with the Abbey of Montmartre; and ever mindful of the dream which had determined his vocation to the ecclesiastical state, he added to his list of patrons the two illustrious doctors of the Church, S. Ambrose and S. Gregory the Great, and celebrated their festivals every year, a custom which has been perpetuated to the present day.

But the principal feast of the seminary was that of the Presentation of the Blessed Virgin, whose dedication of herself in the Temple, in unconscious preparation for the incommunicable dignity of Mother of an Incarnate God, M. Olier loved to regard as presenting the most perfect model to those who, in embracing the clerical state, separate themselves from the world in order to fit themselves for the celebration of the august Mysteries of the Altar. On that day every ecclesiastic in the house was to make a solemn renewal of his engagements, uniting himself in spirit to the interior dispositions of the daughter of the King of kings, when she left her people and her father's house. The first occasion of this observance was in the November of 1650, when (as we have seen) the new chapel was consecrated. M. Olier, with that tender childlike piety which he ever entertained for the Virgin Mother, went to Nôtre Dame to invite her to be present; the eve was kept as a strict fast, a practice never discontinued, and the Papal Nuncio himself presided at the ceremony. It happened that the general assembly of the clergy was being held in Paris at the time, and the Bishops deputed one of their number to express, in the name of their united body, the joy and satisfaction with which they had beheld the happy fruits which the seminary had produced during the eight years of its existence, and the confident hopes they entertained of the good it would hereafter effect for the Church; at the same time bestowing their benediction. An extraordinary fervour was enkindled in the hearts of the whole community, and all felt that the act in which they had been engaged would prove a fresh source of graces to the seminary. M. Olier himself, with gratitude for the favours his Benefactress had obtained, besought her to indicate to him in what way he could best evince his love and homage, and received this answer: "Prepare me hearts;" by which (he says) it was meant that he should learn that what was most pleasing to the Mother was to have hearts to serve her Son in the ministry of His Church.

But he soon received a substantial proof of her watchful care and powerful aid. The letters patent accorded by the crown in 1645 had never been registered by the parliament, and so many obstacles had been thrown in the way, that M. Olier had ceased his applications, without any intention of renewing them. But two days after the ceremony just described, he felt an inward conviction that his petition would be granted. He accordingly sought an interview with one of the principal officers of parliament, on whom the matter chiefly depended. At first the magistrate made many difficulties, but on M. Olier giving utterance to a few words which had been suggested to him in prayer, the heart of him whom he was addressing seemed (as he expresses it) suddenly to expand, and throwing himself into the arms of the man of God, he said, "Yes, I will do it; and I thank you for the occasion you offer me of terminating my official course by rendering God this service." It was the custom for all communities to select some person of influence as their civil protector; but M. Olier, doubting whether it would be pleasing to his heavenly patroness that he should have any earthly helper, went to Nôtre Dame to learn her will; when she (he says) "who loves order, and would have all things done in order," gave him to understand that he should enjoy her protection by taking as his patron the President Molé, who was a relative of his, and whom he had already in intention chosen for the office. This great man received the proposal with the utmost cordiality, responding feelingly to the pious terms in which it was conveyed, and in all respects fulfilling the assurance which had been given, that in him the seminary should find the protector it sought. The parliament registered the royal letters, and the Seminary of S. Sulpice became henceforth a legalized corporation, capable of holding and inheriting property, and enjoying such privileges and immunities as the state could bestow.

CHAPTER XVIII.

M. Olier's Method of Spiritual Training.

THE servant of God had constructed his material building according to the pattern which had been shown him by the Blessed Virgin. But there was a spiritual edifice to be raised, the model of which had also been divinely given, and we are now to see by what process this work was accomplished; in other words, how the holy founder of S. Sulpice formed the ecclesiastics of his seminary to the virtues and perfection of the sacerdotal state. The effects produced by the system he inaugurated were in a short time so remarkable, that when M. Godeau, Bishop of Vence, visited the seminary, and some of the clergy who were with him, admiring the beauty and solidity of the structure, exclaimed, in the words of the disciples to our Lord, *Vide quales lapides* ("Behold what manner of stones"), that prelate replied, "Nay, rather, *Videte quales homines* ('Behold what manner of men')."

That M. Olier had a very exalted idea of the sacerdotal state, and of the perfection to which priests are called, it were superfluous to state. "They are set in the Church," he would say, "to be models of sanctity to all conditions of men; consequently they ought to possess the graces and the virtues of all other states; religious as well as seculars ought to see in them all that is necessary to their own perfection. If priests who are detached from the world are said to live like religious, it is only a sign of the corruption of the age; for it ought rather to be said, in the language of the saints, that religious lead the life of priests, seeing that priests are bound to live in such wise, and religious are bound to imitate the holiness of priests, to follow their steps, and sanctify themselves by practising those rules of perfection which were originally given for the clergy.* Accordingly he would have the course of probation which a priest goes through, as strict of its kind as the noviciate in a religious house. When any applied for admission he would confer with them in person, and examine them as to their dispositions and the motives which led them to embrace the ecclesiastical state, especially whether they had any view to obtaining benefices, or retaining such as they already possessed; and he would sometimes subject candidates to a prolonged suspense before receiving them as inmates of the house. His next object was to inspire them with a desire of Christian perfection. A cleric, he said, is one who, if not already in the state of perfection, at least aspires to it, and to this end he must deny himself and die to the world. "The seminary is the hedge which separates the vineyard of the Lord from the world. This hedge is full of thorns, and the world ought not to approach it without feeling the prick of them; that is, without being made sensible of the horror we have of its execrable maxims. This house ought to be so replenished with evangelical virtues, as to inspire distaste, aversion, and

---

* On the subject of the relative perfection of clerics and religious, the reader is referred to Faber's "Growth in Holiness," chap. ix.

horror of all the contrary vices. We ought to strip ourselves of the world's livery, and its whole exterior, and exhibit nothing in our persons which can serve to attract its esteem."

Anything, therefore, in his ecclesiastics which he deemed wanting in simplicity or modesty, he instantly remarked upon and strove to correct. Thus observing that M. de Lantages had a way of walking which seemed to him to savour of the affected manners of the world, he often begged him in the sweetest manner to carry himself differently. But the habit had become so natural to him, that in spite of all his endeavours to correct himself, he was continually, from inadvertence, relapsing into it. One day M. Olier being in his confessional, saw the young man pass by, carrying himself as usual, upon which he stepped behind him, and taking him by the shoulders, said, "Ah! why do you still walk in that way?" The rebuke proved effectual: M. de Lantages never offended in like manner again. So, too, though he laid much stress on their observing towards each other, and towards every one, all the kindly attentions which are inseparable from true charity, he could not endure in them what he calls "affected civilities, compliments, witticisms, and other little worldly gentilities; studied postures and much bowing, the object of which is simply to please, and to be thought courteous, polished, and well-bred. That which ought to render us welcome in all companies," he adds, "is our being dead to the world; for if we are valued for anything else we can produce no fruit. We shall but inspire an attachment to ourselves, and a certain secret esteem, which in fact is what we are seeking, although perhaps not by any deliberate act of the will. God may, if He please, make us esteemed by others, but it is a gift which He bestows on those who do not wish for it, who avoid and despise it, and who at first attract only the scorn of the world."

To preserve among the young ecclesiastics a spirit of holy equality, and prevent all assumption of superiority, he directed that in the general exercises of the seminary there should be no distinction of places; and perceiving one of them disposed to take precedence, on account of his better birth and position in the world, he reproved him publicly in these terms: "If you love Jesus Christ, you will rejoice to be always near Him or with Him. I would advise you, therefore, to take *this* place" (pointing to the lowest), "for it is the one He loves best, and has chosen for Himself, and where you will be certain to find Him." However, as no community could subsist without distinctions and gradations, to prevent any evil thence arising, he would say to those who occupied any honourable position, "First places in this house are to be taken as humiliations, for they are such as are affected by the children of the world. The desire of precedence belongs to the flesh and the devil; when, then, we have to put ourselves before others, we ought to be ashamed of seeing ourselves in the place which the devil seeks and Jesus Christ shuns." Accordingly, he would have all perform in turn the menial offices of the house: sweep the floors, wash the dishes, wait at table, serve the poor; and in all this he might have proposed himself for an example; for in whatever company he was he seated himself, in spirit, at the feet of others. Nay, M. de Bretonvilliers records in so many words that he has seen him cleaning shoes, and performing many little services of a like kind, with a fervour which it was most touching to witness; and M. de Lantages relates how, on his returning one day from Vaugirard in very dirty plight, M. Olier took a towel, and, kneeling down, wiped his feet and then kissed them, and this with so much sweetness and simplicity, that the act seemed to have nothing of singularity in it. He particularly disliked hearing any speak disparagingly of themselves, knowing how often a secret self-esteem takes the disguise of professed contempt. "Self-humiliation," he would say, "to be genuine, must spring from a sincere desire of losing the good opinion of others." Some one observing in his presence, and before several other persons, that he was a miserable sinner, M. Olier said, "When a man wishes really to humble himself, he is not satisfied with accusing himself in general terms, but mentions some particular fault of which he is guilty." For himself, he would never endure to have a word uttered to his advantage; he instantly said something which might raise the mind to God, or changed the conversation: to be praised was positive torture to him. Neither would he allow any marks of distinction to be shown him which he deemed incompatible with the vow he had made to be the servant of all. One day, hearing some person call him simply *Monsieur*, as usual in designating the master of a house, he said, in a loud tone, "There is no master here except Jesus Christ. I am but a servant, and an unprofitable servant."

Anything that betokened a passion for news or a love of sight-seeing was his particular aversion. Not that he laid any express prohibitions on the seminarists, for he preferred that they should mortify themselves simply from a motive of advantage to their souls, and in this, as in all things, he was careful to avoid excess. Being on a journey, accompanied by some of his ecclesiastics, he had occasion, more than once, to rebuke them for stopping to gaze at the mansions and noble buildings which were visible from the road. On arriving at Bourges, he took them to the cathedral, which is a magnificent specimen of Gothic architecture, and observing that they scarcely ventured to raise their eyes and admire what was before them, he said, "The beauty of churches is not like that of the things of this world. You may look at churches, and at whatever is consecrated to the worship of God, provided you do it in a religious spirit, and not out of curiosity. *I have loved the beauty of Thy house*, says the Psalmist, *and the place where Thy glory dwelleth:* and if subjects rejoice to see their princes in magnificent palaces, what ought to be the delight of Christians at beholding the beauty of the places consecrated to the service of their Master, the King of kings and the Lord of the universe! These vast piles of stone, the music of the bells resounding far and wide, these splendid functions and august ceremonies and rich decorations proclaim, as clearly as is possible here below, the greatness and the majesty of the God whom we serve and adore."

As for himself, so perfect was his mortification of his senses, that they seemed to have abdicated their office. A servant of the house being found fault with one day by one of the community for taking the superior a basin of soup that was quite cold, the man replied, "What does it signify whether it is cold or hot? He does not taste what he eats, and takes no notice of what is set before him." Another time, when he was being vested for High Mass, the subdeacon, in putting on the maniple, ran the pin, without knowing it, into his arm. Finding there was some resistance, he said to M. Olier that he could not get it in any further; on which the man of God, without removing his arm, replied, in his usual gentle way, "It will go no further, because it has pierced to the bone." So great was his abstraction when engaged in any act of devotion, that the most sudden surprises were unheeded. One Holy Saturday, while performing the benediction of the fonts, the burning wax of the Paschal candle kept falling on his hand, and when one of the assistants at last perceived what was taking place, and snatched the candle from him, he did it with such violence that it almost took the skin off; yet all this time the servant of God betrayed no consciousness of pain. It need scarcely be said that a man so mortified would strongly recommend to others the practice of corporal penance, and the use of the discipline was consequently as frequent at S. Sulpice as in many religious houses. An ecclesiastic observing to him one day that, instead of this sort of penance he preferred offering the Holy Sacrifice, which had a wholly different value in the sight of God, M. Olier replied, "Strange that we are so lavish of the Blood of Christ, and so sparing of our own! If it is true that the Son of God supplies for us, yet ought we not to begin by offering to the Eternal Father something of our own before we have recourse to this divine compensation for our poverty and misery?" But in expressing himself thus he was far from approving any indiscreet and excessive fervour; on the contrary, he severely censured those who acted merely in obedience to their own impulses, being used to say that austerities become cruelties when they are no longer prompted by the Spirit of God. It was one of his maxims that the ill-regulated attempts at mortification which are made in youth, without the advice of a director, often injure the constitution for life; and, besides, such imprudent austerities are commonly of short duration.

But while earnestly enjoining "bodily exercise," he did not fail to warn his disciples, that when it has not the mortification of the interior as its base and principle, it "is profitable for little;" nay, it produces in the secret of the heart a certain complacency and self-esteem. He would, therefore, have them apply themselves to the destruction of their vices less by maceration of the body than by the Spirit of our Lord and the practice of Christian virtues. Interior mortification (he said) has none of the disadvantages of bodily mortification. In the first place, it is capable of being more constantly practised; for the body cannot be made to suffer unintermittingly, whereas, the interior can be mortified continually. In the second place, it is more universal in its character and effects. He who wears a hair shirt punishes his sense of feeling, leaving his other senses unchastised, and it is the same with fasting; but interior mortification extends the infliction to the whole man itself. In crucifying the heart, we crucify that which is the universal source of all our appetites and inclinations. From the first, therefore, it was his endeavour to lead the seminarists to mortify their own judgment and their own will; and before admitting them to the tonsure, he spent an entire year in inculcating the necessity of killing self in their hearts. To this end he insisted especially on the duty of being perfectly open and sincere with their director, following his counsels without reserve, and obeying the rules of the institute with most minute exactness. No one on earth (he said) is dispensed from submission, however exalted the lights with which God has favoured him. Such was our Lord's own fidelity to this rule, that in His infancy He was subject to the Blessed Virgin and S. Joseph. With this example before him, who would wish to guide himself? Even though God may have bestowed upon us some extraordinary grace, He would not have us take it as our rule of conduct until we have obtained the sanction of superiors. We are not bound to follow private revelations, but we *are* bound to obey those whom God has set over us. For our greater perfection He may give us some extraordinary light, in order to try our fidelity in sacrificing even it to the duty of obedience. The Spirit of God is not contrary to Itself; and should a superior order that which does not accord with His intentions respecting us, we should do a work most agreeable to Him in obeying. Thus, obedience was one of the virtues on which he laid the greatest stress. He who faithfully obeys the rule, he would say, is invulnerable; whereas he who lets himself follow his own caprices lays himself open to the assaults of the enemy, and runs great risk of falling. No inmate of the house was to step outside the door, or make or receive visits, without leave obtained of the superior; and the observance of silence was so strictly enforced, that M. de Bretonvilliers could say that, except in time of recreation, not a word was spoken, although the community consisted of more than a hundred persons. Fidelity to a rule formed the subject of the last capital lesson which M. Olier gave the young ecclesiastics on their quitting the seminary to enter on their duties in the world: "If you observe a good rule of life, faithfully and out of love for the Lord" (he would say to them), "you have everything to hope: you will live for God. But if you have no rule, or if you are not faithful in observing it, simply from motives of faith, and as far as circumstances permit, you have everything to fear for your salvation: you will not be living for God."

But this habit of mortification and obedience was not its own end: it was wholly in order to the forming in themselves the life of Jesus Christ. Next to the devotion of the Blessed Sacrament, which (as need not be repeated here) he regarded as the perennial spring of that Divine life, the means he prescribed were prayer, and meditation, especially on the Holy Scriptures. "Prayer," he said, "is the supplement of the Most Holy Eucharist, our Lord having given both the one and the other in order to unite us to Himself. In prayer we receive the same benefits as in communion, though not in equal proportion; in prayer, as in the Eucharist, we adore Jesus Christ present in such manner that there needs, as it were, only the removal of a veil to disclose Him to us; in prayer, Jesus Christ nourishes the soul and fortifies it; He unites Himself closely to it; He abides in it, and it in Him; He makes it like unto Himself, inspires it with a disgust for the gross things of earth, fills it with love for those of heaven, and makes it terrible to the evil one." It was his desire that the seminarists should faithfully adhere to the method of prayer * followed in the house; not that he would lay restrictions upon those who felt themselves attracted to any different mode, provided only they obtained the approval of their director; but he judged it to be of the last importance, that in a community there should be one fixed principle and rule from which none should be allowed to deviate except for solid reasons; and he expressly prohibited those who were moved to follow another path, however far advanced in perfection, from making it matter of conversation with others, lest it should have the effect of inspiring distaste for the accustomed method. Neither would he dispense any from the obligation of preparing beforehand the subject of meditation, for fear of illusion; but when once they had faithfully complied with this direction, he would not have them do violence to themselves by pursuing the subject further, but bade them yield themselves in all simplicity to the attractions of God's Spirit.

Another means which he especially recommended to his disciples was the assiduous study of the actions of their Divine Master as recorded in the Gospels, and of the interior dispositions with which He accompanied them. "Our Lord" (he said) "would have us every day receive some maxim from His mouth, and live in the depth of our soul according to what we shall thus have

* See end of this chapter.

learnt. It is this spiritual life, this hidden life, this interior disposition of the heart, which above all He desires in us." To this end, therefore, he taught the seminarists to read a chapter of the Gospel on their knees, with head uncovered; then to consider some one of our Lord's acts or virtues; and, lastly, to examine themselves, and see what their own dispositions were in performing the same act or practising the same virtue. This exercise he called Particular Examination, and to facilitate its practice a book was composed for the use of the seminary, by M. de Poussé and M. Tronson, the groundwork of which was furnished by M. Olier.

Indeed, the study of the Scriptures he declared to be one of God's express commands to the house, and he directed the ecclesiastics of the seminary to treat the Bible, even exteriorly, with all respect and reverence, by giving it the most honourable place in their chamber. "Holy Scripture" (he said) "interiorly nourishes the soul; it is a ciborium in which God has been pleased to hide Himself, in order to give Himself to us and communicate His graces. And, in fact, according to S. Paulinus, there were anciently in the holy tabernacle two compartments, one beside the other, in one of which was the Blessed Sacrament and in the other the Divine Scriptures. One contained the Word of God, under the sacred species, in the majestic silence of His Divinity; the other, the Word of God expounding Himself exteriorly, and rendering audible that which He says in Himself, but expounding Himself after our mode and fashion of expressing ourselves. For the Word of God, that is, what God says in Himself, is incomprehensible, God saying for ever and ever all that He is and all that He knows; and this is immense, infinite! But in the Scriptures we read only a single syllable of what that fathomless Bosom pronounces within Itself; we see the thoughts of God only in a very imperfect manner. While listening to this infinite word, the unfolding of the eternal secret of God, we must keep our mind respectfully attentive to the revealed words, and to that portion of the Divine knowledge which He manifests in His Scriptures, regarding them as the oracle whence God speaks to us, as the ark and the tabernacle where He is pleased to be adored and consulted." Of this devout respect M. Olier was himself a perfect model. He always read the Scriptures on his knees and with head uncovered; his Bible occupied a sort of throne, which he had erected for it in his chamber; and on entering or leaving it, he humbly adored the Divine Spirit residing in the Sacred Book. From a motive of religion, he had its covers adorned with a magnificent design in silver, representing the Word of God worshipped by the Cherubim on the one side, under the emblem of an open volume; on the other, under the Eucharistic veils, with this inscription, which aptly expresses the devotion of the seminary to the Divine Word, in these two states: "*Par cultus et amor utrique.** This Bible is still preserved in the seminary.

The virtue of religion, as being immediately conversant with the service and worship of Almighty God, M. Olier regarded as peculiarly incumbent on ecclesiastics, and he desired that the ceremonies of the Church, as being instituted to this very end, should be observed with the most scrupulous exactness. Herein he had the assistance of men endowed with no common gifts. Besides M. de Bassancourt, of his own community (to whom reference has more than once been made), he enjoyed the active co-operation of the learned Benedictine, Father Bauldry, who volunteered his services to instruct the students in this important department of their duties. So perfect was the knowledge they thus attained, that the seminary came to be regarded as a high authority in such matters; and even M. Bourdoise himself, towards the close of his life, when in doubt on any point, would apply for information to the clergy of S. Sulpice. But the servant of God, as scarcely need be said, did not content himself with familiarizing his ecclesiastics with mere external details; he would initiate them also into the interior spirit and hidden meanings of

---

* Equal worship and love to both.

the ceremonial of the Church, that their acts might be at once intelligent and devout, as well as faithful to the letter. "God the Father," he said, "takes no pleasure in any earthly thing, unless He beholds in it something of His Son. Every act of the Jews was a figure of Jesus Christ: *Omnia in figura contingebant illis.* Why should we be less religious towards Him? Even in their most ordinary actions, as, for instance, the eating of the manna, they were to see our Lord, and to worship Him by faith; much more, then, ought we, who have had the advantage of receiving His Holy Spirit in order that all we do might be filled therewith, to consider Him in our most common acts, and interiorly adore Him in every thing that can represent Him to us." Occupied with this thought he composed his "Explanation of the Ceremonies of High Mass," in which, while inculcating the sublimest doctrine, he indicated, in a manner truly Patristic, some of the many allegorical and mystical senses of which the several actions of the sacred rite are susceptible, with a view of showing the wonderful harmony of the whole, and the importance of not omitting one single item, however insignificant it may appear.

Besides taking part in the ordinary exercises of the seminary, the students assisted in rotation at the different functions performed in the parish church; but some of the directors complaining that this frequent and prolonged attendance was a serious interruption to other avocations, M. Olier, before making an alteration to which he was very averse, consulted M. Bourdoise on the subject, who, in that laconic manner which was peculiar to him, replied, "Monsieur, Monsieur, you must labour *in* the hierarchy, not alongside of it;" meaning that ecclesiastics destined to become parish priests, ought to be trained to parochial duties. And such had ever been M. Olier's practice. As soon as a seminarist had been ordained priest, he passed into the community, and assisted the clergy in the administration of the sacraments; he was then permitted to officiate himself, attended by the superior, who corrected any error he observed, and supplied whatever instruction was required. He had another motive for the practice, and that was the edification of the people, who might profit by the catechetical instructions which the young ecclesiastics gave, as well as by their devout and reverent demeanour. The following little incidents, which are noted by the Abbé Faillon, may serve to illustrate both the religiousness of the master and the fidelity with which his scholars copied him. A young priest who usually served M. Olier's Mass having inadvertently laid his cap upon the altar while making the necessary preparations, was punished by being prohibited from offering the Holy Sacrifice for eight days. The young Prince de Conti, who had entered the ecclesiastical state, happening to attend some public office at S. Sulpice, asked the student beside him what was taught at the Seminary. "My lord," was the reply, "we are taught to keep silence in church." The prince took the rebuke in good part, and thanked the young cleric for his counsel. M. de Sève, who at sixty years of age resigned a high official situation in the parliament of Paris to enter the Seminary of S. Sulpice, which he edified by his childlike humility and obedience, observing a priest who was vesting for Mass put the amice on his shoulders without first putting it over his head, as the rubrics direct, and indeed as the prayers to be used while vesting expressly imply, said to him, "How is it, sir, that you do not scruple to tell a lie at the very moment you are about to offer the Holy Sacrifice? You ask God to place the amice on your head, and you put it only on your shoulders!" Such was the spirit of reverence and strict observance that characterized S. Sulpice.

But perfection was the rule of the whole house, and under M. Olier's direction the Seminary is described as resembling a religious community in the glow of its first fervour. Each new comer, as he entered its walls, felt as if he had been brought into the society of the early Christians: the world was so totally renounced and excluded, that even to speak of it except in terms of condemnation occasioned a remorse of conscience, and such was the love of poverty that the inmates seemed to vie with each other who should have what was worst and meanest, and perform the lowest and most distasteful offices. Everything was virtually in common, for what each possessed was equally at the service of his brethren. Gathered from all classes, and from all parts of the country, there were no differences or preferences among them; and so completely did each one hold himself at the disposal of his superior, that at a word he would have hastened to the other end of the earth. Indeed, so ready were they to follow and almost to anticipate his will, that he was obliged to be careful what he said, lest the hearer should on the instant act upon it to the detriment of his health. Such is the account given by one who, himself a Sulpitian, is familiar with the traditions of the house. One thing they inherited from their founder in a singular degree—a tender, trustful love of Mary. Nothing was undertaken without consulting her; each one saluted her image as he entered or quitted his room, or that of his director. They loved to speak of her to one another, and would fast or perform some other act of mortification on her vigils; need it be added, that they spoke also much and often of union with her Divine Son, and that the crucifix and the image of Mary were never divided? At M. Olier's suggestion, each had one or two monitors, whose business it was to apprise him of his faults. At the first stroke of the bell all the doors were thrown open, strict silence was observed, not a look even was exchanged in the corridors or on the stairs, and often when two saluted as they passed, neither perceived who the other was. At recreation the stranger would have been at once struck with the brotherly affection, frankness, and mutual deference that marked the intercourse of the assembled students; the conversation, though it ran on pious subjects, was invariably cheerful and even lively, and the whole house was redolent of a certain sweet and pleasant air of kindliness and charity, which to one coming from the world without had a charm and an attraction it was impossible to resist. M. de Lantages, who, while M. Olier was testing his vocation was a frequent visitor at S. Sulpice, thus describes his impressions at the time: "Though the distance from my lodging was considerable, the fatigue was nothing to me; I seemed rather to fly than to walk, such was the pleasure I experienced in going to the house. I found there a perfection so far beyond anything we had yet attained, that I said to a friend, Truly ours is a mere playing at being devout; it is only at the Seminary that real devotion is practised."

When the servant of God first undertook the charge of the parish, one of the objects he distinctly proposed to himself (as already mentioned) was the introduction of the highest Christian maxims into the schools of the Sorbonne by means of those students who should go through the necessary acts preparatory to taking their doctor's degree. The very end and design of the Seminary being to form good priests, he desired that piety should be given the pre-eminence over science, and that the studies pursued should be such as were calculated to produce holy and well-instructed pastors of souls rather than learned or brilliant divines. Whether the students of S. Sulpice should prove to be the latter as well, would depend, in his opinion, on their own natural abilities, and on a concurrence of circumstances which it was impossible to foresee and needless to anticipate. But he was far from lending any countenance to the erroneous idea that priests might be content with but a smattering of theological knowledge; on the contrary, he was accustomed to say that, without such knowledge, a priest could never do much good in the Church. To inspire a love of study, he instituted a general theological course for the whole body of seminarists, and particular lectures for those who attended the schools of the Sorbonne. Every week also there was a public disputation between these two classes of students, and he desired that poor scholars who showed any special aptitude for theological science should receive every encouragement and assistance. The Church (he would say) is a body of which priests are the eyes; it is a ship, of which they are the pilots; a school, of which they are the masters; an army, of which they are the captains. In the confessional they sit to render judgment, prompt and decisive, with none to aid or advise, on matters the most momentous on which any judge could be called upon to pronounce; in the pulpit they have to speak to both learned and ignorant, to uphold the truths of the Gospel, to combat vice, to resist the torrent of human opinion, to confound heresy, and expose its evasions, its impostures, and false issues; all which supposes a knowledge higher, deeper, and more extensive than can be acquired by private study, and such as has been exercised and proved in schools and academies. All, therefore, were to be well grounded in philosophy and scholastic theology, dogmatic and moral, as well as in controversy; but the great and primary object was to be the formation of priests,—interior men,—men of prayer, which he called the very life-spring of all virtues, and the indispensable means of attaining sacerdotal perfection.

Study, he said, ought to be but another mode of advancing in holiness and in the love of God, and the reason it is commonly otherwise is that it is not pursued with a view to Jesus Christ alone. "If you study from any other motive than that of piety, all your knowledge will serve only to make you more vain, more full of yourselves, more self-opinionated and attached to your own private judgment; in a word, the more learned you become, the dryer will be your devotion. To be learned without being puffed up is a miracle: *Scientia inflat.** Yes, it is a miracle to see a learned man who does not hold himself in some esteem. The highest archangel was not proof against it; he could not keep his footing on the slippery path: *In veritate non stetit.*† The only true knowledge is to know that we are nothing, and clearly to discern our nothingness in the midst of our gifts. This pride, this vanity of the intellect, is the most dangerous, the most deadly of all; it is a vanity from

---

* "Knowledge puffeth up."—1 Cor. xiv. 1.
† "He stood not in the truth."

which a man scarcely ever recovers, for human learning goes on increasing with age and experience.

"The great evil is that study is not pursued in a Christian spirit. To understand this aright, we must learn that there are three kinds of knowledge. The first is purely human: it is the knowledge of pagans, who studied only from a human motive, and solely in the strength of their own powers. They studied for a merely natural end: the satisfaction of their own mind, their own individual improvement, or the praise and esteem of men. The second, which is infused, is simply divine, and ranks among the gifts of the Holy Spirit. This it is that God anciently gave to the Apostles, and has bestowed on a great number of saints who had neither time for study, nor the means of acquiring the knowledge necessary for their ministry. The third is human and divine together: it is the true and proper knowledge of Christians, and that of which the Wise man speaks when he says, *Dedit illi scientiam Sanctorum, complevit labores illius.** It is not given by infusion and without labour; it partakes of both one and the other. It is not a knowledge like that of Adam; it is of the nature of Christian grace and virtues, which are acquired with labour. By original sin, as we all know, man lost his right to the knowledge and to the virtues with which he was endowed in his state of innocence: Jesus Christ, by His merits, has obtained us the right and the power to acquire, but with labour, both knowledge and virtues."

Hence, to study in a Christian way, there is need of three things: humility, penance, and zeal for God's glory. Convinced that in ourselves we are nothing, we must have recourse to Jesus Christ, in whom God the Father has hidden all knowledge, to be by Him diffused through the Church; and we must look upon books as a sort of reservoir, in which Jesus Christ has stored it for our use. To keep this great truth ever before the minds of the

---

* "She gave to him the science of the Saints, and fulfilled his labours."—Wis. x. 10.

students, M. Olier caused an image of our Blessed Lord to be placed in the library of the Seminary, with this inscription underneath,—*Quæcumque audivi à Patre meo, nota feci vobis;** and in a little book of "Interior Acts" which he composed for their use, he suggested a series of most devout and humble aspirations to Jesus as the Eternal Wisdom and the Light of men. Further, he would have every one in his reading look to his director, both for subjects of study and the time he should devote to it; never retrenching his spiritual exercises in order to have more to give, but, on the contrary, being the more assiduous in devotion, in order to escape the dangers to which intellectual pursuits are liable; renouncing all spirit of curiosity, stopping awhile to lift up the heart in prayer when sensible of overmuch activity and ardour; sighing from time to time for the perfect possession of God, in whom will be found the full and entire knowledge of that which here below we know so faintly and imperfectly.

So, too, in their public disputations he bade them argue, not to display their knowledge, but simply to ascertain the truth, if they were in doubt, or to confirm themselves in it if they were sure of their grounds. To dispute from a motive of vanity, he said, was to pledge ourselves never to yield; it was to act the part of Lucifer, who would be content with nothing short of the highest throne in heaven. To confess one's own ignorance, and acknowledge another's ability, as it was the part of true candour and humility, so it was torture to the proud. In the schools let them keep before their eyes, and adore in their hearts, Jesus Christ in the midst of the doctors. Though He had in Himself all the treasures of wisdom and knowledge, yet He was found *hearkening to them, and asking them questions*. The rules he gave on this subject are at once so general in their application, so simple, yet so noble, and so instinct with the purest Christian kindness, that the writer cannot forbear ex-

---

* "Whatsoever I have heard of My Father, I have made known to you."—John, xv. 15.

tracting some of them. "Before disputing you ought to have an assured conviction of your own ignorance, and to make an interior avowal of it before the majesty of God, and in the presence of the Angels and all Saints; then, ere you begin, invoke the aid of the Holy Spirit to be your guide in an act so full of peril, and in which it is so incumbent upon you to observe the rules of a just and holy moderation. In disputing let it be with the greatest charity, never seeking to confound your adversary, or pressing him hard; on the contrary, contrive to suggest some opening by which he may see his way out of the difficulties that embarrass him; in a word, do to him as you would wish that it should be done to you under like circumstances. If you feel any rising of pride within you, urging you to get the advantage of him, then you may make as though you were unable to solve the objections he proposes, and beg him to enlighten you. This is to give the death-blow to our own judgment, which is naturally so unwilling to submit. You ought to make this your practice, not only in discussion, but whenever you feel a strong desire to show your learning. Nevertheless, there are certain public occasions on which prudence demands a different course, and then you must content yourself with laying the desire interiorly before our Lord, and begging Him to destroy it by virtue of His grace; and our Lord, seeing your fidelity, will not fail to hear you in the moment of danger."

The effect of such a rule of conduct persistently followed soon became apparent, not only in the intercourse of the students one with another, but in their influence upon the world without. M. Blanlo had obtained the highest distinction by his theological proficiency, his profound acquaintance with the Holy Scriptures, and his knowledge of Greek and Hebrew, of the latter of which languages he was made a professor by the University of Paris. At the age of twenty-two he was chosen to fill the chair of philosophy in the College des Grassins, when, deeply impressed with the sanctity of M. Olier, he entered the Seminary of S. Sulpice, there to lead a hidden and mortified life, and to be as remarkable for his modesty and humility, as in the world he had been distinguished for the extent and variety of his attainments. He had a particular devotion to the Sacred Infancy of our Lord, in honour of which he wrote, under obedience, a little work which was published after his death. Once within the walls of the Seminary, his object seemed to be to conceal his extraordinary gifts. Chosen by M. Olier to give lectures in theology, he delivered them, as usual at the time, in the way of dictation, reading them apparently from a book which he held in his hand. One day, however, being called away from the class while thus engaged, a student had the curiosity to look into the book out of which he had been reading, when, to his astonishment, he found that it had nothing to say to the subject in hand, and that the professor had been really composing while he seemed to be merely dictating.

This good man was but practising in detail M. Olier's lesson, and realizing that great primary idea of his, as we have seen it developed in this chapter, the mortification of self—self-love, self-will, self-opinion, self-display—that Jesus Christ may be formed in the soul.

The method of prayer approved by M. Olier has been described as follows :—*

"He divides mental prayer into three parts: the preparation, the prayer itself, and the conclusion. The preparation is threefold: remote, less remote, and proximate; the first being occupied in removing obstacles, the second in preparing what is necessary for praying well, and the third being, as it were, the entrance into prayer. The more remote preparation may be said to extend over the whole life, and is principally occupied with three obstacles—sin, the passions, and the thought of creatures. The less remote preparation is concerned with three times; the time when the subject of prayer is given overnight, the time between then and waking in morning, and the time from waking to beginning the prayer. The first requires attention: the second, a review of the subject, and strict

---

* Abridged from Faber's "Growth in Holiness," chap. xv.

silence; and the third, the affections of love and joy with which we should approach prayer. The proximate preparation is almost a part of the prayer itself. It comprises three acts: 1. The putting ourselves in the presence of God; 2. The acknowledging ourselves unworthy to appear in His presence; 3. The confessing ourselves incapable of praying as we ought without the aid of divine grace. For each of these three preparations he gave very minute rules, all taken from ancient sources.

"The body of the prayer consists of—1, adoration; 2, communion; 3, co-operation. In the first we adore, praise, love, and thank God. In the second we try to transfer to our own hearts what we have been praising and loving in God, and to participate in its virtue according to our measure. In the third we co-operate with the grace we are receiving by fervent colloquies and generous resolutions.

"In adoration we contemplate the subject of the meditation in Jesus, and worship Him because of it in a becoming way. Hence there are two things to be observed in this first point. Suppose, for instance, the subject be humility; we first of all consider Jesus as humble, and in this again are included three things: our Lord's interior dispositions about humility, the words He said, and the actions He did; secondly, we lay at His feet six offerings—adoration, admiration, praise, love, joy, and gratitude, sometimes going through all of them, sometimes selecting such as harmonize with the subject of our prayer. This point is extremely important, as it leads us first to contemplate our Blessed Lord as the source of all virtues; secondly, to regard Him as the original exemplar of which grace is to make us copies; thirdly, of the two ends of prayer—the veneration of God and the petition of man—the first is the more perfect; fourthly, if we look to our own interests, of the two roads which lead to perfection—prayer and imitation—the first is the shortest, the most efficacious, and the most solid. To dip our souls, as it were, in the dye of the Heart of Jesus by love and adoration, is a quicker way to imbue them with a virtue than multiplied acts of the virtue itself would be.

"The second point is communion, by which we endeavour to participate in what we have been loving and admiring in the first. It contains three things. We have first to convince ourselves that the grace we desire to ask is important to us, and we should try to convince ourselves of this chiefly by motives of faith. The second thing is to see how greatly we are wanting in that grace at present, and how many opportunities of acquiring it we have wasted. The third, and chief thing, is the petition itself; and this petition may take four shapes, the types of which are in Scripture:—1, simple petition; 2, obsecration, which is the adding of some motive or adjuration, as by the merits of our Lord, or the graces of our Lady; 3, thanksgiving, for thanksgiving for past graces is the most efficacious petition for new ones; 4, insinuation, as when the sister of Lazarus said no more than, '*Lord, he whom Thou lovest is sick.*' All these petitions must be accompanied by four conditions—humility, confidence, perseverance, and the union of others in our prayers, as our Lord teaches us to pray for *our* daily bread, and forgive us our trespasses.

"The third point is the co-operation, in which we make our resolutions. In these resolutions three things are required: they must be particular, present, and efficacious. They must be particular, because general resolutions are of very little use except in union with particular ones. They must be present, that is, we must have some application of our resolution present to our minds, as likely to occur that day. They must be efficacious, that is, our subsequent care must be to carry them out with fidelity, and we must fully intend to do so by an explicit intention at the time we make them.

"The conclusion of the prayer consists of three things, all of which are to be very briefly performed. First, we must thank God for the graces He has given us in our prayer, the grace of having endured us in His presence, of having given us the ability to pray, and of all the good thoughts and emotions we have experienced. Secondly, we must ask pardon for the faults we have committed in our prayer, negligence, lukewarmness, distraction, inattention, and restlessness. Thirdly, we must put it all into our Lady's hands to offer it to God, to supply all defects, and to obtain all blessings. Then follows the spiritual nosegay of S. Francis de Sales, that is, some thought for the day, to refresh us in the dust and turmoil of the world."

CHAPTER XIX.

M. Olier and Jansenism.

WE should gain but a very inadequate idea of the services which this great man rendered to religion, if we excluded from our consideration the prominent part he took in resisting the insidious encroachments of the Jansenistic heresy, which all this time was spreading like a pestilence through the Church of France, and insinuating its baneful virus among the religious bodies, both of men and women, especially in and about the capital.

The Jansenists, it must ever be remembered, came forward in the first instance in the guise of reformers, protesting loudly against the scandals which all good men deplored and were labouring to remove, and exhibiting an unwonted fervour of devotion and austerity of life. This apparent strictness with themselves, and display of earnestness, had the effect of deceiving many who, if they could have penetrated the true motives of all these ardent professions and the real import of the tenets with which they were accompanied, would have been foremost in their condemnation. Of such was M. Bourdoise, who, captivated by the specious piety and severe morality of the Abbé de S. Cyran, was slow to credit the warnings which keener-sighted friends gave him as to the real character and intentions of the man; and even when his eyes were opened it was some time before he could be induced to exercise that vigilance in the admission of fresh members into his community which the necessity of the case demanded. Towards the end of 1640 a breach had all but occurred in consequence between M. Olier's little society and himself. He was at length completely undeceived, but not before the wolf, who had found an entrance into the fold, had succeeded in carrying off one of the most promising of his flock.

M. Olier, on the other hand, never hesitated for a moment: from the first he had an instinctive feeling of distrust and repulsion for the whole party, and it will ever be one of the chief glories of S. Sulpice that it stood as an impregnable bulwark against the errors of Jansenism, and that this odious heresy could never boast of having gained a footing within its walls. A mortified life, however, and earnestness in the cause of ecclesiastical reform were identified in the minds of many with a leaning to the new opinions, and it was the policy of the sect to encourage the delusion. To those who disliked M. Olier's spirituality and zeal, but who were withheld from condemning, even to themselves, what their consciences told them they ought rather to admire and applaud, it was a kind of relief to be able to set him down as a favourer of Jansenism, and the party itself was only too eager to claim him as an ally.

A public protest which he felt himself compelled to make against a certain confessor, who had been called in to a sick person, and whose practice was in accordance with those maxims of false leniency which, as has been said, were in vogue at the time, was seized upon both by Jansenists and by indifferent Catholics as a confirmation of the suspicion already afloat. "I detest these maxims," said the servant of God, "as I detest everything which is not in conformity with the purity of the Gospel; I have a thousand times more horror of them than of the open suggestions of Satan, and would much rather behold a sick man besieged by a legion of the spirits of darkness, than see him put his trust in a casuist who, to make broader the way of salvation, opens to him the gate of hell." A condemnation so decisive was taken as a judgment in favour of the no less fatal rigorism which was one of the distinctive signs of Jansenistic predilections, and M. Olier, who would have remained silent under any ordinary calumny, considered it his duty, when his orthodoxy was called in question, to rebut in the face of the Church a charge so injurious to his influence as a pastor of souls. This he did, not in the way of passionate self-defence, or of a vehement attack on either of the two opposite errors, but by a simple and forcible exposition of the Catholic doctrine, in language which could admit but of one interpretation. From this moment he became the object of a relentless hostility, which did not terminate even with his life; but he never flinched from the unequal contest,—unequal where one side dealt in unscrupulous falsehood, and the other adhered to the strictest requirements of charity and truth; and the only effect of the persecution he encountered was to make him redouble his exertions to protect his people against the unceasing machinations of the innovators.

Heresy is a fearful thing: open, avowed hostility to the authority of Christ's Church and to the faith it teaches. But there is something still more hateful: heresy, not merely nascent, undeveloped, undeclared, but hidden,—secretly lurking within the Church itself, dissembling its hostility, professing submission, protesting fidelity. Such was Jansenism: insidious, hypocritical, insincere; in a word, dishonest: this it was that made it so powerful for mischief.* A letter, which M. Olier addressed to a lady of his parish, a person of some consideration, who had allowed herself to be entangled in its toils, so clearly illustrates the disingenuousness of these false brethren, and at the same time brings out into such strong relief his own uprightness and sincerity, that a portion of it may here be quoted. " I cannot express to you," he writes, " my grief and my confusion at the tidings I have received. I am assured that you are in private correspondence with the Jansenists, and that in your letters you evince a great zeal in upholding their party. For more than eight months I have continued to refuse credence to the different reports that have reached me, relying on your own assertions in spite of all the testimonies to the contrary; but of late such convincing proofs have been brought before me that I cannot doubt any longer. My very dear daughter, what would you have me do for you? If you have lost confidence in me, you are quite right in believing than I can only be irksome and useless to you. No one can serve two masters, as our Lord says, or obey in simplicity two persons opposed to each other in their sentiments and maxims.... I am sure that my heart is wholly yours in the charity of Jesus Christ to aid you and to serve you; but I doubt very much whether I ought to allow you to practise any longer this feigned confidence and submission. I may safely say that I have never abandoned a soul which Jesus Christ entrusted to me, and that I have always been careful not to give it any just cause for leaving me; but, when I see a soul following two different paths, and joining finesse to concealment, after once making known to it my views and intentions, I let it go its own ways, knowing that it cannot take a more dan-

---

* A rapid, but comprehensive and graphic sketch of the history and spirit of Jansenism is given by Father Dalgairns, in his "Devotion to the Heart of Jesus."

gerous course than one of divided direction, especially
if it incline towards the worse side. . . . What would you
say of persons who assert that the Church is in error,
who profess that their object is to reform her, and are
for ever railing at their mother, tearing her heart, and
filling her with unparalleled affliction and desolation?
You see nothing where you are. You are furnished
only with good books,—such, for instance, as recommend almsgiving, because you have an inclination
that way. Under pretexts the most specious these
gentlemen neglect the most essential works, in order to
further their own malignant views, despise all who do
not enter into them, and even brand them as heretics
and schismatics. Because we preach that Jesus Christ
died for all, they are scandalized. They go so far as to
complain and express their displeasure aloud in the
churches, as they did in our own only three days ago.
In short, in all their proceedings they give frightful signs
of passion, anger, and fury, which make one shudder. . .
Beware! error has always insinuated itself into the
Church under the guise of reform. The last heretics
declared that their doctrine was that of the primitive
Church, founded on the word of Jesus Christ, announcing everywhere a reformation of manners exceeding even
that of the Church herself. When asked who sent them—
where were the signs of their extraordinary mission, and
the approbation of the Holy See—they made no answer,
for they had none to make. Nevertheless, they continued
spreading abroad their doctrine, without mission, without
the approbation of their superiors,—a condition absolutely indispensable, and one which has always been so
in the Church. S. Paul himself, apostle as he was,
took his directions from S. Peter. No, without submission, there is no security; besides, I see in those who
have gained you over to their party so much obstinacy,
impetuosity, contempt of all who do not think as they
do—so much esteem of themselves, to the prejudice of
the Church, and of the whole body of the faithful; and
it is this alarms me about you. Beware, then, of this
dangerous leaven; and however fair the exterior of those

of whom I speak, make haste to separate yourself from them, that you may be united only to Jesus Christ, and to the purity of the faith, which will ever be the same in the Church, because Jesus Christ will ever be with her."

Brother John of the Cross would also have fallen a victim to their artifices but for M. Olier's sharp remonstrances. He had taken to going every Sunday to hear the preaching at Port Royal, his attraction being, not the sermons, which were beyond his comprehension, but a paraphrase of the Gospel, which M. Singlin, who since S. Cyran's death had become the patriarch of the sect, was in the habit of giving in French, a practice which he thought betokened great zeal for the word of God. It required much firmness and not less tact on the part of M. Olier, to keep this simple and illiterate man from the snare. Ever on the watch, and as determined as he was vigilant, this good shepherd used his influence in high places to have the two leading Jansenists, F. F. Séguenot and Des Mares, both Oratorians, interdicted by authority from preaching at Paris. The party retaliated by accusing him of being himself the innovator. This indeed was the line of defence they universally adopted. Condemned again and again by the Holy See, to whose judgment they affected to bow, they impudently persisted in retorting on the Catholics the charge of upholding strange doctrines. To teach that Christ died for all, that the commandments of God are capable of being observed, that grace may be resisted—this with them was heresy; while the contrary propositions they declared to be of faith. Accordingly they publicly accused M. Olier of being the author of a schism, and denounced the Sulpitians as Pelagians or Semi-Pelagians, as though they referred all to nature, and made no account of grace. "On the contrary," writes M. Olier, "we say with S. Paul, that '*we are not sufficient to think anything of ourselves, as of ourselves, but our sufficiency is of God; for it is God who worketh in us both to will and to accomplish according to His good will.*'*" We refer to nature

---

* 2 Cor. iii. 5; Phil. ii. 13.

nothing that is supernatural; in ourselves we are no more capable of willing or accomplishing supernatural things than we are of thinking them. We have need of grace always, and in all things; and we can do nothing without the grace of God. What more can we say?"

Of all M. Olier's opponents, however, the most formidable, as he was personally the most hostile, was M. du Hamel, Curé of S. Merri at Paris, whom the party had brought from the diocese of Sens and placed at the head of that parish for the avowed purpose of making it the rival of S. Sulpice. Here he established regular conferences, in the first instance professedly for the ecclesiastics of his community, but really for the laity, who soon formed the sole audience. The questions discussed were always such as were connected with the subject of grace. The novelty of the proceeding attracted a vast concourse of people, among whom were many persons of rank, and the greatest eagerness and excitement prevailed. Besides the conferences there were catechisings, intended rather for adults than children, as also sermons, which produced no little sensation. Then, too, M. du Hamel became very popular as a director, especially among the ladies of his parish, crowds of whom might be seen waiting to consult him. All this was represented as an extraordinary revival of the fervour, strictness, and purity of primitive times. But the most striking feature in this pretended reform* was the restoration of public penance, as practised in the early Church. This system had already been carried out by M. du Hamel in his former parish on true Jansenistic principles. He divided his penitents into four classes. The first consisted of such as were guilty only of secret sins; these when assisting at the divine office were ranged in the lower part of the church, at four paces distant from the rest of the congregation. The second was composed of such as had

---

* The *vicaire* of Belleville, which was attached to the parish of S. Merri, went so far as to determine to administer the sacrament of baptism only once a year, on Holy Saturday; and taught that immersion was essential to its validity.

been at variance with their neighbour, but without causing scandal; their place was outside the building, in the porch and vestibule. The third class consisted of such as had committed scandalous offences, and these were relegated to the churchyard; while those who had indulged long habits of sin were made to occupy an adjacent hill, from which they had a view of the entrance to the church. All these penitents remained barefoot and bareheaded during the celebration of Mass; they also took the discipline in public, wore a hair-shirt, and added other mortifications. These practices, with some slight modifications, were introduced at S. Merri, and in justification of so startling a proceeding, it was formally propounded that without previous, and even public, satisfaction, sacramental absolution was of no avail. One of the penances commonly imposed, was that of standing at the further end of the church, or outside the gate, and never raising the eyes to the Blessed Sacrament; and it is related, that a pious young woman having accidentally looked towards It, immediately ran out into the street for fear of being led to look again and make an act of adoration. A priest of S. Sulpice, to whom she was brought by her friends, happily succeeded in disabusing her mind of its vain terrors. Another very usual penance was called the hour's tears, from its consisting in making efforts to shed tears, as if of compunction, for that space of time. Then, too, in the early mornings, a strange sight might have been witnessed in one of the chapels of S. Merri—a whole assembly of women scourging themselves with the utmost vigour; so great, indeed, was the ardour and enthusiasm with which they gave themselves to these and similar austerities, that several died or went mad from the effects. Some even left their homes, and went to lead a solitary life in wild and desert places. One in particular is mentioned, who attired herself in penitential garb and took up her abode at Issy, in a sort of natural grotto that was there. She was venerated as a saint by the devotees of her party, who went frequently to visit and consult her. Thus, under the plea of reviving primitive piety, the most dangerous novelties in doctrine and in practice were gradually introduced, to the destruction of all Christian simplicity and genuine devotion. Many of M. Olier's own flock were drawn away, in spite of all his warnings and exertions, and the spirit of disobedience and singularity everywhere excited was productive of the gravest disorders. But that which caused the man of God the deepest grief, was the general neglect and infrequency of communion, which inevitably resulted from the spread of Jansenistic tenets: in S. Sulpice alone, the number of those who approached the Holy Table during the year was three thousand less than formerly.

Seeing the credit which these innovations had obtained in high places, through the specious piety and zeal of those who introduced them, M. Olier chose the festival of S. Sulpice, when not only the Regent and her court, but a crowd of prelates and other distinguished persons were present, to make a solemn protest against the fatal doctrines that were gaining ground. The particular errors he undertook to refute were—1, the necessity of public penance; and, 2, the invalidity of absolution previous to satisfaction, and in the absence of perfect contrition. He showed that the public penance required by the early Church was not of universal obligation; that it was a matter of temporary discipline, the necessity and benefit of which had ceased with the circumstances which rendered it either desirable or suitable.* He added, that if such extraordinary practices were demanded by the age, God would make known His will as He has

---

* "As is always the case when men fall in love with an obsolete discipline, what they reproduced was not even the phantom, but the mere dead body of the past. They sighed for the ancient discipline which the Church found it necessary to establish at a time when men were crowding into it from a pagan world, and had to learn the very first principles of morality; and they forgot the daily communion in the Catacombs, of men and women pursuing their avocations in the midst of the bustle of heathen society. They did not take into account the Blessed Sacrament carried by Christians to their homes, as well as by solitaries into the desert, dwelling with them in their houses, and accompanying them on their travels by land and sea."—Dalgairns: "Devotion to the Sacred Heart," p. 30.

ever done: first, by raising up men endowed with supernatural gifts and powers; and, secondly, by stamping the practices themselves with the approbation of the Apostolic See. Then, with a holy irony he said, " I do not know whether, in the institution of such unwonted penances, these conditions have been observed. I do not know whether all is done in submission to the Holy See, or if the spirit from which they emanate is not the same which makes men write against it and resist its sacred power. I do not know whether those of whom I speak propound their opinions with the humble surrender of their own lights, or with pride and bitterness. Do we see in their proceedings the spirit of a S. Francis, who desired to be thought a fool, an ignorant man, a poor miserable sinner, nay, the greatest sinner in the world? who was the first to give the example of what he taught, and suffered, with pleasure, contempt and insult? Besides, as these penances are for all the world, as is affirmed, it need be that God approve them by gifts more excellent, and miracles more striking, than those which confirmed the mission of the founders of religious orders, seeing that the latter imposed their observances only on certain individuals, and not on the whole body of the faithful." Then, proceeding to the second point, he maintained, in conformity with the doctrine approved by the Council of Trent, and, indeed, expressly taught in the common Catechism, that attrition is sufficient for sacramental absolution, and concluded with these encouraging but solemn words: " Christians, I require from you that which our Lord required. Souls that have not perfect charity, that have but the principle of love, such as is required of adults to be baptized, receive in the Sacrament of Penance a participation in the perfect charity of Jesus Christ dying for us on the Cross. This sacrament is the second plank that saves from shipwreck. Keep then the middle course, and go neither to the one extreme nor to the other, if you would be saved from perishing. There is abuse in the indulgence and facility of many confessors, and there is excess in the rigorism of others. The evil one pretends but to drive away abuses, and his object is either to abolish the use of Sacraments altogether, or to lead men to dangerous extremes, contrary to the Spirit of Jesus Christ."

This discourse irritated the Jansenists to fury, and they strove to weaken its effects by indulging in the most violent invectives against the preacher. They accused him of having declaimed against the necessity of true repentance, and of having in the heat of his harangue torn in pieces a book against " Frequent Communion," which one of the party had composed. Des Mares published an anonymous pamphlet, which bore the title of " A Christian and Charitable Remonstrance, addressed to M. Olier," * but which was distinguished for anything rather than Christian charity. In it the writer asserted that a scandal so public demanded as public a protest, and undertook to show that the superior of S. Sulpice had sinned mortally by having impugned in the pulpit the doctrine of S. Augustine on the subject of grace, and that of the Fathers generally on penance. He charged him with defaming and persecuting the true servants of God who were not of his opinion, and usurping the authority of the Church, the sole judge of controversies; he declared him guilty of favouring the heresies of Luther and Calvin; and, in fine, of profanation and sacrilege every time he ascended the steps of the altar. But even from this publication we may gather the estimation in which M. Olier was held, and the indubitable marks of sanctity which his life exhibited. The writer concludes by protesting that his sole object is to lead his readers "to conceive a deep compassion for M. Olier, and to humble themselves tremblingly before God, who sometimes permits those who are believed to be saints to fall into thickest darkness, and to pray the Lord to open the eyes of those who place a blind confidence in everything he says, that they may see that the Holy Spirit has not committed to him all the treasures of His wisdom."

This pamphlet was widely circulated in Paris, but to all the calumnies it contained, M. Olier replied only by

* It is dated February 18th, 1653.

silence and patience, leaving to God his justification and his defence. He was silent because it was only his own character that was assailed; but when souls were at stake, he knew neither peace nor rest. The Duke de Liancourt, since his conversion, had led so edifying a life, that M. Olier had thought to confer a benefit on his parish by choosing him as one of the wardens of the church. But yielding to the influence of his wife, this nobleman unhappily sought the society of the Jansenistic leaders, and became an ardent defender of the new opinions. They were both persons of literary tastes and highly intellectual, and they loved discussion for its own sake. This proved their snare. The *hôtel* de Liancourt became the head-quarters of the Jansenists, where the Père des Mares, the Abbé de Bourzeis, and other principal writers of the party constantly met to confer together. Alarmed at the perils with which he saw his two parishioners encompassed, and at the injurious example they presented to his flock, he strove to win them from their errors by personal persuasion and pious discourse; but as his endeavours were of no avail, he proposed a discussion on the chief points in dispute, to be conducted by the Father Dom Pierre de S. Joseph, a religious of the order of the Feuillants, who had distinguished himself by his works on the controverted subject of grace. The proposal was accepted, on the condition that the Père des Mares should take part in the debate; and it was mutually agreed that each disputant should be ready to affix his signature to any proposition he advanced, on being required so to do by his opponent.

Accordingly, towards the end of May, 1652, the duke and duchess repaired with their champion to the presbytery of S. Sulpice, accompanied also by the maréchal and maréchale de Schomberg. With F. Pierre was M. Olier, M. Bretonvilliers, and two others. M. Olier opened the conference by going straight to a point which was one of the most critical, as well as most pernicious, advocated by the sect. "My father," he said, "Do you condemn as erroneous and heretical the opinion of those who maintain that there are graces which are sufficient, but which are not efficacious? In other words, Are there, or are there not, sufficient graces given by Jesus Christ which are rendered inefficacious and inoperative by the ill use that is made of them?" For three hours Des Mares used all the artifices of which he was master to evade the question, and instead of making any reply, entered into a long disquisition on the different systems by which theologians explained the nature of sufficient grace, and, among others, that of Molina, which he taxed with heresy and Pelagianism. F. Pierre, in his turn, proceeded to show that the system of the latter had never been condemned, and Des Mares undertaking, on the other hand, to prove his assertion from S. Augustine, M. Olier, who perceived the object of the subterfuge, interposed, and brought him back to the point. "The question," he said, "is not whether, in order to do good, it is sufficient to have the grace of Molina, or of any other theologian, but whether he who does not do the good which he is commanded to do, has, or may have, all the aid necessary thereto, and whether God, on His part, offers it him." The Jansenist still persisting in his distinctions, and M. Olier continuing to press him for a reply, the duke and duchess came to their advocate's assistance, deprecating the attempt to drive him into a corner, on the ground that the term "sufficient grace" was used in different senses by different theologians. M. Olier, therefore, contented himself with asking his opponent whether he held, or did not hold, that there were graces which were not efficacious; and then, as Des Mares still declined to answer, he reduced his question to the simplest possible form, and, in a single sentence, struck at the very root of the new heresy: "Either subscribe," he said, "this proposition, that there is no sufficient grace which is not efficacious, or renounce Jansenius." Instead of replying, the heretic went off into a denial that he had derived his opinions from the writings of Jansenius, and so the conference ended, as such conferences usually end. More than thirty times Des Mares endeavoured to evade a reply, and then, perceiving (as F. Pierre afterwards said) that, with all his stratagems, he could not induce his opponent to quit his position, "he put up his sword into its sheath,—I mean, he put his books and treatises into his bag," and the combatants separated. M. de Liancourt instantly took possession of all the notes of the conference which lay on M. Olier's table, and the party did not fail to publish abroad that their champion had gained a complete victory. The controversy was renewed in writing between F. Pierre and Des Mares, and we may conceive how great was the interest which the public took in the debate, from the fact that hawkers cried about the streets what they called the "confession of faith of the Father des Mares." M. Olier, however, was satisfied with having done his duty as pastor of souls, and pursued the matter no further.

Subsequent to the condemnation of the Jansenistic tenets by Innocent X., the duke de Liancourt went to confession to M. Picoté, who believed that he had submitted *ex animo* to the Papal constitution; but finding that he still kept up his intimate relations with Port Royal, and was not disposed to break them off, he wished to take a few days to consider what course he should pursue, and, for that purpose, deferred absolution. The duke, instead of returning at the end of the time proposed, spoke openly of what had passed, complaining that he had been refused absolution, so that the affair became the common talk of Paris. The whole party was soon up in arms, and M. Arnauld published "A Letter to a Person of Distinction," in which, while misstating the whole facts of the case, he inveighed with the utmost vehemence against M. Olier and his community. The Sulpitians consulted some of the most learned and most experienced doctors of the Sorbonne, who gave it as their opinion that the duke might justly be refused absolution, though he could not be publicly refused communion, if he presented himself. M. Picoté, from the nature of the case, was unable to justify himself without violating the seal of confession, and his adversaries were accordingly able to indulge their imaginations and their inventive faculties to the fullest extent. The delay of absolution became, in their version of the matter, the refusal of communion; and then this supposed refusal of communion was turned into a positive act of excommunication, and the priests of S. Sulpice were consequently charged with the commission of a mortal sin, in having exceeded their legitimate jurisdiction and usurped episcopal authority. And this is the account which the writers of the party have actually given of the occurrence. The letter of Arnauld was brought before the Sorbonne and formally condemned, and on his refusing to retract he was excluded from the faculty of doctors. The duke, unhappily, remained in his errors to the last; but the Abbé de Bourzeis, who resided with him up to the time of M. Olier's death, made a public retractation in the November of 1661.

It were greatly to misconceive the reach and purport of the Jansenistic heresy to suppose that it involved but a metaphysical error, of no vital consequence; and M. Olier knew well what he was doing when he singled out the doctrine which he made his point of attack in the disputation with Des Mares. That doctrine was already bearing fruits most dishonouring to God, and most deadly in its effects on the souls of men. "These innovators" (he writes) "teach that they never do evil except through defect of grace, God withdrawing it from His creature without cause, and thereby making it to stumble. When we fall, therefore, it is through defect of grace, and not by the abuse of our liberty, and the commandments of God are thus impossible to us. Just conceive what a doctrine this is, and what a pretext it furnishes for indifferentists and libertines! . . . making the sinner, not to accuse himself of being the sole cause of the evil he does, but to accuse God, as if He did not wish us to do good, the good which He commands us, and to enable us to accomplish which He died upon the cross, and shed every drop of His blood." This impious doctrine was even imported into the sacred tribunal of penance, and, among other instances, it is related that a person who had violated the most solemn engagements had the audacity to say in so many words, not that he had sinned, but that grace had been wanting to him, on three several occasions.

M. Olier, as strenuous as he was firm in maintaining the integrity of the faith against the innovators, was ever most charitable in his judgment of individuals, and moderate in his conduct even towards the party. On the publication of the bull of Innocent X., when the Jansenists were saying to each other that there would be "fireworks" at S. Sulpice and elsewhere to celebrate the event, this truly great man was deprecating in his letters to his friends all appearance of triumphing over their opponents. To M. de Bretonvilliers he writes, "My idea would be to do nothing to hurt the feelings of the Jansenists, but to treat them with tenderness and great openness of heart, so as to draw them into union and make them subserve the glory of God and the good of the Church." The Jansenists, as we know, were far from sharing these sentiments. They neither submitted nor openly rebelled, but pretending that the judgment of the Holy See did not touch their propositions, sought by a course of systematic concealment and prevarication to escape the consequences of their condemnation, and propagate their doctrines with impunity. They had long desired to avail themselves of some organization, ready formed, by which to undermine the faith of the people with greater secrecy and effect, and but for M. Olier's promptness and energy they would, in all human probability, have gained their end, at least for the time. There existed at Paris a congregation which bore the name of the Propagation of the Faith; it had been formed in 1632, by F. Hyacinthe, a Capuchin preacher, with the approbation of the Holy See, and had been confirmed by letters patent from the crown. Its object was the recovery of heretics, and the care of new converts; and as its ramifications were widely extended through the provinces, and it enjoyed considerable credit with the public, the Jansenists hoped that, under the protection of M. de Gondi, the archbishop, on whom it immediately depended, and who favoured the party, they should be able to intrench themselves in this association, as in a stronghold from which it would be impossible to dislodge them. Many of them, accordingly, had themselves enrolled among its members; and the conspiracy seemed to be succeeding to admiration, when M. Olier, perceiving their design, resolved to defeat the manœuvre by himself seeking admission into the company, with the Curé of S. Germain l'Auxerrois, a man of like spirit to his own. The Jansenists in vain opposed his election, and all their worst fears were realized: M. Olier was chosen to fill one of the highest offices in the association, and almost the first use he made of his authority was to prevent the admission of two priests who had refused submission to the Papal bull. The archbishop supported the candidates, but on the servant of God addressing himself to the Queen and Cardinal Mazarin, who had now returned to the head of affairs, he reluctantly confirmed the exclusion; and then, weak, vain man as he was, on the Jansenists representing the prejudice done to his prerogatives, he, six days afterwards, ordered them to be received, together with three others whom he named. More than this, a majority of the association having decided on appointing M. Olier to the post of director, the archbishop formally opposed the election for special reasons of his own, which he did not think fit to disclose. Upon this the minority proceeded to an election, and in violation of all the laws of the society, nominated M. d'Aubigny, a cousin* of our own Charles II., hoping under shelter of his name—for he held the rank of prince at the court of France—to carry out their intentions without further molestation. M. Olier and his supporters at once absented themselves from the meetings of the society, and appealed to the Council of State to cancel the informal election. The Jansenists, on their side, presented a memorial, and Cardinal Mazarin, who was unwilling to offend an association whose officers might be useful in promoting

* He was fourth son of the Duke of Lennox, and was called M. d'Aubigny, from a *seigneurie* of that name which he had in Berri.

his policy, and who was also on terms of close intimacy with the Abbé de Bourzeis, would fain have let the matter rest, but the Queen was firm, and he found himself compelled to look about for a pretext on which the archbishop might be induced to comply with the royal pleasure without apparently receding from his own position. But as no such expedient offered itself, the cardinal made himself one by pretending that the appointment of a foreign prince to an office which involved so much interest in the country was dangerous to the realm, and forthwith dissolved the society.

We have given these particulars as an illustration of the vigilance and perseverance which M. Olier displayed in confronting and baffling this insidious heresy at every point, and by which he has deserved the gratitude and veneration of every true Catholic, as he certainly earned for himself the implacable and undying hatred of the Jansenists. Thus, M. Nicole, one of the most moderate of the party, attributed the ruin and discredit of his friends to the intrigues of the Jesuits, and also of "a certain great director and his priests," meaning M. Olier and his community; comparing the first to fiends, and the latter to secondary spirits, or, as he ironically designates them, "angelic souls." M. Olier was ever on the alert, and all his movements were characterized by a quickness and a decision which allowed no time for the evil, when once detected, to gain strength and confidence by delay. In the seminary no disputes were permitted which were calculated to introduce division or to foster a spirit of party; all books of a dangerous or equivocal character were proscribed; it was forbidden to hold communication with any who did not avow implicit obedience to the decisions of the Church; and all professions of piety, however specious, were condemned, which were not founded on an entire and unreserved submission to the Holy See. It is unnecessary to add, that if any openly declared themselves in favour of the new opinions, whether in the community or in the seminary, they were instantly expelled.

CHAPTER XX.

The Community of S. Sulpice: its Constitution and Interior Spirit.

JANSENISM, it has been said, never gained even a temporary footing within the walls of S. Sulpice. This honourable distinction was doubtless due, as long as M. Olier lived, to his untiring vigilance and zeal; and that at a time when there was scarcely a religious house into which this pernicious heresy had not penetrated with the most disastrous results, he should have succeeded in preserving his community from its influences, must be reckoned among his strongest titles to our admiration and respect. But, what is still more remarkable, the seminary of S. Sulpice ever continued to enjoy the same exemption from Jansenistic infection; and there are circumstances which seem to show that this was a special favour of Heaven, and one integrally connected with the original mission of its founder.

The reader will recollect that in establishing the seminary of Vaugirard, M. Olier had two associates, who made their solemn act of consecration with him in the church of Montmartre, and might equally have been regarded as founders of the society. These were M. de Foix and M. du Ferrier, the former of whom was for a short time at the head of the community. But from the first the Spirit of God had made known to M. Olier that the work was in some especial way his own and not theirs; that they were his appointed fellow-helpers in inaugurating the design, but that its consummation lay wholly with himself. "I will not give to others the spirit of paternity," was the word that was spoken interiorly to him, and this secret intimation was singularly fulfilled. M. Olier was the actual founder of S. Sulpice: no one could dispute the title with him; and it was his mind, his genius, that ruled and ordered everything. The seminary was the embodiment of his ideas, or rather it was the realization of the divine plan of which he had been made the depository. And, as if to leave no doubt in men's minds as to the authorship of the work, he alone of "the three solitaries of Vaugirard," was destined to remain a member of the community. Nor, as we are about to see, was this the only design of Providence in permitting the departure of his two associates.

On the removal of the society from Vaugirard, M. de Foix was made director of the new seminary; and as M. Olier at first was principally occupied with the reform of the parish, he had almost the sole superintendence of the house; his exhortations and personal example exercised a most powerful influence over the minds of the students, and by M. Olier no less than by the ecclesiastics generally he was regarded as one of the mainstays of the institute. When, therefore, it became known that, on the recommendation of S. Vincent de Paul, he had been nominated by the Queen Regent to the vacant see of Pamiers, the feeling excited at S. Sulpice was one of simple grief and dismay. M. de Foix himself was no less sensibly afflicted at the thought of the burden which it was sought to impose upon him, and protested that in consenting to assume the episcopal office he should be withdrawing from a post to which he had been summoned by a particular attraction of grace, and abandoning a vocation which had been blessed with many and signal marks of the Divine favour. Unwilling, however, to act on his own impulse, he resigned himself entirely to the decision of M. Olier, as his superior, who, as may be supposed, bearing in mind the solemn engagements into which his colleague had entered at the first foundation of the society, and the positive injunctions of F. de Condren as to refusing all ecclesiastical preferments, counselled him to persevere in his resolution and to decline the proffered dignity. The queen, however, continuing to press the matter, at the end of three months

M. Olier began to fear lest his reluctance to lose so useful, and, as it appeared, so necessary a subject, should have insensibly biassed his judgment, and resolved to consult F. Tarrisse, and to be determined by his advice in conjunction with that of S. Vincent. The decision of these two great servants of God was strongly in favour of complying with the queen's behests; and M. Olier, sacrificing at once his own personal wishes and the apparent advantage of the community, submitted to the decision, and bade M. de Foix prepare for consecration. This accordingly took place in the church of S. Sulpice, on the 5th of March, 1645, in the presence of the community and a large number of the parishioners, who were deeply touched by the recollection and devotion of the new prelate; the abundance of tears that flowed from his eyes indicating, as it seemed to them, the well of devotion that lay hidden in the depths of his heart.

M. Olier was much blamed for allowing M. de Foix to quit the seminary, there being a general persuasion that his presence and co-operation were indispensable for the success and, indeed, for the very existence of the institution. But M. Olier, although the loss of such a man was apparently irremediable, had regard simply to the will of God, who, as he said, was the Father and the Master of the house, and would never abandon the work He had begun. So entirely was he absorbed in the one idea of furthering the designs of Providence, that at a time when the community could ill afford any diminution of its numbers, he desired several of his most efficient priests to accompany M. de Foix to Pamiers for the purpose of assisting him in the work of his diocese, which stood in great need of reformation, and in the establishment and direction of his episcopal seminary. The high estimation in which he held this prelate is evident from the terms in which he spoke of him to one of these very priests: "Cultivate," he said, "the advantage you enjoy with Monseigneur de Pamiers in his holy conversation, and in the example of his admirable virtues, which you will not easily find elsewhere. Assist this prelate of rare excellence, who is left without aid, and is so deserving of all help." M. de Pamiers, on his side, ever displayed the greatest respect and affection for M. Olier, whom he did not scruple publicly to call "a man inspired by God to dispense His special graces to the Church of France." Whenever he came to Paris he took up his residence at S. Sulpice, presided at its solemn functions, and occasionally preached in the parish church. It may well be conceived that such a man would oppose with all his energies the spread of the new opinions. Accordingly we find him, and that after M. Olier's death, concerting one while with S. Vincent, at another with the priests of S. Sulpice, the most efficient means of bringing back to their allegiance such as had been seduced into resisting the authority of the Church; and he was in the habit of saying that if these novelties came from God, they would not produce, as unhappily was too apparent, such manifold fruits of rebellion, pride, and apostasy.

Such was the Bishop of Pamiers during the first twenty years of his episcopate. Who then could have supposed that a prelate who was a model of the ecclesiastical virtues should a very few years after the death of M. Olier, and that of S. Vincent de Paul, have become one of the most strenuous defenders of Jansenism! Yet such is the miserable fact. This Abbé de Foix is no other than the too celebrated François Etienne de Caulet, one of the four bishops who opposed the *formulary*, as it is called, of Alexander VII.,* and fomented a most lamentable

* The other three were M. Pavillon, Bishop of Aleth; M. de Buzenval, Bishop of Beauvais; and M. Arnauld, Bishop of Angers. M. Pavillon was one of the ecclesiastics who, in conjunction with M. Olier, commenced the Conferences of S. Lazarus; he long enjoyed the confidence both of the superior of S. Sulpice and of St. Vincent de Paul; through the influence of the latter he was promoted to the see of Aleth, and M. Olier lent him some of his most zealous priests to assist in reforming his diocese. By the high reputation he acquired for self-denial and austerity of life, he may be said to have "made the fortune" of the Jansenistic party; but "obedience is better than sacrifices:" he resisted the supreme authority of Christ in His Church, and all his specious virtues were but as gilding on a mausoleum of the dead. The first symptoms betrayed by this prelate, as by his friend the Bishop of Pamiers, over

division in the Church. That he should have quitted the seminary, and that, too, so soon after its establishment, must therefore be regarded as a visible sign of the Divine protection; for how calamitous might the result have been to that rising institution had he continued to be numbered among its members! Joint founder with M. Olier of the house at Vaugirard, first director of the Seminary of S. Sulpice, his experience, his numerous virtues and unquestionable abilities, and the marked ascendancy which he exercised over the minds of others, would have pointed him out as without dispute the man most capable and most worthy of succeeding M. Olier as superior of the society; and in this case the same misfortune would have befallen S. Sulpice as actually befell the Oratory, in spite of the fidelity and zeal displayed by many of the

whom he exercised a fatal influence, of a leaning towards the Jansenists, was an unwillingness to commit himself by a public condemnation of their tenets, on the plea of promoting peace and preventing schism. By this course both were able for a space to dissemble their opinions; or, as it would probably be more true to say, their want of fidelity in not declaring openly for the truth, which in fact was tantamount to tampering with error, had time to develop into positive resistance to the commands of the Holy See: an act from which they would in the first instance have shrunk with horror. By the *formulary* of Alexander VII. (1665) they were called upon to reject and condemn the five points of the Jansenistic heresy extracted from the *Augustinus* of Jansenius, *in the sense of the author*, as the Holy See had condemned them. But while they declared their willingness to condemn the propositions, they refused to subscribe to the *fact* that the propositions were in substance contained in the book of Jansenius; and on this latter point they claimed to preserve what they called a reverent silence. Under Clement IX., however, they consented to subscribe, and to oblige their subjects to subscribe, the condemnation of the five points without any restriction or limitation; and this is called the *Peace of Clement IX.* It may here be observed that until the five propositions were condemned by the Holy See, the Jansenists held them to be true, and to be contained in the book of Jansenius; but no sooner were they condemned, than they publicly maintained the contrary, while privately adhering to their original opinion. The doctrines condemned, they said, were not true doctrines, but then they were not contained in the book of *Augustinus*. By this subterfuge they thought to be able to hold their heresy while affecting to disavow it.

latter body. S. Sulpice also would have yielded before the demoralizing influences of the Jansenistic heresy, and its end would have been in like dishonour.

The departure of M. de Foix from the seminary was soon followed by that of M. du Ferrier. The motives that led to his removal do not distinctly appear, but from his Memoirs it is clear that it was sorely against his own will, for he speaks of leaving S. Sulpice with as much pain and grief as if he were being led to execution. There is reason, however, to believe that it was a measure of precaution on the part of M. Olier; and this at least is certain, from the Letters of M. Tronson, that M. du Ferrier was one of those who, though not Jansenists in doctrine, were on such terms of intimacy with certain members of the party as to be unwilling to take a side against them, who spoke of them with esteem, and approved, or at least did not discourage, the reading of their books. After filling the office of grand-vicar in several dioceses for the space of thirty-seven years, he fell into disgrace with the court for supporting the Bishop of Pamiers in resisting the encroachments of the civil power, and was committed to the Bastille, where, in fact, he died, in the sixth year of his imprisonment and the seventy-seventh of his age.

After M. du Ferrier several others quitted the seminary, in consequence of their favourable dispositions towards the new opinions, among whom in all probability was his brother, M. de Cambiac, who for some time had entertained thoughts of entering the community of S. Merri. His departure under such circumstances was the cause of much grief to M. Olier, who, in his letters written at the time, speaks of him in terms of the utmost affection and charity. For six or seven years the Jansenistic party endeavoured with the help of the seceders to shake M. Olier's authority at S. Sulpice, but finding all their efforts fruitless, they sought by means of his old friend M. de Pamiers, who, as we have seen, took no decided part against them, to exercise some sort of influence in the conduct of the house. But here again their attempts were entirely unsuccessful. To all that prelate's exhortations to call in the aid of sound advisers, the servant of God replied that they were in the habit of consulting M. Vincent (de Paul) on any extraordinary occasion, and on ordinary occasions they did not fail to convene a meeting of the whole community. "As for those," he added, "who have set themselves up to judge all things, and condemn whatever they have not the ordering of, we have but small need of their advice."

Baffled at every point, and unable to gain the smallest influence within the seminary, the Jansenists determined on bringing the Fathers of the Oratory into the Faubourg S. Germain, many of whom were among the warmest defenders of the new opinions, and as such in direct antagonism to M. Olier and the Sulpitians. Indeed, as we learn from a letter which the servant of God addressed to M. Bourgoing, the then Superior of the Oratory, to whom the motives of his conduct had been misrepresented, one of that society, and he a person of no little consideration (meaning F. Camus), had not scrupled to say, in the presence of one of the priests of S. Sulpice, in reference to a member of the Jansenistic party, "He does not, it is true, do as many works as M. Olier, but—*omnia infidelium opera sunt peccata;*"* a speech, it is needless to remark, as much opposed to orthodoxy as to charity. To secure the success of their project they put in requisition the most powerful influences of which they were possessed, in the persons of the Duke of Orleans and the President de Maison, the declared protectors of the Oratory, with whose assistance they entertained no doubt of obtaining the support of the Queen Regent. The occasion they chose was also a most favourable one for furthering their suit, for the Court was on the eve of re-entering Paris, after the first troubles of the Fronde, and at this time the duke was a firm adherent of the royalist cause. At S. Sulpice, as we are told by M. Olier, the greatest consternation prevailed; its inmates were convinced that the establish-

---

* "All the works of unbelievers are sins."

ment of the Oratory would involve the ruin of the Seminary, and that if in the midst of the thousand contradictions which the enemy of all good was every day raising against them, in order to force them to abandon their work and the reformation of the parish, they should have to encounter a congregation which was at open war with them, they should infallibly be compelled to give way, and betake themselves elsewhere.

M. Olier, meanwhile, preserved his usual calmness, but afraid of acting at his own dictation, he kept himself in complete seclusion for the space of eight days, which he spent in silence and in prayer. He then repaired to the Abbé of S. Germain, in the hopes that through him, as his ecclesiastical superior, God would be pleased to make known His will. That prelate no sooner saw him enter than he at once began speaking of the Oratorians, and declared that nothing would induce him to permit their establishing themselves in the parish, convinced, as he was, that the majority of that body were deeply tainted with the Jansenistic errors. The like happened also in the case of the Regent herself. When M. Olier went to present his congratulations in person, as the other *curés* of Paris had done some days previously, the queen volunteered to inform him, that having heard from the abbé of the design which the Oratorians entertained, she had forbidden his compliance. God seemed thus to have taken the matter out of His servant's hands, and he, therefore, felt emboldened to act with confidence in opposing the movements of the Oratory, a course to which, considering his former relations with the society, he had naturally been much averse. In this resolution he was confirmed by a signal favour which was at this time accorded to him. The Blessed Virgin by a particular manifestation, the manner of which he does not relate, promised him her continued protection, and bade him rest assured that the establishment in contemplation would never take place, although the highest powers in France should conspire to bring it about, and though the whole world should believe or fear that so it would be. As a perpetual acknowledgment of this mercy, she desired that he should engage to render some special honour to her " glories" for the space of a quarter of an hour daily. This was the origin of a practice * which has been strictly observed in the seminary down to the present day. His first visit of thanksgiving was to the church of Notre Dame; but in further token of his gratitude, he repaired also to the shrine of Our Lady of Liesse, where, before her miraculous image, this heavenly Patroness did not fail to confer fresh favours upon her devoted client, and to assure him, with a certain ineffable authority and majesty, that all the devices of his adversaries should be brought to nought. In effect, though the friends of the Oratory took advantage of M. Olier's absence from Paris to renew their solicitations, the Regent stood firm in her determination, and at the instance of the Abbé of St. Germain, the Parliament issued a decree, forbidding the proposed establishment within the parish of S. Sulpice.

In founding his seminary M. Olier had two objects: the first was that of forming young men for the ecclesiastical state; the second, and that which he deemed even more important, was the creation of a society devoted to the education of the clergy, which, in its turn might lend its powerful aid in establishing similar institutions throughout the country. In selecting and forming the subjects of this society, he proceeded wholly on supernatural principles. It was never his practice to invite any one to enter the community, however strongly pronounced a vocation any individual might appear to possess; he left all in the hands of God. He desired that the community should be the simple work of the Holy Spirit, and not the construction of human prudence; to this end he

* M. Faillon says that the custom of reciting the Rosary every day for a quarter of an hour was already established at S. Sulpice when M. Olier received this intimation, and that he added to the recitation a quarter of an hour's meditation on the glories of Mary: a practice which continued to be observed for some years, and is still observed in the general annual retreat. This recitation, with meditation, is given by M. Allies in the order of exercises followed at that time.— *Journal in France*, p. 35.

would employ no constraining influences, nor permit any to be employed by others. The only power he called into operation was that of secret prayer and the Adorable Sacrifice of the Altar, that the will of God might be done, and His name glorified by means of such as He should Himself choose for His ministers. "Better," he would say, "receive one subject from the hand of God, than a hundred thousand in any other way." Accordingly, it was the rule of the seminary to treat a vocation to the community as a matter which belonged solely to God; and if any one showed the slightest inclination towards another kind of life, this alone was sufficient for his director to endeavour to turn his thoughts from entering the society. M. Le Peletier, who became a member of S. Sulpice after M. Olier's death, says, expressly, in reference to his own case, that no inmate of the house ever made the least approach to a proposal that he should join them, or so much as spoke to him of the mode of life, with a view of attracting him towards it; nay, he adds, that he was disappointed in the manner in which his application for admission was received, and that he had to make it several times before the superior appeared disposed to listen to him.

Abandoning himself thus to Divine Providence, M. Olier had, in the course of eight or ten years, without personal effort or persuasion, gathered within the walls of S. Sulpice as many as thirty or forty men whom it would have been difficult to match for intellectual powers, no less than for their piety and zeal, and, above all, for their apostolical detachment from the world; and he seemed to behold before his eyes the literal fulfilment of the promise he had received, that the Goodness of God would raise up a new order of beings sooner than the work he was called on to accomplish should fail for want of assistants. Among other remarkable vocations the following may be mentioned:—

M. Souart was a young man of great ability, in whose education no pains had been spared by his father, who intended to resign to him an appointment which he held in the household of the Duke of Orleans. Brought up at what, in the language of those days, was justly styled the *court* of this prince, he thought only of enjoying the pleasures and advantages which the world afforded, and had been affianced by his friends to a young lady of considerable wealth, to whom he was on the eve of being married. But God had other designs regarding him. One day when he was attending Mass at S. Sulpice, the priest whose duty it was to deliver the sermon, was taken suddenly ill, and on word being brought to M. Olier, he sent and begged M. Meyster,* who hap-

* The effects produced by the preaching of this extraordinary man were such that M. du Ferrier called him "the first missioner of the age;" and F. de Condren, who was little given to praise, said of him that he was "a man to be confronted with Antichrist." He was not a Sulpitian, but spent his life in missionary labours. His death was accompanied with circumstances of the most awful character. He was giving a mission at Metz, and none of the churches being large enough to contain the crowds that flocked to hear him, he addressed them from an eminence outside the town. One day, in proceeding to the place, the heat of the sun being very great, he felt much indisposed, but was preparing to deliver his sermon, when he was seized with a raving fit, during the paroxysms of which he gave utterance to blasphemies against God, and cursed the day on which he was born. He was immediately conveyed to his lodgings, but took advantage of the temporary absence of one of his attendants to stab himself mortally with a knife. Before expiring, however, he recovered his senses, and made his confession to F. Bouchard of the Oratory, who had taken the direction of the mission in his place.

The event, as may be imagined, caused a great sensation at the time, and the most conflicting judgments were passed upon it. On account of his keeping up communications with the Oratory, he was supposed by some to share the errors with which that body had already begun to be infected. But this was not the case, as is sufficiently proved by the respect, and almost veneration, with which M. Olier and others continued to speak of him after his death. The temptation to self-destruction is one with which God, in His mysterious dealings with the souls of His creatures, has permitted the holiest persons to be assailed; and M. Meyster was plainly bereft of his senses, and therefore morally irresponsible, when, in a paroxysm of frenzy he blasphemed God, and inflicted on himself a deadly wound. In the midst of his apostolical labours and astonishing successes, this eminent servant of God had so great a dread of yielding to a feeling of vanity, that he had begged to be humbled in the sight of men, and to lose the good esteem in which he was

pened at the time to be kneeling at the end of the church, to take the preacher's place. M. Meyster, who was always prepared, and able at a minute's notice to preach on any given topic, began by treating of the subject proper for the day; but soon glancing off, as was not unusual with him, he proceeded to insist on the necessity of a man's examining his vocation, showing how difficult it was for any one to be saved in a state to which God had not called him; when, raising his voice, he exclaimed, as if transported in spirit, like one who had received a sudden illumination, "I have one such before me! I have one such before me!" At these words the young man felt as if a thunderbolt had struck him: he saw the peril in which he stood; he was about to engage himself for life, and he had done nothing to ascertain the will of God. His distress and agitation were so great, that M. Meyster had no sooner descended from the pulpit than he went and opened his whole mind to him, and, acting on the advice he gave, made a retreat at S. Sulpice under the direction of M. Olier. The result was that he broke off his marriage, received the tonsure, and offered himself to the servant of God, who (as we shall see hereafter) sent him into Canada with M. de Queylus.

M. de Bretonvilliers, who has been often named in these pages, was the son of a secretary of the Council. Seeing the great esteem with which M. Olier was regarded, he conceived a strong desire to make his acquaintance; and was so moved by his conversation, that he never quitted him without a desire to return. It was not long before he consulted the servant of God on the choice of a state of life; and on the 12th of January, 1643, M. Olier offered the Holy Sacrifice for the determination of his doubts. Immediately after-

everywhere held. And God, it would seem, thus granted his prayer. Or it may be that his death was intended as a monition to others that his eccentric modes of action (for such they seem to have been), though worthy of admiration in his individual case, could not safely be imitated. This opinion accords with that given of him by F. de Condren in Chapter V.

wards M. de Bretonvilliers came and told him that at the very moment of the Elevation he felt himself called to the ecclesiastical state, and begged to be admitted into the society. By M. Olier's direction, the young man's desire was communicated to his father, who at first was astounded at the news, and required time for reflection; but recollecting what had been once said to him by a Capuchin monk, who bade him watch carefully over the education of his son, for that he would one day be at the head of an important ecclesiastical community, he himself, on the 19th of June in the same year, took the young man to S. Sulpice, and after giving him his blessing, confided him to the charge of the superior. Shortly after his admission, the servant of God observed to one of the community that M. de Bretonvilliers was destined to be his successor: a prediction which eventually received a twofold fulfilment, for this ecclesiastic succeeded him first in his pastoral office, and then in the government of the seminary, of which he was the second superior. Of his fitness to take the place of so good and great a man, we may form some opinion from the estimation in which he was held by M. Olier himself. "His charity," he writes, "seems to have no bounds; he has the faculty of infusing sweetness into all things; he carries about with him, as it were, an atmosphere of peace, tenderness, and joy. He is a centre of charity round which his brethren cluster; all feel the charm of his presence; averse to anything like display, he cannot endure that any one should know what he does or what he gives to the poor and unfortunate. A more generous charity was never seen; his hand is ever in his purse for those who are in need. His love of poverty is very great; he will not suffer a servant to accompany him; he delights in wearing shabby clothes; and his only desire seems to be to deprive himself of everything he possesses. His words have a wonderful power of moving souls: they who listen to him never wish to leave him, or that he should give over speaking, so redolent is everything he says of piety and deepest consolation."

Although M. Olier, as has been said, never solicited

any one to enter the community, he did not the less implore the Father of Lights to put the desire into the hearts of those whom He judged fitted for the work. It was thus he acted in respect to M. Tronson, who was his second successor. This ecclesiastic, a son of a secretary of the cabinet of Louis XIII., was distinguished for his profound acquaintance with scholastic theology and the Holy Scriptures, as well as with the Fathers, and the History of the Church; and it was said of him that, if he was not a doctor, he was capable of instructing doctors, being endowed with a particular gift of communicating to others the knowledge he possessed. Attracted by the sanctity of M. Olier, he took him as his director, and under his guidance made rapid progress in the way of perfection. The servant of God, deeply sensible, from the first moment he knew him, of the services he might render to the clergy, if God should call him to the work of the seminaries, continued for several years offering up prayers with this intention. Fearful, however, of running before Divine Providence, he preserved the strictest silence on the subject, while M. Tronson, on his part, who already felt himself drawn towards the community, said not a word to M. Olier, waiting till God should summon him. At length, unable to resist any longer the attractions of grace, he besought permission to try his vocation at S. Sulpice. The day he entered the house, M. Olier, then too ill to leave his bed, ordered all the community to assemble in the chapel, and sing a *Te Deum*, in thanksgiving to God for a particular favour granted to the seminary. This ebullition of holy joy was amply justified by the event. As superior of S. Sulpice, as well as by his writings, M. Tronson won the confidence and respect of the clergy of France in a singular degree, and has left behind him a name which will be ever held in veneration by the society he governed. The great Fénélon, writing to Pope Clement XI., makes it his boast that he had been "nourished with the words of faith, and formed to the clerical life," by one who was never, as he believes, surpassed for "love of discipline, ability, prudence, and piety, and more than all, sagacity in judging of men." Thus wonderfully did God provide for the efficient government of the seminary, as well as for its preservation from the destructive inroads of heresy.

It is in the rules and maxims which M. Olier laid down for the conduct of the noviciate, through which all who sought admission into the community must pass, that we may most clearly discern the spirit and genius of the new institution. The noviciate was, as we may say, the inner sanctuary of the edifice he had begun to rear; it was the school in which the teachers and directors of the Seminary were themselves to be trained and sanctified for the momentous task of forming the future priests of the Church. What these rules and maxims were we are enabled to ascertain with perfect precision from the various writings which the servant of God composed for the guidance of the society. The following meagre specimen can convey to the reader but a very inadequate idea of their exalted spirituality, comprehensiveness, and depth.

The inmates of this "interior Seminary," as he called it, were to be exercised in habits of self-annihilation, abnegation of their own will, patience, mortification, and other similar virtues, that they whose life was to be devoted to the service of priests might be the examples and the sources of the graces which it was their business to cultivate in others. To this end they were to practise, not only simplicity, but poverty. Their rooms were to be meanly furnished, and destitute of anything like ornament: content with a bed, a chair, a table, and a little picture to pray before, they would thus serve God in simple faith, unassisted by any of the helps or appliances of this world. To inspire a love and reverence for the house of God, and for its extrinsic and intrinsic beauty, as well as to nourish in themselves and others a meek and lowly spirit, they were to perform all the lowest offices about the church; to wash the altar-steps, dust the chairs and benches on which the clergy sat, and keep clean the whole interior of the choir. They were to be employed also from time to time in the duties of the sacristy, to put everything in its place, and learn by experience the order which ought to be observed in all that related to Divine worship. As some of their future subjects would be canons of cathedral churches, others would have the cure of souls, or be employed in other ministrations, they were to be trained to all the functions which those for whose service they were destined might hereafter be called upon to fulfil.

But these rules, though calculated to produce an interior spirit of self-abjection and devotion, required, materially at least, only an exterior service; but it was this interior spirit which it was his one unceasing solicitude to form. For himself (as we have seen), he had made a vow of particular and perfect servitude to the Church, and especially its ministers, and he directed that every member of the community, at such time as he seemed capable of doing so, should be called upon to make a personal dedication of himself to the same special end. It was in the shape of a protestation, by which each offered himself to the Eternal Father, with the assistance of the Blessed Virgin and S. Joseph, and in the Person of Jesus Christ, the Perfect Victim, to live, after His example, in perpetual dispositions of sacrifice and servitude to the last moment of his life; and consecrated himself to the adoration of the Most Holy Sacrament, by which these sentiments are nourished and sustained in souls. The import of this profession he thus explained: "The spirit of servitude to Christ and to the Church implies obedience to the least of the members of the Church whose servants we are. It implies poverty, in so far that we have nothing of our own: for that which a serf acquires, he acquires for his lord, not for himself. It implies humility, making us lie in spirit at the feet of all, as the serf must do in respect to his master; and every individual member of the Church must be held to be our master. It implies love of suffering, inasmuch as we must endure every species of contempt, opprobrium, affliction, and pain in the service of the Church. There is nothing, whether of heat or cold, hunger or thirst, toil, slight, or contradiction, which the servant must not endure to further the interests of his master, even though they proceed from the master himself, receiving with quietness and submission all the ill-treatment he may choose to inflict, and endeavouring in all humility to regain his favour.

"The spirit of servitude is, properly speaking, a great purity of intention, with an ardent desire of the glory of our Master. So far from being jealous when He is loved, honoured, and glorified by others more than by ourselves, we experience, on the contrary, a feeling of perfect complacency; and this is a sign that we do not seek ourselves in our labours, and are not acting in the spirit of a hireling. To acquit ourselves, then, as true and faithful servants, we ought at the beginning of an action to remember what our Lord says: *If any man will come after Me, let him deny himself;* for example, in preaching, we must first renounce the esteem of men; in confessing, we must renounce all self-complacency; in prayer, our own satisfaction and our own tastes; in receiving communion, all seeking after the gifts of God; in conversing, we must renounce the desire of being loved by men, or pleasing them; in eating and drinking, sensuality; in study, curiosity; in dress, all self-display; in the practice of virtue, all complacency in our own perfection: in all things we must act by faith in the intentions of Jesus Christ, and unite ourselves to the intentions He had of honouring and pleasing His Father. . . . This implies a great mortification of the natural desires and appetites, which we must have subdued in no little degree; a great love for our Lord, together with an ardent desire to promote His glory,—there being no stronger sentiment in our hearts, nothing which has greater dominion over us; in fine, a sincere love of the cross, of contempt, poverty, suffering, so that in the service of our Master there is no obstacle which can stay our progress.

"From this spirit of servitude comes that of immolation, which implies a disposition to die to self, and to live to God alone, awaiting but the time and the occasion to sacrifice ourselves to Him for the good of His Church. As victims, we are reckoned as no longer belonging to the world, so that we are ignorant of its laws, its ceremonies, its habits, its language, and are conversant only with the ceremonies of the Church, the praises of God, the service of His temple; remembering that of old the victims were separated from the flock, and removed from the fold, that they might abide in the temple of God: they no longer lived for themselves, being destined for sacrifice; and so must we have lost all care of our body, all solicitude about health, all attachment to life. If we eat, it must be as the victims in the temple, awaiting death, and preserving life only for the moment of sacrifice. They ate in order to die, rather than to live; and thus it must be with him who lives in the spirit of immolation. He must be as an angel would be in a human body: he must keep his eyes fixed ever on God, tending to Him incessantly, to love, adore, and serve Him, as a pure flame which rises and tends towards heaven; or rather as Jesus Christ in the Most Holy Sacrament, who would make us partakers of His spirit of immolation by giving us to eat of His Sacred Flesh."

Such, in epitome, were the maxims which M. Olier laid down as the foundations on which the future members of the community were to form their spiritual life; and to these he appended two practical rules, to the observance of which he attached much importance. One was a weekly confession, in common, of the faults which each might have committed against the principal Christian virtues and his clerical profession. The other was a private self-examination every evening, on the points contained in the following schedule, a copy of which in their own handwriting, was to be hung up in their respective rooms:—

"Have you been wanting in the love of the cross?

"Or in the love of poverty, suffering, and contempt?

"Or in the hatred of yourselves, seeking yourselves in your actions, instead of renouncing all self-satisfaction and all self-interest?

"Have you failed as respects the love of your enemies, or interior religion, by neglecting to refer your actions to God, or to our Lord Jesus Christ?

"Have you been wanting in exterior devotion in church, and, in particular, in any of the divine offices, or other duties of religion?

"Have you walked the whole day in the presence of Jesus Christ, having His interior everywhere before your eyes, to adore it, and to form it in yourselves?

"Have you been faithful in recollecting yourselves at the beginnimg of each work, according to the direction?

"Have you lived according to faith, regarding and esteeming all things as Jesus Christ regards and esteems them?

"Have you manifested Jesus Christ in your conduct?

"His sweetness, humility, patience, charity, obedience, and forbearance?

"Have you, among other virtues, practised that which especially becomes clerics, modesty?

"Have you lived in the spirit of servitude towards Jesus Christ and His members?

"Have you lived also in the spirit of immolation?"

Of the devotions by which this twofold spirit was to be derived from its source in the Sacred Heart of Jesus, we need not here speak, as they were sufficiently indicated in the general account that has been given of the interior life of the seminary, and of the great spiritual idea according to which the interior structure was to be reared. We are here concerned only with the particular obligations and characteristics of the community, as distinguished from the seminary. To maintain among his priests that spirit of detachment and disinterestedness which he deemed essential to the existence of the institution, M. Olier would have them receive no sort of stipend or remuneration, however small, but be content with the food and clothing which the society provided. Not that he would have them make a vow of poverty, or strip themselves of such property as they chanced to possess; on the contrary, he would never allow M. de Bretonvilliers to take such vow, or make such renunciation, although he sought permission long and earnestly. "Renounce," he said, "the use of worldly goods, but retain their possession. You will thus abide in the state in which Providence has placed you; your goods will be employed to His glory, and you will possess all the benefits of poverty, which consist in having nothing to prevent your belonging to God only." This, indeed, was the sort of poverty of which he himself gave his disciples the example. For several years he neither disposed of his property, nor made any personal use of it; nay, so little conversant was he with money matters that he could not keep his own accounts, and on more than one occasion showed an absolute ignorance of the value of certain coins, saying with genuine simplicity, "You see I am not fit for these sorts of things." Strict and apparently even severe as he was in requiring from his subjects an entire subjection and immolation of themselves in all that related to their special vocation, he insisted no less strongly on the general duty of taking care of their health. This is evident from his letters, one of which may here be cited. The reader will not fail to observe how perfectly in harmony the advice he gives is with those supernatural principles to which he referred everything. "I pray you may have the grace," he writes, "to avail yourself where you are of all the benefits which the air, the fine weather, and the remedies prescribed are capable of rendering, for the improvement of your health. You have vowed and consecrated it to God; you know that it belongs to Jesus Christ, by the right He possesses over all creatures of employing them to promote the glory of His Father, and in particular by the choice He has made of you to serve Him in His Church. Jesus Christ has made over His rights to His Church, and she may justly claim the service of your body for the good of His children. See, then, to how many masters you belong, to how many you are responsible, and whether you can with justice refuse them the preservation of your health. Therefore be careful of it, forgetting yourself, and simply obeying your superiors."

The noviciate at first was at Vaugirard, but the desire he had to be as far removed as possible from all contact with the world, induced him to transfer it to a *château* at Avron,* belonging to M. de Bretonvilliers, and afterwards to Issy,† where the seminary still has its country house. Here he received all who desired to join the community, and such ecclesiastics as were sent by the bishops to be trained for the direction of similar institutions in the provinces.

---

* At Avron was a chapel with the title of *Notre Dame des Anges.* Tradition assigns its origin to three foreign merchants, who were robbed and then hanged upon trees near the spot, but were miraculously delivered by the assistance of the Blessed Virgin, who appeared surrounded with a multitude of angels. In thanksgiving they erected a chapel, which became one of the most famous places of pilgrimage in the diocese of Paris. It was rebuilt, in 1663, by the canons regular of the congregation of France, to whom the neighbouring abbey of Livry belonged. At the revolution it was demolished, but a new building has since arisen out of its ruins, where Mass is said on all feasts of the Blessed Virgin, and especially on the feast and during the octave of her Nativity, when the concourse of people is still considerable. Near it is a holy well, to the waters of which curative properties are ascribed.

† The house at Issy had belonged to Marguerite de Valois, first wife of Henry IV., and was purchased, with its furniture, of M. de Sève, uncle of M. Tronson, by M. de Bretonvilliers, for the use of the society. It stood within an enclosure of sufficient extent to be styled a park, but was itself of small dimensions. It was subsequently enlarged, and a chapel added, after the model of that of the Holy House of Loreto. The chapel was dedicated to the Blessed Virgin, under the title of *La Reine des Cœurs*, and at the end of the last century contained a vast number of votive offerings in the shape of hearts, all silver-gilt, which had been presented by prelates and other ecclesiastics, and were suspended to the lattice-work which separated the chapel from the Holy House. At the breaking-out of the revolution ninety-six of these silver hearts were sent to the mint. One offering was of a singularly touching character. It had been sent by the savages of Montreal in Canada, and was composed of little stones of different colours, all in the shape of hearts, and equal in number to the Christians in their tribe. The library was remarkable for a large collection of works relating to the Blessed Virgin. It was here that the conferences on Quietism were held, which lasted seven or eight months, and at which Bossuet, Fénélon, and Cardinal de Noailles were present.

CHAPTER XXI.

Establishment of Provincial Seminaries.

As early as 1643, several of the most zealous and distinguished prelates had consulted M. Olier (as we have seen) on the subject of erecting seminaries in their dioceses; but for the first few years the reform of his parish required the presence of so many of his priests, that he was unable to do more than train for the work such clergy as were sent to him. After a time, however, he was in a condition to render more efficient aid by commissioning members of his community to take the direction of a seminary until the newly-trained ecclesiastics were capable of managing it without assistance. The next step was to charge the society itself with the conduct of provincial seminaries; and here an important distinction is to be observed. The seminary of S. Sulpice was never erected into a congregation: such a result would have been totally opposed to the intentions of its holy founder, whose desire was that it should remain in closest union with the whole body of the clergy, and (to use his own expression) be as it were "merged and lost in it." For this reason he gave it no distinctive appellation,—the name it bore being, in fact, bestowed upon it by popular consent, because it was situated in the parish of S. Sulpice and connected with that church; he did not even let his ecclesiastics be called Fathers, as were the members of other secular communities; for instance, that of the Oratory. It was a merely local institution, whose situation was at Paris. When, therefore, the priests of the society, at the call of the bishops, went to labour in the provinces, they remained as long as their services were required, and no longer. Even when, in obedience to episcopal authority, they founded seminaries in different parts of the country, they regarded themselves only as temporary residents, not as settled inhabitants; they claimed no right of possession beyond such term as was assigned them, and held themselves in readiness to surrender the very houses they occupied to other labourers whenever they received the word to depart. In Paris, alone, and in their own seminary of S. Sulpice, had they either permanent habitation or corporate existence. With what fidelity M. Olier adhered to these principles and conditions will appear in the course of the present chapter.

One of the first seminaries the establishment of which was due to his example and instructions, was that of Bordeaux, where for fifty years unsuccessful efforts had been made to meet the urgent need of the Church. Of the assistance rendered to the Bishop of Pamiers, mention has been already made. At Villefranche, in the diocese of Rodez, which was then of large extent, and may be said to have lain desolate for twenty years, the result surpassed all his expectations, as he had occasion to observe when visiting the place in 1647. In the space of only five months, a seminary had been erected, several of the canons of the church emulating the zeal of M. de Queylus by contributing liberally both to the building and to its endowment; monthly conferences had been commenced, at which each ecclesiastic gave written answers to twelve questions in dogma and morals; and the general conduct of the clergy had undergone so marked and rapid a transformation, that M. Olier was able shortly afterwards to withdraw his priests. Returning through Limoges, with the object (as was related at the time) of venerating the relics of S. Martial, the state in which he found the diocese filled his soul with anguish. Many of the gentry, by a fictitious presentation, made over the parishes of which they were patrons to *vicaires*, who were removable at their pleasure, and bestowed the revenues on their own children. Such was the ignorance of the clergy, and their utter disregard of the essential duties of their office, that one of themselves, writing to M. Bourdoise, declared that all that was required in order to be reputed a good ecclesiastic, was " to be able to read, and not to be guilty of any heinous crime." Another thus expressed himself: " If you knew but a hundredth part of what goes on in country churches, you would weep tears of blood." In his grief and desolation the man of God, after saying Mass at the tomb of the saint, remained for five hours in prayer, bathed in tears and beseeching the Father of Mercies to have pity on the poor neglected people. God was not deaf to His servant's call, for as he prayed he received a secret intimation that he should himself be the instrument of the grace which he implored: that the day was not far distant when the diocese should possess its seminary, conducted by his own community, and for its chief pastor, one of his own spiritual children. All which was literally verified when, five years after the death of the holy man, M. Jean Bourdon, a priest of S. Sulpice, was sent to found and to govern the seminary of Limoges, and M. Lascaris d'Urfé,* who was a child of the house, and had a singular veneration for M. Olier, was made bishop of that see. By their united exertions an entire reformation was effected in the diocese.

When, in 1648, M. Olier (as noticed at the time) went to pay his devotions at the tomb of S. Vincent Ferrier at Vannes, the particular grace for which he

* M. d'Urfé, or the Comte de Sommerive (for such was his title in the world), was the eldest son of a noble family, and passed the early years of his life at the courts of France and of Savoy. As bishop of Limoges he was a model of piety, humility, and charity towards the poor. In order to have the more to give in alms he took up his residence at the seminary, where he lived in all plainness and simplicity. In a time of great public distress he stripped himself of all he possessed, even pledging his episcopal ring. During the eighteen years which he spent in the seminary he never failed to be present at the morning prayers of the community; he said his office on his knees; and every day passed whole hours before the Blessed Sacrament. His affection for his priests is described as having in it something not only tender but reverential, so great was his respect for their sacred character; and the feelings he entertained for them they in turn reciprocated. He seemed born to be a bishop and the reformer of his diocese. Such is the testimony which M. Bourdoise has given of him.

prayed was that of preaching with something of the energy and power for which that great apostle of Brittany had been distinguished. But the saint, by an interior communication, gave him to understand that he would obtain for him a gift more in accordance with his vocation: that of training children for God who should perpetuate the work he had begun, and enlarge the kingdom of Christ; and to this end bade him establish a seminary at Nantes, and send some of his ecclesiastics to conduct it. The impression thus supernaturally conveyed received an immediate confirmation; for the grand-vicar of Vannes, as though regardless of the interests of his own diocese, strongly urged him, for the good of the province, to do the very thing which had been enjoined upon him by the saint. Keeping silence, however, as to what had occurred, M. Olier returned to Paris to await a further manifestation of the Divine will. This was not long delayed. The Bishop of Nantes now himself begged the man of God to take the direction of the seminary, which for six years he had been endeavouring to establish in his diocese. M. Olier, wishing to leave the matter entirely in the hands of Providence, suggested that application should first be made to the Oratorians, who had a house at Nantes, and were in the habit of giving retreats to candidates for ordination: adding that his mission led him rather into desert places where labourers there were none. The bishop, however, declaring that to the priests of S. Sulpice and to them alone would he intrust the undertaking, M. Olier yielded to his instances, reserving to himself the liberty of withdrawing his ecclesiastics whenever they were needed elsewhere. At the end of ten or twelve years, perceiving that the dispositions of the bishop had undergone a change, he desired the members of his community at once to remove; but his influence was not altogether withdrawn from the seminary, for at his express recommendation its managers obtained the assistance of one who by birth belonged to the diocese, and had been formed under his own direction while the noviciate was at Avron. This was M. René Lévêque, one of the most laborious and mortified men of the time, who had instituted a sort of community in the parish of S. Sulpice for poor scholars, whose poverty prevented their proceeding to the priesthood. This institution grew subsequently into the seminary of S. Louis;* and when at Nantes he founded a second community, which eventually was united with the seminary of that town.

* The actual founder of the seminary of S. Louis was François Chansiergues. He resigned a prebendal stall which he held in the cathedral church of Uzés, although he was possessed of no private means, and joined the little community of poor priests, formed by M. Lévêque, who lived on alms and by transcribing treatises of theology, and who, on account of their extreme poverty, went by the name of the Brothers of Abstinence. At the time he came to Paris the society was governed by one of the parish priests of S. Sulpice, who at his death was succeeded by M. Chansiergues. Under his management the society rapidly developed; no less than thirty-eight *petits séminaires* owing their foundation to his exertions; as also twelve communities of poor scholars in Paris alone. But his humility was equal to his zeal, and with a touching simplicity he always referred the success with which his labours had been attended to the prayers of pious persons interested in the work, especially to M. Bauin, director of the Seminary of S. Sulpice. As his efforts prospered he redoubled his austerities; his abode was in a sort of turret, to which it was necessary to ascend by a ladder, and all the furniture of which was a couple of boards with a miserable coverlet which served him for a bed, a table to write at, a crucifix, an image of the Blessed Virgin, and a little picture representing the death of S. Francis Xavier. He took but two hours' sleep; the remainder of the night being spent in prayer, answering letters, and drawing up memorials for seminaries. In the day he went about begging alms for his poor clerks, in the course of which he had to endure many rebuffs and insults, but he would laughingly say that the alms were for his communities, the rebuffs were for himself. His poor scholars cost him, as he declared, no more than three sous each a day, but the number was so large that the expense was considerable. Being of a lively, humorous disposition, he invented numerous dignities and offices which he affected to sell to bishops and abbots in order to raise money. Thus one was made a general of the order; another, superior; a third, visitor; a fourth, assistant. Louis XIV. learning with astonishment at how small a sum a man was able to support himself in the heart of Paris, became a benefactor to the institution, and his example was followed by several about the court. He died in 1691, at the age of fifty-five, having, from humility, never proceeded beyond the diaconate.

So one good work produced another, and all may be said to owe their origin to the founder of S. Sulpice. To the distress of M. Lévêque* the seminary of Nantes became infected with the Jansenistic errors, but in 1728, at the urgent and repeated requests of the then bishop of the see, the Sulpitians again undertook its direction, and have continued it to the present day. These particulars have been given in detail, though in as succinct a form as possible, in order to show the wide-spread influence which M. Olier indirectly as well as directly exercised; and how, without corporately going beyond the limits which it occupied in the Faubourg S. Germain, the Seminary of S. Sulpice was able to extend its operations throughout the Church of France.

Wherever he went some good seed was let fall which afterwards germinated and fructified, or some salutary impression was left which sooner or later made itself felt: his mission, as he knew, was to his brethren of the clergy, and he neglected no opportunity of fulfilling it. Meeting a young ecclesiastic one day on the road, he asked him what he was thinking of, and the other saying in reply that he was thinking of nothing, " Eh, what!" he exclaimed in a voice which betokened grief as well as surprise, " has not an ecclesiastic God to think of, and some worship ever to pay Him in the secret of his heart?" When, in the course of his journeys, he found himself in a parish where the priest was diligent in instructing the people, he seemed unable to show him respect enough, or to testify all the joy and satisfaction he felt. " But alas!" he writes, " it is a wonder to meet

* This holy man went every other year from Nantes to make a retreat at S. Sulpice. It was his custom to perform the journey on foot, but towards the close of his life, being no longer able to bear the fatigue, he took boat on the Loire. His provisions by the way consisted of a little bread and butter which he carried with him, the water of the river served him for drink, and for an occupation he used to twist cinctures for albs, which he gave to poor priests. Such was his spirit of mortification, that having a painful ulcer in his leg he paid no attention to it until the wound became gangrened. At his death, which took place at S. Sulpice, a rough hair-shirt was found upon him, which he wore day and night.

with one good pastor in a whole province. My only solace amidst the almost universal desolation is in a few ecclesiastics who are established in a solid virtue and in the prudence of a fervent zeal." In Provence, however, his addresses to the clergy produced a most powerful effect. "They cannot cease talking of them," wrote F. Yvan; "they declare they never heard anything which moved them so much, and only wish they could have listened to you longer, that their reformation might have been the more perfect." Encouraged by these indications, M. Olier sent M. Philippe, an ecclesiastic of learning and judgment as well as virtue, and a native of those parts, to found a seminary at Aix, which, on account of its university, was frequented by a large number of students. The see was vacant at the time, owing to the death of the Cardinal de Sainte-Cecile,[*] brother of Cardinal Mazarin, but on the accession of Cardinal Grimaldi, he immediately proposed that M. Olier should undertake the conduct of the house. Several priests of the country joined M. Philippe's community, after having spent a certain time at S. Sulpice, but from causes which do not appear, the seminary was not formally placed under the direction of the Sulpitians until the year 1805.

In 1651, M. Olier took advantage of the general session of the clergy to submit to the collective episcopate the particular rules together with the entire plan and constitution of the society, in order to obtain their solemn approbation. In a letter which he at the same time addressed to them, he in the most unconditional manner surrendered the whole conduct of the seminary into their hands, as alone capable of judging whether in its design and interior spirit the institution was in accordance with the true ecclesiastical idea. "The house," he said, "was called into being simply for your service, and it will go on as it has begun if it merits your approbation. If not, it is ready to change everything, being convinced that there is no security for it, save in

---

[*] See note at p. 292.

implicit obedience to your holy counsels. "He at the same time laid before the assembly the principles and rules which his ecclesiastics had hitherto observed in the several diocesan seminaries they had founded, with a view of obtaining the benefit of their united counsels as well as their formal sanction. The sublimity of the views he propounded may be gathered from the following summary:—

"As every religious order has its particular spirit, which diffuses itself copiously among its novices, so the magnificent order of the holy clergy, which alone is formally commissioned to render to God all the duties, exterior and interior, of the religion of Jesus Christ, has in itself the universal Spirit of the religion of that Sovereign Pontiff, who lets fall the seeds of His life abundantly in the sacred houses of the seminaries, in order to form therein the ministers of the Church. Hence we may learn the reason of that abiding grace and that abundance of light and spirit which God pours down upon them. .. The true and only superior of the seminary is the Bishop, who, containing in himself the plenitude of spirit and of grace which is to be diffused among his clergy, can alone communicate to it its spirit and its life. What the head is in the natural body, the holy prelate must be in the mystical body of his clergy; and it is but to labour in vain to attempt any other mode of sanctifying clerical colleges. However exalted may be the sanctity of those distinguished persons, eminent for their virtues, who are to be found scattered here and there throughout a diocese, inasmuch as they do not possess that capital grace which belongs to the divine character of prelates, we cannot expect in them that plenitude of spirit and life which is capable of replenishing and vivifying the body of the clergy; seeing that, according to S. Paul, it must flow from the head into the members by those "joints and bands," the veins and nerves and ligaments, which have been provided for the communication and distribution of life and spirit. These are the priests united to their holy prelate, according as Jesus Christ prescribed in the first formation of the clergy. To some He has given to receive life, to others to communicate and diffuse it; and that by an order of parts fitted and compacted together in an admirable structure, for which no human invention can be substituted without destroying and ruining the whole Church. Seeing, however, that bishops have not the leisure to attend personally to the direction and instruction of their clergy, they must have under their control priests whom they can set in their place to conduct their seminaries, and to whom they can communicate of their spirit and grace, as did Moses of old to the seventy ancients. They thus satisfy the most important obligation of the episcopate, which is to sow the seed of divine life in the hearts of their principal subjects, who, in their turn, may fill cathedral chapters with their religion, altars with their sanctity, pulpits with their doctrine and piety, sacred tribunals with their justice, and the hearts of the people with the holy fire of their love. Herein principally consists the pre-eminent function of the hierarchical dignity in the communication of the Spirit and the life of God. O how admirable is the mission of good priests, who have a share of this Spirit, that they may distribute it among the noblest and the holiest portions of the Church! They ought to be as reservoirs, deep and wide, to receive the abundance of grace necessary for an office so sacred. They ought to be by their virtue what a holy prelate is by the dignity of his character, that, filled with his light, his spirit, and his grace, they may distribute it among all the members of the clergy, dividing to each according to his needs. A human exterior they must have, but in their heart of hearts they ought to be wholly divine; and their life must be human only that they may diffuse the life of God among men. They ought to have the interior of a bishop under the exterior of an ordinary life, endeavouring to transform the pupils of the sanctuary into themselves, even as they have been themselves transformed into the interior of their holy prelate.

" When the Son of God was preparing His Apostles and disciples for the spirit of their vocation, He kept them three years near Himself, leading them continually to the annihilation of their own will, and the stripping themselves of the gross things of this world. This very preparation it is which the Church of Christ, the depositary of His secrets, demands of all its priests, and especially of those whom the prelates, the true successors of the Apostles, call to them to take the direction of their seminaries and to fill them with their spirit. These good priests, who, in their ordinary life, ought to be the models of their holy flock, must renew in themselves all that the Church has ever demanded of what is most pure and holy for the perfection of the priesthood; they must have immolated and annihilated their own will, being assured that the emptying themselves of self is the only disposition which will attract the Spirit of Jesus Christ, which cannot co-exist with their own individual spirit; and that, unless they give place entirely to this Divine Spirit, they will never afford Him the means of manifesting in them or in others the surpassing effects of Apostolic grace. I think, too, that they ought to renew in the presence of their bishop the renunciation they had already made of all wordly goods, when, on entering the clerical state, they took God for their portion, and the riches of heaven for their only possession.... Seeing also of how much importance they are to a diocese, they ought to renounce all benefices, and not allow themselves to be withdrawn from an occupation which, as it is public and universal in its character, is likewise of wider influence and higher consideration than any mere individual office.

" As few are to be met with who are willing to enter on a life of self-denudation, and who at the same time are possessed of the necessary zeal, prudence, and capacity, pains must be taken to keep them when the goodness of God has provided them." They must be relieved (he continues) of all exterior occupations, otherwise their attention to the work of the seminary will be in some degree relaxed, and its spiritual interests will proportionably suffer. They must be supplied with such food and clothing as is strictly necessary, but without having any personal concern in the matter. When death shall have removed any of the directors, the survivors shall choose two or three priests whom they shall present to the bishop for his selection. Besides the directors, there ought to be in every seminary a number of priests thoroughly formed, and ready to go at a moment's notice into any part of the diocese to which the bishop may please to send them. These need not, like the first, make renunciation of ecclesiastical benefices or dignities, inasmuch as they ought to hold themselves at the disposal of their prelate, to be employed in such way as shall seem to him good. The third class, which is far the most numerous, will consist of the seminarists, properly so called. As they are of every rank and condition, care must be taken to observe such simplicity in the matter of food and clothing that, on the one hand, the poor may not be over-provided for, and, on the other, the rich may not be too hardly treated. He then insists on the great importance of inuring all alike to habits of mortification, in terms similar to those which we have seen him employ in a former chapter.

A copy of this memorial having been presented by one of the priests of S. Sulpice to each of the bishops in the assembly, as well as of the deputies of the second order, their lordships, not content with simply approving the rules of the society, at once accepted its proffered services in behalf of themselves and their clergy, and bestowed upon it the name of the "Company of the Priests of the Clergy of France." But even when fortified by the general approbation of the episcopal body, M. Olier did not the less scrupulously await the personal invitation of each particular bishop before seeking to exercise his mission within his diocese: a tacit or implied consent did not suffice. Thus, in 1652, while at the waters of Bourbon, he was solicited by many influential persons to lay the foundation of a seminary at Avignon, but finding that the archbishop was himself lukewarm on the subject, he at once abandoned the design, although one which his devotion to the Apostolical See, to which Avignon at that time belonged, strongly urged him to undertake. True to the principle which was the polestar of his life, he would not forestall by one moment the leadings of Divine Providence. "We must walk step by step," he said, "following the majestic and eternal decrees of God in all things;" and God in His own good time brought about the fulfilment of the object which His servant had so much at heart. Two priests of the country, both Sulpitians, established the needed institution, the direction of which was subsequently accepted by M. Leschassier; and at this very day, the seminary of Avignon is conducted by the children of M. Olier.

In 1650 the servant of God had sent M. de Queylus to aid the Bishop of Viviers, M. de Suze, in founding a seminary; but the attempt had met with an embarrassing opposition on the part of those from whom it ought rather to have received the readiest support. The establishment was represented as a sort of respectable prison, the inmates of which were made to lead a life of perpetual slavery, and to practise mortifications beyond human endurance. On his way to Avignon M. Olier stopped at Viviers; he arrived, as it happened, two days before the opening of the diocesan synod, and his presence seemed to have the effect of not only healing all dissensions, but of inspiring the clergy with a most lively zeal in behalf of the infant seminary. The bishop made over to it some dilapidated buildings which had anciently formed the episcopal residence, and the ecclesiastics who were present contributed largely towards the necessary repairs, as well as for the support of the house. A great number, also, of the parish priests sought admission into the seminary, in order to be more perfectly instructed in the duties and virtues of their state, or at least to go through the exercises of a spiritual retreat. Besides the personal advantage to themselves, this act of theirs was of the greatest immediate benefit to their flocks, as during their absence ecclesiastics of piety and experience were sent to supply their places, who entered on their office with all the ardour of missionaries. Sermons were preached, and the people invited to make a general confession, an invitation the more necessary that many, never having had the opportunity of disclosing the state of their souls to any but their own pastor, had unhappily been tempted to make sacrilegious confessions, or had deserted the tribunal of penance altogether. The difference between the clergy who had received ecclesiastical training and those who had never enjoyed that advantage very soon attracted attention, and the seminary became the object of general admiration. Some, indeed, of those who, either from ignorance of their vocation or from unworthy motives, had offered themselves for the clerical state abandoned their design and embraced other professions; but the greater part, when they quitted the seminary, exhibited an amount of devotion, enlightenment, and laborious zeal to which the people had been hitherto little accustomed. The bishop, overjoyed at the changes which he saw effected, extended the term of residence: candidates for the tonsure were to remain eight days, and those who sought minor orders, ten days; while such as aspired to the higher orders were to spend three months in the seminary preparatory to receiving each of them. Clergy from other dioceses also came for spiritual retreats or for a longer course of instruction; so that in a short time the house at Viviers became a fruitful source of grace to the extensive *cantons* of Auvergne, Dauphiné, Comtat, and Provence. According to his wont, M. Olier professed to have no more than a temporary connection with the seminary, although he and his community had borne a portion of the expenses, and for more than fifty years there was no formal act of union between it and S. Sulpice; but in 1706, the bishop and the clergy of the diocese, fearing that if the establishment ceased to be conducted by those who had founded it their withdrawal would be fatal to its existence, begged the society to undertake its direction in perpetuity.

From Viviers M. Olier repaired to Puy, without any thought, however, of contributing to the foundation of a seminary in that town. Such an establishment had been in contemplation for ten years, and he had been repeatedly solicited to commence the work, but he had been unable to spare any of his priests; and besides, the necessary funds were wanting. But now a sudden en-

thusiasm was kindled in the breasts of both clergy and
laity before which all obstacles disappeared. The bishop,
M. de Maupas, convened a meeting of ecclesiastics and
others, and begged M. Olier to lay before them the
necessity of making personal sacrifices for an undertaking of such paramount importance. The servant of
God recollected himself for a few moments, and then
addressed the assembly with so much energy and fervour,
that a seminary was resolved upon as by acclamation.
M. de Maupas, himself one of the greatest orators of
the day, though he had often had experience of M. Olier's
extraordinary powers, was astonished at the burning
torrent that issued from his lips; and long afterwards,
when speaking of the circumstance, he said that his
address on the occasion "abounded not only in grandeur,
force, and light, but in that fire of the Holy Ghost
which warms the coldest hearts and stirs the most insensible." As for the servant of God himself, he attributed
the result to the powerful interposition of Our Lady of
Puy, to whom he cherished a particular devotion. For
her sake, and in his zeal for the glory of God and the
good of the diocese, he not only contributed towards the
establishment out of his private means, but undertook
its direction. A pious layman of the town put his house
at his disposal, until such time as a suitable building
could be provided, and M. Olier summoned M. Tronson
and M. Le Breton to inaugurate the work. But the
man on whom the bishop had set his eyes to be superior
of the new seminary was M. de Lantages. This ecclesiastic was one of M. Olier's best subjects, for whom he
entertained the tenderest affection, and whom of all the
members of his community he could least afford to lose;
but true to his engagement of making his society the
handmaid of the episcopate, he yielded at once to the
bishop's request, declaring, however, that in surrendering
M. de Lantages to him he was giving him his heart.
The engaging qualities of this young priest soon gained
him the confidence of all with whom he came in contact,
and M. de Maupas, thinking to render his remarkable
gifts the more available to the benefit of the diocese,

insisted on appointing him his vicar-general. This design, however, he reluctantly abandoned, on M. Olier representing that he should be obliged to recall M. de Lantages to Paris. In adopting this course, the servant of God was determined by the consideration that the clergy would be less disposed to open their hearts as freely to one who was invested with such authority over them, and would be tempted to act rather from motives of human respect than of confidence and love. Nowhere, it may be added, were the blessings of heaven poured forth with more abundance than on the community of Puy. In a few years the face of the diocese was so completely changed, that the bishop, after M. Olier's death, declared in the fulness of his feelings to M. de Bretonvilliers, that since the establishment of the seminary, no one would recognize his clergy as the same men.

We have seen with what zeal and self-devotion M. Olier laboured as a missionary for the sanctification of the provinces in which at the time he held benefices, Vivarais, Velai, and Auvergne. He felt that it was a work to which he had been called by God, particularly as regarded the diocese of Clermont; for being in prayer one day in the cathedral church of that town, the blessed Virgin had been pleased to make known to him that she desired him to do a work there for the glory of her Son. Though fully assured in his own mind that in no way could that glory be more effectually promoted than by the establishment of a seminary, yet as no intimation had been given him as to the nature of the services he was to render, he awaited in patience a fuller disclosure of the Divine will. It came at length, when nothing was less in his thoughts, in the ordinary way of an invitation from the bishop to found a seminary in his diocese. Hitherto nothing more had been required of candidates for ordination than a retreat of eight days, and even this was a practice only of recent institution, for which the piety of the Cardinal de Rochefoucauld had provided the funds. Once assured of the Divine intentions, he lost no time in sending M. de

Poussé to Clermont, but he took no measures to secure the direction of the house for the priests of the society, and the seminary he founded remained independent of S. Sulpice until 1659, two years after his death. He contributed also towards the reformation of the clergy of Auvergne, by assisting in the establishment of the seminary of S. Flour. The deplorable condition of this diocese, which was of great extent, may be estimated from the fact that it was computed to have within it from 6,000 to 7,000 ecclesiastics, who had no competent knowledge of the duties of their state. M. Olier, who, from his connection with the abbey of Pébrac, had long been aware of evils which he was powerless to remedy, felt himself called upon to make some sacrifices for a prelate whose zeal deserved all the assistance he could render him. M. de Mont-Rouge, finding himself utterly at a loss for coadjutors among his clergy on whom he could rely, had collected forty or fifty young men in his own episcopal residence, and placed others under the instruction of such priests of his diocese as by their piety and knowledge seemed best fitted for the task. M. Olier's first thought was to send M. Couderc to the bishop's aid, but his choice eventually fell on M. Planat, of whom a writer of the time says, "by his piety and doctrine he gained the approbation of all who were most enlightened in the science of the saints." Under his direction the seminary of S. Flour became at once the recipient and the source of abundant blessings from heaven.

Nothing, however, more strikingly exhibits M. Olier's respect for the episcopate, and the attitude of entire dependence which he maintained towards it, than the course he adopted in the case of M. du Bosquet, Bishop of Lodève. The former occupant of the see, M. de la Pause, had assigned the priory of S. Paul to the priests of S. Sulpice, for the commencement of an ecclesiastical seminary, and M. Couderc had been made superior of the house. Finding, however, that M. du Bosquet, whether on account of his Jansenistic predilections, or from some other cause, did not bestow the same marks of confidence in this ecclesiastic and his colleagues as had been shown them by his predecessor, M. Olier desired him to resign his office into the hands of the bishop, and to put the whole community at his sole disposal. At the same time he addressed a letter to M. du Bosquet, in which he says he has reminded M. Couderc that it is not fitting to remain in any house without the master's cordial assent, and that no blessing could be expected where this condition was wanting. "It is on this maxim," he continues, "that the seminary of S. Sulpice reposes as on a foundation. It has reserved to itself no other rights over such of its subjects as go out from it at the call of their lordships the Bishops, than that of continuing to remind them of the absolute dependence which they must maintain towards them, and of reproving them in case they should fail in this respect. This is why, amidst the pain which I suffer at seeing one of the subjects of the house no longer meriting your regard, I nevertheless experience a real joy in making the entire sacrifice of this benefice, in order to testify, in one of our first establishments, that the members of the community have no life, no proper end, no directing principle of conduct, but in obedience to their lordships the Bishops. They may call for us, and they may send us away, at their pleasure; and the house professes to be nothing, and to possess nothing, save in pure and simple dependence upon them. A work of God ought never to be the cause of aught that is unbecoming, or contrary to the simplicity and justice of the Gospel; and if I thought there would ever go forth from S. Sulpice a single subject of the house who should oppose the mandates of their lordships the Bishops, or lend his countenance to any violation of that reverence which is their due, I would pray that the seminary might be destroyed, and become an object of anathema in the face of the whole world." These words, followed as they were by an immediate abandonment of the seminary and of the whole work which had been attended with such signal success, are sufficient to show that in the conduct of his institute, as in all his other acts, public and personal, this great man continued true to the principle which had ever guided him, of following simply the will of God, and looking for the indication of that will in the command or the assent of ecclesiastical superiors.

From the brief enumeration that has been made, the reader will be enabled to infer how much M. Olier was able to effect in a few short years for the Church of France; but his influence began speedily to spread beyond the confines of the realm, and as early as 1651 several bishops of other countries begged him to send them priests to aid in the erection of seminaries and in the general reformation of their clergy. Before making any reply to these applications he resolved to go to Rome, for the purpose of soliciting in person the approbation of the Holy See. In this he was encouraged by the king, who directed his ambassador to support the petition with all his influence; but the servant of God was withheld from pursuing the matter further by the consideration of the great demand there was for such auxiliaries in the kingdom itself, and the object he sought was not attained until after the foundation of the seminary of Ville Marie at Montreal; when, in the year 1664, seven years after his death, the Seminary of S. Sulpice was, on the petition of M. de Bretonvilliers, approved and confirmed by letters patent from the Cardinal Chigi, Legate *à latere* for France. Thus was fulfilled—and the terms of the Apostolic brief are express on this point—the prediction of M. Olier, to which he gave utterance while at Vaugirard, that the Seminary of S. Sulpice should be open to all the provinces of France, and devoted to the service of the universal Church. Nor must mention be omitted of the remarkable testimony borne to the mission of M. Olier by the assembly of the bishops when, in 1730, they solicited from the Pope the canonization of the Mother Agnes. "We desire," they said, "with the more earnestness the public veneration of this pious virgin, inasmuch as, if we may so express ourselves, she brought forth in the Lord that excellent priest, the glory and ornament of our clergy, and by leading him to a more perfect life conferred incalculable benefits upon the

Church. For, to say no more, what abundant fruits are not every day reaped from the foundation of the Seminary of S. Sulpice, which owes its existence to this holy priest! From this seminary, as from a fortress of religion and a school of all virtues, goes forth a countless multitude of prelates and ecclesiastics of all ranks, powerful in word and example, strong in faith, *rooted and founded in charity, and furnished to every good work.*"

CHAPTER XXII.

Various Missionary Enterprises.

M. OLIER's zeal for the sanctification of the sacerdotal order did not terminate in this object. If he would form holy and devoted priests, possessed with an habitual sense of the dignity and sacredness of their office, it was that souls might be more abundantly gained to God. This thirst for souls had led him to form the design of resigning his parish and his seminary, and quitting France for ever, to go and labour for the conversion of the infidel nations of the East. When, therefore, the Papal nuncio at Paris urged him to accept the bishopric of Babylon, which the Shah of Persia desired might be conferred upon a Frenchman, in preference to a native of Spain or Portugal, with which countries he was at war, the servant of God willingly lent himself to the proposal, and was only dissuaded from carrying his design into effect by the strong opposition he encountered on the part of all the members of the community.

A few years afterwards, when it was in contemplation to send Vicars-Apostolic into China, M. Olier, in spite of his declining health, offered himself, with all the ardour of his soul to the Jesuit Father Alexander of Rhodes, one of the most celebrated missionaries of the time, who had been charged by the Pope with the selection of fit subjects for consecration at Paris. Convinced, however, that the work in which the founder of S. Sulpice was engaged was one to which he had been specially called by God, the missionary would not accept the sacrifice. Throwing himself on his knees, M. Olier conjured him, by all the motives which a burning love for souls suggested, to grant him his desire; but on the father still persisting in his refusal, he humbly adored the will of God, and acknowledged himself unworthy of the favour for which he had pleaded. "Eight days ago," he writes, "I let the pride of my heart appear, in testifying the desire I had of accompanying this great apostle of Tonkin and Cochin China. The holy man, or rather our Lord in him, judged me unworthy. So I am obliged to remain here in my nothingness, engaged in the work which the Divine Majesty has given me to do . . . . receiving with love and joy the crosses and sufferings I meet with in the service of the Lord. Charity crucified is the safest . . . . This hidden life keeps me more in my own centre, which is littleness of spirit and nothingness. Those other employments have something brilliant about them which would inspire me with apprehension; but that to which our Lord has graciously vouchsafed to call this poor sinner, is more hidden, more unknown. It is more closely associated with the self-annihilation of our Master, who departed not out of Judea, to do all the good He might have done by the preaching of the Gospel, but, leaving to His disciples to display the hidden, unknown zeal of His soul for the glory of God, was content to labour in that little country, and amongst the people to which He had been sent."

Unable to satisfy his own devotion, M. Olier had the consolation of seeing several priests of the community accompany the missionary to China, where they spent their lives in the propagation of the faith; but the project of sending Vicars-Apostolic to the Indies met with many discouragements, which were a sore trial to his ardent zeal. To comfort him in this affliction, God was pleased to favour His servant with a presentiment of what He would ere long bring about in furtherance of the object which lay so near his heart. For in a letter to his director, still preserved, he says, that being one day transported, as it were, out of himself by his desire to spread abroad the faith among all creatures, he exclaimed, " O my All, whom I would send through all the world! " and at the same moment there seemed to rise before his eyes a seminary having for its object the conversion of the heathen nations, and supported by a few liberal souls whom God had inspired with the thought. This prevision was fulfilled when, in the year succeeding his death, three Vicars-Apostolic were sent to China and Siam, and, shortly after, the Seminary of Foreign Missions, whose glory is in all the Church, was established in his own parish of S. Sulpice.

He endeavoured, however, to indemnify himself for not being permitted to carry the Gospel to the heathen by another enterprise of laborious charity, the objects of which were nearer home. In the spring of 1652, this zealous pastor was seized with a violent fever, which reduced him to such extremity that the physicians despaired of his recovery; and on the 20th of June, in the same year, he resigned his cure. This act was no sooner accomplished than he suddenly rallied, and was pronounced to be out of danger. For the restoration of his health he was sent to spend the ensuing winter in the south; but instead of passing the time in complete repose, as was recommended by his medical advisers, and as his state of convalescence demanded, he employed himself in organizing a mission on an extensive scale for the conversion of the Protestant populations of the Vivarais and the Cevennes. The design was one he had long formed, and he was moved to its execution by two considerations—the extreme spiritual destitution of those particular districts, and the charge which, as he believed, God had specially laid upon him of rekindling the torch of faith and piety in Velay, Vivarais, and Auvergne. From Geneva, the heresy of Calvin had made successful inroads into these quarters, where it still held its ground, in spite of all the endeavours of Louis XIII. and Cardinal de Richelieu, who, after the taking of La Rochelle, had sought to expel it from its fastnesses by force of arms. The servant of God resolved to wage a war of quite another character. On his way through Lyons he conferred with his friend M. Crétenet, who has been already mentioned as the founder of an association of missionary priests, and proceeding thence to Viviers, where he arrived on the eve of a diocesan synod, he could no longer doubt that Providence was opening a way to the fulfilment of his long-cherished desire. His proposal was received with acclamation, and many of the clergy solicited a mission for their parishes. Full of joy, he wrote to M. de Bretonvilliers, telling him that Viviers was on the point of yielding to the Lord; that at Lyons he had found a flying camp of missionaries, all filled with the spirit of apostles; and that on the morrow he was starting for Puy, to see if there, also, the fire were ready to be applied. He ended by bidding him send labourers into the harvest, as many as he could collect: "I want," he said, "only hearts devoid of self, simple virtuous souls; from such we may look for miracles."

At Puy the enthusiasm with which his proposal was received by the chapter and the clergy generally was not less ardent than at Viviers. The bishop would have resigned his see in order to secure such a pastor for his flock; and his desire increasing with the earnestness of the other's refusal, he threw himself at M. Olier's feet and implored him not to deny him a favour, the greatest that could be conferred upon him. Nor was it until the holy man, astonished and confused, protested his unworthiness in the most moving terms, and declared that no considerations whatever could change his resolution never to accept an office which demanded virtues so exalted and supernatural light of so high an order, that the bishop ceased to urge his request. M. Olier, as may be remembered, had established at Puy clerical conferences after the model of those of S. Lazarus, and the ecclesiastics now invited him to reanimate their flagging zeal, and many offered themselves with alacrity and fervour for the labours of the mission. From Puy the man of God wrote again to M. de Bretonvilliers, begging him to contribute towards the work out of his private means, and to urge his brother to do the same. "He must be saved," he writes, "and saved magnificently, by making him co-operate in saving thousands of souls... Ah! my son, if Jesus counted His Blood as nothing for our sakes, shall our goods, which are ashes and dust of the earth, be anything to us, when it is question of mingling them with His divine treasures that we may co-operate with Him for the salvation of so many souls?" To this appeal M. de Bretonvilliers generously responded by praying to be allowed to offer not only his goods but also his person and his life, if they could be of use; declaring that as to any share he might have in the merit of the enterprise, he prayed God to place it to M. Olier's account, for that it was his wish that to him should accrue all the grace of it in this life, and all the glory of it in the other.

Another priest of S. Sulpice, who contributed largely towards this important mission, was M. de Queylus, whom M. Olier had sent, as we have seen, to establish a seminary at Viviers. The first object was the evangelization of the large towns occupied by Protestants, the influence of which was powerfully felt among the neighbouring populations. Privas, situate in a country intersected with numerous deep valleys, and in the midst of thickly-scattered villages, had become one of the strongholds of Protestantism in France. It had stood a desperate siege, conducted by Louis XIII. and Cardinal Richelieu in person, in which 25,000 men had been engaged, and many officers of mark had perished. Compelled to yield to overwhelming force, the people had shown themselves none the less, perhaps all the more, strongly attached to their errors, and there were now but forty Catholic inhabitants. This stronghold once gained, the adjacent places, it was hoped, would yield a comparatively easy victory; and M. de Queylus was commissioned to inaugurate the campaign by taking on himself the spiritual charge of the town. He was made Curé of Privas.

The appointment was hailed with lively satisfaction, which was shared even by the Protestants themselves, who had already, during his residence in the province, learnt to regard him with esteem and admiration. His very acceptance of such a charge tended further to conciliate their respect and confidence. For that a man of high birth and independent means, who was also Abbé of Loc-Dieu, should be willing to enter on a field of labour so unattractive in itself, and which offered no compensating advantages, seemed to them a mark of extraordinary disinterestedness and zeal. He was accompanied by another priest of S. Sulpice selected by M. Olier, and under his directions preparations were at once made for opening schools in which the children of the place might receive a gratuitous education. The Protestant ministers, however, took the alarm, and wrought with so much effect on the prejudices of the people that no suitable building could be obtained for the purpose. Six months elapsed before one of the chief persons of the town had the courage to disregard the denunciations of the dominant powers so far as to let his own house to Catholic priests.

Active operations then commenced, with the aid of four additional ecclesiastics from the seminary, the Lyonnese auxiliaries, and an ardent band of preachers who volunteered from various quarters. All the usual resources of a mission were brought into play: sermons and catechisings, public instructions and private conferences; but these were accompanied, or rather pervaded, with that without which arguments are weak and instructions profitless, a winning sweetness and charity towards all men, and the constraining example of an irreproachable life. Soon the little flock of Catholics had increased to three hundred souls, the church began to be filled, not only with auditors, but worshippers; the sacraments, which had been to many from childhood the objects of contempt and abhorrence, were now frequented with a compunction and a devotion most touching to witness; the

God who had once been banished from the town, and for years had lain concealed even from the eye of His faithful few in obscurity and dishonour, was reinstated on His throne and reposed once more within His tabernacle; nor was it long before a Calvinist conventicle was consecrated to Catholic use amidst the sobs and tears of crowds who remembered with what blasphemies its walls had resounded against the Lord of glory in the Mystery of His love. Nay, so rapid and complete was the change that came over men's minds, that on the Feast of Corpus Christi the Blessed Sacrament was borne in triumph through the streets, with all the pomp which the circumstances of the case allowed. The oldest inhabitant of Privas had never before beheld a procession or other public ceremony of the Church, and now in a town which for more than sixty years, previous to its capture by Louis XIII., had not tolerated so much as the presence of a priest within its walls, there walked, in open day, no less than thirty ministers of the once proscribed religion, clothed in surplices, preceding the Most Holy amidst the smoke of swinging censers and the sound of many instruments of music. More than 5,000 persons, attracted from all parts, assisted at the solemnity; the utmost decorum and respect was observed by the populace along the whole line of march; and from that day the procession was annually renewed without giving occasion either to profanation or to scandal.

A victory so glorious (it scarcely need be said) had not been gained without great conflicts, and the endurance of many insults and many acts of violence on the part of the sectaries. The converts were treated as apostates and traitors, furious outcries were often raised against them, and they were threatened with having their houses burned over their heads and themselves thrown into the flames. These, however, were but the acts of individuals; no popular commotion was excited, and the rage and violence that displayed itself only served to exhibit in brighter colours the patience and constancy of those who were the objects of attack. Among the priests whom M. Olier despatched to the aid of the Curé of Privas was M. Couderc, son of a counsellor of the parliament of Toulouse, and brother of the superior of the community at Magnac. He had not as yet received holy orders when he was sent to take charge of the schools of the town, and he proved, as the servant of God had anticipated, to possess popular talents of the highest order. It was his custom to station himself near some Protestant conventicle, and as the people came out from the preaching he would mount upon a bench and refute the arguments to which they had just been listening, in language so felicitous, and with a flow of eloquence so natural and simple, that the crowds that thronged about him could not refrain from testifying their admiration. Great numbers of Huguenots, among whom were several ministers of the sect, were converted through his efforts; and so acknowledged were his powers and so signal his success, that the very members of the consistory shrank from meeting him in public disputation. The mission occupied M. Olier for the five remaining years of his life, and was continued by his successors at S. Sulpice with unabated zeal. The result is evident in the fact, that Protestantism, which held almost exclusive sway at Privas, now numbers but a thirtieth part of the population among its adherents.

Under the direction of M. Olier, troops of missionaries passed from town to town, who in five years changed the entire face of the diocese. Wherever the pure faith was preached by men filled with the Spirit of God, prodigies of grace followed, and it seemed as if they had but to show themselves in places where Protestantism most prevailed to see the partisans of error become transformed into ardent children of Holy Church. At Jaujac, the houses were closed as long as the mission lasted, and the inhabitants spent the entire day in the church, listening to instructions, praying before the altar, or preparing themselves for a general confession. At Viviers, the piety of the people led them to forego, of their own accord, all the gaieties of the carnival. Nor were the effects of the revival of a transitory character.

At Thueyts, a town notorious for the irreligiousness of its population, so fervent was the devotion of the inhabitants, three years after the departure of the missionaries, that on Sundays and festivals there were not priests enough to hear the confessions of the multitudes that desired to approach the sacraments; and M. de Bretonvilliers, writing from the Vivarais at a later date, declares, on the authority of a doctor of the Sorbonne resident in the place, that no one who had known them in their former condition would have believed them to be the same people. And these instances are given as only particular exemplifications of a great general result.

During his stay at Puy, M. Olier had desired to see a house set apart for the instruction of Protestant children, and as a place of refuge for such as were driven from their homes by their relatives on announcing their intention of embracing the Catholic faith. With this view he established an association of the Blessed Sacrament on the model of that at Paris, and this was the beginning of the numerous institutions for the same object which were subsequently founded in different parts of France. Writing to M. de Saint-Antoine, who had asked whether a sum of money which he had left at Puy might be applied to this purpose, the servant of God replied, "Not only that, but everything I have in the world; and if my blood could be of any avail, I would drain it to the last drop."

From Puy he was summoned to Paris on a business which he calls the most delicate which our Blessed Lord had ever intrusted to him, and fraught with most important consequences to the Church of France. By some he has been supposed to allude to his endeavours at this time to win to God and to the faith one in whom, with all his faults and vices, English Catholics must ever feel a deep and compassionate interest—our own Charles II. The supposition, however, seems hardly compatible with the terms he uses. Be this, then, as it may, the religious state of England had long been the object of his most earnest solicitude. We learn from his own memoirs that as far back as 1642, when he was laying the foundations of his society at Vaugirard, he had been moved to offer himself to God as a victim for the salvation of this country. It was on the 12th of March, the feast of St. Gregory the Great; and he had begged his young associates to make their communion that day instead of Thursday, as was their habit, and to pray for the conversion of England, where (he says) he had heard within the last few days that certain priests and others had just suffered martyrdom. From that time he had never ceased imploring the mercy of God for this distracted kingdom, not only with fervent supplications but with bodily mortifications of the most rigorous kind. When Father Alexander of Rhodes refused his services for the Chinese missions, M. Olier would fain have accompanied him on the still more perilous mission to England, which he was then proposing: "If I dared aspire," he writes, "to something of that solid glory which is found in the service of our Divine Master, by giving one's life and shedding one's blood for Him, I should look upon England as the one object of my hopes." No sooner, then, did he learn that the royal exile had taken refuge in Paris, than he sought an opportunity of holding personal communication with him. To one so easy-natured as Charles, access was at no time difficult, and M. Olier found a ready way to his confidence by his liberality in providing for the necessities of his followers, many of whom were destitute of all means of subsistence. Charles took evident pleasure in his conversation, but on the one subject to which the man of God desired to lead his thoughts he was quite unapproachable. The young king was all the less disposed to listen to his advice, because the Pope, to whom he had written to beg his aid in recovering possession of his kingdom, seeing that he evinced no intention of returning to the faith of his ancestors, had made him no reply. His resentment, however, at length began to yield before the charm of an address which few were able to resist, and the conversations he held with M. Olier, assumed more and more the character of a conference on the tenets of the Catholic religion. The servant of God, as need not be said, relied less on argument than on prayer, and he called in other devout persons to his aid: "I earnestly beseech all our brethren," he wrote to the priests of Puy, "to recommend to our Lord, in our Blessed Mother, the affair of the king of England, with which Providence has again charged me. He now shows himself disposed to have his religious difficulties removed: yesterday I had the advantage of speaking to him. So far as I can urge one thing upon all in common and on each in particular, I do so in this matter. Some prayers, some petitions, and intentions at Mass daily I must have, for they are absolutely needed in order to obtain so great a boon. I leave all to the love which you have for Jesus, and for Mary, who once had that kingdom for her dowry. I say no more."

That M. Olier's expositions of the Catholic faith produced a most powerful impression on the mind of Charles, and that the impression, though overlaid for a time, was a lasting one, there can be no doubt. The king himself is known to have declared to one of his friends, that although many distinguished persons had spoken to him on religious matters, from none of them had he derived so much enlightenment as from M. Olier; that he felt his words to be endued with a power quite extraordinary; and that, in short, he had fully satisfied his mind. Indeed, there has always been a belief among the Sulpitians that, under M. Olier's direction, Charles made a formal abjuration of Protestantism preparatory to being received into the bosom of the Church, and that he transmitted it secretly to the Pope, promising at the same time to make his conversion public on being reinstated in his kingdom. With that generous ardour, which he ever displayed where the interests of religion were concerned, the servant of God undertook to put 10,000 disciplined soldiers at his disposal, if Charles on his part would engage to re-establish the Catholic faith. Nor shall we consider the proposal as the mere heedless expression of an enthusiastic zeal, when we recollect the extraordinary influence exercised by this holy man over some of the boldest military spirits of his time; how he had defeated single-handed the tyranny of public opinion in the suppression of duels, and had actually despatched the Marquis de Fénélon and two hundred other gentlemen to defend Candia against the Turks in the capacity of volunteers. Such an expedition, however, would have been little in consonance with the policy of Cardinal Mazarin; and besides, Charles himself had very soon changed his mind. The solicitations of divine grace were no longer heeded amidst the vicious indulgences to which he had abandoned himself in the gay city of Paris, and his degradation was completed by renouncing the convictions of his conscience for a political advantage. Yielding to the counsels of the interested advisers by whom he was surrounded, he publicly announced his determination to live and die in the Anglican communion for which his father had suffered so much. And live accordingly he did ostensibly a Protestant while a Catholic in belief; but, by one of those miracles of grace which our merciful God sometimes vouchsafes, as though to show forth His longsuffering for sinners, he was to die in the faith which, during life, he lacked the courage to profess. For M. Olier his esteem remained unaltered, as was shown when, on hearing of his death, he observed with manifest sorrow that in him he had lost one of the truest friends he had ever possessed. Two papers also in the king's own handwriting, which were found in his cabinet after his decease, and which testify to the strength of his religious convictions, were probably preserved as containing a summary of the arguments advanced by his saintly instructor during the earlier portion of his residence at Paris. Two noblemen, his fellow-exiles, came under the same salutary influence while staying in that city. Edward marquis of Worcester went so far as to engage, in a document which was deposited in the seminary of S. Sulpice, April 22nd, 1650, to maintain a priest at his own private expense in the event of his regaining his patrimonial estates. But unhappily, like his royal master, the world proved too strong for him, and in the day of prosperity he forgot both his engagement and his God. He forgot also to repay a loan of money which M. de Bretonvilliers had made him, and the acknowledgment of which, signed with the marquis's own hand, might long have been seen, and perhaps may still be seen, among the archives of the society. It was now also that the earl of Bristol had the happiness of embracing the Catholic faith.

Allusion has been made in the course of this history to the part taken by M. Olier in the foundation of the seminary of Montreal in Canada. The circumstances under which it was undertaken are no less extraordinary than those with which so many of his pious enterprises were attended. His soul was filled with grief and shame that while commerce had its numerous associations, all busily engaged in extracting from the natives whatever could minister to wealth and luxury, so little had been done or even attempted towards supplying them in exchange with the infinitely more precious treasures of the faith; and in 1634, but for the intervention of F. de Condren, he would himself have crossed the Atlantic to their succour.* He resolved, however, to establish a company devoted solely to the salvation of these poor neglected tribes. It was while he was meditating on the execution of this design that God inspired a gentleman of La Flèche in Anjou with the same holy thought. This was Jerome Le Royer de la Dauversière, a married man, but one who to great detachment from the world and constancy in prayer united an ardent love of mortification. He conceived the idea of founding a community of *sœurs hospitalières* (hospital nuns) with the view of planting a colony in the Isle of Montreal, then nothing but an uninhabited desert. With the permission of his director he repaired to Paris, and being in the gallery of the old château of Meudon, whither he had gone for the purpose of obtaining the necessary authorization from the keeper of the seals, an ecclesiastic entered whom he had never seen before. The two looked at each other for a moment, and the next, urged by an uncontrollable

* See *supra*, chapter iv. p. 52.

impulse, they had thrown themselves into one another's arms, and each was calling the other by his name with every demonstration of the tenderest affection. It was the mutual attraction of two holy souls given to God, and, though strangers in this world, united in the Heart of His Divine Son, and recognizing each other with the instinct of a supernatural love. M. Olier—for that the stranger was he the reader does not need to be informed —congratulated M. de la Dauversière on the object for which he had come, and putting into his hand a *rouleau* of 100 *louis d'or*, said sweetly, "Monsieur, I wish to go shares." He then celebrated Mass, at which the other communicated; after which they walked in the grounds about the château discussing for three hours the particulars of the plan; finding themselves perfectly in accord, they were the more convinced that it was the will of God that they should labour in common for the object they had both so closely at heart.

An association was at once formed, afterwards known under the name of the Society of Our Lady of Montreal. M. de Lauzon, intendant of Dauphiné, made over to M. de la Dauversière the Isle of Montreal, which had been bestowed upon him by the great Canadian Company, with the condition of his founding a colony there; and M. de la Dauversière, in his turn, transferred the grant to M. Olier and the other members of the association. By the end of 1640 the transaction was concluded and the society legally incorporated. Mlle. Manse (to whom allusion was before made) accompanied the first band of emigrants, and was followed, in 1653, by that heroine of charity, Marguerite Bourgeois, who, amidst privations and sufferings of no ordinary kind succeeded in forming a large community of religious women devoted to works of love and mercy. The fortunes of this missionary settlement form no part of this history; it must be sufficient to mention shortly the share taken by M. Olier and the Sulpitians in its foundation and support. Before the colony took possession, the servant of God consecrated * the island to the Holy

* See *supra*, chapter ix. p. 144.

Family, and placed it under the particular protection of the Blessed Virgin, by whose sweet name the town was to be called (*Ville Marie*). It was his wish to constitute Montreal an episcopal see, and the matter was so far concluded that it awaited only the royal assent, when unexpected obstacles arose, and M. de Queylus, who had been destined for the episcopal office, was, in 1657, nominated by M. Olier the first superior of the missionary college, and despatched with three other ecclesiastics, one of whom was M. Souart, to Canada. The Sulpitians grudged neither money nor life itself for the glory of God in the salvation of the heathen; two of their number, M. Le Maitre and M. Vignal, suffering death at the hands of the savages, while engaged in the peaceful duties of their calling, under circumstances of peculiar horror. Indeed, but for the unfailing liberality of the priests of the Seminary, the colony would have been unable to maintain itself amidst the continual alarms and disasters to which it was subjected, and at length, in the year 1663, the Society of Our Lady of Montreal, finding itself burdened with an enormous debt which it saw no prospect of being able to liquidate, made over the whole domain, and with it the whole of the heavy charges, to the Seminary of S. Sulpice; M. de Bretonvilliers, alone, out of his private means, furnishing a sum little less than 400,000 livres.

The work commenced by M. Olier with the express sanction of Heaven, and maintained at so many sacrifices by his successors, was not allowed to come to nought. The Seminary of Ville Marie has continued to subsist down to the present day; and when Canada came into the possession of England, an arrangement was made with the government by which the Sulpitians were enabled to retain their house and property, on condition that the Seminary of Montreal, though still remaining one with the Seminary of the *faubourg* S. Germain-les-Paris, should be separated, in all that concerned its temporalities, from the parent institute.

CHAPTER XXIII.

M. Olier's Last Illness and Death.

GOD's ways are not as man's ways: it might have been thought that a servant so devoted to his Master's interests would have been granted a lengthened term of service; but it had long been revealed to this holy pastor, that at the end of ten years his public ministry would close. This was the assurance he had given to several of his priests; but as, at the beginning of the year 1652, there was no appearance of the prediction being verified, one of them said to him, as they were taking the air in the country, "The ten years will have soon expired, yet how can you resign your cure? and, even if you could, ought you to do so?" "It is for God," replied M. Olier, " to fulfil His own words, and accomplish His own designs." In March his health underwent a considerable declension: rest was the only remedy, but his zeal would not tolerate either repose or abatement of labour. In June the shrine of S. Geneviéve was carried in solemn procession to the Church of Notre Dame, and M. Olier, regardless of his enfeebled state, spent the whole night in prayer before the sacred relics. A few days after, he was seized with a violent fever: such was the intense internal heat from which he suffered, that it seemed at times as if his very bed were on fire. His soul meanwhile enjoyed a profound peace, and he never ceased making acts of love, thanksgiving, and self-renunciation. He never prayed to be restored to health, or begged others to make it the subject of their prayers: one thing only he desired—to do simply the will of God. The physicians declared there was no hope of his recovery, but the sick man knew he was not then to die; and a pious person coming to visit him, he said, "Be under no apprehension on my account: the Blessed Virgin has assured me that my end is not yet come; but there is another thing which has been made known to me, and it is a fault you have fallen into in neglecting a certain practice of devotion which was profitable to yourself and pleasing to our Lord." From God alone could this intimation have come, for the person in question assured M. de Bretonvilliers that he had not mentioned the omission to any human being.

But this holy man was accustomed never to take the extraordinary lights with which he was favoured as the rule of his exterior conduct; and though assured of his recovery, he proceeded to dispose all his affairs as if he were at the point of death. He received the last sacraments, and on the physicians announcing that he would not live through the morrow, he, on the 20th of June, made a formal resignation of his parish to the Abbé of S. Germain, and of his priory of Bazainville to the Abbé de Marmoutiers. At noon of the same day he dictated his last will and testament. No sooner were these formalities completed, than his health immediately improved, as though the malady had been sent only to be the occasion of his relinquishing his charge. He had been installed on the 25th of June, 1642, and his resignation took place on the 20th of the same month, 1652: thus was the word of the Lord fulfilled, as His servant had foretold. Another prediction, uttered eight years before, now, also, received its accomplishment, by the appointment of M. de Bretonvilliers to be his successor at S. Sulpice, notwithstanding the existence of reasons which, according to that ecclesiastic, rendered such a choice on the part of the Abbé of S. Germain morally impossible.

While all good men were lamenting the loss which the parish would sustain by being deprived of so indefatigable a pastor, M. Olier was himself filled with grief and confusion, as though, owing to his innumerable faults, he had retarded rather than promoted the work of God; and one of his own priests relates, that, passing through Lyons a few months after in his company, and happening to kneel on one side of a confessional while

M. Olier was kneeling on the other, he heard him accuse himself, in so loud a tone and with so many sobs and tears, of having undertaken the charge of a vast parish, while devoid of all the necessary qualifications for so responsible an office, that any one might have supposed he had been guilty of the grossest dereliction of duty; and the confessor was obliged to have recourse to all those consoling topics which faith suggests in order to relieve his fears.

M. Olier had recovered from a dangerous fever only to be visited in succession by three of the most distressing disorders to which humanity is subject. So great were his sufferings, that his friends, seeing the efforts it cost him to bear them in silence, were astonished at the perfect tranquillity of spirit he was able to maintain. No murmur or complaint escaped his lips: in the midst of the most racking pains he might be heard saying repeatedly, "Love, love, love!" and such was the sweetness and devotion with which the words were uttered, that the bystanders were moved to compunction, and retired resolving to lead a more holy life. It was during his subsequent convalescence that he organized the great mission of the Cevennes, and laid the foundation of several seminaries, as narrated in the previous chapter.

On the return of spring, instead of repairing again to the south, as he had intended, he was ordered by his physicians to take some repose in the country, and for this purpose he retired to a house belonging to Madame Tronson at Péray, near Corbeil, where that pious lady tended him with a sort of religious care. Thence he went to Argenteuil,[*] near Paris, a celebrated place of

---

[*] The object of this pilgrimage was to venerate a robe of our Saviour's which had been sent (such was the tradition) by Constantine, son of Irene, to Charlemagne, and had been presented by that monarch to the convent of Argenteuil, when his daughter Theodrada made her profession there. As a perpetual memorial of the fact, three strokes of a bell were sounded every day at half-past twelve at noon, that being the time at which the holy relic had arrived. This robe is known in history as *Cappa Salvatoris nostri inconsutilis*, or *Tunica Salvatoris inconsutilis*. The Abbé Chaste-

pilgrimage, which attracted a large concourse of devout persons during the octave of the Ascension; but fearing that people would be coming to confer with him as usual on their spiritual concerns, he resolved to leave the place. "They do not know how weak I am," he writes; "yet I cannot and ought not to deny myself, as I do not look so very ill." He had a strong desire to visit once more the shrine of Notre Dame des Ardilliers, where he had received so many favours, and this desire he was permitted to satisfy, although an inability to sleep and the excessive heat of the season obliged him to stop some days on the way. After trying the waters of several mineral springs, and staying for a short time at the houses of attached friends, who vied with each other in tendering him hospitality, he at length returned to Madame Tronson's château at Péray, where he was seized with the malady which was to complete his sanctification and terminate his life.

Four or five months before, he had received what he recognized as a warning of the state to which he was to be reduced. He was on a journey in the country for a spiritual object, when a person who was seated with him in the carriage said to him, "Ere long, your condition will be such that you will be staying in the world as if you were no longer living in it;" to which he had replied, "I shall be content to be in whatever state God wills: I desire and wish for nothing else." From this

lain, canon of Paris, who examined it in 1672, describes it as being of a thick sort of crape, of the colour of a dead rose-leaf; and Robert du Mont, an old author, adds that it appears from written documents to have been made by the hands of the Blessed Virgin for the infant Jesus. The pilgrimage was a favourite one, not only with the common people, but with the highest personages in the realm: S. Louis, Henry III., Louis XIII., Mary of Medicis, Anne of Austria, our own Mary of Modena, Cardinal Richelieu, and many others going to venerate the holy relic. It was anciently enclosed in a silver reliquary, but on the Huguenots plundering the shrine, it was kept in one of wood, until, in October 22nd, 1680, Mdlle. de Guise caused another of costly materials to be made for it. This precious relic is still preserved in the church of Argenteuil, and pilgrims continue to resort to it, especially on the feast of the Ascension.

moment he was possessed with an ardent love of the cross, so that he was for ever speaking of the blessings it brought into the world and the love we ought to feel for it. In his fear, lest the threatened blow should fall before he could reach Péray, he made all the haste his weakness permitted, and arrived, as he wished, before the 8th of September. On the feast of the Nativity of the Blessed Virgin, as well as on that of the Exaltation of the Holy Cross, his devotion found its gratification in making little cradles in which the infant Mary was represented holding crosses in her hands, which she distributed among ecclesiastics according to the love she was supposed to bear them and the excellence of the works which her Divine Son desired to perform through their ministry. He reproached himself for not having insisted sufficiently on the love and reverence which is due to the Holy Cross, in his instructions and conferences at the Seminary, and resolved for the future to inculcate on all hearts a greater devotion to it.

The man of God was now ready for the protracted trial through which he was to pass. On the 26th of September, 1653, while alone in his room engaged in prayer, he had a paralytic stroke, which deprived him of the use of the whole of his left side. His first thought was to offer himself to God, in union with Jesus Christ dying on Calvary, to meet death in such manner and at such time as should please the Divine Majesty. Having still the use of his right side, he knocked on the floor to attract attention, but no one heard him, and he lay as he was, adoring the Justice of God, and content to be abandoned by all, even in his last moments, after the pattern of his Lord. At last, some one entering the room found him extended on the ground, incapable of moving, but with a tranquil smile upon his face. Being lifted up and laid upon a bed, he bore the remedies that were tried not merely with patience but, as those who were present testified, with joy and even exultation. This joy, however, was nothing sensible: it was the simple effect of his ardent love for the adorable will of God, and his entire abandonment of himself to Divine

Providence. The treatment to which he was subjected was of the most cruel kind, and may not be inaptly compared to the torments inflicted by the savages of America on their captured foes. First he was cupped and scarified; lancets were then thrust deep into his shoulders: his limbs were not so far paralysed but that he was acutely sensitive to pain, and as the surgeon gave him no intimation of what he was about to do, he made an involuntary start, and said mildly, "I had better have been warned; one is not so much startled when one expects it." Accordingly, a priest who was present apprised him when the operator passed to the other shoulder, and the sufferer made no more movement than if he had been an indifferent spectator; not even a sigh escaped him. Apprehensive of a second seizure, whenever they saw an inclination to drowsiness out of his accustomed time for sleep, they began tormenting him anew, and plied him continually with nauseous medicines, for which he felt an extreme repugnance. Owing to his disabled state, he could take only a spoonful at a time, and was obliged to swallow drop by drop, thus adding indefinitely to the bitterness of the draught. But his patience remained unaltered; he smiled sweetly on all who brought him anything to take, bidding them not to spare him, but to administer whatever was prescribed by the physician. Unable to move, so much as to turn on his side, he had to be fed like a child: a state of helplessness, which, far from adding to his affliction, was the source of a particular joy to this holy man, who, with fervent acts of love, adored the Infant Jesus, subject to all the feeblenesses of childhood, and receiving in perfect obedience whatever was given Him by His Virgin Mother.

In about three weeks he was in a condition to be conveyed to Paris, where he could have the advantage of all the advice and attention which his case demanded. But the one desire of his heart was to suffer in union with Jesus: "So great was his love of the cross to which God had fastened him," says M. de Bretonvilliers, "that I saw him shed tears more than once when he was told that he would soon be cured." Incapable of making a continued meditation, he was nevertheless able, to the astonishment of every one, to keep himself in that interior disposition of a victim which it had been his endeavour to preserve all through life. It seemed as though, by a special gift of God, no effort was necessary to him: it was sufficient to abandon himself simply to the operations of the Lord Jesus dwelling in him. A thousand times a day would he adore the Divine Justice, ready to accept whatever crosses God might be pleased to lay upon him, so only that while His justice afflicted him on the one hand, His goodness would uphold him on the other: "for without this," he said, "I should not be able to bear them." The peace of his soul showed itself so strikingly in the serenity of his countenance, that S. Vincent de Paul, coming to see him, remarked aside to the ecclesiastics who were present, that it was perfectly marvellous to see a man so full of joy under the crushing effects of such a malady.

But soon to his bodily affliction there was added an interior cross far heavier to bear. The light in his soul went out and he was left in utter darkness, bereft of all joy and consolation, and tormented with a dread that he had lost the favour of God. He could no longer speak of divine things as heretofore, and in the sadness of his heart he would sometimes ask his confidential friends if they did not think that our Lord and His Blessed Mother had abandoned him. And yet, if any one had recourse to him for spiritual counsel, all his former gifts seemed to be at once restored. The same phenomenon had been remarked during a previous illness; and on a person afterwards expressing his astonishment, M. Olier had replied with a smile, that it was as if he had two heads, one of which was his own and was devoid of all capacity, the other given him by God for the service of his neighbour. In this state he lay during the greater part of a year, regarding himself as a barren tree which was to be rooted up to make room for another. On first resigning his *cure*, his intention had been to devote himself more completely to the work of the Seminary, which he desired to raise to the highest point of perfection. But now he abandoned all to the Divine pleasure, saying to those who expressed the regret they should feel at the work being left unfinished, that God in His own time would supply what was wanting; and adding, that much as he prized the Seminary for the object it was intended to fulfil, he should only rejoice at its destruction if thereby God were ever so little glorified.

Unable to occupy himself with prayer, or reading, or anything which could afford his mind the least relief, and oppressed with a feeling of dryness and desolation, he would say, " It is the will of our Lord that I should find pleasure in nothing: I must be content, and submit to His appointments with a good heart." On the malady abating in intensity, his friends suggested some little employments which would give light occupation for his hands; but though he thanked them for their kindness, everything was a weariness to him which did not help to raise his heart to God: he could not pay it even a passing attention without a feeling of distress and pain. God, as he said to some of his most intimate friends, seemed to have fixed a cross for him on all created things, so that if for a moment he sought his consolation in any one of them, he was sure to find it. He was given a little bird, so tame that it would sit and eat on the table while he was taking his repast, and prove its familiarity in a hundred pretty ways. Like S. John with his partridge, M. Olier was pleased with his little friend; but some one having inadvertently opened the window, the bird flew out and never returned. His great love for the Holy Scriptures made him esteem it a particular happiness that God had left him the use of his eyesight at times when his malady permitted him to read. But knowing that his sanctification was to be consummated by the loss of everything in which he took a pleasure, he one day said, " I have still this consolation left me; God will deprive me of it;" and, as he spoke, there was a smile on his lips, and his countenance wore an expression of peculiar contentment. No longer capable of saying Mass, he was nevertheless able to assist at the Holy

Sacrifice, and to communicate either in the tribune of the chapel or in his own room. He had the satisfaction also of visiting his beloved church of Notre Dame, in pursuance of a vow he had made while at Péray, to perform that act of devotion eight times in the space of a year. These were the only expeditions that afforded him any real recreation: if his friends took him for an airing into the country, it was observed that his mind appeared preoccupied, and neither the fineness of the day nor the pleasant scenery could rouse him from his apathy.

The reader will not need to be informed that M. Olier was compelled to relinquish the numerous works of charity in which he was engaged, and to resign into other hands the different institutions of which he had the direction. But he will hardly be prepared to learn that the Bishop of Grenoble, who was far advanced in years, chose this time, of all others, for petitioning the Queen, through S. Vincent de Paul, to appoint M. Olier his coadjutor; convinced that in spite of his great infirmities his diocese would derive no less benefit from the presence of such a pastor than from the active exertions of a more efficient man. It does not appear, however, that the Queen renewed her solicitations, or that M. Olier was even made aware of the bishop's design.

In the spring of the year 1654, his condition was so far improved, that his physicians again advised his having recourse to the waters of Bourbon. Though assured that his malady would never leave him but with death, he obeyed with all the simplicity of a child. During his journey, which he performed by easy stages, he never let a day pass without receiving the Holy Eucharist. As some of the inns at which he stayed the night were at a distance from a church, his friends would have had him sometimes abstain; but he replied, in tones that touched their very hearts, "Ah! deprive me of everything, so that you but leave me holy communion, the only consolation I have remaining." On one occasion, during a similar journey, he was left without this divine food, and through the whole day he remained in a state of depression and sadness. The next day his manner was altogether changed, and as he was not subject to these variations, one of the ecclesiastics with him could not refrain from evincing his surprise. That morning M. Olier had communicated: "How is it possible not to feel joy," he said, "when one possesses Him who is the Way, the Truth, and the Life!" At Bourbon he obtained from the Capuchins a room in their monastery, where he could hear Mass and communicate at such hours as suited him. From Bourbon he visited the duchess of Montmorency, who had retired to the convent of the Visitation at Moulins,* and took occasion to deliver a short instruction to the inmates. In this address he spoke of the duchess (who at the time was not even a nun) in terms which were afterwards regarded as a prediction of the exalted virtues to which she attained in this house, of which she became superioress, and where she died in the odour of sanctity.

From the waters of Bourbon M. Olier derived but little benefit: such relief as he was to experience emanated from another and a supernatural source. While at Moulins, being one Sunday in the church of the Augustinians, he made a vow for the future to hear Mass, and, if the power were granted him, to say it, for the intentions of the Blessed Virgin: from that day his health underwent a sensible change for the better. On his way to Bourbon, later in the same year, he renewed his vow in the chapel of Our Lady of Briailles ;† and so pleasing to the Virgin Mother was this pious act, that she obtained for him a boon for which his soul longed, that of offering the Holy Sacrifice on the feast of her Nativity, after having been deprived of this privilege for little short of an entire year. The hope with which he was now animated of being able to say Mass daily filled

---

* See *supra*, chapter xiv., p. 251.

† The little village of Briailles possessed a miraculous image of Our Lady, which attracted numerous pilgrims to the spot, particularly on the Mondays in Easter and Whitsun weeks, and on the 16th of August. At the time of the Revolution the image was destroyed, and the place ceased to be frequented. The chapel is now a private dwelling.

him with more abundant joy than if he had returned from his journey in the most vigorous health; and his love of Jesus in this august mystery overcoming his reluctance even to appear wanting in external respect, he consented to celebrate with his head covered until the canon, as otherwise he would have been unable to say Mass during winter.

Every year until his death he went to Bourbon, and in the early part of 1655, conscious that his end was approaching, he desired for the last time to make the pilgrimage of Our Lady of Puy.* It was that for which, of all the holy places in France, he felt the most attraction, as being the spot where he had been favoured with so many graces. Unable to be always in the church, yet desirous of being ever so in spirit, he caused a silver image of himself to be made, in the attitude of a suppliant, and deposited at the feet of his beloved Mother. To this he added a gold medal representing the Seminary of S. Sulpice, which he thus recommended to her unceasing patronage. He remained at Puy about six weeks, during all which time he had the happiness of saying Mass in the cathedral every day except two, on which, however, he was not debarred the consolation of receiving communion.

The order and fervour which he found prevailing in the Seminary at Puy were so grateful to his heart, that he desired to profit by his visit to place the establishment on a permanent and solid basis. As yet it had neither house of its own nor endowment, and he now united to it the *cure* of the parochial church of S. George, the only benefice which he had retained in his possession. In this church were preserved the relics of S. George, apostle and first bishop of Velay, together with those of S. Hilary of Poitiers; but they had ceased to be the objects of

---

* This was one of the most celebrated shrines in France, and was frequented by such vast multitudes of people as on more than one occasion to lead to loss of life. The place is still the resort of numerous pilgrims, and a colossal bronze image of our Blessed Lady, more than fifty feet high, has very recently been erected on Mount Corneille.

popular veneration until the servant of God, who took particular delight in restoring to His saints the honour which is their due, caused them to be formally authenticated* and commended to the public devotion of the faithful. The Bishop of Puy presided at the ceremony, which took place in the presence of the clergy and judicial authorities of the town and a vast assemblage of people.

Before quitting Puy, M. Olier wished to testify his gratitude to all who had taken an interest in the establishment of the Seminary, and especially to the nuns of the Visitation, who had rendered the directors so many kind offices, that these in their turn had given them all the spiritual assistance in their power. M. Olier had sanctioned this proceeding under certain important restrictions, and when he went to take his leave and

---

* According to documents existing at the time, the relics of these two saints had been deposited 700 years before, under the altar of the church dedicated to S. George, by the then Bishop of Puy. Three hundred years afterwards they were again uncovered by the bishop, and replaced as they were found. When again exposed to view, at the instance of M. Olier, in 1655, a large coffin was found, divided into three parts. In the first part lay the bones of S. George, with a little marble tablet, on which were inscribed the words, "Here repose the bones of the glorious Saint George, first bishop of Velay." In the second part was the body of S. Hilary, with the exception of the head, of which only a small portion remained. The bones were all black, as if charred with fire, the tradition at Poitiers being that the body of the great bishop had been burned. They had been transferred to Puy for better security during the wars of the middle ages, by a Count of Poitiers, brother of the bishop of the former town. In the third division were the cloths in which the bodies had been found wrapped when the altar stones were removed 400 years before, together with a box enclosing a parchment, in which were described the circumstances of the opening and the state of the two bodies at the time. A duplicate of this document had also been deposited in the archives of the church. At the request of the Chapter of Poitiers a bone of each saint was subsequently conveyed in solemn procession to the church of that town, where the precious relics are still an object of pious veneration. The portion of skull mentioned above was formally authenticated only a few years ago by M. de Bonald, Bishop of Puy, and is still preserved in the cathedral church.

thank the religious for their charity, the superioress begged him to extend the permission he had previously given. He refused four or five times in succession, and as she continued repeating her request and urging reasons for the relaxation, he said in a decided tone of voice, "My mother, I cannot permit what you ask of me: let us say no more on the subject, I pray." The superioress then turned the conversation, and the interview terminated with mutual satisfaction. The servant of God, however, was troubled at having answered, as he thought, rather warmly, and to the surprise of the priests of the Seminary, who saw the state of excessive weakness to which he was reduced, he expressed a wish to pay the nuns another visit. But greater was the astonishment of the religious themselves, when this holy priest began to accuse himself in the most humble terms of the disedification he had caused them, by the manner in which he had refused a request with which he felt unable to comply.

Among other instances of his humility, the following is related. A religious of Puy, in preaching to a community in that town, had inveighed in severest terms against certain ecclesiastics whom he did not otherwise designate, but whom his audience did not fail to recognize as the priests of the Seminary. The confessor of the monastery, who was their devoted friend, was filled with indignation, and scarcely allowed the preacher to leave the pulpit before he gave free expression to his feelings. "I said hardly anything," answered the other; "if I had given them their deserts, I should have said a great deal more:" a reply which only added fuel to the flame. At this juncture M. Olier visited Puy, and the confessor, going to see him, began eagerly to relate the whole circumstance, and to show how zealously he had taken the part of the Seminary. "Monsieur," said the holy man, "will you do what I am going to tell you?" "You have only to speak, to be obeyed," was the reply. "Then," said M. Olier, "go immediately and beg the good monk's pardon for the way in which you have treated him." A judgment so unexpected excited no small surprise; and the Père de Serres, guardian of the Cordeliers, did not scruple to tell M. Olier that the preacher, so far from being the person to receive an apology, ought himself to have played the humble part and asked forgiveness. "My father," replied the man of God, "when we have made reparation for all the insults we have offered to the Divine Majesty, then we may think of demanding satisfaction for ourselves."

On his return to Bourbon he passed through the village of Langeac, for the purpose of visiting, for the last time, the remains of the Venerable Mother Agnes. In 1652 he had, with the permission of the ordinary, caused her tomb to be opened, and had possessed himself of a portion of her relics. He now obtained leave to transfer the body of the saint to a new and more suitable depository. As he entered the inclosure, supporting himself with difficulty on his staff, he said with a smile to the Mother des Cinq Plaies, then prioress, "You see how I am: it is Mother Agnes who has done me this good turn;" meaning that she had been faithful to her promise of obtaining crosses for him. On beholding once more the precious remains of one who was now in the company of Jesus and His saints, he experienced an interior joy far surpassing any he had felt during their converse together on earth; and as he looked again on that right hand which had disciplined her body with such holy courage, his thirst for mortification and penance became more burning than ever. On leaving he bestowed numerous gifts upon the community, and, among the rest, a silver chalice, which is still religiously preserved among the treasures of the convent.

Returning to Paris in the spring of 1656, he profited by the fine weather to perform two pilgrimages which he had promised to God; that of Notre Dame des Anges, near the château d'Avron, and that of Sainte-Fare,* in the diocese of Meaux. He then retired to the Seminary

---

* The remains of this saint were preserved in the abbey of Faremoutiers, in the little village of Brie. They are still the object of popular veneration, particularly on the 10th of May.

of S. Sulpice, disappearing for ever from the eyes of the world. From this time his life was one continued succession of bodily and mental sufferings, a sort of protracted martyrdom. Such was the state of depression under which he laboured, that one day, feeling how utterly incapable his lengthened illness rendered him, he complained in tender accents to his Divine Master, and entreated Him to restore him to health, if only it were for His glory, promising to employ it wholly in His service and that of His Church. At the same instant he beheld our Blessed Lord, stooping and well-nigh bent down to earth under the weight of a heavy cross. The sight seemed to lend him supernatural strength, and rising from his seat, he prostrated himself on the ground as though at the very feet of Jesus bearing the wood of salvation; then, filled with shame and confusion, he bitterly reproached himself for his weakness and cowardice, and with a profusion of tears, besought the Lord's forgiveness for the request he had made. From this moment he never allowed himself to desire either restoration to health or a diminution of his pains. On the contrary, it was his joy henceforth to see himself conformed to the sufferings of Jesus; and the better to confirm himself in these dispositions, he had a picture made representing our Blessed Lord bending under the weight of His cross in the very manner he had seen Him. Nay, thinking that he did not suffer enough, and desiring to make expiation for the weakness of which he had been guilty, he begged his director's permission to renew his accustomed mortifications, and to discipline his body on the side which was not affected with paralysis.

As his end approached, it was observed that his thoughts ran constantly on the subject of our Lord's Resurrection, a mystery for which he had always felt a peculiar attraction. He had a picture of it placed in his room, and one day, enfeebled as he was, he placed himself on his knees before it, and remained in that posture for a full hour. At last his attendant begged him not to fatigue himself any longer, and helped him to rise: "Ah!" replied the holy man, "how can one feel fatigue while contemplating this mystery?" From time to time he might be heard crying, "O dear Eternity, thou art not far off;" then, taking his own hand, he would add, "Body of sin, thou wilt soon be rottenness!" A priest, with the view of diverting his mind, once began telling him the news of the day, but M. Olier stopped him, saying, "This does not taste of Eternity." The one desire of his heart was to go and enjoy the presence of God. He often implored to be freed from the chains of the body; and on Easter Day, in particular, he earnestly besought the Holy Virgin to call him to herself, that with her and all the company of the blessed he might celebrate the resurrection of her Divine Son in heaven. But it was God's will that he should suffer yet awhile, and he offered himself without ceasing as a victim desirous of living only in order to die a daily death on the cross to which he was fastened. "If I could produce as much fruit by suffering as by preaching," he once said, "I should prefer the way of suffering, because I should thereby give more to God." Indeed, his thirst for suffering seemed only to be equalled by his longing desire to behold the Face of God. One day that a dose was brought him, the very smell of which was enough to create disgust, he sipped it slowly drop by drop, without betraying the least repugnance. If any one expressed pity for his state, he would reply, "It is nothing: Jesus endured far more; and what happiness, what joy, to suffer something for love of Him!" His excessive weakness incapacitating him for continued application of the mind to God, it was necessary from time to time to divert his thoughts to other things. He would try and second his friends' endeavours; but in a few moments, as though transported out of himself, he would renew his heavenly aspirations, which sometimes found their expression in such ejaculations as the following: "O how faint and feeble is love on earth! how full is it of self-interest and self-seeking! O my God—the misery of seeing oneself in such a state! Let us sigh for heaven, the only place of true and solid love! O land of love, how dear art thou to the heart that longs to love! Thou alone canst satisfy the poor soul, which here below is stifled with its own ardent desires of loving."

Yet, great as was the joy with which he contemplated the near approach of death, his tender consideration for the priests of his community had made him refrain from speaking of it. But, on the first day of Lent, 1657, when alone with M. de Bretonvilliers, he said, "We must make our preparations; for soon we shall see each other no more: at Easter we must part." He then designated that ecclesiastic as his successor in the government of the house, and every day held long conversations with him on the direction of seminaries, the spirit that ought to pervade them, and the rules necessary to be followed. M. de Bretonvilliers committed these instructions to writing, and it was from them that M. Tronson drew up the regulations for the use of superiors and directors of provincial seminaries. Jesus dying naked on the cross, abandoned by all, was ever before his eyes; and the nearer he came to his last hour the stronger grew his desire to deprive himself of every human satisfaction, even of a spiritual kind. There was one friend from whose conversation he derived particular comfort, but for a month before his death he ceased asking him to come and see him. His friend felt the change, and inquired the cause. "My child," he answered, "I shall soon die; I wish, therefore, to strip myself of everything, and to have no longer any consolation in this world. I would look only to that which I hope for from the Divine Mercy in a blessed eternity." Lent was now drawing to a close, and the man of God, as was afterwards remembered, seemed to know that the hour of his departure was at hand. A person who was under his direction told him he wished to make his confession to him, and would choose such time as should be least inconvenient. "Let it be before Easter Sunday, then," he said. As another person, also under his direction, was leaving the room, M. Olier turned and bade him farewell, at the same time giving him his blessing unperceived, a thing he was not in the habit of doing to visitors. On the morning of the 26th of March, being Monday in Holy

Week, while getting up, he was seized with a trembling in all his limbs, and had another paralytic stroke, without, however, losing consciousness. This was at Issy, to which place he had gone in order, as he said, to prepare for death, but it was deemed advisable to move him again to Paris. From this time it was observed that he had lost the recollection of almost everything except what related to God. On the Thursday, a person coming to see him, M. Olier received him with a more than usual tenderness of manner, and disclosed to him certain secrets of his conscience which he could have known only by an interior revelation. On the same day he gave some excellent instructions to one of the directors of the Seminary, both for his own guidance and for that of the house, exhorting him expressly never to act from motives of human prudence, but always in the simplicity of faith. About the same time, when announcing his own speedy departure, he bade certain of his ecclesiastics be prepared soon to follow him. M. Blanlo, hearing his beloved master ask who amongst those present wished to make the journey of eternity, answered blithely, " I do." "Then begin your preparation," said the holy man. That very day M. Blanlo was obliged to take to his bed, and he died before the servant of God was buried.

On Holy Saturday some one begged M. Olier to remember him when he had entered into glory, and at the same time let fall some expressions in his favour. "Ah," replied the dying man in a tone of poignant sorrow, "what you say pierces me to the heart." These were the last words he ever uttered. Shortly after, it being nine o'clock in the morning, he suddenly lost the power of speech, which he never after recovered. About

his soul enjoyed and its entire absorption in the thought of God. In this extremity his zeal for the honour of Mary was still conspicuous; for, unable to speak, he intimated by signs, to one who stood near, his wish that the decorations of the chapel designed to illustrate her glories should be completed without delay.

During all that night his frequent stupors caused renewed alarm; but he returned to himself, and, seeing near his bed one who had always enjoyed his especial confidence, he embraced him affectionately and bade him farewell. At three o'clock on Easter Day he again lost his consciousness, and lay in this state when the Archbishop of Bourges, the Prince de Conti, and other persons of rank came to see him; the queen-mother, Anne of Austria, had paid him this mark of respect on a previous occasion. However, he once more rallied, and remained as before till the next day, which was to be the last of his life. And now this saint-like man was to have the happiness of being conducted to the verge of eternity by one whom the Church with authoritative voice has pronounced to be a saint. S. Vincent de Paul, on learning the state to which he was reduced, came to visit him, and it was under the eyes of this angel-guardian, to whose aid he had so frequently had recourse during life, that he rendered up his soul to its Creator, about a quarter past five in the afternoon, on Monday in Easter week, being the 2nd day of April, the feast of S. Francis of Paula. His biographer, M. Baudrand, assures us that he retained his senses to the last, and that the loving transports of his soul never ceased till they found their perfect fruition in the bosom of God. M. Olier died aged forty-eight years, six months, and twelve days. Abelly,[*] in his Life of S. Vincent, testifies to the singular veneration which that great apostle of charity entertained for the founder of S. Sulpice; and Collet, another biographer, relates that the saint, during the three years he

---

[*] The Abbé Faillon, at the end of his second volume, gives a chapter from Abelly's "Life of S. Vincent de Paul," not published in the work itself, on the relations that subsisted between the saint and M. Olier.

survived, was in the constant habit of invoking him, as indeed he himself mentions in a letter addressed to Mdlle. d'Aubray, in July, 1660; that is to say, two months before he went to join his friend before the throne of God.

For three days the body of the holy man lay exposed to view in his priestly vestments in the chapel of the Seminary, where it was visited by crowds eager to satisfy their devotion and obtain the benefit of his prayers. Some might be seen kneeling at his feet, humbly recommending themselves to his remembrance; others soliciting, or, without waiting to solicit, appropriating something that had belonged to him, or touching the venerated remains with their rosaries and medals. His countenance, as he lay, looked so beautiful and calm, that to the spectators it seemed as though he had but sunk into a gentle slumber. About the time of his departure the event was notified in a dream to a devout person, living at some distance from Paris, who had been united to the man of God in the bonds of a holy friendship. He appeared clothed in a purple robe, and by his side was a radiant figure, which said, "He is a martyr, and more than a martyr." Some years before his death there had been observed on his forehead the print as it were of a red cross, a sign, for so it was regarded by all, of the predilection shown to this mortified soul by the Father of Mercies, and of his conformity to Jesus crucified. During his last illness he had taken pains to conceal this favour from the eyes of his friends, but not with entire success; and one of those who were most frequently with him, M. de la Pérouse, perceiving that one arm of this cross, which seemed to spring from the midst of a heart in flames, was imperfectly formed, once said to him, "Father, your cross has only one arm." "My child," answered the sick man, "that is because my cross is not yet finished;" meaning that he had still much to suffer. M. de Bretonvilliers, who wished to ascertain the truth, deposes that on the second or third day after M. Olier's death he saw this cross distinctly marked upon his forehead, and that many others were also eye-witnesses of the fact.

On the 5th of April, the body was conveyed to the parish church of S. Sulpice, and on the 9th was celebrated a solemn service, at which all the ecclesiastics of the Seminary and of the community assisted, together with a large number of the parochial clergy of Paris. M. de Maupas, Bishop of Puy, preached the funeral sermon, in which, after extolling the prudence, zeal, and courage of the deceased, he did not fail to recall that instance of his disinterestedness which has been mentioned in this life, how he had begged him, even on his knees, to accept his bishopric, but without avail. The body was deposited in the upper chapel of the Seminary, under a mausoleum of wood covered with black velvet, but in the year 1684, the then superior, M. Tronson, in fulfilment of M. de Bretonvilliers' request, caused it to be laid in the ground in the centre of the chapel, which was at the same time paved with black and white marble. His heart was preserved in a silver casket, on which were engraved the monograms of Jesus, Mary, Joseph, encircled with flames; and in another vase of the same material was enclosed his tongue. These two portions of the mortal remains of their holy founder are all that have been left to the seminarists of S. Sulpice. In the evil days of 1795, the coffin was carried away for the sake of the lead and its contents thrown into some neighbouring cemetery, notwithstanding all the precautions that had been taken by the then superior, M. Emery, to prevent the desecration. As some sort of compensation (observes the pious biographer of M. Olier), the Seminary possesses the remains of another disciple of Father de Condren, the Cardinal de Bérulle, who, as institutor of the French Oratory, which was destined to have but a brief existence, was the first to labour for an object which to M. Olier it was given to realize, and which the Society he founded continues at this day, with unremitted energy, to fulfil.

CHAPTER XXIV.

Supernatural Gifts and Graces.

M. BAUDRAND, who was M. Olier's fourth successor in the *curé* of S. Sulpice, has left the following description of his personal appearance. "He was of middle height, with a distinguished air and an easy carriage. His complexion was of the sanguine order, and he was delicately constituted, although he would have been by no means deficient in strength and vigour if he had not impaired his health by his fasts, long watchings, and severe penances. He was fair, with a rather florid colour, a full face, an aquiline nose, and a broad and serene brow. His eyes were bright, and there was a fire in them tempered with an engaging sweetness. The whole expression was refined and intelligent, his mouth of moderate size, his lips red; he had a good voice, the tones silvery and flexible; his utterance was distinct and agreeable; his gesture, while expressive of devotion, was perfectly natural, and gave effect to an eloquence that was both manly and elevated, and so captivating, that, at once and without effort, he delighted the mind and won the heart. To sum up this description, he had handsome regular features, and a pleasing countenance, to which was added an air of so much grace, majesty, and modesty, that it was impossible to approach him without conceiving sentiments of esteem and respect, and having one's heart raised to God. His intellect," adds M. Baudrand, "was quick, ardent, and penetrating, rapid in its conceptions, and endowed with a large capacity for the acquisition of knowledge. The lights which were divinely communicated to him in prayer were of a far higher order than those which he had acquired by his own labour. To hear him expatiating on the deepest mysteries of our religion, it would have seemed to you that the speaker could not be a man living an ordinary life on earth, but a S. Paul rapt to the third heaven, or a S. John the Evangelist in his desert island. Not only were his conceptions most sublime, but he had the gift of expressing them with so much brilliancy, clearness, and grace, that you could not fail to recognize in them something more than human."

Of his marvellous force of eloquence, several proofs have incidentally been given in the preceding pages, but it deserves a mention among those extraordinary graces, some account of which remains to be presented to the reader. Of these, none was more remarkable than his gift of reading the secrets of men's hearts and foretelling the future, of which M. de Bretonvilliers says that he witnessed innumerable instances. One day, in particular, when he was walking with him in the street, they met a person, who, in conversation, concealed something from him: M. Olier at once told him of it, to the other's great astonishment; and on M. de Bretonvilliers asking him afterwards how he had become acquainted with a circumstance of which he could not possibly have had any previous knowledge, he made this reply: "All things are visible in God, and with a far greater clearness than they can be seen in themselves." M. Leschassier has left the same testimony: "He could see into the very bottom of the heart" (he writes), "and often told persons, still living, of thoughts they had had which they had never communicated to any human being, and which from their very nature he could not have inferred by any process of natural reasoning." A young lady, who was under his direction, had resolved, after much prayer to God, on going into religion; but when all had been arranged for her reception, she was assailed with so violent a temptation to return to the vanities of the world as to persuade herself that she had no true vocation, and even to doubt whether she would continue to take him for her spiritual guide. The next day M. Olier sent for her, and scarcely allowing the first salutations to be over, he said, "The question, my child, is not whether you can save your soul as well in the world as in religion, but simply of doing God's will." He then repeated in detail all that had passed in her mind, and with such particularity, that, amazed and confounded, she would not let so much as another day pass without fulfilling her intention. Her vocation proved a true and solid one, and for seventeen years she practised all the austerities of her rule with fidelity and fervour.

Brother John of the Cross also left a similar attestation in writing. For six months he was tormented with a dread that he had intruded himself into an office to which God had not called him; that all his exertions in behalf of the poor were the effect of mere habit; and that, if he would save his soul, he must abandon his present employment, and take to manual labour. His interior distress was so great that his health was affected to a degree which excited remark, and M. Olier's attention was directed to the fact. The servant of God sent for him, and before the other could utter a word on the subject, thus addressed him: "Are you to be for ever the sport of the devil? .... I know very well what it is that afflicts you: you think that God has not called you to the service of the poor; but I tell you in His name that it is His will you should thus employ yourself: yes, I assure you in the most positive manner; never doubt it again." In an instant (as he himself deposes) his mind was at rest; it was filled with calmness and peace, and he never after experienced the slightest temptation on the subject.

On several occasions the man of God reminded persons of secret acts of mortification which they were in the habit of practising, but for some reason or other they had deferred or omitted: "It is not enough," he said, "to do the things that God requires of us; we must do them at the time prescribed to us." M. de Bretonvilliers relates an instance of a person who had made a promise to God which he gradually ceased fulfilling. To his astonishment, M. Olier one day reproached him, with tears in his eyes, for his infidelity, and at the same time showed an intimate acquaintance with other particulars, the knowledge of which he had supposed to be confined to his own breast. Throwing himself at the feet of the servant of God, he confessed his fault and lost no time in repairing his omission. Another who had been consulted on an affair of some importance under an engagement of secrecy wished to have M. Olier's advice in the matter, but was met with the objection that to suggest anything to the purpose it was necessary to be made acquainted with the exact facts of the case. On the other replying that he was not at liberty to speak more particularly, the holy man made two or three turns in his room, then, as if he had received the requisite instructions, he entered into the whole circumstances of the case, and gave his advice accordingly. After a conference, in which he had spoken to his clergy on the subject of poverty, one of them retired in much distress of mind, not feeling in himself the heart to aspire to a perfection so difficult. "Ah, monsieur," said M. Olier to him shortly after, "this poverty causes you a great deal of trouble," and he began forthwith to tell him all that had been passing within him.

The following is an instance of a different kind. A priest had under his direction a person who pretended to have arrived at the highest degrees of perfection, and whom he looked upon as quite a saint for revelations and other extraordinary graces. One night he dreamed that he saw M. Olier, who warned him that his penitent was deceiving him, and exposed all her cheats and impostures. On awaking he thought no more of the matter; but great was his surprise when, chancing to meet M. Olier a few months afterwards, the man of God, as if he wished to confirm what he had previously described in detail, bade him in general terms beware of the person in question. It was not long before the priest acquired a perfect knowledge of all the arts which the miserable creature had practised upon him, and found them to be exactly and in all particulars such as had been communicated to him in his dream.

The secret influences which this saintly man exercised over other holy souls were not among the least astonishing of his supernatural gifts. So many examples have been incidentally given in the course of this history, that one in addition may here suffice. The Mother de Saint-Gabriel, superioress of the nuns of La Miséricorde at Paris, relates that frequently while conversing with him, or merely being in his presence, she experienced such powerful impressions of divine grace, that, not only for the time but for a month afterwards, her only desire was to be separated from creatures, that she might occupy herself with God alone. It not unfrequently happened that these effects lasted till she saw him again, when they would be renewed with such abundance and intensity, that at times she was unable to utter a word. She adds, that after speaking to him she often found herself delivered from habitual imperfections of which she had not said a word to him, and which she had used no particular effort to overcome.

The power he possessed of relieving mental suffering was no less wonderful. Sometimes he would tell persons so afflicted to go to such or such a church and beg our Lady's blessing, and they found themselves perfectly delivered. Mdlle. de Roguée, who afterwards became a Sister of Christian Instruction, and eventually superioress of the house, has left a written attestation of what happened to herself. For five or six months she endured interior trials of the most distressing kind: feelings of rebellion against God, thoughts against faith, temptations of every description. She began to despair of her salvation, and fell into a state of melancholy and despondency, the more strange and inexplicable, that hitherto she had enjoyed the sweets of a most tender and sensible devotion. Nothing could administer consolation, and her confessor was powerless to assist her. While in this miserable condition she was taken to the Seminary by Mdlle. de Richelieu, who wished to consult M. Olier. When the interview was over, Mdlle. de Roguée went to beg his blessing, and he asked her whether she wished to devote herself to the service of the Lord. She replied that she had long had a desire to do so, but had not as yet made a beginning. Then looking

earnestly at her, he said, "My daughter, I should wish
to speak to you in private: when I am able to see you
I will send to you." A few days after he did so, and
acting on the advice of her confessor, she resolved to
tell him all she suffered. But for this M. Olier gave
her no opportunity; he began speaking of the interior
of Mary,* and of the ways of honouring it. As he
spoke, his words seemed to ravish her heart, and the
sufferings under which she had been so long labouring
ceased as completely as if (to use her own expressions)
they had been removed bodily, and the peace and joy of
the blessed had been put in their place. She so utterly
forgot them, that she went away without saying a word
on the subject; nay, for several months she had no present recollection of what she had endured, and the distressing feelings never returned. In their stead she
experienced a love of our Lord and His holy Mother and
an interior joy such as it was impossible to describe.
He bade her tell no one but her confessor what he had
said to her, but to go to our Lady's altar at S. Sulpice and
make an offering of herself to that good Mother. "As
I returned," she says, "I was so absorbed in the
thought of what I had heard, that my friends could not
extract a word from me; my happiness was almost too
great to bear; my feet seemed not to touch the ground,
and my companions had difficulty in keeping up with
me.... What astonished me most was that our blessed
father said nothing to me about my sufferings, and yet
I was delivered instantaneously. What I have here
written," she adds, "is so true in every particular, that I
am ready to sign it with my blood."

After such proofs of his power in the matter of
spiritual infirmities, it need cause no surprise that he
possessed also the gift of healing bodily diseases. The
Mother de Saint-Gabriel was afflicted with a spitting of
blood, for which all remedies had proved unavailing.
M. Olier going to see her, found her in such a state of
debility that she had been obliged to take to her bed.

---

* See *supra*, chapter xvii., p. 301.

"My daughter," he said to her with all simplicity, "I won't have you spit blood any more: I forbid you doing it." On the instant the disorder ceased, and during the eighteen years that had elapsed up to the time when she made her deposition, it had never once returned. M. Olier has himself recorded the following:—M. de Villars, who became Archbishop of Vienne, while a student at S. Sulpice, was seized with what appeared a mortal illness. The physicians gave him up, but (writes the man of God) "our Lord said to me, 'I will restore him to you;' and so it really came to pass, the physicians themselves regarding it as a miracle." Many similar instances are related in his memoirs; the sick whom he visited finding themselves cured while he was speaking to them, although he had not asked God to restore them to health. Upon which he says, with that piety and humility which distinguished him, "This shows me how little part the ministers of Jesus Christ have in the operations of His goodness and power, seeing that He produces the most holy effects by means of those who are most imperfect and most unholy, waiting for neither their concurrence nor their desire. The numerous cures which were wrought by his prayers, or, as it seemed, by his mere presence, inspired the sick of the parish with such an extraordinary confidence in his power to succour them, that many thought themselves sure of recovering if once they were recommended to his assistance; and this confidence, it need scarcely be said, was in no way diminished after his death. A few extracts will here be made from the mass of authentic declarations, the originals of which are preserved in the Seminary of S. Sulpice.

Mlle. Manse, of whom we have already heard in connection with the colony of Montreal, broke her arm by a fall on the ice, and through the unskilfulness of the surgeons, who set the limb but did not perceive that the thumb was dislocated, she entirely lost the use of her hand. After nearly two years of much suffering she returned to France for the purpose of obtaining the best advice, and at the same time expediting the departure of the *Hospitalières* of La Flèche, who had been prevented leaving for Canada by want of funds, and also by the opposition of certain persons in power, who wished to substitute another community in their place. Unable to travel alone, or even to dress herself, she was accompanied on her voyage by the Sister Bourgeois, who has left a circumstantial account of the whole case. On reaching Paris, the friends of Mlle. Manse called in the aid of the most experienced surgeons of the capital, but after trying various measures, they one and all declared that the recovery of the limb was perfectly hopeless; and for eighteen months she employed no remedies whatever. Submitting to what she believed to be the will of God, she directed all her thoughts to the affair of the *Hospitalières*, although there appeared but small prospect of being able to procure from the charity of the faithful the necessary funds for their establishment. However, she had a desire to visit the chapel in which lay the body of M. Olier, for whom she entertained a great veneration, not with any view of obtaining a cure, but simply to honour one whom she regarded as a saint of God, and to obtain the benefit of his prayers for the accomplishment of a work in which he had taken special interest when alive. She went accompanied by the Sister Bourgeois, and the day she chose was the feast of the Purification (1659), a mystery for which she knew that M. Olier had a particular devotion. The account of what followed shall be given in her own words.

"As I was on the point of entering the chapel in which his body reposes, the thought came into my mind to beg of God, by the merits of His servant, that He would be pleased to grant me a little strength and relief in my arm, that I might have the use of it for the most necessary things, as dressing myself and arranging our altar at Montreal. 'O my God,' I said, 'I ask not for a miracle, for I am unworthy of it, but for a little relief, and that I may have the use of my arm.' As I entered the chapel a gush of joy came over me, so extraordinary that I never experienced anything like it in my life. My heart was so full that I have not words to express what I felt; my eyes were like two unfailing fountains of tears;

and all this was accompanied with so much sweetness, that I felt as though I were wholly dissolved in tenderness, without any effort or exertion on my part to excite in myself emotions to which I am not naturally disposed. I can only express it by saying that it was an effect of the great pleasure I felt at the thought of the happiness enjoyed by this blessed servant of God. I spoke to him as though I beheld him before me, and with even greater confidence, knowing that he had a far more intimate acquaintance with me than when he was in the world; that he saw my needs, and the sincerity of my heart, which had concealed nothing from him.

"I assisted at the Holy Sacrifice, and communicated, still enjoying this extraordinary interior sweetness; I never gave my arm a thought till Mass was over, when M. de Bretonvilliers going away to the parish church to take part in a procession, I begged him to give me the heart of M. Olier that I might touch my arm with it, telling him that I wished to have nothing more to do with *the blood of bulls and heifers* for my cure. From this moment I had a confident assurance that my prayer would be heard. He brought it to me and departed: for myself, thinking of all the graces which God had put into this saintly heart, I took the precious deposit in my left hand, and laid it on my right, enveloped as it was in a scarf. At the same instant I felt that my hand was set free, and that it held up the weight of the leaden casket without support: this surprised, or rather exceedingly amazed me, and I felt moved to bless and praise the Divine Goodness for vouchsafing me the grace of showing forth in myself the glory and the merit of His holy servant. At the same time I felt an extraordinary heat spread through my whole arm, to the very tips of the fingers, and from that moment I recovered the use of my hand; although the dislocation still continues, I am able to use it without pain, which is even more wonderful.

"I declare that what I have here set down is a true and sincere account, in proof whereof I have written and signed it with the same hand the use of which was restored to me. Paris, February 13th, 1659."

On returning from the procession, M. de Bretonvilliers found Mlle. Manse bathed in tears, and transported with joy to such a degree that she could not speak a word. The fame of the miracle was soon spread through Paris, and so great was the veneration excited among the populace for her who had been the subject of it, that they would cut off pieces of her dress as she walked in the streets, and she was obliged to go about in a carriage in order to escape the crowds that pressed upon her. Of all the attestations to the fact, not the least important is that of the surgeons of Montreal, who certified to the reality of the cure eighteen months after it had taken place. The author of the memoirs of M. de Laval, first bishop of Quebec, states that Mlle. Manse retained the use of her hand till the day of her death.

This miracle became the means of accomplishing the other object which had brought her to Paris, and that in a manner which surpassed all her hopes and expectations. In the number of those whose attention was now directed to her were some generous souls, who came forward with funds enough, and more than enough, to supply all she wanted for her foundation; and on her return to Canada, she had the happiness of taking back with her the *Hospitalières* of La Flèche. The history of these devoted women furnishes us with another instance of the assistance rendered by the servant of God after death to those who commended themselves to his prayers. It has been said that the establishment at Ville Marie had encountered strong opposition in influential quarters; scarcely had they arrived before they received an order to retire, and but for having brought with them the contract signed by M. Olier, they would have been compelled to resign the management of the hospital into other hands. At this juncture M. de la Dauversière was ruined by an unexpected reverse of fortune, and the funds that had been raised for the hospital, having been put to his account, were irrecoverably lost. Their condition in consequence became most pitiable: for five-and-twenty years their almost sole subsistence was a little black bread, and salt meat of the worst description.

Their clothes were so repeatedly patched and mended that it would have been difficult to say of what materials they had been originally made. Their loghouse, ill put together, was so open to the outward air, that it was impossible for them to keep themselves warm. During the severest part of the winter their beds were covered with snow four inches deep, and their cells so filled with it, that immediately on rising they were obliged to carry it away in shovels. To these terrible privations were added continual alarms from the Iroquois, whose practice it was to roast their prisoners over a slow fire, sometimes keeping them thus cruelly tortured for eight days together. The alarm-bell was for ever ringing, and affrays with the savages would take place within musket-shot of their miserable dwelling. In this deplorable condition they were encouraged and supported by the servant of God, as appears from a circular letter written on occasion of the death of one of their number, the Sister Maillet, a native of Saumur. Several times, while engaged in prayer, she beheld M. Olier in glory, who consoled her in her interior sufferings, and bade her abandon all fear for the safety of the house. Once when she was more than usually afflicted, he appeared to her, with M. de la Dauversière, and assured her that the work was of God, and that it would subsist in spite of the violence and opposition of men; that God would extract glory to Himself out of the persecutions raised against a house founded on the cross; that, in fine, being Daughters of S. Joseph, and consecrated to the honour and imitation of the Holy Family on earth, they were called to walk by the way of humiliation and contradiction. This prediction received the fullest accomplishment, for in spite of the terrible assaults to which it was exposed, their house was solidly established; and to this day, after all the changes through which the country has passed, the hospital nuns of Ville Marie continue to serve the colony by their charitable labours, and to live in strict accordance with the spirit of their rule.

From the many other duly authenticated miracles

wrought by his intercession, space forbids more than a brief selection.

A priest who owed to M. Olier, under God, his vocation to the ecclesiastical state, was afflicted with deafness for three years, so as to be able to hear confessions only on one side. On Holy Saturday, 1660, having been thus engaged a long time without changing his position, he left the confessional in order to recover a little from his fatigue, when the thought came into his mind to beg the servant of God in all simplicity, as he had been the cause of his entering the ministry, to obtain for him the power of discharging its duties more efficiently. After making his prayer he returned to his confessional, and found, to his surprise, that his petition had been granted. M. Tulloue, regent of the faculty of medicine at Paris, who had attended the priest in question, made formal attestation that a cure so instantaneous and complete had not been effected by natural means.

Pierre Trescartes, a sailor, was desperately wounded in an engagement with the English, September 29th, 1666. His left arm was fractured by a splinter in the most frightful manner, and the hand nearly severed from the wrist. The surgeon would have amputated the limb at once, but seeing the man's reluctance, deferred the operation until landing, which was not effected for ten or twelve days, when he was conveyed to the hospital at Havre. The wound meanwhile had assumed an alarming character; the surgeons took out several pieces of bone, and would have proceeded to amputation but that the man, notwithstanding the excruciating pains which he suffered day and night, refused his consent. He was shortly after pronounced to be in so dangerous a state, that it was feared he would die under the operation, if attempted. One of the nuns of the hospital had preserved, out of devotion to the man of God, a bit of linen which had been dipped in his blood; she spoke to the wounded sailor of the great holiness of M. Olier, and proposed that he should make a novena to him. The man readily consented, only expressing a wish first to confess and communicate. On applying the linen to the wound, the sister bade him say nothing to the surgeon, but remove the relic when he came to dress it. While she was engaged in performing her pious office the man fell into a peaceful slumber, as though no longer sensible of the pains he had been enduring; in fact, from that moment they entirely ceased, the fever subsided, and by the next morning the wound had assumed an appearance so completely different that the surgeons, astonished at the rapid change that had taken place, no longer recommended amputation. On the last day of the novena (November 26th), he left his bed, and went into the chapel to return thanks to God; four days afterwards he quitted the hospital perfectly healed. The fact was formally attested, not only by the sister, but by two medical men and one of the surgeons of the house, who declared that the cure appeared to them altogether extraordinary and marvellous. This was also the testimony which Trescartes himself rendered in the chapel of the Seminary of S. Sulpice, whither he went to thank the man of God at his tomb for the favour accorded to him.

Marguerite Vieillard, a nun of this same hospital, suffered violent pains in her eyes, which no remedies relieved. Removing the bandages, she substituted a rag stained with M. Olier's blood. The pain immediately ceased; she heard Mass the same morning with her eyes unbandaged, and the next day was about her duties in the town.

M. Boucaut, a canon of S. Nicholas of Craon, lay dying, when Marie Gabrielle Rousseau, who was held in high consideration at Angers for her charitable zeal, sent him, by the hands of M. Rigault, one of the canons of S. Peter in that town, a piece of M. Olier's *camisole*,* which she had obtained from the master of ceremonies at

---

* This *camisole* is still preserved at the Seminary, together with an attestation, signed by M. Louis Tronson, certifying its authenticity. Among other relics of the servant of God are a surplice, a *camisole* of cotton, a portion of a towel stained with his blood, and the napkin that was used to tie up his chin immediately after death.

S. Sulpice. At the moment he reached the house, prayers were being recited as for a person in his agony: M. Rigault approached the bed and said, "I bring you something of M. Olier's: have confidence in God, and you shall obtain relief through the intercession of His servant." The dying man, raising his eyes to heaven, took the relic, and dipped it in some broth, of which he drank a little. On the instant he experienced relief; his malady, which was of a most distressing kind, rapidly disappeared, and in spite of the prognostications of the physicians, who considered his case past remedy, he perfectly recovered.

At Puy many extraordinary cures took place, which were regarded as miraculous. Among others may be specified those of M. Colomb and M. de Béget, both canons of the cathedral, with the latter of which a touching incident is connected. M. de Béget had spoken one day to M. Olier of a certain priest, whose poverty was such, that he possessed only one old cassock. The servant of God immediately sent him his own; but M. de Béget, from a motive of veneration, kept his friend's cassock, and gave the priest another of equal value in its stead. God, it would seem, would show how pleasing to him were the charity of the one and the devotion of the other; for being afflicted with a pleurisy which confined him to his bed in a state of complete helplessness, M. de Béget was perfectly restored to health by applying to his side the cassock that had belonged to the holy man. So great indeed was the estimation in which this relic was held, that it was cut into several pieces; and by these, many incontestable cures were wrought, as was certified by M. Antoine de Fornel, the vicar-general, whom the bishop appointed to make formal inquiry into the facts. One of the most remarkable cases was that of Anne Feulha, an Augustinian nun, at S. Didier. A priest of the place, named François Néron, ridiculed the whole affair, declaring that the cure was all imaginary, and that the best that could be said about it was that the nun in question was a weak-headed visionary. However, a week had not elapsed before he was seized with a violent pain in his head, accompanied with a burning fever. In this state his mind underwent a complete revolution; he humbled himself before God, and asked for a piece of the cassock, which he applied to his head, at the same time fervently invoking the aid of God's servant. M. Olier revenged himself in the way he was wont to do while on earth: the priest who had doubted his merits was instantly cured, and made deposition in person before the vicar-general of the fact as it had occurred.

With one other instance, which shows us M. Olier once more in the company of that sainted nun who exercised so extraordinary an influence on his life and mission in the world, this narrative shall close. There lived at Auzon, six miles from Brioude, a woman of the world, by name Françoise de l'Espinasse du Passage, who was devoted to its vanities in no ordinary degree. This lady, coming to Puy the year M. Olier died, went to confession at the church of the Seminary, and was so touched by divine grace, that from that day she became as remarkable for her piety as she had hitherto been for her worldliness. She converted five of her sisters, and taught them mental prayer, in which she herself spent three hours every day: the whole family was transformed into a sort of religious community. In the May of 1661, she became alarmingly ill, and the physicians declared that she had not an hour to live. As she lay apparently at the point of death, her sisters made a vow for her to M. Olier and the Mother Agnes de Langeac; and shortly after falling asleep, she thought she saw two persons coming towards her clothed in garments of a marvellous whiteness, one of which seemed to be the servant of God and the other the venerable mother; but before she could distinguish their features they vanished. On awaking she found herself free from fever and every other ailment, although no crisis had taken place to account for a change so rapid. Her brother, the *seigneur* of Silloux, and all who were present when she awoke, attributed her recovery to a supernatural cause, and she ever after declared her firm conviction that she was indebted for her life to the intercession of the blessed servant of God.

The whole number of authenticated cases of miraculous cures wrought through the intercession of the holy founder of S. Sulpice (including that of Mdlle. Manse) amounts to sixteen.

All that now remains is for the present writer to declare, in the words of the Abbé Faillon, that "to Holy Church alone does it belong to discern infallibly the finger of God in operations which are of an extraordinary character; and in conformity with the decrees of the Apostolic See touching this matter, we submit anew to its judgment whatever we have written concerning the virtues of M. Olier, as also whatever in this history appears to surpass the laws of nature."

APPENDIX.

NOTE A, PAGE 126.

Notwithstanding his protestation, the Cardinal had taken care to provide himself with the abbeys of Citeaux and Cluny, and nearly all the great abbeys of France; and that in direct violation of the decrees of the Council of Trent, which had forbidden that any of the principal abbeys of an order should be held *in commendam* (Comte de Montalembert:—*Les Moines d'Occident; Introduction*, p. clxvi). It may be that he considered himself an exception to the rule, as being "the most worthy and most capable" man in the kingdom.

NOTE B, PAGE 171.

The Abbé Faillon says simply that M. Olier laid it down as a rule, that in the case of habitual sinners (*pécheurs d'habitude*) absolution should be deferred for eight or fifteen days. This statement requires explanation. No theologian now holds that a person who for the first time confesses a habit of sin is to be refused absolution. Yet such a person is technically called *habitudinarius*. Therefore, it would be incorrect to state broadly that habitual sinners ought not to be absolved. The principle of S. Alphonsus is this: Absolution ought always to be refused to *recidivi* (relapsing sinners), unless they show extraordinary signs of contrition, to counterbalance the *primâ facie* presumption against them, arising from the habit. However, amongst these extraordinary signs of contrition he reckons some which are by no means extraordinary, in the sense of being infrequent; as, for instance, spontaneous confession, that is, the penitent's coming to confession without external motive: *e. g.* at any other time than Easter, or Christmas, or such great feast. On this principle, absolution may at once be given to a *recidivus* who comes to confession of his own free will; supposing, of course, that the priest also sees in him the ordinary signs of contrition. No such rule, therefore, as M. Olier made, could possibly be made now, however justifiable it may have been under the particular circumstances at the time.

NOTE C, PAGE 277.

It is scarcely necessary to remind the reader that the Parliament of Paris had nothing in common with that which in England forms an integral part of the constitution, being, not a legislative, but a judicial assembly. The historical student, who would learn something of the origin, functions, and progressive political importance of the Parliament of Paris, may consult with advantage Gabourd :— *Histoire de France*, vol. vi., pp. 233-238 ; vol. xiii. pp. 7-14.

NOTE D, PAGE 344.

Madame de Choisy describes the practical results of Jansenistic teaching in terms which bear a remarkable resemblance to those of M. Olier. After protesting that the effect of Arnauld's writings and conduct was to unsettle people's minds and favour libertinism and impiety, she continues : " I speak of what I know, seeing as I do how many courtiers and men of the world have broken loose from all restraint since these propositions about grace came into vogue. 'Well,' they say, 'what does it signify what one does! If we have grace, we shall be saved ; and if we have not, we shall be lost.' And then they conclude by saying, ' The whole thing is a pack of nonsense.' Before these questions arose, when Easter came round, they were dumbfounded, not knowing what hole to creep into, and full of all sorts of scruples : now they are quite jolly, and never dream of going to confession, saying, 'What is written is written.' This is what the Jansenists have done for people of the world."—Extract from letter to Madame de Maure ; Cousin :—*Vie de la Marquise de Sablé*, p. 59.

A LIST OF M. OLIER'S WRITINGS.

1. Explication des Cérémonies de la Grande Messe.
2. Catéchisme Chrétien pour la Vie Intérieure.
3. La Journée Chrétienne.
4. Introduction à la Vie et aux Vertus Chrétiennes.
5. Traité des Saints Ordres.
6. Lettres Spirituelles.

The following remain still in manuscript :—1. Traité des Attributes de Dieu ; 2. Des saints Anges ; 3. De la Création du Monde ; 4. Le Maître des Exercices ; 5. Sur l'Oraison Dominicale ; 6. De la Vie Divine ; 7. Panégyriques de plusieurs saints ; 8. Mémoires, 9 or 10 vols.

www.ingramcontent.com/pod-product-compliance
Lightning Source LLC
Chambersburg PA
CBHW032010300426
44117CB00008B/976